D0231224

THE PLUMPTON LETTERS AND PAPERS

THE PLUMPTON LETTERS AND PAPERS

edited by

JOAN KIRBY

CAMDEN FIFTH SERIES
Volume 8

FOR THE ROYAL HISTORICAL SOCIETY
University College London, Gower Street, London WC1E 6BT
1996

Published by the Press Syndicate of the University of Cambridge
The Pitt Building, Trumpington Street, Cambridge CB2 1RP
40 West 20th Street, New York, NY 10011–4211, USA
10 Stamford Road, Oakleigh, Melbourne 3166, Australia

First published 1996

A catalogue record for this book is available from the British Library

Library of Congress cataloguing in publication data applied for

ISBN 0 521 57394 7 hardback

SUBSCRIPTIONS. The serial publications of the Royal Historical Society, *Royal Historical Society Transactions* (ISSN 0080–4401), Camden Fifth Series (ISSN 0960–1163) volumes and volumes of the Guides and Handbooks (ISSN 0080–4398) may be purchased together on annual subscription. The 1996 subscription price (which includes postage but not VAT) is £35 (US$56 in the USA, Canada and Mexico) and includes Camden Fifth Series, volumes 7 and 8 (published in July and December) and Transactions Sixth Series, volume 6 (published in December). There is no volume in the Guides and Handbooks series in 1996. Japanese prices (including ASP delivery) are available from Kinokuniya Company Ltd, P.O. Box 55, Chitose, Tokyo 156, Japan, EU subscribers (outside the UK) who are not registered for VAT should add VAT at their country's rate. VAT registered subscribers should provide their VAT registration number.

Subscription orders, which must be accompanied by payment, may be sent to a bookseller, subscription agent or direct to the publisher: Cambridge University Press, The Edinburgh Building, Shaftesbury Road, Cambridge CB2 2RU, UK; or in the USA, Canada and Mexico: Cambridge University Press, 40 West 20th Street, New York, NY 10011–4211, USA. Copies of the publications for subscribers in the USA, Canada and Mexico are sent by air to New York to arrive with minimum delay.

SINGLE VOLUMES AND BACK VOLUMES. A list of Royal Historical Society volumes available from Cambridge University Press may be obtained from the Humanities Marketing Department at the address above.

Printed and bound in Great Britain by Butler & Tanner Ltd, Frome and London

CONTENTS

PREFACE

The Plumpton letter collection, the least well known of the four early collections of English letters, precedes by more than a century other Northern collections of lay correspondence. Not only a unique source for Northern history, it is of value for political, social and legal history generally. The present edition, made possible by the rediscovery of the main text, contains material unavailable to Thomas Stapleton, whose edition of 1839, though remarkable for its date, is by present standards deficient in many respects, and may have obscured the interest, significance and value of the texts.

I am deeply grateful to Mr G. C. F. Forster and Mr John Taylor of the University of Leeds for checking the text and for their most generous help in many ways; also to Professor M. W. Beresford for bringing material to my notice. I am indebted too to Mr Robert Frost, Archivist to the Joint Committee of the West Yorkshire Archive Service, and to Mr W. J. Connor, Archivist to the Leeds District Archives, for making a photocopy of the Plumpton Letter Book available to me for transcription, and for permission to include the transcripts of this and other material in the present edition; also to Mr Brett Harrison and the staff of the Leeds District Archives for their willing help, and to Mrs Sylvia Thomas, Archivist to the Yorkshire Archaeological Society, whose Council has authorized the inclusion of material from the Society's collections. The Keeper of Western Manuscripts in the Bodleian Library and the Curator of the Manuscript Collections in the British Library have kindly granted permission for the inclusion of transcripts of material from these collections.

ABBREVIATIONS

Bodl. Lib.	Bodleian Library
BL	British Library
BIHR	*Bulletin of the Institute of Historical Research*
CB	Plumpton Coucher Book
CCR	*Calendar of Close Rolls*
CFR	*Calendar of Fine Rolls*
CIPM	*Calendar of Inquisitions Post Mortem*
CPR	*Calendar of Patent Rolls*
CSPD	*Calendar of State Papers Domestic*
DNB	L. Stephens and S. Lee (eds), *Dictionary of National Biography* (63 vols, 1885–1900)
*Econ.*HR	*Economic History Review*
EHR	*English Historical Review*
GEC	G.E.C.(ed.), *Complete Peerage* (13 vols, 1910–59)
HBC	Sir Maurice Powicke and E. B. Fryde (eds), *Handbook of British Chronology* (2nd edn, 1961)
L&P	*Calendar of Letters and Papers Foreign and Domestic, Henry VIII* (21 vols, 1864–1920)
NED	Sir James A. H. Murray (ed.), *A New English Dictionary* (11 vols, 1888–1919)
NH	*Northern History*
OED	*Oxford English Dictionary* (2nd edn, 19 vols, 1959)
PRO	Public Record Office
RP	*Rotuli Parliamentorum ut et Placita in Parliamento* (6 vols, 1767–77)
Somerville	R. Somerville, *History of the Duchy of Lancaster*, i (1953)
Stapleton	Thomas Stapleton (ed.), *The Plumpton Correspondence* (Camden Society, o.s. IV, 1839)
SS	*Surtees Society*
Test.Ebor.	J. Raine and J. T. Clay (eds), *Testamenta Eboracensia*, Surtees Society, IV (1836); XXX (1855); XLV (1865); LIII (1869); LXXIX (1884); CVI (1902)
TRHS	*Transactions of the Royal Historical Society*
VCH	*Victoria History of the Counties of England*
WYASL	West Yorkshire Archive Service (Leeds)
WYASYAS	West Yorkshire Archive Service (Yorkshire Archaeological Society)
YAJ	*Yorkshire Archaeological Journal*
YASRS	Yorkshire Archaeological Society Record Series

The Later Plumptons (Abbreviated)

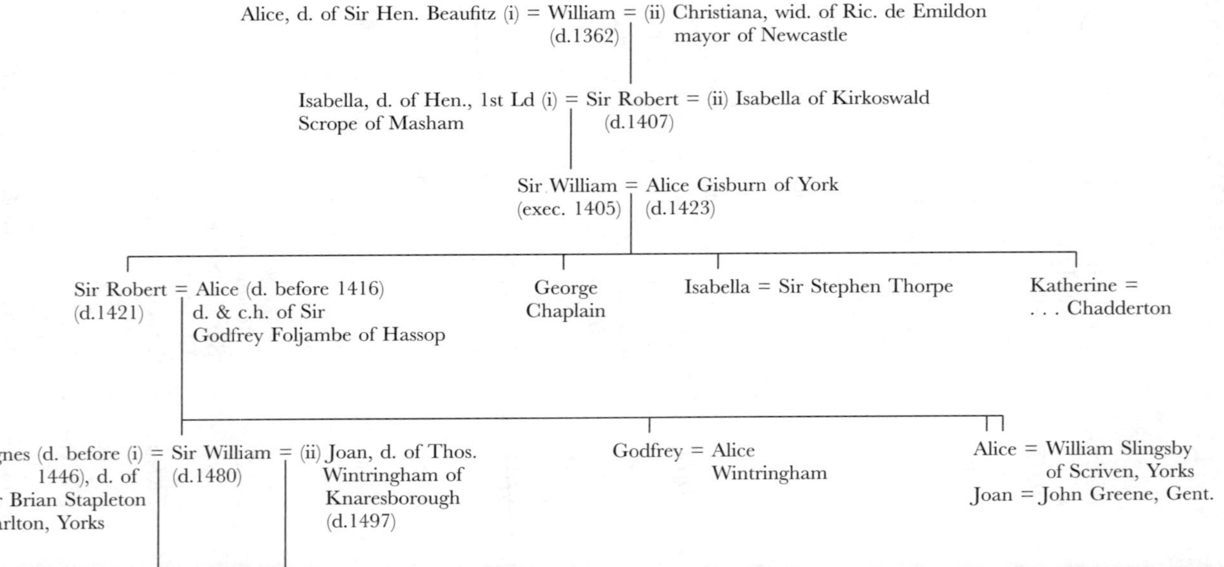

Alice, d. of Sir Hen. Beaufitz (i) = William = (ii) Christiana, wid. of Ric. de Emildon
(d.1362)
mayor of Newcastle
Isabella, d. of Hen., 1st Ld (i) = Sir Robert = (ii) Isabella of Kirkoswald
Scrope of Masham
(d.1407)
Sir William = Alice Gisburn of York
(exec. 1405)
(d.1423)
Sir Robert = Alice (d. before 1416)
(d.1421)
d. & c.h. of Sir
Godfrey Foljambe of Hassop
George
Chaplain
Isabella = Sir Stephen Thorpe
Katherine =
. . . Chadderton
Agnes (d. before (i) = Sir William = (ii) Joan, d. of Thos.
1446), d. of
Sir Brian Stapleton
Carlton, Yorks
(d.1480)
Wintringham of
Knaresborough
(d.1497)
Godfrey = Alice
Wintringham
Alice = William Slingsby
of Scriven, Yorks
Joan = John Greene, Gent.

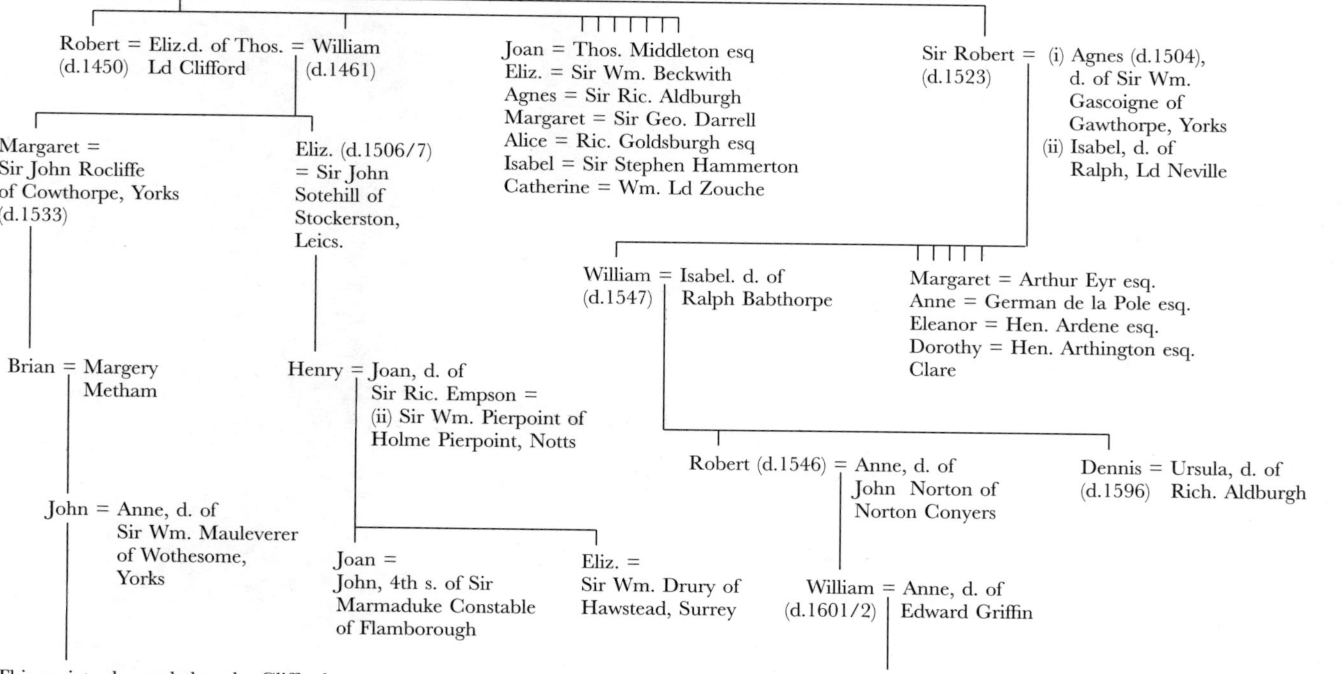

Robert = Eliz.d. of Thos. = William
(d.1450) Ld Clifford (d.1461)
Joan = Thos. Middleton esq
Eliz. = Sir Wm. Beckwith
Agnes = Sir Ric. Aldburgh
Margaret = Sir Geo. Darrell
Alice = Ric. Goldsburgh esq
Isabel = Sir Stephen Hammerton
Catherine = Wm. Ld Zouche
Sir Robert = (i) Agnes (d.1504), d. of Sir Wm. Gascoigne of Gawthorpe, Yorks
(d.1523) (ii) Isabel, d. of Ralph, Ld Neville
Margaret = Sir John Rocliffe of Cowthorpe, Yorks (d.1533)
Eliz. (d.1506/7) = Sir John Sotehill of Stockerston, Leics.
William = Isabel. d. of
(d.1547) Ralph Babthorpe
Margaret = Arthur Eyr esq.
Anne = German de la Pole esq.
Eleanor = Hen. Ardene esq.
Dorothy = Hen. Arthington esq.
Clare
Brian = Margery Metham
Henry = Joan, d. of Sir Ric. Empson = (ii) Sir Wm. Pierpoint of Holme Pierpoint, Notts
Robert (d.1546) = Anne, d. of John Norton of Norton Conyers
Dennis = Ursula, d. of
(d.1596) Rich. Aldburgh
John = Anne, d. of Sir Wm. Mauleverer of Wothesome, Yorks
Joan = John, 4th s. of Sir Marmaduke Constable of Flamborough
Eliz. = Sir Wm. Drury of Hawstead, Surrey
William = Anne, d. of
(d.1601/2) Edward Griffin
This moiety descended to the Cliffords
Sir Edward (will dated 26 Jan. 1654)

INTRODUCTION

Because of the instability of the Borders the northern counties were more highly militarized than those of the Midlands and South, and the martial *esprit de corps* of the northern gentry, fostered by frequent border skirmishes and more prolonged periods of conflict, earned them a widespread reputation for bellicosity and savagery. But despite their portrayal by John Whethamstede and others as 'alien and barbarous',[1] northern magnates and greater gentry were not a provincial race apart. Like their great rivals the Nevilles, the landed estates of the Percies, stretching southward into Sussex, gave them a significant presence in the South. Similarly, those greater knights who held lands in distant counties usually found it necessary to establish a second residence as a centre for the estate, and a political presence for its protection, whilst their social horizons were further extended by military and administrative service abroad. Sergeants-at-law and other leading lawyers from northern gentry families, like John Vavasour, Brian and Guy Palmes, Robert Constable and Richard Pigott, operated at Westminster, accumulated fees and retainers from many sources, and served on a variety of royal commissions. In the West Riding of Yorkshire the king, as duke of Lancaster and lord of the honors of Pontefract, Knaresborough and Tickhill, was by far the greatest nobleman, albeit an absentee, whose lordship was therefore exercised by the local noble and gentry élites functioning as its brokers and managers.[2]

The chance survival of a single, late medieval northern letter collection is of obvious interest and importance for the study of a region whose political influence was disproportionate to the size of its adult population, which was only 15 per cent of the total recorded for the poll tax of 1377.[3] Although concerned largely with matters of business, the Plumpton Letters, addressed mainly to Sir William Plumpton (1404–80) and his son Sir Robert (1453–1525), show that the northern gentry shared to the full the concerns and characteristics of contemporary

[1] Thos. Wright (ed.), *Political Poems and Songs* (2 vols, Rolls Ser., 1859–61), ii, 262–3; J.S. Davies (ed.), *An English Chronicle of the Reigns of Richard II, Henry IV, Henry V and Henry VI* (Camden Society, LXIV, 1856), 107, 109; N. Pronay and J. Cox (eds), *The Crowland Chronicle Continuations 1459–1486* (1986), 191.

[2] S.J. Gunn, Review of C. Carpenter, *Locality and Polity: A Study of Warwickshire Landed Society, 1401–1499*, *The Historical Journal*, xxxv (1992), 999.

[3] H.M. Jewell, 'North and South: The Antiquity of the Great Divide', *NH*, xxvii (1991), 17–18.

landowning society: acquisitiveness, ruthless exploitation of the law, use of credit to sustain an opulent life-style and the burden of crippling marriage portions – components in the unending struggle to maintain and increase the family's wealth and standing: to avoid at all costs its descent into 'the bottomless pit of oblivion'.

First heard of in 1166 as holders of a knight's fee of the Percy barony of Spofforth, the Plumptons are known in the earlier period through their numerous charters. The family's Yorkshire estates lay in Plumpton, a riverside settlement on the eastern boundary of the forest of Knaresborough, and in and around Steeton, Idle, Grassington and Studley.[4] In *c*.1402 a turn in their fortunes raised this ancient, but comparatively modest, knightly family to the front rank of the county gentry: the marriage of Sir William's father, Sir Robert (d.1421) to the sole heiress of the Nottinghamshire knight Sir Godfrey Foljambe, of Kinoulton. Alice Foljambe brought her husband some eleven manors and numerous scattered estates in Nottinghamshire, Derbyshire and Staffordshire, of which only the valuable manor of Kinoulton, where the family had established a second residence as an administrative centre, continued to be held in demesne by the mid-fifteenth century.[5] When the manor was eventually leased meticulous arrangements were made with the tenant for the occasional accommodation of the Plumptons and their officials.[6] An incomplete valuation of 1479 assessed the estate, including the Yorkshire lands, as worth a clear £290 14s 3½ d.[7]

The family attracted the notice of the chroniclers as a consequence of the execution in 1405 of Sir Robert's father for complicity in the ill-fated rebellion of his uncle, Richard Scrope, archbishop of York. Notwithstanding the gruesome aftermath – Sir William's head displayed on Micklegate Bar at York – the family avoided the penalties of attainder, and were soon receiving favours from the king, who treated them with remarkable clemency.[8] Sir Robert himself sailed with Henry

[4] Th. Hearne (ed.), *Liber Niger Scaccarii* (1774), i, 317. The early history of the family is recounted in Stapleton, ix–xxxvi. See also J.S. Purvis (ed.), *The Chartulary of the Augustinian Priory of St John the Evangelist of the Park of Healaugh* (YASRS, XCII, 1936); E.M. Holt, 'Study of Ancient Fields (Medieval) with Specific Reference to Early Estate Maps in the Pennine District' (unpub. M. Phil. thesis, University of London, 1974), 105.

[5] CB, 294, 313; **17** below. Kinoulton was let at farm by 1476, CB, 681–2.

[6] App.II, 50.

[7] App.I, 4.

[8] G.L. Harriss and M.A. Harriss (eds), 'John Benet's Chronicle for the Years 1400 to 1462', *Camden Miscellany*, XXIV (1972), 176; C.L. Kingsford (ed.), 'A Northern Chronicle 1399–1430', in Idem, *English Historical Literature in the Fifteenth Century* (Oxford, 1913), 282. The inscription on his tomb, formerly in Spofforth church, is recorded in CB, 664. The question arises why Plumpton incurred the death penalty when a number of other knightly insurgents were pardoned, C. Given-Wilson, *The Royal Household and the King's Affinity: Service, Politics and Finance in England 1360–1413* (1986), 218.

V on the king's first expedition to France, in company with John, duke of Bedford, returning thither in 1418 accompanied by a man-at-arms and two archers, this time under Lord Fitzhugh, whom, earlier the same year, he had appointed one of his feoffees in indentures for securing the provisions of his will. At home he succeeded his grandfather Sir Robert Plumpton (d.1407) as steward, castellan and master forester of Knaresborough, and was returned three times to Parliament, twice for Yorkshire and once for Nottinghamshire and Derbyshire. As he did not obtain possession of Plumpton until his grandmother's life interest ceased with her death (1419/20), he and his wife settled at Kinoulton. He died in 1421, probably in France, leaving an eighteen-year-old son, the future Sir William.[9]

Sir William Plumpton

Born on 7 October 1404, William, aged twelve, was betrothed to the twelve-year-old Elizabeth, daughter of Sir Brian Stapleton of Carlton (d.1417), his father paying 20 marks a year for the pair to be brought up together in Sir Brian's household.[10] On the death of Sir Robert the earl of Northumberland held custody of the family's Yorkshire estates during the few remaining years of William's minority.[11] Between 1427 and 1430 the young man saw service in France and received knighthood; five years later he enlisted under the duke of Bedford, distinguishing himself sufficiently to be rewarded with the *vicomté* of Falaise.[12] In accepting knightly status Sir William incurred, as its ineluctible burden, the 'obligatory grandeur' imposed upon knightly families by the expectations of society. Though in this period a dubbed knight was usually one whose ancestors had traditionally taken knighthood and could still afford it,[13] the margin between income and expenditure for even the wealthiest gentry was small. All suffered from an endemic shortage of cash, and many tried to make a profit out of usury, whose prevalence was reflected in the business of the court of common pleas, which was overwhelmingly concerned with cases of debt.[14] Sir William's creditors

[9] Somerville, i, 523, 525, 527; A. Gooder (ed.), *The Parliamentary Representation of the County of York, 1258–1832* (2 vols, YASRS, XCI, 1935; XCVI, 1938), i, 174; *CPR, 1416–20*, 250; CB, 368, 384, 397, 399; Stapleton, xlvii–ix; J.S. Roskell, L. Clark and C. Rawcliffe, *The House of Commons 1386–1421*, iv (1992), 90–2; App.II, 4–6.

[10] CB, 361, 374, transcript in Stapleton, xliii–iv.

[11] App.II, 7.

[12] Joseph Stevenson (ed.), *Letters and Papers Illustrative of the Wars of the English in France* (2 vols, Rolls ser., XXII, 1861, 1864), i, 433; *CPR, 1441–46*, 203.

[13] C. Given-Wilson, *The English Nobility in the Late Middle Ages* (1987), 18.

[14] Margaret Hastings, *The Court of Common Pleas in Fifteenth-Century England* (Ithaca, NY, 1947), 26–27; **165**.

grew tired of prevarication, clamoured for money and issued writs of *exigi facias de novo*, whilst he himself engaged in the same tortuous business of pursuing defaulting debtors through the courts.[15] Nevertheless, their crenellated mansion, enclosed park,[16] private chapel and commemorative chantries[17] proclaimed to all the wealth, pride, and credit-worthiness of the Plumptons. But with predators always on the look-out for chinks in the security of titles, and the hazards of a political crisis, stretching from the mid-century onwards, that aggravated the discords and uncertainties of a society based on land Sir William forged defensive alliances with important local families through the marriages of his three sons and seven daughters. Thus were the Cliffords, Darrells and Middletons, Aldburghs, Goldsburghs, Beckwiths and Gascoignes,[18] traditional allies of the Plumptons, drawn into a kinship network intended to provide him with reliable feoffees and well-willers. He was supported also by kinsmen whose sons were employed as stewards – Godfrey Greene, steward of the Yorkshire estates, Geoffrey Towneley, German de la Pole and Robert Girlingham came of minor gentry families related to the Plumptons – and by his illegitimate son 'Robinet' a shrewd lawyer with a practice in York, who served the family's interests loyally as confidante and adviser. The household included a number of trusted upper servants like Thomas Bickersteth, Henry Fox and Oliver Diconson, who acted as counsellors, witnesses and executors, confidential messengers and estate officials, whilst two clerks, John Ellis and John Whixley may have been employed as secretaries.

Furthermore, the letters suggest that both Sir William and his successor not only had the degree of familiarity with writs and the intricacies of legal process deemed necessary for self-preservation, but also exerted themselves by summoning influence and favour, labouring jurymen, and, in general, preparing the ground. Lawyers feed by them from time to time included luminaries like Sergeants Yaxley, Fairfax

[15] E.g. **6–8**; *CPR, 1467–77*, 327; *ibid., 1476–85*, 185; Joan W. Kirby, 'A Fifteenth-Century Family, The Plumptons of Plumpton and their Lawyers', *NH*, xxv (1989), 107–8.

[16] The licence for crenellation and emparkment is dated 17 Feb. 1473, CB, 585.

[17] The chapel at Plumpton, dedicated to the Holy Trinity, was said to be near the manor house, *Test. Ebor.*, iii, 335, 209. Sir William Plumpton (d.1362) founded a chantry dedicated to the Holy Trinity behind the high altar in the minster church of Ripon, App.II, 1. Ellen de Gisburn, mother of Alice Plumpton, widow of Sir William (exec.1405), founded the chantry of the Blessed Nicholas in St Martin's church, Micklegate, York in May 1396, App.II, 2. In his will, dated 14 Nov. 1450, George Plumpton, clerk, endowed a chantry at the altar of St Mary Magdalene at the east end of the north aisle of the nave in the parish church of Spofforth, known as the Plumpton Quire, CB, 520; George E. Kirk, *The Parish Church of All Hallows (All Saints), Spofforth, Yorkshire, and the Chapels of Follifoot, Little Ribston, Plumpton and Stockeld* (Shipley, 1958), 12–13; University of Leeds, Brotherton Library, Archives of the Dean and Chapter of Ripon, MSS, 1.1.

[18] CB, 541, 570, 555, 579, 534; App.II, 11, 13, 17.

and Frowyke, and other experienced men of court with local practices and Westminster connections, such as Edward Plumpton, William Elleson and Thomas Strey. Sir William's attorneys included his nephew, Godfrey Greene of Newby, who juggled with his client's numerous lawsuits, making brazen use of suspect procedures, like the *supersedeas*, and such legal loopholes as would further his client's matters and impede the ploys of his adversaries. Sir William, like most gentlemen, preferred, for the most part, to pursue his social inferiors – the prior of St Robert's, Parson Dromonby, Hargreve of Fewston, Robert Dykeson, husbandman, and John Daste, labourer, for example, rather than embark on the hazardous path of legal proceedings against the great and powerful.[19]

Disaster struck in March 1461 with the death on Towton field of Sir William's last surviving son, also named William, leaving two daughters by Elizabeth, daughter of Thomas, Lord Clifford. In consequence, the Plumptons were faced with partition of the estate between the two co-heiresses. Although tail male may not have been the generally accepted practice among landowners that it became towards the end of the century, the passing of an inheritance to a female heir or heirs was a prospect dreaded by those for whom the preservation of the family name was thought to be of overmastering importance. As an infant Elizabeth Clifford had been carried into the chapel of Skipton Castle for her betrothal to William's elder brother, Robert, who died in July 1450.[20] Her marriage to William followed in 1453 in accordance with a clause in the first marriage contract which provided for such a contingency.[21] By this time Sir William's first wife was dead and he was living with a lady named Joan Wintringham, to whom he afterwards claimed to be clandestinely married. Their son, afterwards Sir Robert, was born in 1453.[22]

Not lacking the egocentricity that 'often lay behind the devotion men of his kind gave to local affairs', Sir William became the quintessential administrator-knight, wielding local influence as steward, castellan and forester of Knaresborough and steward of the Percy lordship of Spofforth (for which his fee was increased from £10 to £20).[23] He also served in the three major public offices of justice of the peace for the

[19] **18**, **27**, **28**; *CPR*, *1467–77*, 327; *ibid.*, *1476–85*, 185.

[20] CB, 437; App.I, 2.

[21] App.II, 16. There is no record of the second marriage in the CB.

[22] See below, p.9.

[23] *DNB*; Somerville, i, 524, 525; App.II, 10, 12. He had been granted the stewardship etc. of Knaresborough for life, *RP*, v, 347. Until 1308/9, when they acquired Alnwick, Spofforth had been the caput of the Percys' northern estates, E.J. Fisher, 'Some Yorkshire Estates of the Percy Family 1416–1537' (unpub. Ph.D. thesis, University of Leeds, 2 vols 1955), i, 12.

West Riding (which enhanced his local standing as the only justice resident in the Knaresborough area),[24] MP for Nottinghamshire (1436–7), Yorkshire county representative at the abortive Great Council summoned for May 1455,[25] sheriff of Yorkshire in 1447–8, and of Nottinghamshire four years later.[26] As a royal commissioner he was entrusted with a variety of tasks, including array, river management, and inquisition into the estates of attained Yorkists.[27] But he lacked the formidable combination of influence at court and power in the country that led to the aggrandisement of such contemporaries as the Stanleys, Cliffords and Tiptofts; perhaps his prime loyalty to the Percies caused him to be regarded with suspicion by kings who mistrusted the earls but had perforce to suffer them. Moreover, private acts of violence in the interests of his patrons earned him the disapproval of the government, as when he and others, at the behest of the third earl of Northumberland, executed Richard Neville, earl of Salisbury, in revenge for the death of the earl's father at St Albans.[28] Some twenty years earlier, during a protracted quarrel between the Percies and John Kemp, archbishop of York, he was called to account for having encouraged the rebellious foresters of Knaresborough, intent on asserting their immunity from payment of toll, in bloody combat with the archbishop's towns of Otley and Ripon.[29]

The Plumptons were probably uncharacteristic, even in the north-east, where the gentry 'were more successful than some at balancing loyalty with self-interest', in their commitment to their lords and patrons, which drew them into the Lancastrian orbit and cost them loss of life, liberty and office. Elsewhere many gentlemen were more pragmatic – even cynical – in their response to claims on their loyalty, and showed a 'marked reluctance to become involved in the dangerous

[24] *CPR, 1436–41*, 594; *ibid., 1441–46*, 482; *ibid., 1446–52*, 598; *ibid., 1452–61*, 683; *ibid., 1467–77*, 638; *ibid., 1476–85*, 579–80; Carol Arnold, 'The Commission of the Peace of the West Riding of Yorkshire', in R.A. Griffiths and James Sherborne (eds), *Kings and Nobles in the Later Middle Ages: A Tribute to Charles Ross* (Gloucester, 1986), 119–20.

[25] *Return of Members of Parliament*, 330; R.L. Storey, *The End of the House of Lancaster* (1966), 160–1.

[26] *A List of Sheriffs for England and Wales* (PRO, Lists and Indexes, ix, 1898), 103, 162.

[27] *CPR, 1429–36*, 520; *ibid., 1441–46*, 369; *ibid., 1446–52*, 88; *ibid., 1452–61*, 408, 560; *ibid., 1467–77*, 55, 349, 355, 408, 572; *ibid., 1476–85*, 50; *CFR, 1430–32*, 350, 355; *ibid., 1445–52*, 169; CB, 545 (enquiry concerning the lands of the attainted Richard, duke of York, 1 May 1460).

[28] Storey, 194; P. Jalland, 'The Influence of the Aristocracy on Shire Elections', *Speculum*, xlvii (1972), 47, 487; *CCR, 1461–68*, 135.

[29] Catherine Pullein, *The Pulleins of Yorkshire* (Leeds, 1915), 45; R.A. Griffiths, *The Reign of Henry VI: The Exercise of Royal Authority, 1422–1461* (1981), 578; *CCR, 1441–47*, 98; *ibid., 1454–61*, 101; CB, 455–58. There is a transcript of this account of the riots in Stapleton, liv–lxii.

national politics of the day'.[30] By contrast, Sir William Plumpton was one of the few to be ejected from the commission of the peace in August 1460 because of his hostility to the Yorkists.[31] After the rout of the Lancastrians at Towton in March 1461, with the third earl of Northumberland slain and his son attainted and in custody, Sir William resorted to self-preservation. Brought before Edward IV at Newcastle, he agreed to pay £2,000 as a recognizance for good behaviour, but was unable to raise the sum and in July was confined in the Tower.[32] The following February he obtained a pardon, and in September release from his bond on condition that he remained in London.[33] Further trouble befell him, however, for he was accused by an informer of treasonable words, tried, acquitted, and pardoned anew by signet letter, dated 20 January 1463/4.[34] Meanwhile, Warwick having been granted the stewardship of Knaresborough for life, Sir William hastened to make his peace with the earl, possibly through the good offices of the latter's brother-in-law, Henry, Lord FitzHugh, and was rewarded by appointment as Warwick's deputy.[35] It appears that he also resumed the stewardship of Spofforth, presumably replacing Sir Robert Constable who had been granted the office on 8 August 1461.[36]

The restoration of Henry Percy as fourth earl of Northumberland in March 1470 doubtless revived Sir William's latent Lancastrianism. For some reason, possibly an injudicious move during the crisis of 1469–71, whilst the earl shrewdly 'sat still', he was ousted from the deputy stewardship of Knaresborough,[37] but looking for reinstatement on Percy's succession to Warwick as steward of the honor, his fury on discovering that the earl had chosen instead to confer the favour on his brother-in-law, Sir William Gascoigne, gave rise to a deluge of

[30] Susan Wright, *The Derbyshire Gentry in the Fifteenth Century* (Derbyshire Record Society, VIII, 1983), 75, 101; Keith Dockray, 'Sir Marmaduke Constable of Flamborough', in J. Petre (ed.), *Richard III, Crown and People* (Richard III Society, 1985), 218; Christine Carpenter, *Locality and Polity*, 498–514.

[31] Arnold, 122, 125–6; J.R. Lander, *English Justices of the Peace, 1461–1509* (1989), 44.

[32] CB, 549 (recognizance, 13 May 1461), 550 (imprisonment, 12 July 1461), transcripts in Stapleton, lxviii and n. He was said to have been captured by the earl of Warwick, James Gairdner (ed.), *Three Fifteenth-Century Chronicles* (Camden Society, 2nd ser., XXVIII, 1880), 161.

[33] **8** App.II, 19.

[34] App.II, 26.

[35] A.J. Pollard, *North-Eastern England During the Wars of the Roses* (Oxford, 1990), 288–9, 293.

[36] E.J. Fisher, 'Some Yorkshire Estates of the Percy Family', i, 36; *CPR, 1461–67*, 39.

[37] J. Bruce (ed.), *Historie of the Arrivall of Edward IV in England and the Finall Recouerye of his Kingdomes from Henry VI A.D. Mccccl xxi* (Camden Society, I, 1838), 7. Pollard suggests that Sir William's dismissal followed Warwick's loss of office, *NE England*, 139. He received a pardon for offences committed before 30 Sept. 1471, CB, 578, transcript in Stapleton, lxxv n.

instructions to his attorney to urge his cause in the highest quarters.[38] Northumberland remained unmoved, but did intervene to secure Plumpton's reinstatement on the commission of the peace.

After his acquittal in January 1463/4 Sir William turned his attention to an important domestic matter: he received 400 marks and £333 respectively, from Brian Rocliffe and Henry Sotehill for the marriages of Margaret Plumpton, aged four, and her younger sister Elizabeth, the daughters of his deceased son William, on the understanding that they were co-heiresses to the Plumpton inheritance. The tightly-drawn Sotehill marriage contract, with its protective indentures, conditions, deadlines and contingency clauses, included a clause forbidding the alienation by enfeoffment of any part of the Plumpton estate. Hence Sir William was precluded from providing other than a life annuity for a future son. Should there be a son, his wardship and marriage were guaranteed to Henry Sotehill on payment of 100 marks on the day of his delivery into Sotehill's keeping, and 100 marks within the year following.[39] By this time, however, Sir William had indeed a second wife (if later testimony can be believed) and a son, aged about ten.[40] Understandably, he had been in no hurry to reveal the secret of his marriage, but on being summoned to appear before the Official of the civil court at York on 26 January 1468 to account for the irregularity of his private life, he then declared that Joan Wintringham had for long been his lawful wife, and that their only child had been born in wedlock.[41] Proceedings were interrupted by the political disturbances of 1469–71, and it was not until 6 July 1472 that the case was resumed, and the court heard the crucial deposition of the parish clerk of Knaresborough who claimed to have witnessed the ceremony.[42] Upon this evidence Dr William Potemen (significantly, perhaps, Northumberland's godfather) certified the validity of the marriage and the legitimacy of the young Robert, who was thereafter recognized as his father's heir apparent.[43] The cartulary contains copies of the deeds of conveyance and settlement, dating from October 1475, by which Sir William enfeoffed all his estates to his own use, with reversion to his son. Having thus supplanted the heirs general,[44] he defaulted on the final clause of his contract with Henry Sotehill by signing indentures, dated 13 July 1477, for Robert's marriage with Agnes, sister of Sir

[38] **28**,**29**.
[39] App.I, 3; II, 23.
[40] See below, p.14.
[41] App.II, 30.
[42] CB, 582, 631, transcripts in Stapleton, lxxvi–vii.
[43] App.II, 33.
[44] App.II, 35, 36.

William Gascoigne.[45] In the following year he made absolute dispositions of his entire estate, real and personal, to his son, so precluding the necessity for a will.[46]

By these means Sir William's carefully-contrived purpose was accomplished. Impelled by pride of lineage and determination to secure its continuance in undiminished standing, he subjected his second wife to years of humiliation (although in the circumstances she might not have been an altogether unwilling accomplice) and defrauded his granddaughters. Their disposal has indeed been much criticised on the ground that it was motivated merely by greedy concern for financial gain; but whatever the motive, the sin of the father was amply visited upon the son.

Sir Robert Plumpton

Through the good offices of Sir William Gascoigne[47] the escheators, William Nettleton, for Yorkshire, and Edmund Pierpoint, for Nottinghamshire and Derbyshire, acted quickly to hold their inquisitions and return their findings to the court of chancery. The deeds of settlement of 1475 having been submitted in evidence, Robert Plumpton's title as his father's heir was admitted, and the status of Margaret Rocliffe and Elizabeth Sotehill, then aged about twenty and nineteen, respectively, as heirs general acknowledged.[48] Not surprisingly, however, the latter, their husbands and supporters were already embattled, and a few months before Sir William's death Northumberland and Gloucester agreed to arrange a settlement through the good offices of their respective councils.[49] Sir William's death, and political events supervened to postpone a determination of the cause, and it was another three years before Richard of Gloucester, now King Richard III, delivered his judgement, which awarded to the heirs general a lawful estate in Grassington and Steeton and in twenty-one Derbyshire lordships, whilst the Plumptons were to retain the residue,

[45] App.II, 37.

[46] App.II, 38, 39.

[47] CB, 625 (30 Nov. 1481), transcript in Stapleton, lxxxvii.

[48] App.II, 42–44.

[49] App.II, 41. On 7 Nov. 1476 the heirs general obtained exemplifications of fines made respectively by Sir William Plumpton's paternal and maternal grandparents. A copy of the former, dated Oct. 1326, is in CB, 173. The latter was made in Trinity 1366, *CPR, 1467–77*, 601–2. In neither case were the lands entailed in the male line.

including the valuable Nottinghamshire manor of Kinoulton.[50] Unhappily for the Plumptons this did not prove to be the last act in the drama.

As closely identified with the Percies as his father had been, Robert was knighted by Northumberland in August 1481 while on campaign against the Scots.[51] Succeeding his father as steward of Spofforth, he was also appointed deputy steward, castellan and master forester of Knaresborough under the earl – offices Sir William may have regained before his death.[52] Unlike his kinsmen Sir Christopher Warde, Sir Stephen Hammerton and Sir Piers Middleton, Sir Robert received no favours from King Richard, and therefore easily transferred his allegiance to Henry VII in 1485. In the following year he rode in Northumberland's train to meet the new king at Barnsdale during the royal progress to York, and afterwards was in attendance on the earl at the coronation of Henry's consort, Elizabeth of York.[53] In April 1489 he performed his latest personal service to his patron during the mysterious affair at Cocklodge, near Topcliffe, where the earl was lynched by the mob within sight of his formidable retinue. Contemporary writers cried shame on all but the few, including Sir Robert, who attempted to rescue him; but it is suggested that many of his followers as former annuitants of Richard of Gloucester bore a deep grudge against Northumberland for his inaction on the battlefield at Bosworth.[54] In May 1492 Sir Robert received his sovereign's special thanks for service in the field, under Thomas Howard, earl of Surrey, against the northern rebels at Ackworth.[55]

Soon after the betrothal of his eldest son, William, aged twelve, in May 1496, to Isabel Babthorpe, the young heiress to Sir Ralph Babthorpe of Osgodby, Sir Robert heard from his attorney, Edward Plumpton, the unwelcome news that the powerful lawyer-administrator Richard Empson, seizing, perhaps, the opportunity afforded by the fifth earl of Northumberland's minority, proposed to bring an action of

[50] App.II, 48. The original document, with the king's sign manual and the seal of the privy signet (now missing) is preserved among the Hastings MSS, *Historical Manuscripts Commission*, Series 78 (4 vols, 1928–47), i, 283, transcripts in R. Horrox and P.W. Hammond (eds), *British Library Harleian Manuscript 433* (Richard III Society, 4 vols, 1979–83), iii, 133–6; R.B. Smith, *Land and Politics in the England of Henry VIII: The West Riding of Yorkshire: 1530–46* (Oxford, 1970), 292.

[51] M.A. Hicks, 'Dynastic Change and Northern Society: the Career of the Fourth Earl of Northumberland, 1470–89', *NH*, xiv (1978), 107.

[52] **52**; Given-Wilson, *Nobility*, 101.

[53] **47**; *DNB*; John Leland, *De Rebus Britannicis Collectanea*, ed. Thomas Hearne (6 vols, 1874), iv, 185–7, 229–33.

[54] M.A. Hicks, 'The Yorkshire Rebellion of 1489 Reconsidered', *NH*, *XXII* (1986), 39–42; **74**; John Skelton, *Complete English Poems*, ed. V.J. Scattergood (1983), 31.

[55] **107**.

novel disseisin to oust him from the estates reserved to him under the arbitrement of 1483.[56] Empson's prizes were to be the manors of Kinoulton and Mansfield Woodhouse, but he soon increased his stake in the enterprise by securing the hand of Elizabeth Sotehill's son, Henry, for his daughter, Joan. Since the case for the plaintiffs is discussed below, it is sufficient to note here that having obtained the legal estate of the surviving feoffees under the deeds of settlement on the marriages of the heirs general, Empson conveyed it to two clerks, Robert Bubwith and Richard Burgh as feoffees to the use of Sir John Rocliffe and Margaret his wife, and Elizabeth Sotehill, widow. Because the assize could not be heard at *nisi prius*, writs were issued on 4 August 1501 to John Vavasour and John Fisher to hear the case at Nottingham, and to Humphrey Coningsby and James Hobart for the trial at York, with Vavasour specially appointed as clerk of assize, temporarily replacing Thomas Strey, one of the two regular clerks, who was known to be favourable to the Plumptons[57] – a blatant perversion of the law, which could perhaps be excused on the ground that there were reasons for suspecting that Sir Robert possessed his estates as a result of his father's deliberate fraud. In spite of an impressive array of legal talent retained on his behalf[58] the weight of influence was against Sir Robert, and the letters reflect his premonition that he and his advisors would be no match for the great minister who opposed him,[59] and had drawn into his conspiracy not only the justices, but also, through his close interest in Nottinghamshire politics, the many knights, gentlemen and yeomen who were to ride with him to the assizes to maintain his cause.[60] Inevitably, both verdicts were returned in favour of the plaintiffs – at Nottingham in September 1501 and York a year later. Sir Robert, thus dispossessed, spent the following years in fruitless efforts to have the verdicts reversed – his predicament the more intractable because the perversity and incompetence of his young patron, the fifth earl of Northumberland, had nullified his influence at court and antagonised

[56] **119**.

[57] *CPR, 1494–1509*, 291; E.W. Ives, *The Common Lawyers of Pre-Reformation England, Thomas Kebell: A Case Study* (Cambridge, 1983), 311–12; App. II, 61. For Thomas Strey, see **181**. For a note on *nisi prius*, see **126**, n. 9.

[58] Sergeants John Yaxley and Thomas Frowyk, with Richard or John Brook and Gregory Edgar as counsel, **152**. Frowyk was unable to appear because of his appointment as CJCP, **153**, **165**. For Yaxley's retainer, see App. II, 60, transcript in Stapleton, 152–3.

[59] **152**, **156–7**, **159**. Sir Humphrey Coningsby was one of Henry VII's feoffees, Somerville, i, 276 n.

[60] He obtained the support of the influential Sir Henry Willoughby, whom he subsequently rewarded with a fee, A. Cameron, 'Sir Henry Willoughby of Wollaton', *Transactions of the Thoroton Society*, lxxiv (1970), 17; Idem, 'A Nottinghamshire Quarrel in the Reign of Henry VII', *BIHR*, xlv (1972), 29–30; **206**.

Archbishop Savage, president of the Council in the North.[61]

About a year after his wife's death in 1504 Sir Robert married Isabel, daughter of Ralph, Lord Neville, and the unfortunate girl was immediately thrust into her predecessor's uncomfortable shoes. The two women laboured loyally and energetically, sometimes against their better judgement, to defend Plumpton and finance Sir Robert's ruinous litigation, whilst giving occasional expression to their impatience with his unwillingness to face reality.[62] Henry VII responded to his appeal against the injustice of the court proceedings by making him a knight of the body – thus affording him immunity from arrest for debt;[63] but shortly after the king's death in 1509 the withdrawal of the immunity enabled his creditors to close in, and he and his wife were confined for almost four months in the Counter.[64] A few days after their release on 5 August 1510 the execution of Sir Richard Empson brought an adventitious change in their fortunes by clearing the way for a more equitable settlement, but it was a further five years before the parties, now represented by Sir Robert and his son, William, Sir William Pierpoint, second husband of Empson's widowed daughter, Joan Sotehill, Sir Marmaduke Constable, who had purchased the marriage of one of Joan Sotehill's twin daughters, and Sir John Rocliffe and his co-parcenors, were brought together by Sir William Gascoigne.[65] Both sides having entered into recognizances of £1,000 to abide by the judgement of a panel of arbitrators headed by Richard Fox, bishop of Winchester,[66] their award, announced in 27 March 1515, included the reinstatement of the Plumptons in their ancestral lands within the parish of Spofforth.[67]

Unlike his father, Sir Robert never held any of the county offices, but as the earl's deputy at Knaresborough, and farmer of the corn-mills there and at nearby Killinghall, he exercised considerable influence

[61] M. Condon, 'Ruling Élites in the Reign of Henry VII', in Charles Ross (ed.), *Patronage, Pedigree and Power in Later Medieval England* (1979), 118; M.L. Bush, 'The Problem of the Far North: A Study of the Crisis of 1537 and its Consequences', *NH*, vi (1971), 42.

[62] **162**, **188**, **200**. His son was also critical, **176**.

[63] *L&P*, I (i), 207; **186**.

[64] CB, 836; **196**n. Their imprisonment lasted from 24 April to 5 Aug. 1510, Stapleton, cxviii.

[65] **210–11**.

[66] **209**; App. II, 74.

[67] App.II, 75–77, 79, 80. The midlands estates became the property of the descendants of the co-heiresses, and were held in undivided moieties. The Rocliffe moiety descended through the marriage of the heiress Anne Rocliffe to Sir Ingram Clifford, through whom it came ultimately to the earls of Cumberland, and the Sotehill moiety through Henry Sotehill's twin daughters Joan and Elizabeth to Sir John Constable and Sir William Drury, R. Meredith, 'The Eyres of Hassop, 1470–1640', *Derbyshire Archaeological Journal*, lxxxv (1964), 12, 83; see App.I, 8.

locally, and was not a man to be crossed.[68] No less unscrupulous than Sir William, he embarked on what was to be a lengthy, abortive dispute over the Babthorpe estates, and his attempt to deprive the widowed Joyce Percy of her land in Arkendale, frustrated by the intervention of her late husband's patron, the earl of Shrewsbury, was a misuse of his office as steward of the Yorkshire estates of Lilleshall Abbey.[69] His lack of prudence and judgement irritated both his wives, in spite of their loyal support, whilst his heedlessness drove his daughter Dorothy to the edge of despair. In May 1515, shorn of most of his former realty, he passed the management of the Plumpton estate to his eldest son, reserving accommodation for himself, his wife and three servants, and the right to be consulted on management policy. It was further agreed that causes of serious discord should be submitted for arbitration to two local clerics.[70] But in his turn, Sir Robert bequeathed a troublesome legacy to his heir, saddling William with the obligation to continue the legal battle over the spurious claim to lands belonging to his wife's family, the Babthorpes, which had been specifically exempted from the marriage contract of 1496. After William's death in 1547, his son Robert having predeceased him, the claim, revived by Robert's son William on achieving his majority, was not finally settled until 1567, when a decree of the court of wards and liveries set the seal of legality on the Babthorpes' claim to their patrimony.

The Plumpton Inheritance

The disposal by Sir William of the marriages of his granddaughters for substantial sums on the understanding that they were co-heiresses to his estates was a dangerous deception, which left his successor vulnerable to legal attack. In their submission to the commissioners in 1501[71] the heirs general cited a series of transactions beginning with a feoffment, dated 24 September 1420, by Sir Robert Plumpton (d.1421) of his Yorkshire estates in Plumpton, Idle, Steeton and Nessfield, with the advowson of his chantry of the Holy Trinity in Ripon Minster. Among the feoffees was Sir Thomas Rempston, second husband of Margaret, widow of Sir Godfrey Foljambe. Nineteen years later, on 10 April 1439, Rempston was again a feoffee in a conveyance by Sir William himself of Kinoulton, and estates in Derbyshire and Staffordshire. The trustees

[68] **66**, **78**, **128**. He appears to have lost the office by 10 Nov. 1505 when it was granted to Thomas Fairfax of Finningley during pleasure, Somerville, i, 524.

[69] **106**, **108**.

[70] App.II, 78, transcript in Stapleton, cxxiii–xxv.

[71] App.I, 6.

to whom seisin was delivered a week later included another kinsman, Richard Redman, senior, of Harewood, and Levens.[72] On the betrothal of his eldest son, Robert, to Elizabeth Clifford, Sir William settled all his estates on the couple and their heirs, but after Robert's death in 1450 Sir Thomas Rempston, as sole surviving trustee under the deeds of 1420 and 1439, by feoffment dated 23 August 1452, entailed all the estates upon Sir William and his heirs male, with remainder to Godfrey Plumpton, his younger brother.[73] The only record of Elizabeth Clifford's subsequent marriage to the new heir, Sir William's younger son, also named William, is to be found among the transcripts made by Roger Dodsworth and Christopher Towneley of the manuscripts surviving in Skipton Castle. These include the testimony of witnesses to both marriages and a memorandum in French of the case for the plaintiffs, Bubwith and Burgh, in 1501.[74] According to this evidence the terms of the settlement made by Sir William on the second marriage were similar to those pertaining to the first. But by this time he had secretly remarried and had a son, the future Sir Robert, who, even as he negotiated the marriages of his granddaughters, he was doubtless determined should succeed to the Plumpton estates.

Of the two settlements dated 1 June 1464, following the betrothals of Margaret and Elizabeth Plumpton, only one, that of the Yorkshire estates, is included in the Coucher Book; the second, significantly, perhaps, since the feoffees included Brian Rocliffe's clerk Richard Fawberg, through whom Richard Empson was later to acquire the legal estate of the feoffees in the midlands properties, survives in Christopher Towneley's book of transcripts in the British Library.[75] In neither is the intention of the enfeoffment specified. For the purpose of re-conveying and resettling his estates after the certification of his second marriage, Sir William's chosen feoffees, although led by the eminent pluralist Richard Andrews, dean of York, were of rather less social consequence than those brought together for the marriage settlements of the heirs general, and, after the dean's death in 1477, may have been unequal to their obligation to defend his dispositions.[76]

Sir William's death on 15 October 1480 followed quickly by official acknowledgement of Robert's title provoked the opposing parties to action: on 26 April 1481 Brian Redman, son of Richard Redman, senior, deceased, appointed John Sotehill and others his attorneys to

[72] App.II, 6, 8, 9; **219**n.

[73] App.II, 11, 13–15.

[74] App.I, 2, 6.

[75] **120**; App.II, 28, 29.

[76] E. Acheson, *A Gentry Community: Leicestershire in the Fifteenth Century c1422–c1485* (Cambridge, 1992), 85; App. II, 35, 36. Much of the argument centred on the question whether the estates were entailed to the heir male, **152**.

enter the manors of Plumpton, Grassington, Idle, Steeton and Little Studley, and on 10 July following he conveyed the same properties to Sir Thomas Burgh and others, including, significantly, John Ingilby, to the use of the heirs general.[77] Meanwhile, according to the memorandum, Richard Fawberg and his co-feoffees entered the midlands estates 'before the statute of Richard III'. The king's award settled matters until Richard Empson secured the legal estate of the surviving trustees, namely Richard Fawberg and John Ingilby, in the midlands and Yorkshire estates, respectively, and conveyed it to Robert Bubwith and Richard Burgh. The assize of *novel disseisin*, though falling into disuse, had the advantage of requiring an immediate verdict, and in September 1501 Sir Robert was there and then ejected from his midlands lordships after the verdict had gone against him.[78] The following year at the York assizes John Vavasour exhibited in open court a fine, exemplified under the great seal, presumably as proof that the manors of Plumpton and Idle had not been entailed to the heirs male. Sir Robert, who produced evidence to the contrary and condemned the fine as spurious, was not permitted to examine it. He thereupon rejected an attempt at mediation, and Empson's powerful maintenance ensured a favourable outcome for the plaintiffs.

Whether the arbitrement of 27 March 1515 represented justice tempered by mercy or injustice it is impossible to say. In a world where there were few certainties Sir William's gamble might well have succeeded, and the family survived into the next century in undiminished wealth and standing: he must have believed it was a chance worth taking.[79]

The Babthorpe Inheritance

Contemplating the state of the Babthorpe family in 1496 when he negotiated a contract for the marriage of his son with Isabel Babthorpe, Sir Robert must have been aware of the latent possibilities attaching to the alliance. Of the four surviving sons of Sir Robert Babthorpe (d.1466) only one had produced a male heir: the eldest, Sir Ralph

[77] App.II, 45.

[78] How Empson was able to defy the terms of Richard III's settlement is not clear; there was remedy to be had in chancery against such transgressions, e.g. *Early Chancery Proceedings*, iv (Lists and Indexes, xxix), 373.

[79] App.II, 64. On the question of Sir Robert's legitimacy it appears that not until 1472, when he witnessed an enfeoffment, did he act as heir apparent. On 30 May 1530 a jury was summoned to pronounce on the matter, and consequentially on his son's fitness to present a clerk to the chantry in Ripon cathedral, *Yorkshire County Magazine*, i (1891), 272; CB, 857.

(d.1490),[80] was the father of Isabel, wife of Sir John Hastings, who died without issue a few weeks before the marriage contract was signed, and whose heir, her cousin Isabel, daughter of Robert Babthorpe, would soon be the wife of William Plumpton; it was the third brother, William, who was the father of a young son. After her death Isabel Hastings's lands continued to be held by her husband by courtesy of England, with reversion to her heir, Isabel Plumpton.[81] As enumerated in the marriage contract Isabel Plumpton's inheritance included the manors of Sacombe and Waterton, with appurtenant lands in Hertfordshire and Lincolnshire, and certain smaller properties in Yorkshire. Reserved to William Babthorpe and his heir were the manors of Osgodby and Babthorpe and lands in Hemingborough, all held of the bishop of Durham as of his manor of Howden, with properties elsewhere in East Yorkshire.[82] The ink can hardly have been dry on the indentures before Sir Robert laid claim to the whole estate on the ground that all the properties had been entailed to the heirs general. William Babthorpe countered with evidence of their having been entailed to the heirs male, and with a claim of his own to the manor of Waterton.[83]

In January 1498/9 John Pullein and William Elleson informed Sir Robert of William Babthorpe's intention to have the issue over the lands in Hemingborough tried at *nisi prius*.[84] Accordingly, the case was heard at the Michaelmas assizes in York,[85] apparently without result, because a new *venire facias* was awarded by the justices of the court of common pleas the following November.[86] Whatever the outcome, William Babthorpe was declared seised of all his legal estate at his death on 10 February 1500/1. Having previously leased Babthorpe and the lands in Hemingborough to Sir John Hastings for a term of years yet to expire he had made a feoffment of the manor of Osgodby to the use of his wife, Christian, for life, remainder to the use of himself and his heirs male.[87] Soon afterwards Christian married William Bedell, to whom the bishop of Durham had sold the wardship of her young son, William. Shortly after the death of Sir John Hastings on 28 June 1504 the youngest of the four brothers Thomas Babthorpe, provost of Hemingborough, took forcible possession of Babthorpe on behalf of the eleven-year-old William, whose wardship he had purchased from

[80] *CIPM, Hen. VII* (3 vols, 1898–1956), i, 258–9.

[81] App.II, 63.

[82] App.I, 5.

[83] BL, Add. MS 32,113, fols 216–18v. This evidence was taken *c.* 1512, probably during one of the attempts at arbitration, App.II, 65, 66, 69–72.

[84] **126**, **129**.

[85] BL, Add. MS 32,113, fols 230v.–233.

[86] **142**.

[87] *CIPM, Hen. VII*, ii, 595–6. Christian was the daughter of Henry Sotehill of Stockerston.

Bedell.[88] But the following year William Plumpton obtained livery from the king of the manors of Sacombe and Babthorpe and the lands in Hemingborough, in right of his wife, as heiress of the late Lady Isabel Hastings, in which he received seisin from the escheator for Yorkshire, William Crouch, on 3 April following.[89] The Plumptons promptly invaded Babthorpe[90] and held it until Thomas Babthorpe counter-attacked a year later and, as related by William Plumpton in his complaint to the court of Star Chamber, forcibly removed Isabel from the premises.[91] The court instituted an enquiry by four Yorkshire JPs, Sir William Gascoigne, Sir William Scargill, Sir John Everingham and William Elleson, instructing them to report their findings to Sir Edmund Dudley. Depositions and replications were taken and a grand jury was summoned to make presentments, but of thirty rioters named in the indictment only three of the most insignificant were presented.[92] On 29 April 1511 the parties were bound in penal sums to abide by the award of Thomas, Lord Darcy and Sir Marmaduke Constable in respect of William Plumpton's claim to Babthorpe and that of Thomas Babthorpe to Waterton.[93] The arbitrators failed to reach agreement. William Babthorpe came of age *c.* 1511, and the quarrel simmered on, each side dispossessing the other, until the failure of a second attempt at arbitration in the summer of 1519.[94] A third attempt in 1524, the year before Sir Robert Plumpton's death, was equally unsuccessful.[95]

The year 1540 saw the death of William Bedell; William Plumpton died seven years later and Isabel Plumpton in 1552, seised, *inter alia*, of the manor of Babthorpe and the lands in Hemingborough;[96] whereupon the Babthorpes forced an entry on the disputed premises and they were forthwith taken into the queen's hand.[97] After the death of Sir William Babthorpe in 1555 his son and namesake brought the interminable affair to a successful conclusion. On 21 November 1563 he obtained from chancery the farm of the manor and lands,[98] and traversed the finding of the court of inquisition on the estate of Isabel Plumpton that

88 App.II, 63.

89 *CPR, 1494–1509*, 481; App.II, 65, 66.

90 App.II, 69.

91 C.G. Bayne and W.H. Dunham (eds), *Select Cases in the Council of Henry VII* (Selden Society, LXXV, 1956), cxxxv; App.II, 70.

92 App. II, 70, 71.

93 App. II, 73.

94 The obligation is dated 27 June 1519, CB, 850. Sir Robert Brudenell and Sir Humphry Coningsby made the attempt.

95 The obligation is dated 2 May 1524, prior to arbitration by Sir Lewis Pollard and Sir Richard Brook, CB, 855.

96 App.II, 88.

97 App.II, 88.

98 App.II, 85.

she was seised of the properties; a jury was summoned to view them and William appeared in chancery on 23 November 1564 to plead his cause. The following February young William Plumpton came of age, received livery of the lands inherited by him in right of his grandmother, and lost no time in reviving his claim.[99] A fourth, and finally successful, attempt at arbitration followed on 20 October, when two justices of the court of common pleas, Richard Weston and John Walsh, awarded the manors of Babthorpe and Osgodby, with the lands in Hemingborough to William Babthorpe, and the manor of Waterton, with the other lands to which he was entitled under the terms of the marriage contract of 1496 to William Plumpton.[100] A decree of the court of wards and liveries was awarded to Babthorpe in the Michaelmas term 1567 after Sir Nicholas Bacon, keeper of the great seal, had appeared before the justices of the bench and accepted his plea. The traverse was thereupon declared justified.[101]

The Manuscripts

The Plumpton archive comprises eight items, all compiled during the first half of the seventeenth century: the Letter Book, Coucher Book, five books of transcripts and abstracts of evidences, mainly from the Coucher Book, and an unbound volume of transcripts, possibly in the hand of Christopher Towneley, which includes copies of nine letters, of which three are not now to be found in the Letter Book (**107**, **162**, **166**).[102]

Sir Edward Plumpton's Book of Letters,[103] originally a small, unbound paper volume of some 216 pages with a fragment of a parchment cover adhering to the spine, has recently undergone repair, so that the pages adhere to stout paper, which also provides the cover. Compiled between 1612 and 1626, the first twenty-six pages and certain pages from the end of the book are now missing, and a number of leaves are badly damaged. The letters were transcribed in three separate sections and stitched together, with those addressed to Sir William Plumpton forming the middle of the book.

The Letter Book is made up as follows:

pp. 1–26 Missing. 37 letters missing.

[99] App.II, 85.

[100] App.II, 87.

[101] App.II, 88. Visiting Plumpton, Leland observed that there was 'a park and a fair house of stone with 2 towers longging to the same. Plumpton is now owner of it, a man of fair land and lately augmented by wedding the daughter and heir general of the Babthorpes', Lucy Toulmin Smith (ed.), *The Itinerary of John Leland in or about the Years 1535–1543* (5 vols, 1907–10), i, 87.

[102] WYASL, Acc 1731/2–9. See John Taylor, 'The Plumpton Letters', *NH*, x (1975), 74–81.

[103] Acc 1731/2.

pp. 27–149 Letters to Sir Robert Plumpton (176 letters), transcribed 1612–13, for the most part in a flowing, secretary hand, though with two or three other transcribers, one with a somewhat laboured, unprofessional hand, intervening. In the margins Stapleton has noted the number assigned to each letter in his edition.

Between pp. 72 and 73 A fragment (see **181**n.).

pp. 149–50 Blank space between the series, filled with a letter to Sir Richard Plumpton, priest. Page 150 is headed: *Letters to Sir Robert Plumpton who died 25 year of King Henry the eyght.*

pp. 151–79 Letters to Sir William Plumpton (30 letters), transcribed in 1612 in a neater, much more formal secretary hand, by possibly two transcribers, with a third, perhaps the same unprofessional writer, intervening occasionally.

Thirteen of these letters were copied into the CB between 15 and 20 July 1616 (611–23). Each page is headed: *Letters written to Sir William Plompton who died 20 year of R.Edward the fowrth.*

p. 180 Blank save for a note in a different hand: *A letter written conserning Mr William Plompton*, to which another writer has appended the words *Blessed by thy holy Name*

pp. 181–216 Letters to William Plumpton, Mrs Isabel Plumpton and others (35 letters), transcribed in 1626 in a single, neat secretary hand similar to that of the previous section, which can be detected also in some of the entries in the CB (e.g. no. 781). Pages 181–84 are headed: *Letters written conserning Mr Wm Plompton who dyed primo Ed: 6*; pp. 185–92: *Letters written to Mrs Isabel Plompton who dyed 6 Ed. 6*; pp. 193–5: *Letters written to Mr Robert Plompton esquire who dyed 38 of Hen: 8*; pp. 196–216: *Letters written to Mr William Plompton esquire who died primo Ed: 6.* The marginal notes in all three sections are written in a variety of hands, in some cases apparently much later.

Although the manuscript was complete when Roger Dodsworth saw it in 1633, he copied only five letters (**108**, **162**, **166**, **185**, **206**) from the missing pages. One more may be found in the Chambers MSS (**79**), and another in Stapleton's edition, transcribed by him from a source as yet unidentified (**105**).[104] The earliest letter, addressed to Sir Robert Plumpton (d.1421) in 1416 by a group of York citizens, which may not have been included in the Letter Book, appears only in the CB (App. I). It is said to be one of the earliest surviving letters in English.[105]

[104] The letter from the earl of Surrey to Sir Robert, 9 May [1492] (**105**), is cited erroneously by Stapleton as in Dugdale's *Yorkshire Arms*, among the MSS in the College of Arms (Stapleton, 96n). A search failed to locate it. Thus 8 letters from the missing pages are included, viz. nos **79**, **105**, **107**, **108**, **162**, **166**, **185**, **206**.

[105] John Taylor, 'Letters and Letter Collections in England, 1300–1420', *Nottingham Medieval Studies*, xxiv (1980), 67. Idem, *English Historical Literature in the Fourteenth Century* (Oxford, 1987), 210.

Minor emendations in the text suggest that the copyists probably adhered closely to the originals, although a comparison with the thirteen letters copied into the CB reveals numerous small variations. Each letter is written continuously, with haphazard sub-punctuation limited for the most part to occasional oblique strokes and a very few full points, and with inconsistent use of capital letters. The salutations and commendations, which vary from the terse to the profuse, form part of the opening sentence, and although the present participle is sometimes used to lead into the narration, such phrases as 'please you to witt', or, more commonly, the lumpish 'it is so that' are generally preferred. However, the conclusion is often reached more elegantly by such conventions as 'with the grace of Jhesu, who you and yours long preserve in prosperous felicite'. The Deity and the Holy Trinity are sometimes invoked, especially by ecclesiastics, but Edward Plumpton's frequent invocations to Jesus seem to reflect devotion associated with the newer cult of the veneration of the Holy Name (**38**, **93**). The recipients are unnamed within the text of the letters.

The narration is almost always severely practical, the lawyers frequently packing information, advice and instructions on a number of disparate matters into a single, comparatively short, letter. Phrases which doubtless had the authority of dictamen abound, though occasional reported conversations perhaps capture 'the unforced note and movement of the lost spoken language' (e.g. **2**, **18**).[106] The warmer emotions have little place in the correspondence: Sir Robert's few words of endearment to his wife (**162**, **185**); young Robert's gratitude to his mother (**230**), and German de la Pole's obvious desire to establish an affectionate relationship with his parents-in-law (**138**), possibly as a counterweight to his tight-fisted grandmother, are among the very few such insights. For the rest, we have, for example, Sir William's cold-hearted trifling with a lady's affections (**12**); the calculated enthusiasm of Edward Plumpton's stratagem to secure the hand of an eligible widow (**121**); the exasperation of Dame Agnes and Dame Isabel (**188**, **199**); Dorothy Plumpton's appeal to her father to show some interest in her concerns (**201**); the desperation of King Henry VI, hardly concealed under his peremptory summons (**3**), and the bluff heartiness of that sporting knight Sir Henry Savile (**244**). In her drily unsentimental letter to her daughter, Lady Neville may have relied upon the assistance of the bearer, who 'loues you full wele', to express the maternal consolation which she had not committed to writing (**200**). Indeed, reliance on the credence frequently deprives the letters of information necessary to a full understanding of the text.

[106] N. Davis, 'Style and Stereotype in Early English Letters', *Leeds Studies in English*, n.s., i (1964), 15.

Whilst some letters are stated, or appear, to be autograph (e.g. **14**, **42**, **44**, **46**, **135**, **138**), these do not differ materially in style from those dictated to, or written by, clerks or secretaries. Even the letter from John Eyre (**192**), which has been described as the work of an unlettered man, is nevertheless expressed in accordance with the accepted formularies. The date, where this is given, is incorporated into the final sentence, usually the day of the month, perhaps with reference to the nearest saint's day or other church feast. The signature and introductory words of the subscription are written separately at the end, usually spread over two lines. The endorsement appears at the head of the letter, sometimes at the foot of the previous page. Whilst some order of precedence was observed in the arrangement of the letters there was no attempt at chronology. The period covered (1460–1552)[107] is slightly longer than that of the *Paston Letters* (1422–1509), but whereas much of the Paston correspondence relates to the reigns of Henry VI and Edward IV, the greatest concentration of dated Plumpton letters occurs between 1480 and 1510.

Correspondents range widely from kings, magnates, senior churchmen, abbots and judges to lawyers, men of affairs, friends, relations and servants, enemies and creditors. The great majority are 'incoming' letters; only four were written by Sir Robert himself (**162**, **166**, **185**, **206**), although members of the immediate family, Dame Agnes (**168**, **170–2**, **186**, **188–90**), Dame Isabel (**199**), Sir Robert's son and daughter, William (**232**) and Dorothy (**201**), and William's son Robert (**229–30**) are represented.

The Plumpton Coucher Book[108]

A bound parchment volume with a paper section inserted, the limp cover lined with a paper fragment from a fifteenth-century theological MS.[109] The first two pages, containing entries 1–19 are missing and the following three pages are eaten away. The contents, comprising about 1,000 entries, include Plumpton deeds and other evidence (n.d.–1555), and copies of thirteen letters addressed to Sir William Plumpton, all transcribed between 15 and 20 July 1616. In addition there are extracts from the Knaresborough Forest records (1432–83) and from the Fountains, Healaugh, Bridlington, Bolton and Embsay Coucher Books; a Studley rental of 1483; extracts from the Plumpton court rolls (1440–1509); a copy of an exemplification of proceedings in the common pleas

[107] The earliest extant letter in the Letter Book is dated 1433 (**1**).
[108] WYASL, Acc 1731/3.
[109] I am indebted to Mr J.W. Connor for this information.

in a case relating to the manor of Ryther (1555) and certain notes made for Sir Edward Plumpton by Roger Dodsworth (1633).

Entries up to p. 149 are written in a uniform hand; thereafter they appear in various hands, some of which are detectable in parts of the Letter Book. The parchment leaves are ruled horizontally with lines one cm. apart, although the copiers did not always observe the rulings.

On the completion of the Letter Book the original letters appear to have been destroyed. The book itself, however, together with the CB and other material, survived the extinction of the family in the eighteenth century through acquisition by Christopher Towneley (1606–74), a noted antiquarian and transcriber, whose family were related to the Plumptons by marriage, and who himself transcribed a number of the Plumpton sources. In 1839 Thomas Stapleton's edition of the Letter Book, augmented by material in the Towneley collection, was published by the Camden Society. Forty-four years later a Nottinghamshire gentleman, Mr J.E.F. Chambers, acquired certain Plumpton manuscripts at a sale of the Towneley collection by Sotheby's and they were henceforth unavailable to scholars until in 1972 his descendant, Mr Jowett of Southwell, gave to the WYASL the items now included in the Chambers MSS.[110]

Editorial Method

The texts, with a few exceptions noted below, rest on new transcripts; they are unaltered save for modern capitalization and minimal punctuation, and retain the inconsistencies of spelling of the originals. Paragraphs have been introduced into the longer letters.

The u and v, c and t and the ampersand are retained as in the originals, as is the use of þ and ȝ (the latter appears rarely, the former frequently but inconsistently). The capital I and J, for which all writers used a single form in both functions, are distinguished in printing. Abbreviations have been slightly extended. Supplied text and lacunae are placed between square brackets, interlined words and phrases

[110] No vestige of Plumpton Hall remains, though the well which may have supplied the house survived for a time near the entrance to Plumpton Rocks. The house was demolished by the purchaser, Daniel Lascelles, who used the stone to build a new residence designed by John Wyatt of York, on a different site. It remains unfinished because he decided to live instead at Goldsborough. A drawing of the south aspect of the old house, then known as Plumpton Towers, is in a collection of drawings made by John Warburton, J.W. Clay (ed.), 'Journal in 1718–19 of John Warburton, Somerset Herald', *YAJ*, xv (1900), 80; Ely Hargrove, *History of the Castle, Town and Forest of Knaresborough with Harrogate* (1st edn 1775, repr. 1789), 356–61. I am indebted to Professor M.W. Beresford for bringing to my attention a map dated 18 April 1587, of the manor of Plumpton and its environs, PRO, MPC 230.

between angled brackets, and in **53**, **54** and **220**, where the paper of the original is so damaged that the text is now indecipherable, the missing words, taken from Stapleton's edition, are placed within round brackets.

Two letters and a fragment of a third (**222**, **246**, **247**), now missing from the end of the Letter Book, are reproduced from Stapleton's edition (pp. 225, 252–3). A comparison of the lacunae as they appear in Stapleton with the damaged pages in the Letter Book suggests that Wyvill's letter was the first of these, and that Besey's was the last letter in the book as Stapleton saw it. Letter **107**, from Henry VII to Sir Robert, can now be reproduced only in abbreviated form. The reference given at the head of each letter relates to its number and page in the Letter Book.

The thirteen letters copied into the CB in July 1616 (**3**, **5**, **8**, **13**, **16**, **18**, **19**, **21–4**, **28**, **29**) reveal numerous differences in spelling, but as these are insignificant and do not affect the sense, they have been ignored for reasons of space.

Internal evidence, where this is now available, frequently supports Stapleton's chronological sequence, which has therefore been retained as a framework within which the order of groups of letters has been changed. In particular, some effort has been made to distinguish the 4th earl of Northumberland's letters from those of his son and successor, for example, those despatched from Seamer can probably be attributed to the latter (**74**n.).

In Appendix II (Calendar of deeds from the CB and other sources) each item has been numbered separately and the original language and location noted at the end, together with the copyist's note of the date of copying. Marginalia which merely indicate the subject of the deed and the date have been omitted. Standard clauses of warranty, distraint and power of attorney have been curtailed or merely noted, and clauses of sealing omitted, unless of particular interest. 'Etc' is used in the text only where it appears in the original unless it is enclosed within square brackets. The few editorial insertions are likewise enclosed within square brackets, and in a few places suspension points indicate illegibility of the original.

Place-names are given in their modern equivalents where these can be identified, but have otherwise been left in the original within inverted commas. Christian names have been modernized but not surnames, which appear as in the manuscript. Dates have been modernized and Arabic numerals used.

SIR EDWARD PLUMPTON'S LETTER BOOK

1 *John, Lord Scrope of Masham*[1] *to Sir William Plumpton, 19 February [1433]* *(No. 8, p. 154)*

Trusty and welbeloued I greet you wel,[a] praying you that you wil haue in tendernesse and faour my welbeloued cousin George of Plompton,[2] your nepew, as towching his annuity, in such wise as he may know this my writing may turn into auail; certifying me wherin that I may shew you as much kindness or ease, the which I wold do with al my harte, as God knowes, who haue you in his keeping. Written at London, the ninetenth day of Feueryear.

The Lord Scroop, treasurer of England

Endorsed: To my right trusty and welbeloued cousin Sir William Plompton

[a] *Marginal note*: 8 letter.

[1] John, Lord Scrope of Masham (d.1455), lord treasurer of England 6 Feb. 1432 to 11 Aug. 1433, *CPR, 1429–38*, 187; **2**.

[2] George Plumpton, clerk, Sir William's uncle and brother of the writer of **2**, App. III.

2 *Katherine Chadderton*[1] *to George Plumpton, [c.1450 × 1455]* *(No. 30, p. 178)*

My best brother, I am sory, by my troth, that I shall nott see you & cum thus far as to York. God knoweth my intent was not for no great gud þat I thoght to desire, but I wott wele now ye trusted the contrary. But, brother, it is not vnknowne þat I am right sickly, & my hart wold haue bene gretly comforted to haue spoken with you, but I trow, & so doth my daughter, that ye be disp[l]eased, denyeing that my writing afore, because she desired a booke of you, and as euer I be saved, she praied me write for either salter or primmer, and my hosband said, halfe apley, 'prey my brother to gett somwhat to my new chappell'. God wot, he ment neither gold nor siluer, but some other thing for said awter. But I had knowne ye wold haue bene displeased, I wold not haue writt, for as much as I haue speuled my best brother.

My sister, Dame Isabell,[2] liueth as heauy a life as any gentlewoman borne, the which cause me I faired neuer well sence I saw her last month. Hous such, hath nether woman nor maide with her, but her selfe alone. And her hosband cometh all day to my hosband and seyeth the feyrest langwage that euer [...][a] ye hard. But all is rong, he is euer in trouble,[b] and all the ioy in earth hath she when my hosband cometh to her. She sweareth there is noe creature she loueth better. Also, brother, I beseech you intirely, if there be any goodly young woman [*p. 179*] that is a good woman of her body, & pay iiij and xx or more, and I would haue one of my owne kin, an theare were any, for my selfe. And, deare brother, and ye or any for you <can> espie, I beseech you to gitt her for me as hastely as you may, soune upon Easter, and it may be. I can no more, for great hast of my iorny, but I beseech þe blessed Trinitie, with all þe saints in heauen, give me grace to se you or I die, to God's pleasure & your bodily health.

And, brother, I yede to the Lord Scroope[3] to haue sene my lady, & be my trothe I stood thear a large houre, and yet I might neither se lo[rd] nor ladye; and þe strangest cheare that euer I had of my Mistres Darsie,[4] and yet I had 5 men in a suit. There is noe such 5 men in his house, I dare say.

Be your sister Ka: Chadyrton

Endorsed (p. 178): To Master Georg Plompton att Bolton Abbey

[a] *Two words deleted.*

[b] *Marginal note*: Lanc Plompton. King H. IV.

[1] Katherine, sister of Sir Robert Plumpton (d.1421), Stapleton suggests her husband was a Chadderton of Chadderton Hall, Lancs. Two possibilities are (1) Richard Chadderton who entered Henry V's retinue in 1415 in the following of Sir Ralph Staveley, (2) Henry de Chadderton to whom Sir William de Assheton owed a debt in 1431, Stapleton xl; J.S. Roskell, *Knights of the Shire for the County Palatine of Lancaster* (Chetham Society, n. s., 96, 1937), 111, 177; *VCH of the County Palatine of Lancaster*, ed. Wm Farrer, v (1911), 98, 109n.

[2] Katherine's elder sister, Isabel, married a Lincolnshire knight, Sir Stephen Thorpe, George Plumpton being one of the parties to the contract, 10 March 1425. Their mother, Alice Plumpton (d.1423), had made provision for their marriage portions, and bequeathed to each a number of devotional and household items, CB, 424, 456, 381, 411; Stapleton, xxxi–ii.

[3] John, Lord Scrope of Masham married, before 24 Aug. 1418, Elizabeth, daughter of Sir Thomas Chaworth, of Wiverton, Notts, *GEC*; **I**.

[4] Eleanor Scrope, daughter of John, Lord Scrope, married Richard Darcy (d. before June 1452), son and heir of Sir John Darcy of Hirst, *Coll(ectanea) Top(ographica) et Gen(ealogica)* (8 vols, 1834–43), ii, 148–9; C.B. Norcliffe (ed.), *The Visitation of Yorkshire in the Years 1563 and 1564 made by William Flower, esquire, Norroy King of Arms* (Harleian Society, xvi, 1881), 91–2, 279.

3 *Henry VI to Sir William Plumpton, 13 March 1460/1* *(No. 1, p. 151; CB 611)*

By the King R[ex] H[enricus]. Trusty and wellbeloued we greete you well, and for as much as we haue very knowledg that our great trator the late earle of Mearch hath made great assemblies of riotouse and mischeously disposed people; and to stirr and prouocke them to draw vnto him he hath cried in his proclamations hauok vpon all our trew liege people and subiects, theire wiues, children & goods, and is now coming towards vs. We therfor pray you and also straitely charge you that anon vpon the sight herof ye with all such people as ye may make defensible arraied come vnto us in all hast possible wheresoeuer we shall bee within this our realme, for to resist the malitious entent and purpose of our said trator. And faile not herof as ye loue the seurty of our person, the weale of your selfe, and of all our trew and faithfull subiects.[1] Geuen under our signet at our cyty of York the thirtenth day of March.[a]

Endorsed: To our trusty and welbeloued knight Sir William Plompton

[a] *Marginal note*: 1 letter. Ano 1612, copied 8 December.

[1] The death of Sir William's son and heir, William, probably on the field of Towton, 29 March 1461, was to have far-reaching consequences for the family. He is last recorded as living 19 Feb. 1460/1, CB, 547.

4 *Brian Rocliffe to Sir William Plumpton, 5 November [1461]* *(No. 10, p. 155)*

My right reverent & honorable maister,[a] all humble recomendation praemised, please you that I receaued of your servant John Smith xl marks and your letter to the tresorer[1] and barons of the exchequer for respitt of your day to xvna Hillary,[2] which would not be graunted but soe I haue gotten that one shall appeare for you att the day of account, & soe to be appeared for in the pipe, and then for to be prepared in the next tearme. And soe I haue labored a felow of mine to be your attorney in the court, for I may nought be but of counsell;[3] and he & I shall shew you such service att that time and afterwards that shall be pleasing vnto you. And soe shall ye haue day or respitt to the xv of Hillary next coming, then to be opposed of your greenwax,[4] at which time ye may nott faile to send hider all your bookes and some readie man for to answer vnto him, for I nor my said felow may nott attend thereupon, and also to be here your selfe tha<n> or before to pursue for your pardon, and to gree all your demandes att once. And I trust to God for to gett you downe your greenwax, if that I may, thof it cost you money, soe ye wrote vnto me. Beseeching our Lord to gif you good speed against all your enemies and in all your matters. Written in hast at Westminster ye fift day of November.

Your servant Bryan Rocliff[b]

Endorsed: Vnto my right reuerent and worshipfull maister Maister Sir William Plompton knight

[a] *Marginal note*: 10 letter.
[b] *Marginal note*: Copied 12 of December 1612, Sunday.

[1] Henry Bourchier, re-appointed 18 March 1460/1 held office until April 1462, *HBC*, 103.
[2] Sir William had been sheriff of Yorks in 1448 and of Notts and Derbys in 1452, *List of Sheriffs*, 103, 162.
[3] Brian Rocliffe's appointment as third baron of the Exchequer was ratified 2 Nov. 1458; his office precluded his appearance as counsel in the exchequer court, *CPR, 1452–61*, 482; App. III.
[4] The summons of greenwax particularized those items for which the sheriff was held responsible. He might be called to account years after the end of his term in office, M. Blatcher, 'Distress Infinite and the Contumacious Sheriff', *BIHR*, xiii (1935–36), 149–50; A.L. Brown, *The Governance of Late Medieval England, 1272–1461* (1989), 63.

5 *Sir Richard Bingham to Sir William Plumpton, 8 January [1461/2] (No. 14, p. 158; CB 619)*

Right worshypfull and reverent coussin, after dew and hartyly recommendations, be the advise of my master, Sir John Markam, chiefe iustice,[1] I comonde with Henry Pearpointe, esquire, for the variance that is betwixt you and him,[2] and he is agred, if it please you, to put all things that is in variance betwixt you and him in the said Sir John and me,[3] and if ye will doe the same, we, for the ease of you both and the rest of the contry, will take the matter vpon us, and we will apoynt you bothe, and apoynte you to be at Notinggam vpon the Mondey next after Law Sunday next coming, at euen, you to be lodgd theare vpon the Long Raw in the Satterday market, at your pleasure, and the said Henry against St Mary Kirke; and every of you not to excede xij persons, and ye and every of your persons to be single arrayd, and in noe other forme; and the place of metting for you and vs to be at St Petter Kirke. And if this please you, I trust to God the matter in variance betwixt you and him shall take good conclusion. And therfore how ye will agre in this matter I pray you send word in writing to my son, Richard Bingham, that he may let my master, Sir John Markam, Henry Perpoint, and mee haue knowledg of your disposition in the said matter. The day of your trety shall bee at Notingham upon the Tewsday next after Law Sunday betimes, and my said master and I shal so behaue us [*p. 159*] betwixt you that yf you both wil bee ruled by reason, ye shall both bee wel eased, with the grace of God, which keep you euer. Written at Midlton the eight day of January.[a]

Your poor cosin Rich: Bingham knight

Endorsed (p. 158): To my right honnorable and reverant coussin Sir William Plompton knight

[a] *Marginal note*: 14 letter. Variance betwene Perpoint and Plompton, month other.

[1] Sir John Markham, CJKB 1461–9.

[2] In the 1450s the Plumptons were in dispute with the Pierpoints, of Holme Pierpoint, Notts, over land in Mansfield Woodhouse. Whilst process was pending in the courts Sir William Plumpton's brother-in-law and steward, John Greene of Newby, murdered Henry Pierpoint on 21 July 1457, and was in turn murdered at Pannal, near Harrogate, by Henry's brother John. Crown proceedings against those involved were supplemented by appeals of homicide by Henry's widow, Thomasin, and John Greene's nephew and heir, Richard Greene. A previous attempt at arbitration had failed, S.J. Payling, *Political Society in Lancastrian England* (Oxford, 1991), 200–1; App. III.

[3] Sir Richard Bingham, JKB. His award was given 21 May 1463, Apps II, 22; III.

6 *Brian Rocliffe to Sir William Plumpton, 14 October [1462] (No. 9, p. 154)*

In speciall my verray good maister,[a] after due recomendations, my maister the chief baron[1] comuned to my lord treasorer[2] of certaine matters, and soe my lord opened that Thomas Beckwith was his awntes son, and he would make him eshetour, saying that he loved you right wele and would fayne an end were taken betwixt you and Beckwith,[3] willing my said maister to take vpon him the rewle; and would undertake Beckwith to be ruled by him, if he would take it upon him, who disclosed this vnto me, nott certaine that ye would agree. And I answered that I supposed ye would agree to all reason, enforming him of the trewthe of the matter, to my cuning, after your information. Soe that if such writing be had vnto you by the advize of your trewe in reason, in reason it is to be agreed with reason, as my simplesse seemeth, saueing your better advise.

And, Sir, Beford hath spoken with me sayeing that the matter is broken up in the default of Sir Harry that kept no tyme, and soe he purposes to continue and take out his suite, whom with sobernesse I entreate, affirming that ye will be here this tearme, and as long as I may, but I haue noe grant of him. And Colt[4] hath spoken to me for the remainder of the money which ye should send with the bill of issues and for costes. And Beford hath spoken with Plomptree[5] for the other obligation under sewertee, and soe in manner of a certante of payment; but now it is deatt the lyeing att large. Thus matters remitted to your

said discretion, whom our Lord govern and haf in his keeping. Written in hast in the Temple the fourtenth day of October.[b]
Endorsed: Unto his reuerent maister Sir William Plompton knight in hast

[a] *Marginal note*: George Plompton, Sir William, refer *ut supra*.
[b] *Marginal note*: Copies 10 December 1612.

[1] Richard Illingworth, lawyer, of Kirby Woodhouse, Notts, appointed 10 Sept. 1462; knighted by 1466, *CPR, 1461–67*, 22, 198.
[2] John Tiptoft, 1st earl of Worcester (exec.1470), lord treasurer in April 1452 and again in 1462 and 1470, J.S. Roskell, *The Commons and Their Speakers in English Parliaments 1376–1523* (Manchester, 1965), 248.
[3] The quarrel arose out of the terms of a contract for the marriage of Sir William's daughter Elizabeth, and William, son of Thomas Beckwith of Clint. Thomas may have been escheator for Yorkshire in Nov. 1462, as Stapleton states, but there is no record of the appointment for that year, *Index of Escheators for England and Wales* (PRO, L and I, supp. ser., lxxii), 189; **68**; App. II, 17, 54.
[4] Probably Thomas Colt (d.1467), a lawyer retained by the Duchy as apprentice 1452–66 chamberlain of the Exechequer, App. III.
[5] John Beford (or Bedford) and John Plumtree, citizens and fishmongers of London, and merchants of the Staple of Calais, *CCR, 1454–61*, 15, 412.

7 *Brian Rocliffe to Sir William Plumpton, 19 May [1463]* *(No. 13, p. 157)*

Right reue[r]end and honorable Sir[a] and mine especiall good maister, after all humble recomandations, with dew regraces and hartly thankinge of your kind mastership vnto me vndeserved, effectualy my trust is desiring continuance. Please you that I haue communed with Beford[1] in your mater, as ye wrote to me, and I cannot find him disposed that he will eyther grant you any yeares of payment, or els <to> be content by any soum yearly to be paid, and he will agre to no[...][b] treate but if he have some money in hand, and so he haith taken his *exigi facias de nouo*[2] and is with us called in the hustengs; maruelling me that after writing by letter and comunication by [*p. 158*] mouth, ye tender not hartyly that matter, considring the other obligation which might be executed against Plumtre of Nottingham, if ye wold doe your deuor; beseching you to remember your honestie and wellfare.

And, Sir, I have tretied with Wigmore, and, at few words, I find him right hard and strange, and soe ye bene iij called in Middlesex;[3] wherfore ye must purvay hastely remmedy, for he will noe more trust faire wordes, as he saith. Thus remiting matters to your discrett wisdom, whom the Holiest enspire to your profit and pleasure, my advis being allwaies [...][c] redy. Written in hast [...][d] at London, the 19th of May.[e]

Your servant Brian Roclife

Endorsed (p. 157): Vnto his right reuerend and honorable master Sir William Plompton knight in hast

[a] *Marginal note*: 13 letter.
[b] inn *deleted.*
[c] written *deleted.*
[d] the *deleted.*
[e] *Marginal note*: Coppied the 13th December *Anno* 1612.

[1] See **6**.
[2] A writ, sued out with a return day, which allowed the sheriff sufficient time to proclaim outlawry in four successive courts before pronouncing it in a fifth, M. Blatcher, *The Court of King's Bench, 1450–1550: A Study in Self-Help* (1978), 74.
[3] The Bill of Middlesex was the procedure whereby the court of King's Bench acquired jurisdiction in civil cases between subject and subject.

8 *Brian Rocliffe to Sir William Plumpton, [December 1463] (No. 11, p. 155; CB 618)*

Right worshippfull my singuler good mastre,[a] as my dewtie is, with intier regraces, I recomend me vnto you, whose honor, ioy & prosperitie I beseech the blessed Trinitie to encrease dayly, as I would haf of my simple person. Sir, I thank you, among inumerable other of your comfortable letters, that you now take your disport[1] att your libertie. And as touching my lord,[2] I shall ride to M. to him within these 4 daies and doe my parte, and as I shall find him [*p. 156*] so shall I certifie you. Sir, as anenst Scatergood, I hafe yett taken a longer continuance vnto New Yere Day, and I would fayne that it were att an end, thof it cost you money for countermaunding and noysing that would be had by priuy seales, for they go light cheape; and send me your will therein.

Sir, it is necessary that T[homas Beckwith] be content at t[h]is time x *li* for losse of money by suites makes more payments.[3] Sir, if it like you that Richard F. aftre this Yoole might entend vpon me toward London, seing your presence now here, and ye might forgo him, I would haue of you knowledge, for other haue labored me whome I respite therefore. Butt dissease or displease would nott I you in any wise. As for Gouldesburgh, yett mett we nott, but now I trust that ye shall confirme all that first was named,[4] and for God's sake perform it (*qua mora trahit periculum*), or his brother Edward[5] goe to London att twentie day of Yoole, and ellis will it straunge and delay. And think how ye lost Robart Ros son.[6] Your daughter & myn with humble recomendations, desireth your blessing and speaketh prattely and French, and hath near hand learned her sawter. Sir, Henry Suthill hath knowledge of her feofment, as a man tould me secretly,[7] but for all that, I trust all shalbe well, with the grace of the blessed Trinity, who quyte you and send you all your desires. Writen in hast att Colthrop on Fryday.[b]

Your serviseable brother Bryan Roucliffe

Endorsed (p. 155): Vnto his singuler good maister Sir William Plompton knight

[a] *Marginal note*: 11 letter.
[b] *Marginal note*: Copied 12 of December 1612, Sunday.

[1] A reference to Sir William's acquittal in 1463 on a charge of spreading treasonous rumours. Pardons were issued to him on 30 Aug. 1463 and 20 Jan. 1463/4, *CPR, 1461–67*, 285; App. II, 19, 26.

[2] Probably the earl of Warwick, whose stronghold was Middleham castle, Richmondshire. Plumpton was reinstated as the earl's deputy at Knaresborough after coming to terms with him, Introd., above p. 7.

[3] See **6**.

[4] The bond for the marriage of Sir William's daughter Alice with Richard Goldsburgh is dated 1 Oct. 1465, CB, 586.

[5] Edward Goldsburgh later became a baron of the Exchequer, *Test. Ebor.*, iv,49; S.B. Chrimes, *Henry VII* (1972), 158; Rosemary Horrox, *Richard III: A Study of Service* (Cambridge, 1989), 199.

[6] Robert Roos of Ingmanthorpe, near Wetherby, whose son's projected marriage with another of Sir William's daughters was aborted, WYASL, Acc.1731/6, fol.208.

[7] Margaret, daughter of William's deceased son and heir was contracted to marry Brian Rocliffe's son John, 26 Nov. 1463. The following Feb. her sister Elizabeth was contracted to marry John, eldest son of Henry Sotehill of Stockerston, Leicestershire. Significantly the two prospective fathers-in-law were servants of the earl of Warwick, Apps I, 3; II, 23; III.

9 *Godfrey Greene to Sir William Plumpton, 14 February [1463/4]* *(No. 26, p. 171)*

Right worshipfull maistre,[a] I recomend me vnto you. Please it you to witt the minister of St Roberts[1] has taken 2 suits, one of trespas for deluing his ground att St Roberts,[2] another of debt & detinue both in a writt, debt 12 marks, which was, I vnderstand by Horberey, should be lent to you. Be the place[b] of the detinue [*p. 172*] for a chalise shold be lent to you, also the writts were out but I caused Horberey *per album breue*.[3] So the sheriff shall haue none paid for the writts, by the avise of Mr Rocliff. I pray you send answerre against the next tearme; also had I understood for certain what goods Folbaron [...][c] and Walker had of yours, I shold haue bene answerd this tearme by Horberey not guilty, which is the best issue you can haue. I pray you send word against the next terme. Also Whele had sent out *exigi facias de nouo* against Holden, Hanworth & West[4] or I came here, & said they were returned *quarto exactus*: he had giuen them to short a day. Whearfore he said he wold write vnto you for an excuse, and pray the *exigi* against West may be withdrawen: I promised he shold take no hurt by the proces. Also White sends you a *capias utlegat*[5] against Harldre by Rauf Annias, but he deliuered it to the sheriff. I shall send you another with the copie of your new suites and a *venire facias*[6] against þe ministre.

Mr Rocliff hath labored effectually this tearme for your matter of Stamford[7] and for my Lady Inglestrop, for your sake, and to Pa[s]ke also; and also he dined with my lady & thanked her hartely for your sake.[8] I trust by his labour your matter of Stamford shall take a good end, with the grace of God, who haue you euermore in his keeping. Written at London, 14 February.[d]

Your servant Godfrey Grene[9]

Endorsed (p. 171): To my right worshipfull maistre Sir William Plompton kt

[a] *Marginal note*: 26 letter.
[b] *MS* plea.
[c] had *deleted*.
[d] *Marginal note*: Copied 1 of February 1612, Monday.

[1] Robert Bolton, minister of the house of St Robert, of the Order of the Redemption of Captives at Knaresborough, is known to have been in office in 1491. His successor was appointed in 1499, *VCH Yorks*, ed. Wm. Page, iii (1930), 296.

[2] Sir William claimed some rights over this ground. The use of a plea of trespass instead of one of *novel disseisin* enabled a straightforward question of title to be put, as opposed to the complexity of the rules of pleading which had grown up around the petty assizes, Hastings, 203–4, 237–8; **10**, **18**.

[3] A slang expression for returning a writ without an endorsement, Hastings, 228.

[4] A judicial writ of mesne process issued by the filacer and aimed at getting the defendant into court, J.H. Baker, *An Introduction to English Legal History* (1979), 52.

[5] Writ for the arrest of an outlaw. The minister and certain members of the community were indicted and outlawed during these proceedings. The process did not bring the defendant into court to answer the plaintiff unless he found himself inconvenienced by the outlawry, Hastings, 240; App. II, 31.

[6] Writ to summon a person against whom an indictment for a misdemeanour had been found, **18**.

[7] See **10**, **11**.

[8] Sir William may have been seeking a place in Lady Ingoldesthorpe's household for Isabel Marley, **12**.

[9] A trusted kinsman and lawyer, one of Sir William's feoffees in the conveyances etc. of 1472–5, **5**; App. II, 35, 36.

10 *Godfrey Greene to Sir William Plumpton, 14 June [1464]* *(No. 28, p. 174)*

Reuerend and worshipfull master,[a] after all due recomendacions had. Sir, as for your suites against the minister and others, they shalbe called vpon as effectually as I can, and, with the grace of God, shall take as good speed as the law will suffer. Howbeit that Horbury sais that ye and the minister stand in comprimise to abide the award of Sir John Maliuera[1] and others, and that he hath in command to continue the suite of the minister by reason of the same. Notwithstanding, your suit shall proceed [*p. 175*] untill the time ye send otherwise in command. And as for the byeing of the veluett, the mony vpon the obligation of Mr Suthill is nott paid;[2] he sais Barnby wilbe here with it this tearme, God send grace it be so, for Mr Byngham, Thomas Eyr and Chapman of Stamford,[3] each one of them attends after his part this tearme. And as for the suits, I shall borow untill the time the other come.

There is [a] young man, a mercer in the Chepe, the which a Michaelmas purpose to sett vp a shop of his owne, the which mercer makes great labor to my lady and to Jeffrey Dawne[4] for my sister, Isabell, to marry with her. Lyuelode he hase none; a Norfolk man, and of birth no gentleman, as I can vnderstand. What he is worth in goods I cannott wytt; mercers deals nott all together with their owne proper goods. How be it, My Lady P. hath preferred him faire, that is to say xl *li* in money of my Ladys & her frends, and my lady to find her thre yeare if he will, & Jeffrey hath proferred to lend him for iij yeare a hundreth merce, the which mony is ready in a bag [if][b] the[y] agre. I moued vnto my lady & Jeffray, as far as I durst, for displease, that the mony was much without she had some twentie of other of lyuelodes or of goods, to the which my sister, as fare forth as she durst, abode upon; by the which they brake & Jeffrey agreed well to the same, notwithstanding my sister ne I cannot think it is for her to deny or refuse my ladies labour nor agreement, but wholie to put her to my ladies rule & ordinance, and so she did att all times; how be it, my lady said to her it shold come of her selfe, and she answered þat of her selfe she could nott, ne wold nothing do without the advise of you & her freinds; but whatsoeuer my lady thought she shold do, she wold do it, vnwitting you or any of her freinds. Whearfore I beseech you, as hastely as it please you, [*p. 176*] to send me word of your entent, for she & I wold faine do that at might be most to your pleasure & <her> profitt.

Also, Mr Byngham hath spoken to Mr Rocliff & me to witt what day ye wold be in Nottinghamshire, & I could not answere thereto; ye may send him word as it please you. Also I am not very certaine of þe day and yeare that your milne dam was broken. I pray you send þe certaintie this terme, and ye may, that it may be amended, if it be wrong; & all your other matters shalbe called vpon with the grace of God, who haue you euermore in proteccion. Written at London, ye xiijth day of June.

Also, as for þe mercer, I understand he profers now to find surety that if he die, she to haue a c *li* besides her part of his goods, after þe custome of the cittie.[c]

Your servant Godfrey Grene

Endorsed (p. 174): Vnto my reuerend & worshipfull master Sir William Plompton kt

[a] *Marginal note*: 28 letter.
[b] *MS* of.
[c] *Marginal note*: Copied 1 of February 1612, Munday. Edward Bickerdick.

[1] Sir John Mauleverer, of Allerton Mauleverer (d. by 1483), **16**.
[2] Henry Sotehill, whose first instalment of the balance of the purchase price of his son's marriage was now due, **8**; App. I, 3.
[3] See **11**.
[4] Geoffrey Downes (d.1494), who styled himself a 'gentleman of London', was Lady Ingoldesthorpe's steward, and co-founder with her of a chantry and lending library at Pot Shrigley, Cheshire. It is therefore probable that Joan, Lady Ingoldesthorpe, is the Lady P. referred to here, G. Ormerod, *History of the County Palatine of Cheshire* (3 vols, Chester, 1882), ii, 325–37.

11 *Brian Rocliffe to Sir William Plumpton, 3 December [1464]* *(No. 12, p. 156)*

Right reuerend worshipful Sir,[a] intirly beloued brother and singularly my good master, after al faithful and due recommdations premised and special regraces and thankings, as I haue mo causes than I can write, which our Lord acquit, where I by non power am restrained, desiring him dayly for your honor, prosperity, ioy and longanimity to be encreased to your pleasure. Sir, like you to remember the conclusion of the matter taken betwixt you and Chapman of Stamford by Husse[1] and mee, that yee, for to haue his releas general, shall pay 100*s*, wherof I paid 4 marks in hand [*p. 157*] which you paid mee again and now, this term, by the aduise of Huzze, thorowh importune clamor of Chapman, and you to bee in quiet deliuering your acquittance, I paid 33*s*4*d* afore Husze to Chapman, so that now you be utterly out of his dammage.

And Sir, I conceiued, by the remembrance of my cosin Mr Midleton[2] that yee willed mee to buy to you black velvet for a gown, but, Sir, I pray you herin blame my non power but not my will, for, in faith, I might not doe it but gif I should run in papers of London which I did neuer yet, so I haue lived poorly therafter; for and I might els haue doon it, I should not have spared. But the wis man saith to us: *Impedit omne forum carentia denariorum.* And that prooves here now: I dare not write al my complaint.

Sir, Sir Thomas Eyr clamoreth upon mee importunly for money, so that gif I had any of my own I wold haue stopped him, and so as I might have promised him this next term, which I like you for to send hither than: for and hee begin his first suit now he wil not bee so easily entreated.[3] And also, Sir, I pray you specially for to send mee money fro Nessfield, according to your appointment and saing at our last departing, for and ye know how it stands with mee here, I trust uerily yee would tender mee the more. And, Sir, the rather I pray you, for I purpose to haue your son John Roclif[4] to court [...][b] at beginning of this next terme, where my charge of him in array and other expenses shal encreas to the drible, as God knowes, whom I beseech entirly for to haue you in his keeping, and graunt you all your desires. Written in hast in the Middle Temple, *tertio die Decembris*. Sir Henry Uausor[5] was gone hence, or I wist, so that I might not speak to him for the wapp. My Thomas may go to him and speed, I trow.

Your seruisable brother Brian Rocliff

Endorsed (p. 157): Vnto the reuerend and right worshipful Sir William Plompton knight my singular good master be this deliuered

[a] *Marginal note*: 12 letter.
[b] *Marginal note*: Map.

[1] William Hussey, of Gray's Inn (d.1495), king's attorney, 1472, sergeant, 1478, CJKB, 1481–95, Ives, *CL*, 374–5, 466; John, Lord Campbell, *The Lives of the Chief Justices of England* (3 vols, 1858), i, 154–5.
[2] The lawyer, Thomas Middleton, of Stockeld, near Plumpton, **14**; App. III.
[3] Thomas Eyre, a London merchant, acknowledged receipt of 10m. on account, 10 May 1465 and 15 Nov. 1465, CB, 567, 569.
[4] The writer's son, later Sir John, **8**.
[5] Sir Henry Vavasour, of Hazelwood (d.1500), whose wife, Joan, appears to have been Dame Agnes Plumpton's sister, *Test. Ebor.*, v, 164.

12 *Hugh Pagham to Sir William Plumpton, 21 June [?1465]*[1] *(No. 18, p. 162)*

Myne owne speciall & singuler master,[a] with all my hole heart and service I recomend me vnto your best beloued good mastership, humblie thanking it for all that I am bound to thank itt for. Please it the same to knowne that from my departure out of London after Christmas <in> to Good Fryday last was, kam I not to my lodging were ye saw me last, ne neuer since that time herd I word nor wryting from you; nor ouer that, I vnderstand not by any wryting that my brother, the tresurer,[2] hath sent me sith that time, that he receaued the letter which I sent him by your mastership. Wherefore I send John Hawkins, bearer hereof, now to se your greatliest desired welfare, trusting that by him againward I shall hastely be ascertained thereof withall your commaundments & desires, which I shall euer be desireous to obserue, as fer as my simple power may to atteine, with the mercy of the Lord, whom I beseech to haue your singuler and best betruted mastership in his most [*p. 163*] safe gard and gouernment, graunting it as much prosperitie, hertes comfort, and welfare as your gentl heart, with his pleasure, best shall like to desire.

Scribbled in hast with mine owne hand, in default of other helpe, att London, the 21 of June, which day your dayly bedewoman my huswif desired þat by this sedule she may humblie be recomended to your most loving mastership; and to signify you how God bred her to be deliuered of <her> son, Nicholas, on Tewsday the 4 <of> this month; and how that on Saturday last was my daughter Agnes accepted into the habitt of St Dominikes ordre att Dertford, like as the said bearer kan enforme your mastership; which also lyke to knowe how that now of late I was with my Lady Ingols[t]horpe, whose ladyship is well recouered of the great sicknes that she endured many day past; at which time my mistris Isabell Marley[3] was in good hele, thankid be God, and lett me witt how she likes right wele and greatly is bounden to my lady.[4]

My master Rauf Haukins & mistresse his wife, now being lodged att þe Lions, my mistres F.S. now being att Wulwich with her brother & sister kin and others your wellwillers, servants & bedfolkes in this country were in hele att the mekeing hereof, thanked be God. I conceiue th<ere> is displesure hanging that ye saw not my lord chamberlaine[5] vpon his being in the North, aswell for that ye comfort not my said maistresse S., ne none of her frends, in the matter ye know of, for the which I haue bene often called upon sith Paske. It were to be done, as me seemeth, to mak writing from you to my maistres S., thanking her of her trew and loving heart, excuseing the non accomplishment of her desire, in such wis as ye can well enough, and soe to put her out of dispaire; for as I vnderstand, she hath offers great by right worshipfull in the matter. Touching the 48*li* 13*s* 4*d*, I haue opened the specialties thereof vnto John Hawkins, to whom in that behalfe please your maistership to giue vaith and credence.[b]

Hugh Pagnam

Endorsed (p. 162): To my right especiall & singuler good mastre Sir William Plompton kt

[a] *Marginal note*: 18 letter.

[b] *Marginal note*: Copied 12 January 1612, Tewsday.

[1] The letter must have been written before 1469 when Sir William acknowleged his secret marriage to Joan Wintringham, and after the death of Sir Edmund Ingoldesthorpe in 1456, note 4, below; App. III.

[2] The writer and his brother, John, treasurer of the cathedral church of York 1459–77,

probably came of a Kentish family, hence his daughter's profession in the Dominican convent at Dartford Abbey, J.W. Kirby, 'Women in the Plumpton Correspondence: Fiction and Reality', in I. Wood & G.A. Loud (eds), *Church and Chronicle in the Middle Ages: Essays Presented to John Taylor* (1991), 229; Idem, *NH*, xxv, 114.

[3] Probably the daughter of Richard Marley and Sir William's niece, Alice, daughter of Godfrey Plumpton.

[4] Godfrey Greene's letter 14 Feb. 1463/4 suggests that Sir William desired a place for his kinswoman in the household of Joan, Lady Ingoldesthorpe, **9**; App. III.

[5] William Hastings, chamberlain of the household 1461, Ross, *Edward IV*, 74–5 and *passim.*

13 *Richard Neville, earl of Warwick and Salisbury*[1] *to Sir William Plumpton, 19 September [?1465] (No. 7, p. 153; CB 617)*

Right trustie and welbeloued[a] I gret you wele. And whereas I am enformed ye pretend clayme and title to a closse called Spencer Close belonging to my welbeloved Thomas Scarbroughe, whearin with others, I stand infeoffed,[2] I therefore desire and pray you that ye will suffer the said Thomas the said closse in peaceable wise to haue and occupie without vexation or trouble vnto time that, by such persons as therevpon by your both assents being elect and chosen, the matter be thoroughly determined whether of you the same ow<e>th to haue of right. And our Lord haue you in his keeping. Written att Toplife the ninetenth day of September.[3] Therle of Warwick and Salisbury, grete chamberlaine of England and captaine of Calais.[b]

R. Warwick

Endorsed: To my right trustie and welbeloved Sir William Plompton knight

[a] *Marginal note*: 7 letter.

[b] *Marginal note*: Copied December 9 *Anno* 1612.

[1] Warwick had been Great Chamberlain of England since 1461, and captain of Calais since 1455. Granted the Percy manor of Topcliffe in the spring of 1462, he may at this time have been looking after the interests of George, duke of Clarence in Spofforth, a lordship granted to the duke in 1461, but for which he did not do homage until 1466, *CPR, 1461–67*, 45, 71, 86, 189; *GEC*; Pollard, *NE England*, 287.

[2] Visiting Kildwick church in 1666 Dodsworth saw the arms of the Scarboroughs of Giusburn in the east window of the north choir, and an inscription recording the death of William Scarborough, in 1528, Whitaker, *Craven*, i, 212, 216.

[3] Topcliffe, worth £90 a year in 1478–9, was granted to Warwick by Edward IV in April 1462, *CPR, 1461–67*, 186, 189; J.M.W. Bean, *The Estates of the Percy Family, 1416–1537* (Oxford, 1958), 47.

14 *Thomas Middleton to Sir William Plumpton, [16 November 1466]*[1] *(No. 15, p. 159)*

Right worshipfull Sir, I recommend me to your good mastership,[a] letting you wit, as touching the matter betwixt my coussin Golfray Greene and Nyccoll Gotman, that my lord chauncler[2] has giuen in commaundment vnto Mr Patman[3] to make prossis against my cousin Godfrey to bring the issues and profits that he hath receiued of the chauntre, for which the varience shold begin, and else to cours him from day to day. And therefore provide by your wisdome such remmede in his behalfe as you semes best. Also, if ye speake with my Lady Stapleton,[4] if it please you to commend me vnto hir gud ladyship, and let hir vnderstand that I deliuered hir letters that she sent me, and that Mr Borough[5] desired hir, in any wise, that she shold kepe it secret and let no person haue knowledg, but that he shold kepe stil the ward of my master's son, not withstanding he is, and wil be, redy to kepe all appoyntements that ar made in every article.

The king, my lord chauncler, and earle of Warwick ar at London; he came to the towne with 3 horse and more, as it is said. My lord of Clarence is riden to Tutbery and the earle of Woster to Walles,[6] to Denbie, as it is said. I sopose Sir James Harington shall be sherife of Yorke shire,[7] Sir John Conyers[8] and Sir Henry Vaueser[9] is in the bill; Sir Robart Constable[10] is sherif in Lincoln shire. As for tidings, I can none wryte, but I haue sold both my horses, good Morrel and his felow; and as for my bay horse at your neighbor had fro Harwod Park, by his commaundment I purpose to take no such as yet. No more at this tyme, but the holy Trinitee haue you in his blessed keeping. Written at London the Thursday after Alhallow Day.[b]

Your servant Thomas Midleton[11]

Endorsed: To my worshipful maister Sir William Plompton knight bee this bil deliuered

[a] *Marginal note*: 15 letter.
[b] *Marginal note*: Copied 14 December 1612, on Tewsday.

[1] The letter is dated by Sir James Harrington's shrievalty, see note 7, below.
[2] George Neville, archbishop of York, dismissed 8 June 1467, *HBC*, 85.
[3] William Poteman, archdeacon of the East Riding and godfather to Henry Percy, 4th earl of Northumberland, who bequeathed him 2 tuns of Gascon wine annually for life, *Test. Ebor.*, iii, 304–10; App. II, 33.
[4] Isabella, Lady Stapleton, widow of Sir Brian Stapleton, of Carlton (d.1464), and sister-in-law of Sir William. Her son Brian was apparently still a minor, F.W. Dendy (ed.), *Visitations of the North, or Some Early Heraldic Visitations of, and Collections of Pedigrees Relating to the North of England* (SS, cxxii, 1912), 115n.
[5] Sir Thomas Burgh of Gainsborough (d.1496), **219**.
[6] John Tiptoft, earl of Worcester (exec.1470), **6**.

[7] Sir James Harrington, of Brierley (d.1487), sheriff of Yorkshire, Nov.1466, *List of Sheriffs*, 162; App. III.

[8] Sir John Conyers, of Hornby (d.1490).

[9] Sir Henry Vavasour, **11**.

[10] Sir Robert Constable, of Flamborough (d.1488), App. III.

[11] Thomas Middleton, of Kirkby Overblow, lawyer, married Joan, daughter of Sir William Plumpton, CB, 570; **11**; App. III.

15 *John Johnson to Sir William Plumpton, [1465 × 1469]*[1] *(No. 16, p. 160)*

Right worshippfull & reuerent Sir & maister,[a] I recomende me vnto you. And please your good mastershipp to witte there is a clerk att York, the whilke purposes to say his first mes the Sunday next after the feast of the Natiuitie of our Lady the Virgin, and if ye would vouchsafe that he might haue a morsal of venison aganst the said Sunday, for Robart Manfeld sake.[2] And trewly I shall lett him wytte both how ye did to his kinswoman against her wedding, and now for this said priest, for he is full brother to the said woman and they are both right neare of his kin. I am siker he thank you full hartely fro I lett him witt, and that shalbe in all the gudly hast at I may; with the grace of God, who encrease your good estate to his pleas<ure>.[b] Written in hast att York, the Friday next before the said feast.[2]

Your owne servant and bedeman John Johnson of Yorke

Endorsed: To my worshipfull & reverent maister Sir William Plompton kt

[a] *Marginal note*: 16 letter.

[b] *Marginal note*: Coppied 12 January 1612, Tewsday.

[1] The letter was probably written before 1469 when Sir William was dismissed from his office as master forester.

[2] The writer, who was asking a considerable favour, must have known that Manfeld's gratitude would be useful to Sir William, C. Dyer, *Standards of Living in the Later Middle Ages: Social Change in England c.1200–1520* (1988), 61.

16 *Godfrey Greene to Sir William Plumpton, 9 December [1468]* *(No. 25, p. 170; CB 622)*

Right reuerend & my most especiall gude maister,[a] I recomend me vnto your good mastership, and as touching your *nisi prius*[1] against Fulbaron, it were well doon that ye appointed with Mr Danby[2] at what place and what day in his comeing home after the next tearme ye would haue it serued, so that I might haue word the beginning of the next tearme to take out the writt according to your appointment. Also as for þe writt [*p. 171*] against Geffray Maliuera, John Cockle, Richard Croft, Hanson and other, I stand in doubt whether Mr Midleton[3] & Mr Ros greed you and Sir John Maliuera thereof,[4] or no, because they are all his men. Notwithstanding, if they aggreed you nott, and ye send me word, I trust to haue an *exigent* the next tearme.

My lord of Oxford[5] is committ to the Tower, and, it is said, kept in irons, and that he has confessed myche thinges; and on Munday afore St Andrew Day one Alford and one Poiner,[6] gentlemen to my [lord] of Northfolk, and one Sir Peirs Skinner[7] of London were beheaded, and on the morne after was Sir Thomas Tresham[8] arest and is comitt to the Tower, and it is said he was arrested upon the confession of my lo: of Oxford; and they say his liuelhood, and Sir John Marneys[9] liuelhood, and diuers other liuelhuds is giuen [...][a] away by the king. Also there is arest Mr Hungerford the heir vnto the Lord Hungerford[10] & one Courtney[11] heir vnto the earl of Devonshire and many other whose names I know nott, & it is said that Sir Edmund Hungerford is send for, and also the yeomen of þe crowne bene riden into diuerse countries to arrest men that be appeched. Also it was told me that Sir Robert Ughtred[12] was send for but I trust to God it is not so, who haue you euermore in his blessed proteccion. Written at London 9 December.[b]

Your servant Godfrey Greene

Endorsed (p. 170): To my right reuerend and most especiall gud maister Sir William Plompton kt

[a] *Marginal note*: 25 letter.
[b] *Marginal note*: Copied Feb. 1612, Munday.

[1] The assize justices hearing a case at *nisi prius* were empowered only to proceed on issues referred to them for convenience out of one of the benches, and had to send the results back to the relevant court for judgement, Baker, 19–20.

[2] Robert Danby, of Thorpe Perrow (d.1474), CJCP.

[3] Thomas Middleton, **14**.

[4] See **10**.

[5] John de Vere, 13th earl of Oxford (d.1513) turned king's evidence, James Gairdner (ed.), *Three Fifteenth-Century Chronicles* (Camden Society, 2nd ser., xxviii, 1880), 78–9.

[6] John Poynings and William Alford, Ross, *Edward IV*, 122–3.

[7] Richard Stairs, a London skinner, *ibid.*

[8] Sir Thomas Tresham was eventually freed, but beheaded after Tewkesbury, 1471, Roskell, *Commons*, 368–9; M.A. Hicks, 'Edward IV, the Duke of Somerset and Lancastrian Loyalism in the North', *NH*, xx (1984), 34.

[9] Sir John Marney, of Layer Marney, Essex (d. by 1472), *CPR, 1467–77*, 151, 155, 329, 344–5; J. Wedgwood and A. Holt, *History of Parliament: Biographies of Members of the Commons House 1439–1509* (1930), 575.

[10] Thomas Hungerford, executed 1469 at Salisbury in the king's presence, M.A. Hicks, 'Piety and Lineage in the Wars of the Roses: the Hungerford Experience', in R.A. Griffiths and James Sherborne (eds), *Kings and Nobles in the Later Middle Ages: A Tribute to Charles Ross* (Gloucester, 1986), 94–5.

[11] Henry Courtenay, brother and heir of Thomas, earl of Devon (exec. 1461), whose

lands and honours were still forfeit, J.A.F. Thomson, 'The Courtenay Family in the Yorkist Period', *BIHR*, lv (1972), 31–2; *GEC*.
[12] Of Kexby, near York (d.1472), **161**.

17 *Thomas Billop to Sir William Plumpton, 21 August 1469* *(No. 22, p. 166)*

Right worshipfull Maister,[a] I recomend me vnto [you], praying you that you will cause the clothe that the wooll was packed in for to come againe with the shipp, for I borrow it wheare that ye saw that I borrow <it>, of that of your servants aforetime haue borrowed two packcholthes and other geare, which they had neuer againes. Letting you vnderstand that I haue giuen the shipman of [...][b] his hier x*s*, and he for to haue his whole payment when he deliuers the goods which he receaued, which is xxxiij*s* iiij*d*. Whereafore I pray you that ye see that he be content of the said some, for I am nott in store, att this time, of money for to gett your harvest with, withoutyn I might gett it of your tenants, or ells for to take of your shepe siluer, and that I ware right lothe for to do. Letting you witt alsoe that I haue bene in the Peake, and there I cannott gett no money of Harry Fulgram, nor of John of Tor, nor no other that [...][c] owes you, but if I shold take of your cattell, and soe I think for to do, for I haue no oxen to gett your corne with, nor none I cannott gett carryed, for euery man is soe busie with their owne. For whether is so latesum in this cuntrey that men can neither well gett corne nor hay. Letting you witt that your tenant Nichole Bristow hath not gotten but xij foder of hay, and it is nought good, and the corneland is ouerflotin with water. Letting you witt that I haue gotten the hay in Hesththorne meen that was left after Lammas Day, as ye commanded me for to do. Letting you witt that I haue a counterpais [...][d] wheith of the wheight stone that the wooll was weyed with, & that ye se that the stone be kept that the shipman brings. Also letting you witt that I deliuered the shipman viij paire of blanketts that is nott in þe bill indented, and a hanging of old linen cloth that the couerletts are trussed in.

Letting you witt that I was on St Lawrence Day att Melton [*p. 167*] with iiij[x] of your shepe to sell, and could sell none of them but if I wold have selled xx of the best of them for xiij*d* a peece, and therefore I seld none. Letting you witt that I sent vnto you with William Plompton[1] & with William Marley[2] v*li* and also xxv*s* which was borrowed of Bryan Smith, which I must pay againe; & therefore I am not perveyed of money for to gett your harvest with. Also that you gar the malt be windowd, or it be laid in any garners, for ells there will brede wyvills in it, for I could not gett it windowd before it went to

the ship, because that I could not gett no helpe; and therefore I upheaped with a quarter, xxj quarters for xx quarters; and also six of your cheeses hase two markes that I trow be the best of them.[3] Noe more I write to you at this time, but that the holy Trinity haue you euer in his keeping. Written in hast by your servant, Thomas Billop, att Kinoulton, the Munday afore St Bartholomew Day, 9 Edw. 4.[e]
Endorsed: Vnto my worshipfull master Sir William Plompton knight

[a] *Marginal note*: 22.
[b] her *deleted*.
[c] he *deleted*.
[d] *An illegible word deleted*.
[e] *Marginal note*: Copied 21 January 1612, Friday.

[1] Sir William's illegitimate son, **86**; App. II 53.
[2] Probably brother of Isabel Marley, **12**.
[3] Given-Wilson comments on the propensity of the lesser nobility for stepping in and out of direct management as need required, *English Nobility*, 95; Richmond, *John Hopton*, 31.

18 *Godfrey Greene to Sir William Plumpton, 5 December [1469] (No. 27, p. 172; CB 623)*

Right worshipfull maistre,[a] I recommend me vnto your good mastership. Sir, I have sent to you by þe bringer of this letter a *venire facias* against the minister [*p. 173*] of St Roberts,[1] for he hath pleaded not guiltie for fishing your ponds att Plompton. If so be your writt be well served and the issue tried for you, þe punishments wilbe greuieous to them, for it is gyffin by a statute. Also I haue sent you a *venire facias* against Dromonby, parson of Kynalton; he hath pleaded he withholds you nothing in accion of detynue of the goods deliuered him by Heynes. Also the copie of the pleadings betwixt you and the minister for your milne att Plompton; it were wele don that ye had a speech with Mr Midleton[2] of the forme of the pleadings, and of the matter both of the title of his milne and your milne, and of the freholds of both sides the water, soe that your counsell may haue instruccion thereof [...][b] next tearme at the pleasure of þe partis.[3]

Mr Midleton had great labour thereof; I profferd him no rewards because ye may reward him yourselfe as it please you. Maister Fairfax had x*s* for that matter allon,[4] Mr Suttill laboured effectually;[5] I tould him he shold be rewarded of the mony in his hands, and said lightly he would haue none, so I wot whether he will take, or no: he hath not all paid yett. I pray you, against the next terme, send me word how I shalbe demened in rewards giueing, for and it go to matter in law it will cost mony largely. Also I haue sent you a *capias ut legat*[6] against

Hargreaue of Friston; Sir John Maleuerer[7] gaue me a chalenge for him, and said he was outlawd under my treaty: I told him I treted neuer; I bare your message to him, and that was [*p. 174*] a continuance for the matter against Fulburn, but nott for Hargreave. And he said ye had sued all the trew men to the king, to my lord, and to him in the Forest, sith that ye come home; and that he shold complaine to the king and to the lords thereof. And I said I trust to God ye shold come to your answere, & he said that shold not lyg in my power to bring you to, for he wold deele with you & yours, both be the law and besides the law; and said he wold cutt þe clothes norwithstanding. He was full angrie and hastie, what time he said soe, and I was with Mr Roclif the same time ye gaue me this chalenge, and Myles Willestrop[8] was with him, and said no word. And Maister Roclif asked him what þe matter was, if he might any ease, & he answered him that ye desseyued him and all that ye dellyd withall, and Mr Rocliff said he trust to God, who haue you euermore in his proteccion. Written at London, the vth day of December.[c]

Your servant Godfrey Grene

Endorsed (p. 172): To my right worshipfull maistre Sir William Plompton kt this letter be delivered

[a] *Marginal note*: 27 letter.

[b] *CB* 'it hath cost you money this tearme, & yett no conclusion but to change the pleadings the next tearme...'

[c] *Marginal note*: Copied 1 of February 1612, Munday.

[1] The writ sent by Greene with this letter was returned unexecuted by the sheriff in the following Hilary term because of lack of time. Another was issued 12 Feb.1469/70, returnable at Easter, Stapleton, 22n.

[2] Thomas Middleton, App. III.

[3] Sir William's disputes with the convent were eventually resolved by arbitration, 20–25 June 1471, CB 571, 572; App. II, 31, 32.

[4] Guy Fairfax, of Gray's Inn, king's sergeant 1481, App. III.

[5] Henry Sotehill had been king's attorney at the trial of Hungerford and Courtenay, App. III.

[6] Writ for the arrest of an outlaw.

[7] Sir John Mauleverer's challenge related to forest prosecutions initiated by Sir William as chief forester, **26**.

[8] Miles Wilstrop, of Wilstrop in the Ainsty, escheator of Yorkshire, 1469–70, married to Eleanor, daughter of Guy Fairfax, *List of Escheators*, 189; *Flower's Visitation*, 355.

19 *John Neville, Lord Montague, earl of Northumberland*[1] *to Sir John Mauleverer, 7 December [1464 × 1469] (No. 5, p. 152; CB 615)*

Right trusty and hartily welbeloued, I greet you oft tymes wel.[a] Letting you wete that Sir William Plompton, knight, hath sent vnto me and complayneth him that Thomas Wade and Richard Croft dayly threaten to beat or slay his servants and seeketh them about his place.[2] Whearfore I desire and pray you to cause the said Thomas and Richard to surcease & leaue their said threatnings; and if they haue any matters against the said servants lett them complaine vnto me therof, and I shall see that they shall haue such a remedy as shall accord with reason. And that ye faile nott hereof, as my speciall trust is in you. And God keepe you. [p. 153] Written att my castle att Warkworth the seaventh day of December. The earle of Northumberland and Lord Montague, warden.[b]

Northumberlan

Endorsed (p. 152): To my right trusty and hartely welbeloued Sir John Mauliuerer knight

[a] *Marginal note*: 5 letter.
[b] *Marginal note*: Copied 9 December 1612.

[1] John Neville, Lord Montague (d.1471) married Isabel, daughter of Joan, Lady Ingoldesthorpe. Created earl of Northumberland, 27 May 1464 after the posthumous attainder of the 3rd Percy earl, he was induced to surrender the earldom on the reinstatement of the 4th earl in March 1470, for a 'pies nest': the title of Marquis Montague, and Courtenay lands in Devon, *CPR, 1461–67*, 332, 341; M.A. Hicks, 'What Might Have Been: George Neville, Duke of Bedford 1465–83: His Identity and Significance', in Idem, *Richard III and His Rivals: Magnates and their Motives in the Wars of the Roses* (1991), 294; **23**.
[2] Sir John Mauleverer and Thomas Wade (or Ward) were as ardently Yorkist as Sir William was, at heart, Lancastrian, and they had probably been exploiting their political advantage since 1461, Hicks, *NH*, xiv, 81; **10**, **16**.

20 *John Felton and John Warde to Sir William Plumpton, 14 September [1464 × 1469] (No. 21, p. 165)*

Worshipfull and reverend Sir[a] and our right good mastre, we recomend us vnto you. And please you to haue knowlech that our trustie frend Thomas of the Logge hath of late time bene greueously vexed and troubled for certain matters that ye haue knowlich of, so that yett, without that he trusteth specially aboue all things vnto you, he dare not come at his owne house, vnto his right great hurt & hindring; and as we have knowledge, the matters are in your will and throughe your good lordshipp <(quere)> [...][b] Whereafore we beseech you [...][c] <in the> lowliest wise we can or may, that ye vouchsafe to shew vnto him your good lordshipp and mastershipp,[1] for if the matter shold be tryed by his neighbours we deem the countrey should be found of his appeale, soe that, because of this our simple writing and request, he may, vnder your protection, haue his goods vnto his proper use vnder sufficient baile, & that [he] be not put into the wrongs that may cause his vndoing. Wherein you shall deserue thanks of God & your good lords at [...][d] <your> coming to the kings house, with our dayly service att all times. Written att Windsor þe 14 September. And it please to deliuer vnto Robert of Tymble a stub,[2] the which Mr Controller[3] granted vnto his ward for him and his wife.[e]

By your servants John Felton, groom of þe chamber[4] and John Ward, groom of the eurey[5]

Endorsed: To the right worshipfull and right reuerend Sir William Plompton kt custos of the castle of Knaresburgh

[a] *Marginal note*: 21 letter. Sir William that died 20 of Ed. 4th was custos of the castle of Knaresb.

[b] *The original was either illegible or blank at this point.*

[c] through *deleted.*

[d] the *deleted.*

[e] *Marginal note*: Copied 21 January 1612, Friday.

[1] Sir William had been reinstated in office at Knaresborough under Warwick in 1464; dismissed *c.* 1469, **28**.

[2] A timber tree.

[3] Sir John Scott held the office, 1461–70, Ross, *Edward IV*, 324.

[4] John Felton was still a member of the royal household in Jan. 1480, *CPR, 1476–85*, 171.

[5] A younger brother of Sir Christopher Warde of Givendale, he was in office in the royal household in 1469, when he was granted tronage and pesage at Southampton, *CPR, 1467–77*, 166; Horrox, *Richard III*, 241; *Test. Ebor.*, iv, 274.

21 *Henry Percy, earl of Northumberland,*[1] *to Sir William Plumpton, 17 August [?1470] (No. 3, p. 152; CB 613)*

Right trusty and with all myn hart my welbeloued cossine,[a] I grete you hartily wealle, and desire and pray you that my welbeloued seruant Edmund Cape may haue and occupie the office of the baliship of Sesey, as his father did to fore in time past.[2] My trust is in you that, the rather for this mine instance & contemplation, ye will fulfill this my desire, and I will be as well-willed to doe thinge for your pleasure, that knoweth our Lord, who haue you in his blessed keping. Written in my manner of Top<c>life, the seuententh day of August.[b]

Your cossin H. Northumberland

Endorsed: To my right trusty and welbeloued coussin[a] Sir William Plompton knight

[a] *Marginal note*: 3 letter.

[b] *Marginal note*: Copied 9 December 1612.

[1] Henry Percy was released from the Tower, 27 Oct. 1469 and restored to the earldom

of Northumberland at York, where he swore allegiance, 25 March 1470, Thomas Rymer, *Foedera* (20 vols, 1704–35), x, 648.

[2] Sir William's son-in-law Sir George Darrell, of Sessay, died in 1466. His son, Marmaduke, was presumably still a minor and probably in Sir William's custody, *VCH, Yorks: North Riding*, ed. Wm Page, i (repr. 1968), 447; App. III.

22 *Richard, duke of Gloucester*[1] *to Sir William Plumpton, 13 October [?1472] (No. 6, p. 153; CB 616]*

R: Glocestre. Right trustie and welbeloued,[a] we grete you well and whearas att the freshe pursuit of our welbeloued Christopher Stansfeild, one Richard of the Burgh that had take and led away feloniously certaine ky and othe cattell belonging to him, was take and arested with[in] the said manor att Spofford, wheras they yett remaine. Wheafore we desire & pray you that vpon sufficient suerty found [...][b] by the said Christopher to sue against the said felon, as the law will for that offence, ye will make deliuery vnto him of the said cattell, as is according with right, showing him your good aide, favour and benevolence, the rather att the instaunce of this our letters. And our Lord preserue you. From Pontefrett vnder our signett, the thirtenth of October.

Endorsed: To our right trustie & wellbeloued Sir William Plompton knight, stuard of the lordshipp of Spofford, and to the bailife of the same, and to ether of them the duke of Glocester, constabl and admirall of England[c]

[a] *Marginal note*: 6 letter.

[b] found *repeated.*

[c] *Marginal note*: Copied 9 of December 1612.

[1] After Edward IV's resumption of the crown in April 1471 Gloucester recovered the offices of constable and admiral of England, which he held before the Readeption. In the same year he was made chief steward of the North Parts of the Duchy of Lancaster and great chamberlain of England, but surrendered the latter in favour of Clarence, May 1472. This letter was therefore probably written after that date, and before the 'appointment' with Northumberland, May 1473, *CPR, 1467–77*, 178, 262; Ross, *Edward IV*, 186, 200.

23 *The earl of Northumberland to Sir William Plumpton, 25 September [1473 × 1475] (No. 4, p. 152; CB 614)*

Right trusty & withal my hart my right welbeloued cosin, I gret you wel,[a] and desire and pray you to labor Sir Richard Aldborough, to caus him[1] to deliuer unto my cosin Dame Isabel Ilderton[2] such beasts and cattel as he retayneth and witholdeth from her; for she hath no other mean to help herself with unto that a determination be had betwixt Thomas Ilderton and her of the liuelyhed that standeth in trauers betwixt them. Cosin, as ye loue mee, that ye wil endeuor your selfe for the performance of the praemisses, wherin you shal deserue great thank of God, and to mee right great pleasure; that knoweth our Lord, who haue you, cousin, in his blessed keeping. Written in my manor of Lekingfield, the twenty fiue day of September.

Your cousin H. Northumberland

Endorsed: To my trusty and welbeloued cossin Sir William Plompton knight

[a] *Marginal note*: 4 letter.
[b] *Marginal note*: Copied 9 December 1612.

[1] Sir William's son-in-law Sir Richard Aldburgh, of Aldburgh, near Knaresborough, App. III.
[2] Dame Isabel Ilderton, widow of Sir Thomas Ilderton, of Ilderton, near Wooley (d. before 1470), brought an action against her husband's cousins, Thomas (d.1478) and John Ilderton in 1472–75 for removing her deceased husband's evidences 'to the disenheritance of the heirs of the said Thomas and Isabel,' M. Hope Dodds (ed.), *History of the County of Northumberland* (15 vols, 1893–1940), xiv, 274; *CFR, 1452–61*, 113, 274; *ibid., 1461–71*, 196; *ibid., 1471–88*, 151.

24 *The earl of Northumberland to Sir William Plumpton, 6 June [1471 × 1479] (No. 2, p. 151; CB 612)*

Right trusty and welbeloued cossine, I grete you wele,[a] and wheras varience dependenth betwixt you and my right welbeloued servant Robart Birnand,[1] I therfore right hartyly desire [...][b] and pray you therin nothing to doe vnto that I come into the contry. As my trust is in you, confirme you to the performing of this my desire, as ye intend to doe my pleasure; and our blesed Lord haue you, kussin, in his blessed kepping. Wryten in my maner of Lekingfeild the sixt day of June.[c]

Your cossine H. Northumberland

Endorsed: To my right trusty and wellbeloued coussin Sir William Plompton knight

[a] *Marginal note*: 2 letter.
[b] you *deleted*.
[c] *Marginal note*: *Anno* 1612, copied 9 December.

[1] A man of some standing in Knaresborough, Robert Birnand held substantial properties in and around the town in 1462, including burgages and land in the town fields. Concurrently the family leased the mills, market tolls and borough court, B. Jennings (ed.), *A History of Nidderdale* (Huddersfield, 1967), 73, 90.

25 *Richard Banke to Sir William Plumpton, 24 March* *(No. 20, p. 165)*

Right reverent and my full worshipfull maister,[a] I recomend me vnto [you] in the hertelyest wise I kan. And for asmuch as a poore widow called Ellen Helme is my son in law William Nesfeildes[1] tenant, is greeueously vexed in her sons; whearfore I pray you hartely to be their tender and especiall maister, as I and my said son may haue cause to doe you service, the which we shalbe ready to doe with Gods grace, who haue you in his blessed keeping. Written att Newton on St Cudberts Day[b]

By your awne Rich. Banks[2]

Endorsed: To my reverent & worshipfull maister Sir William Plompton knight

[a] *Marginal note*: 20 letter.
[b] *Marginal note*: Copied 21 of January, Friday.

[1] William Nessfield, of Nessfield in Craven, possibly the father of John Nessfield, esquire of the body to Richard III, W.E. Hampton, 'John Nessfield', in J. Petre (ed.), *Richard III, Crown and People* (Richard III Society, 1985), 178–9.
[2] Richard Banke, of Bank Newton in Craven. A retainer of Richard III, he joined the earl of Lincoln's rebellion and was attainted after Stoke, Hampton, 187; *Collectanea*, vi, 321.

26 *Robert Plumpton, senior, to Sir William Plumpton, 1 April [1477]* *(No. 17, p. 160)*

After all lowly & dew recomendations, I lowly recommend me vnto your good mastershipp,[a] certifieing your maistership I sent you by one Wil: Atkinson a letter & the copie of the answerre of the priuie seale, and a box with 6 peeces, 5 sealed & one vnsealed. And, Sir, the box sealed for your maistershipp took me no more. First, they took me 7 & 2 filed together that were of one: the graunt of Stutvill[b] and the peticion thereon,[1] and they tooke away the petition, and soe I had but 5, whilk I sent your mastershipp by the said William in the said box, sealed. And if it were more so, and the letter deliuerd to you with the copie, I desire you send word.

As for your say, I haue sent you a peice of 2 yards and a halfe broad by Grethum of York the first of Lent. As for the other peice, there is none of lesse bredth then 2 yards, for if I could haue any I should haue sent it with the other. And as for the cloth of my ladies, Hen: Cloughe putt it to a sheremn to dight, and he sold the cloth and ran away, and yett after, Hen: mett with him and gart him be sett in the countrie till he founde [*p. 161*] sewerte to answer at the gild hall for the cloth. And soe he hath sewed him till he had iudgment to recover, which cost him large money. And when he shold deliuer it, he deliuered another peice, but that Henry hapned to understand, after the recouery, wheare he had sould it, and soe it is had againe and it is put to dyeing. And as soune as it is readie I shall sendit by the carrier, for it [...][c] was Fryday in the second week of Lent or it was gettin again.

And as for suites in the kings bench again them in Brereton,[2] and in the common place again Will: Pulleyne and his suites are in process, and fro they be in *exigent* ye shall haue the *exigent* sent you as soun as it will be sped. And for the day of appearence of Ailmer wife is mense Paske,[3] I shold haue sent you word or that, but that I had nott the *habeas corpus* against John Esomock and Robart Galaway; and for to see that we were nott beguiled by the day of returne & day of appearance, be it my day, & soe I send you now the *habeas corpora* & a coppie thereof, & you must desier the sheriffe to serue it,[4] if so be that ye agre not. And also, Sir, that ye will send word as soon as ye can, if the principalls were deliuered not att York, and what way is had betwixt you and them, and if there be any towne or hamlett in Craven that is called Medilton,[5] & that ye send word.

And as for your cope, I have cheaped diuerse, and under a hundred shillings I can by non that is ether of damaske or sattin with flowers of gold; and I send you a peice of baudkin and another of impereal to se whether ye will hafe of, and the price. And the bredth of it is elme broade; 3 yards, besides the orffrey, will make a cope – to haue of whilk it please you, ether to be made [?here] or there. And if ye will haue it to be made here, it will stand ye to 6 marks or more, with the orfrey and making, & that is the least that I can driue it to. [*p. 162*] The orffrey 32*s*, the lining and making 8*s*, and as for a broderer, I can find none that will come so farre, but any work that ye would haue, to send hither and they will do it, and in no other wise they will as yett grant me, but I shall that I may to gett one.

Alsoe, Sir, I send your mastership the bill of the expenses and costs that I haue made since I came hither, and please you to see it and send money the next terme. All other thinges whilk ye will I do, and I shall doe therein, that I ether may or can. I beseech your mastership to recomend me lowly to my lady. And if I durst, Sir, the matter betwixt my brother Robart and Mr Gascoines sister me think is so long in makeing up, for in long tarrying comes mekell letting.[6] And I beseech the blessed Trinitie haue you in his continuall keeping. From London, the fift day of Aprill.[d]

Your servant in all Robenett P.[7]

Endorsed (p. 160): To my most reuerent & worshippfull maister Sir William Plompton knight be this deliuered

[a] *Marginal note*: 17 letter.

[b] *Marginal note*: Stutavel deed.
[c] is *deleted*.
[d] *Marginal note*: Copied 12 January 1612, Tewsday.

[1] Undated grant to Nigel de Plumpton *pro servicio suo et pro uno equo precio centum solidorum*, of part of the waste of the forest of Knaresborough, with licence to course the fox and the hare throughout the forest – a right jealously guarded by subsequent generations of the family, CB, 72; BL, Add. MS. 32, 113, f.6.
[2] Brearton, near Knaresborough.
[3] 5 May.
[4] The responsibility for getting his writ to the sheriff lay on the plaintiff, Hastings, 162.
[5] Middleton, near Ilkley.
[6] The contract for the marriage of Robert (later Sir Robert) Plumpton with Agnes, sister of Sir William Gascoigne of Gawthorpe was signed 13 July 1477, Apps II, 37; III.
[7] Robert Plumpton, of York ('Robinet'), attorney, one of Sir William's two illegitimate sons, App. III.

27 *Godfrey Greene to Sir William Plumpton, 10 July [?1477]* *(No. 29, p. 176)*

Right worshippfull Sir,[a] I recomend me vnto your good mastershipp. Sir, as for a *supersedias*[1] for your selfe, there will not begotten without I shold put in sufficient men to be suerties, for there is a new rule made in the chauncery, now late, that no sureties shalbe accepted but such as be sufficient, and twenty of þe old common sureties dischardged; so it is hard to gett suerties for a yoman; & as for the supliants I have dayly labored, sith your man come, to gett a man to aske þe suretie, & so I fand one which hath bene of old a supersedias mounger and was agreed with him that he shold gett me a man to aske it, & he and the man shold haue had vs for their labor. And so he said vnto me and Thom: on Saturday last that it was done, & desired mony for þe mans labor and for the sealing, & we shold haue them forth withall; & also he hath driuen us from morne to euen, & in conclusion deceyued <us>, & hath receued vj*s* vj*d*. And I may nott arreast him nor striue with him for þe mony, [*p. 177*] nor for the decept, because the matter is not worshipfull. And so there is none odere meane but dayly to labor him to gett þe writts, & so I shall, & send them to you asoune as they may be gotten. The labor is great & perillous and the a<n>ger is more because of þe decept. As for the suit of Tulis executor, it is delaid for this terme, but the next terme it cannot be delaid. Therefore it were well done ye sought up your writtings and all the sircumstances of making þe obligacion & whear it was made, for there is none will make a plea without he haue some matter to make it of; & also the court will nott admitt a forreine plea[2] without þe matter be somewhat likely to be true.

As for all your oder suits, they haue the speed the law will giue them, as Horbury will enforme you when he comes home. As for the *supena*, the writt is nott retorned in: it seemes it will take a delay. I have sent you a copie of þe letter & a *supesedias* for Ward of Breeton.[3] And as for your awne, if so be ye will that I put in sufficient suerties for you <ye may haue one>, but, saueing your better advise, methink it not necessary so [to] do without oder cause shold require; for as strong in the law is a *supersedias* of a justice of the peace as in the chauncery.

And as for your bottles, there came no samon men here of all this sumor, but I understand they will come now hastely; by the next at comes they shalbe sent, with Gods grace, who haue you euermore in his blessed proteccion. Written att London, the xth day of July. Thomas can enforme you of nouelties in this countrie better than I can writte.[b]

Your servant Godfrey Grene

Endorsed (p. 176): To my right reuerend worshipfull maistre Sir William Plompton kt

[a] *Marginal note*: 29 letter.
[b] *Marginal note*: Copied 1 of February 1612, Munday.

[1] A writ of supersedeas was a means of blocking the process of outlawry, Hastings, 210.
[2] A plea outside the judgement of the court.
[3] **17**.

28 *Godfrey Greene to Sir William Plumpton, 8 November [?1477] (No. 23, p. 167; CB 620)*

Right worshipfull Sir,[a] I recommend me vnto your good maistershipp. Sir, as for the suit against you by the executors of Parson Tuly, had not it fortuned that there was a default founden in the writt,[1] it had been so that ye had bene condemned, or els an *exigi*[2] awarded against you; for as for the matter of your plea, there would noe man plead it, ne it would not haue bene except if it had bene pleaded. Sir, there is an indenture upon the same *oblige*, the which wold serue much of your intents, and it might be found.

Also, Sir, now of late I have receaued from you diuerse letters of þe which the tenure and effect is this: one, that I shold labour to Sir John Pilkinton[3] to labor to my lord of Glocester or to the king, they to moue my lord of Northumberland that ye might occupie still in Knaresborough. [*p. 168*] Sir, as to that, it is thought here by such as loues you at that labour should rather hurt in that behalue then availe, for it is as long as my lord of Northumberlands patent thereof stands good, as long will he haue no deputie but such as shall please him and kan him thank for the gift thereof, and no man els, and also doe him servise next the king. So þe labour shalbe fair answered and turne to none effect but hurt.

And as to another point comprised in your writing, that is to enforme the lords and their counsell of the miscouernances of Gascoin[4] and his affinitie. Sir, ye understand that in euery law the saying of a mans enemies is chalengeable, and rather taken a sayin[g] of malice then of treuthe, whereby the correction of the [...] <same> default, the complainer hath no availe. And so, certainly by your counsell, is thought here that it wold be soe taken, and in no other wise, how be it that it be trew, and also a disworship to my lo: of Northumberland that hath the cheif rule there vnder the king. And as for the matter to enforme my lord of Northu[mberlands] counsell how ye were entreated at Knaresboro: Sir, we enformed my lords counsell, according to your commaundement, and they enformed my lord, and my lord said he wold speak with us himselfe, and so did, and this was the answerr: that the cause why he wrote that no court of sheriff turne shold be holden was <for> to shew debate betwixt you & Gascoins affinitie[b] vnto time he might come into the cuntry and se a deraction betwixt you; & that he wold that the 3 week court were holden for discontinuance of mens actions; & that he entended not to dischardge you [*p. 169*] of your office,[5] ne will not as long as ye be towards him; and that as soune as he comes into the cuntry he shall see such a direction betwext his brother Gascoin and you as shalbe to your harts ease & worship. And that I vnderstand by his counsell that it shalbe assigned vnto you by my lord & his counsell what as longes to your office, & Gascoin nott meddle therewithall; & in likewise to Gascoyne.

And as for the labour for þe bailiships & farmes: Sir, your worship vnderstands what labour is to sue therefore: first, to haue a bill endorsed to the king, then to certein lords of the counsell (for ther is an Act made that nothing shall passe from the king vnto time they haue sene it) and soe to the privie seale & chauncellor. So the labour is so importune that I cannot attend it without I shold do nothing ells, and scarcely in a month speed one matter. Your mastership may remember how long it was or we might speed your bill of iustice of the peace, & had not my lord of Northumberland been, had not been sped, for all the fair promisses of my lord chamberlaine. And as for the message to my lord chamberlain,[6] what time I labored to him that ye might be iustice of the peace,[7] he answerred thus: that it seemed by your labor & mine that we wold make a jelosie betwixt my lord of Northumberland & him, in that he shold labor for any of his men, he being present. Sir, I took that for a watch word for medling betwixt lords. As for any matter ye haue to do in the Law, how be it that it be to me losse of time and costly to labor or medle, as yett I am & always shalbe readie to doe you service & pleasure therein. With the grace of God, who haue you euermore in his lessed protection. Written att London, the eight day of Nouember.[c]

Your servant Godfrey Greene

Endorsed (p. 167): To his right worshipfull maistre Sir William Plompton kt

[a] *Marginal note*: 23 letter.
[b] *Marginal note*: Deference betwene Gascoine & Plompton but Northumberland pacifies them.
[c] *Marginal note*: Copied 30 of January 1612, Saturday.

[1] The plaintiff was therefore not-suited, Hastings, 158.
[2] Order to appear in court because there was a case to be answered.
[3] Sir John Pilkington of Chevet Hall, near Wakefield, knighted at Tewkesbury, 1471; chamberlain of receipt of the Exchequer, April 1477, dead by 8 March 1479, App. III.
[4] Sir William Gascoigne, of Gawthorpe (d.1487), brother-in-law of the 4th earl, appointed deputy at Knaresborough after the earl's appointment as steward etc., in 1470. In Oct. 1471 he gave a bond to keep the peace towards Sir William, Kirby, *NH*, xxv, 111–12.
[5] The bailiwick of Knaresborough, granted to Sir William by Gloucester, 29 Sept. 1472 for 12 years, App. II, 34.
[6] Sir William Hastings, appointed king's chamberlain for life, 31 July 1461, raised to the peerage 1467, *CPR, 1461–67*, 55; *ibid., 1467–77*, 26.
[7] Having made his peace with the Yorkists, Sir William reappeared on the commission in Feb. 1472, but was dropped in Nov. 1475 when the number of JPs was reduced. His reappointment in Dec. 1476 was due to Northumberland's good offices, *CPR, 1467–77*, 638; Arnold, 117–25.

29 *Godfrey Greene to Sir William Plumpton, [Michaelmas term, ending 25 November 1477] (No. 24, p. 170, CB 621)*

Right reuerent & worshipfull Sir,[a] I recomend me vnto your good mastership. Please you to witt that I labored to Mr Pilkinton[1] & to the chauncelor diuerse times for your letter fra the king,[2] and promissed me to moue my lord to speak to the king therefore; neverthelesse it was not doon; but when the king comes to London I shall labour therefore again. Your writts & *certiorare*[3] are labored for & shalbe had, how be the iudges will graunt no *certiorare* but for a cause. Ailmer wife was like to haue bene non suit in her appeale,[4] for her day was *Octabis Martini*,[5] but Whele [and] I certified the iudges that she wold come if she were in hele & out of prison. The iudges gifnes her no favour, for they say they vnderstand by credible informationes that these men be not guiltie, & it is but onely your mainetenance. And so one of them said to me out of the court. And Guy Fairfax[6] said openly att the barre, that he know so verily they were not guilty, that he wold labor their deliuerance for almes, not takeing a penny, and I, seeing this, took Mr Pygott[7] and Mr Collow.[8]

Godfrey Grene[b]

Endorsed (p. 170): To the right reuerend and worshipfull Sir William Plompton this be deliuered

[a] *Marginal note*: 24 letter.
[b] *Marginal note*: Copied [illeg.] of February 1612, Munday.

[1] Sir John Pilkington, **28**.
[2] Thomas Rotherham, bishop of Lincoln, resumed the chancellorship, 29 Sept. 1475, *HBC*, 85–6.
[3] The statute of 10 Hen. VI c.6 was intended to stop plaintiffs from using the writ of *certiorari* to remove indictments to the king's bench 'unknown to the Party so indicted or appealed', thus procuring outlawry of the defendant. It might also be sued out by a defendant in order to display a pardon already purchased, Philippa C. Maddern, *Violence and Social Order: East Anglia 1422–1442* (Oxford, 1992), 44–5.
[4] Judges disliked the malicious appeal, C. Whittick, 'The Role of the Criminal Appeal in the Fifteenth Century', in J.A. Guy & H.G. Beale (eds), *Law and Social Change in British History* (Royal Historical Society, 1984), 58–9.
[5] 18 Nov. A missed return day might result in the discontinuance of the action, Baker, 53.
[6] Counsel usually demurred at speaking gratis through fear of being accused of barratry or maintenance, J.H. Baker, 'Counsellors and Barristers', *Cambridge Law Journal*, xxvii (1969), 27, 212, 222.
[7] Richard Pigott, called sergeant 1463, App. III.

30 *The earl of Northumberland to William Gascoigne, esq., 19 June [1478]* *(No. 55, p. 33)*

Right trusty & right hartely beloued brother, I greet you well. And forasmuch as I vnderstand that ye haue put vnder arrest in the castell of knaresbrugh one Thomas Ward, for suerty of peace; he finding sufficient suertie to answere to the king our soueraigne lord, I will þat ye suffer him to be at his larg without longer empresonment. Not failling herof as my trust is in you. And our Lord haue you in his kepping. Written in my mannor of Lekingfeild, the xix day of June.

Your brother Hen: Northumberland.[a]

Endorsed: To my right trusty and hartely beloued brother William Gascoygne

[a] *Appended*: Copied the 4 day of March 1612.

31 *Tenants of the lordship of Idle to Sir William Plumpton, [before 15 October 1480]*[1] *(No. 19, p. 164)*

Beseketh your good maistershipp,[a] all your tenants and seruaunts of your lordshipp of Idell,[2] Wil. Rycroft, elder, William Rycroft, yonger, John Rycroft, Henry Rycroft, and John Chalner except. And it please your good mastershipp to heare and consider the great rumor, slaunder, and full noyle of your tenants of your said lordshipp, att they shold be vntrew peopell of their hands, taking goods by means of vntrewth. And for as much as the said Wil. Rycroft, elder, Wil. Rycroft, yonger, John Rycroft, Henry Rycroft and John Chalner are dwelling within your said lordship, they all not hauing any kow or kalves, or any other gude whereaby they might liue, or any other occupise; and fair they are beseen, and wel they fair, and [...][b] att all sports & gamies they are in our country, for the most part, and siluer to spend & to gameing, which they haue more readie then any other <with> in your said lordship; and to the welfare of our soueraigne lord the king and you, nothing they will pay without your said tenants will fray with them. Wherearfore they are in regage to diuers of your graues; and by what meanes they in this wise, with 5 persons being in houshold, are found, God or some euil angel hase notice hereof. And as for geese, grise, hennys, and capons, your said tenants may none keepe, but they are bribed and stolen away by night, to great hurt to your tenants. And for as much as these persons afore rehersed are not laboring in due time, as all other of your tenants are, but as vagabounds live, your said tenants suppose more strangely by them. Whereafore att reuerence of God and in way of charetie, your said tenants besketh you to call all them before you, and to sett such remedy in these premisses as may be to your worshipp, and great proffitt to your tenants, and in shewing of mikle vnthriftiness, which without you is likely to grow hearafter, and your said tenants shall pray to almighty God for your welfare and estate.[c]
Endorsed: Complaynts of your servants of Hidell, John Rycroft and William Rycroft to our maister and lord Sir William Plompton knight

[a] *Marginal note*: 19 letter.
[b] are *deleted*.
[c] *Marginal note*: Copied 21 of January 1612 Fryday.
[1] Sir William died 15 Oct. 1480.
[2] The Plumptons had held 1/4 of a knight's fee (3 carucates) of the Percies in the Lordship of Idle at least since 1166, Sir C.T. Clay (ed.), *Early Yorkshire Charters* (YASRS, extra ser., ix, 1963), 266.

32 *The earl of Northumberland to Robert Plumpton, 7 September [1480] (No. 53, p. 32)*

Right welbeloued frinde, I greet you well. And wheras the Scotts in great number are entred into Northumberland, whose malice, with

Gods helpe, I entend to resist;[1] therfore on the king owr soueraigne lords behalfe, I charg you, and also on myne as wardeyn, [that] ye[a] [with] all such personnes as ye may make in there most defensible array, be with me at Topliffe vppon Munday by viij a clocke, as my trust is in you. Written in Wresill,[2] the vij day of September.[b]

Your cousin Hen: Northumberland.[b]

Endorsed: To my right welbeloued Robart Plompton esquier

[a] *MS* ye þat.

[b] *Appended*: This letter hath a seale. Copied the 3 day of Marche 1612.

[1] Gloucester and Northumberland called out the northern levies for a counter-raid after a Scottish attack had ended in the burning of Bamburgh in the summer of 1480, Ross, *Edward IV*, 279.

[2] Wressle castle, built by Thomas Percy, earl of Worcester, in the king's hand after the 3rd earl's posthumous attainder in 1461, was in the following year granted jointly for life to Lawrence Booth, bishop of Durham and William Neville, Lord Fauconberg, R.L. Storey, 'The North of England 1399–1509', in S.B. Chrimes, C.D. Ross, & R.A. Griffiths (eds), *Fifteenth-Century England, 1399–1509* (Manchester, 1972), 140, 143; *The Itinerary of John Leland*, i, 52–53.

33 *The earl of Northumberland to Robert Plumpton, 31 December [1480] (No. 45, p. 29)*

Right welbeloued I gret you well, willing & charging you to be with me in all hast possible after the sight of this my writting, not failing hereof, as ye will answere to the kings highness and to me at your perill. Written at Lekinfeild, the last day of December.[1]

Henry Northumberland.[a]

Endorsed: To my welbeloued Robart Plompton

[a] *Appended*: this letter hath a seale at ... Copied the 25 day of February 1612.

[1] Preparations began in Dec. 1480 for open war with Scotland, Ross, *Edward IV*, 279–80.

34 *William Joddopken to Joan, Lady Plumpton,*[1] *[?6 July 1481] (No. 115, p. 69)*

Right worshipful and my especial good Lady, I recommend me unto your good Ladiship, euermore desiring to wit of your welfare. And, Madam, I pray you to call to your Ladyship how gude precher I haue been to my master as gon is, and to you. And, Madam, there is one duty awing unto me, part wherof was taken or my master deceased, whose soul God haue mercy, and most part taken to yourselfe since he died; taken by Henry Fox,[2] and by Henry of Sealay, your seruants, of whilk I send you one bill with Henry Fox. The sum is 19*li* 2*s* 9*d*, wherof I haue receiued by Henry Fox, in money, 3*li*, and in 2 fat oxen, price 36*s*. Sum at I haue receiued is 4*li* 15*s*; so remains there behine 14*li* 6*s* 9*d*. Madam, if case be þat ye will haue sende word for Sir John Wixley[3] at drawes 6*li* 6*s* viij*d*; so is ther owying over to me 9*li* j*d*. And I besech you, Madam, þat I myght haue my money. I haue forborne it long. Ye know well, Madam, þe great troble þat I was in, and the great cost and charges þat I had this last yere past; &, Madam, ye know well I haue no lyfing but my bying and selling. [*p. 70*] And, Madam, I pray you sende me my money as ye will I doe you service, or els to send me word when I shall haue it, for it cost me much money sending for. And Henry Fox bad me send my rakning at Ripon, and I should be answered to my money, for Harry receiued most part of stufe of me. And if ye will not answere me therfore, Henry must answere therfore.

Madam, þar is one Casson in taking, of þat towne to; considring of gud service [...] at Sir John Dedyser, my master, and you in your great troble. For sute, Madam, I lost all þat I payd for him, and þat was long of your Ladyship. For when I wold haue followed him, ye dyside me nay, for ye said ye had rather lose þe towne; & therfor I besech you to loke if þer be any thing [I] may dow for your Ladyship or for my master your son, I shalbe redy, with grace of God, who preserue your Ladyship. Written at York on Friday after St Peter Day.

Be your owne William Joddopken

Endorsed (p. 59): To my old Lady Plompton be this bil deliuered

[1] Sir William Plumpton's 2nd wife, and mother of Sir Robert.

[2] Henry Fox, valet, and Sir John Whixley, chaplain, were among the trustees for the settlements made by Sir Robert to increase his mother's life estate, 25–27 Oct. 1480, CB, 701–3.

[3] Sir John Whixley and Richard Plumpton, clerk, were appointed by the official of York to collect the debts and take an inventory of the effects of Sir William Plumpton who died intestate, 10 Jan.1480/1, CB, 628.

35 *The earl of Northumberland to Sir Robert Plumpton,*[1] *9 October [1481]* (*No. 50, p. 31*)

Right trusty and welbeloued I greet you well, & will and charge you on the kings our soueraigne lords behalfe, and also on myne, that ye, with all such persones as ye may make defensibly arrayed, be redy to attend vpon the kings highness & me, vpon our warnying, as ye loue me, and will answere to the king at your perill. Written at Lekingfeild, the ixth day of October.[2]

Your cousin Hen: Northumberland[a]

Endorsed: To my right trusty and welbeloued friend Sir Robart Plompton kt

[a] *Appended*: This letter hath a seale. Copied the 27 day of February 1612.

[1] Robert Plumpton was knighted by Northumberland Aug. 1481, Hicks, *NH*, xiv, 107.
[2] Not until some time in Oct. 1481 did Edward IV announce his decision not to lead the army against the Scots. Gloucester and Northumberland were therefore left to besiege Berwick during the winter of 1481–2, Ross, 282–3.

36 *The earl of Northumberland to Sir Robert Plumpton, 14 February [?1481/2] (No. 51, p. 31)*

Right hartely beloued cousin, I commend me vnto yu. And wheras I conceiue þat wheras award was ordred in the matter of variance depending betwixt John Polleyn,[1] on the one partie, and George Tankard,[2] with other taking his part, or the other party, I am enformed þat ye said parties bene now at trauerse in that behalfe, contrary to such derections as were taken. I, willing ye pacefying and reformation hereof, by the aduyse of you and other of my counsell, desire & pray you, cousin, at your comying to me at Yorke vppon Thursday next comying, to cause the sayd Georg & the other persones to com with you, and þat ye shew your good will for the performance herof, as my very trust is in you, whom God kepe. Written in my castell of Wresell, the xiiij day of February.

Your cousin Hen: Northumberland[a]

Endorsed: To my right hertely beloued cousin, Sir Robart Plompton kt

[a] *Appended*: This letter hath a seale. Copied the 27 day of February 1612.

[1] Possibly John Pullein, of Scotton (d.*c.*1519), sergeant of the kitchen to Richard III, W.E. Hampton, 'Sir Robert Percy and Joyce his Wife', in *Richard III, Crown and People*, 185 & n; **53**.
[2] Presumably a kinsman of the Tancreds of Boroughbridge, George Tancred witnessed a deed dated 15 Dec. 1480, CB, 708; **55**. Feudal settlements by magnates such as Northumberland were known as 'derections', J.G. Bellamy, *Criminal Law and Society in Late Medieval and Tudor England* (Gloucester, 1984), 79.

37 *Master Anthony to Sir Robert Plumpton, 11 March [?1481/3] (No. 173, p. 112)*

Right worshipfull master, I recommend me vnto you, euermore desiring of your prosperity & welfare, þe which I besech almighty Jhesu to mercy to his pleasure & to your most hartiest [. . .][a] ease; & also praying you to comend me vnto my lady your moder & to my lady your wyfe.

And also praying you to be my good master, for I vnderstand a man of Spofforth,[1] which I had his wyfe in cure, will arest me, for I can not goe fourth of place of Master John Fous,[2] nor without his lordship, but your baylaies will arest me, as I vnderstand by them þat loues me. Wherfore I pray you take this matter into your hands, Sir; & also praying your mastership þat I may haue a letter of this man, by you, þat I may goe where I shall. Ye vnderstand þat I haue receved x*s* & xx*d*, & of þat silver I haue spent x*s* of medcins; & also, Sir, as you & this man agres of this siluer, what he shold haue againe, he shalbe contented. As fast as I haue siluer I will come to you & pay you, with grace of God, who haue you in his keping. Wrytten at the place of Master St[eward], aleffant day of moneth of March.[3]

By your well loued seruant Maister [...][b] Antony[c]

Endorsed: Vnto my master Sir Robt Plompton knight

[a] ioy *deleted.*
[b] Mr *deleted.*
[c] *Appended*: Copied þe 29 of Apryll 1613.

[1] Sir Robert succeeded his father as steward of the Percy lordship of Spofforth, **53**.
[2] John Fawkes (*fl.*1494–5), son of John Fawkes, of Farnley, receiver of Knaresborough 1438, Somerville, i, 526; R. Thoresby, *Ducatus Leodiensis* (1st edn, 1715), 130; Pullein, 55.
[3] The writer was probably a university-trained physician with an itinerant practice. Under the terms of his contract with his patient, which probably defined the disease and its cure and was entered into before the commencement of treatment, he could have received a down-payment for medicines etc., and the rest on completion of the cure. Patients were often extremely active, sceptical and well-informed, C.H. Talbot, *Medicine in Medieval England* (1967), 138; M. Pelling, 'Medical Practice in Early Modern England: Trade or Profession', in W. Prest (ed.), *The Professions in Early Modern England* (1987), 91, 101, 106.

38 *Edward Plumpton to Sir Robert Plumpton, 30 June [1483] (No. 192, p. 128)*

After all due recomendations premysed, pleaseth your mastership to wyt þat I haue receiued my fee xxvj*s* viij*d* for Pentycost last past, sent to me by my fadr seruant William Coltman, in my most humbly wyse thanking your mastership therfore. Neuerthelesse, I maruell greatly þat your mastership wrote not to me comaunding me to doe you some service at London, Sir, you know my mynd & service, & I am right sory & any synister wayes of my aduersaryes be shewed vnto you, & not of my deseruing; if þat be so, your wryting had bene to me more comfortable then much goods, considryng althings done aforetyme.[1] Such as be your aduersaryes in your old matters[2] hath bene with me at London. Mr Bryan Roclyfe, Palmes[3] & Topclyffe,[4] comyning &

desyring further to proced in our matters, & saying ye clame suyt, seruice of the maner of Colthorpe,[a] [*p. 129*] and for the same merce him in your court at Plompton; & if yt be so, in my mynd yt is necessary to aske, destreyne, and levie þe sayd amerciment.

Pleaseth it your mastership, in my most humble wyse to recomend me vnto my good ladyes, & to my power service, as I haue bene & euer wylbe to my lyfe end, as more at þe larg the brynger of this shall shew vnto you by mouth, to whom I pray you giue credence. In short space ye shall know more for the best, with þe grace of Jhesu, who your mastership preserue.[5] At London, þe last day of June.

Your humble seruant Edward Plompton[b]

Endorsed (p. 128): To the ryght honorable my especiall good master Sir Robt Plompton knyght

[a] *Marginal note*: Colthorpe plieth to Plo: courts.

[b] *Appended*: Copied þe 6 day of May 1613.

[1] Edward was Sir Robert's young kinsman and legal adviser, Apps.II, 49; III.

[2] Since the death of Sir William the heirs general, Margaret Rocliffe and Elizabeth Sotehill, and their respective husbands, John Rocliffe and John Sotehill, had been in dispute with Sir Robert over his right to the Plumpton inheritance. Richard III's arbitration award is dated 16 Sept. 1483. It held until contested at the instigation of Sir Richard Empson, BL, Harl. MS 433; App. II, 64; **119**.

[3] Brian Rocliffe was Margaret Plumpton's father-in-law; his sister was married to William Palmes, of Naburn, father of two future sergeants, Brian (d.1519/20) and Guy (1516), **8**; Ives, *CL*, 452, 472.

[4] A Thomas Topcliffe was clerk of the receipt to the receiver-general of the Duchy of Lancaster, 1480–4, Somerville, i, 401.

[5] Prof Colin Richmond suggests that Edward Plumpton's habit in the 1480s of confiding his correspondents to the protection of Jesus may mark a changing convention: the name of the Lord is seldom mentioned in the *Paston Letters*, 'Religion and the Fifteenth-Century English Gentleman', in R.B. Dobson (ed.), *The Church, Politics and Patronage in the Fifteenth Century* (Gloucester, 1984), 200.

39 *Edward Plumpton to Sir Robert Plumpton, 18 October [1483]* *(No. 191, p. 127)*

The most humble & due recomendations premysed, pleaseth your mastership to recomend me vnto my singuler good lady your moder, & my lady your wyfe, humble praying your good mastership to take no displeasure with me þat I sent not to you afore this, as my duty was. People in this country be so trobled, in such comandment as they haue in the kyngs name & otherwyse, marvellously, þat they know not what to doe. My Lord Strayng[1] goeth forth from Lathan vpon Munday next with x ml men, whether, we cannot say. The duke of Buck: has so many men, as yt is sayd here, þat he is able to go where he wyll, but

I trust he shalbe right [*p. 128*] withstanded & all his mallice, & else were great pytty.[2] Messingers comyth dayly both from the kings grace & the duke into this country. In short space I trust to se your mastership. Such men as I haue to do with be as yet occupied with my sayd lord. Sir, I find my kynsmen all well dysposed to me. If your mastership wyll command me any service, I am redy & euer wilbe to my lifes end, with þ grace of Jhesu, who euer preserue you. Wrytten at Aldclife vppon St Luke Day.

Your seruant Ed: Plompton[a]

Endorsed: To þe right honorable & worshipfull Sir Robt Plompton knight these be deliuered

[a] *Appended*: Copied þe 6 of May 1613.

[1] Edward Plumpton was secretary to George, Lord Strange (d.1503), eldest son of Thomas, Lord Stanley (d.1504), created earl of Derby 27 Oct. 1485, *GEC*; B. Coward, *The Stanleys, Lords Stanley and Earls of Derby 1385–1672* (Chetham Society, 3rd ser., 30, 1985), 13, *GEC*.

[2] Henry Stafford, 2nd duke of Buckingham (exec. Nov.1483) was in rebellion against Richard III. Lord Stanley's 2nd wife Lady Margaret Beaufort was implicated, Michael K. Jones and Malcom G. Underwood, *The King's Mother* (1992), 147; M.K. Jones, 'Richard III and the Stanleys', in R. Horrox (ed.), *Richard III and the North* (University of Hull Studies in Regional and Local History, 6, 1986), 40, 49n. There was uncertainty as to whether Lord Strange was responding to the king's summons or to the duke's appeals, M.J. Bennett, *The Battle of Bosworth* (1985), 48.

40 *Halnath Mauleverer to Sir Robert Plumpton, Miles Wilstrop, John Pullein and Robert Birnand, 13 May [1480 × 1486]* *(No. 133, p. 80)*

Worshipfull Sires, I recomend me to you. My nephew Halnath hath bene with me, & shewed to me a wyll made upon a feftment, at my brother Sir John[1] goying over see, on whose soule Jesu have mercy, by þe which I vnderstond þat my nephew Halnath & Robart[2] shold have, ether of them, iiij*li* by the yere, term of ther lyfes. If they can shew the wylle vnder seale according to the copie, the must neds have ther iiij*li*. Also they shew þat Myles Wylstropp,[3] John Pullan,[4] Robart Barnand[5] & Nycholas Ward was with my brother [*p. 81*] at his death, to whom my sayd brother sayd þat he wold þat this will were fulfilled & performed. If this be trew, it is a great evydence. As for my sister enterest, I shall comyn with wyse learne men, & shew to them how þe matter stands betwene my sayd sister[6] & my nese as nere as I can. I shall shew them of the exchang and of þe closser byside Sober Hell,[7] and also what þe Law will, if my sayd sister was agreed afore wytnesse þat my nephew shold have my sister iointer and dower for terme of hir lyfe, if yt be by indenter.[8] I remitt þat to your wysdomes, besechying you all to se þat ther be no troble amongst them so I send þe certayne of all þe premisses. Gylbard shalbe with you by Trente Sunday, or sone after, & bryng you the certaynte of everything, by the grace of Jesu, who preserue you. Wrytten at Klerkinwell, the xiij of May.[a]

Halnath Maliuerey[9]

Endorsed (p. 80): To the right worshipfull Sirs Sir Robart Plompton, Myles Wylstrop & to John Pullan, Robart Barnand be this letter deliuered

[a] *Appended*: Copied þe 17 day of Aprill 1613.

[1] Sir John Mauleverer, **18**.

[2] In his will, proved 12 April 1502 in Doctors' Commons, Robert Mauleverer bequeathed to Our Lady of Walsingham a diamond ring given to him by Richard III. His brother Halnath (or Alnathus) was named executor, *Test. Ebor.*, iv, 182n.

[3] See **18**.

[4] John Pullein, of Scotton, married Grace, daughter of Sir John Mauleverer, Pullein, 128–29; **36**.

[5] Robert Birnand, of Knaresborough, Sir John Mauleverer's brother-in-law, described in a deed of 1499 as 'learned', *Flower's Visitation*, 201; D.J.H. Michelmore (ed.), *The Fountains Abbey Lease Book* (YASRS, CXL, 1981), 105; **24**.

[6] Alice, daughter of Richard Banke of Newton (d.1496), *CIPM*, *Henry VII*, iii, 389.

[7] Sober Hill is the name of two farmhouses in Newby Wiske, North Yorkshire, Stapleton, 47n.

[8] It appears that Lady Mauleverer had made over her jointure and dower to her son, Sir Thomas, in exchange for an annuity, **41**.

[9] Halnath Mauleverer, of Allerton Mauleverer, near Knaresborough, App. III.

41 *Halnath Mauleverer to Sir Robert Plumpton, John Pullein and Robert Birnand, 20 May [1480 × 1486]* *(No. 134, p. 81)*

Right worshipfull Sires, I recomend me vnto you, letting you wytte þat I have comond with lerned men to vnderstamd wher my syster in law may enter into her ioynter & dower, or no. They say forasmuch as the erytance & right of þe same was in my neveu after the death of his father, <on> whose soule Jesu have mercy; at whose death my sayd sister let to ferme hir iointer & dower to my sayd nephew, hir son, afore wyttnese, terme of hir lyfe, the which is thought, by them that be learned, is a surrender in the law. Wherfore she must byd by such comonds as was betwyxt hir son & hir.[1] As for my brother William, if it may be shewed vnder his seale or synmanuell, [*p. 82*] or if the sayd wyll be lost, if ther be iiij worshipfull men þat will swere vpon a booke þat they saw the wyll, & þat my sayd brother at his death desired them þat the same wyll myght be performed, my nephewes must needs have ther porcion, & every person to have after thayr porcion. Also yt is thought by the forsayd lerned men þat if my sayd nevew had a *cli* of his father goods, if yt were spended afore his death, his father seckturs may have no accion agaynst his seckturs. Ye haue right wyse & descret learned men in Yorkshire, ye may enquere of them, if it please you. Jesu preserve you. Written at Clerrkynwell the xx day of May.

Yor owne Halnath Mallyverer[a]

Endorsed (p. 81): To the right worshipfull Sir Robart Plompton, John Pullan & to Robart Byrnand & to euery of you be thes deliuered

[a] *Appended*: Copied the 18 of Aprill 1613.

[1] Strenuous efforts were sometimes made to persuade widows to accept a cash annuity in place of dower in order that the whole estate might be brought back into single ownership, for example Dame Isabel Plumpton, widow of Sir Robert (d.1407), was persuaded to accept a rent charge of 40m out of the manor of Plumpton in lieu of dower, App. II, 6.

42 *Thomas Betanson, priest, to Sir Robert Plumpton, [13 December 1485] (No. 148, p. 91)*

Sir, if it please your mastership,[a] on the Satterday after our Lady Day[1] the Parlament was prolonged vnto the xxvj day of January,[2] & then it begineth again. Sir, my lord schanchler publyshed in the Parlament house the same day þat the kings gud grace shall weede my Lady Elizabeth, & so she is taken as quene, & þat [at] the marage ther shalbe great iustying.[3] Also, Sir, ther [be][b] divers lords & gentlemen attended by the Parlament, which be these: & first, Richard, late duke of Glouceter, John, duke of Norfolk, Thomas, earle of Surrey, Francis, Lord Lovell, Watter, Lord Ferris, John, Lord Such; knights, Sir James Hereryngton, Sir Robt Heryngton, Sir Richard Ritliff, Sir William Barkley, Sir Robt Brakenbery, Sir Thomas Pilkynton, Sir Robt Mydleton; and squires, Walter Hopton, [*p. 92*] Wylliam Catisby, Roger Wake, William Sapcott, Homfray Stafferd, Wylliam Clarke, Galfryd Seryng<men>, Watter Watkin, herold of hermes, Rich: Revell of Darbyshire, Thoms Pultor of Surrey, John Walste, John Kendall, secretory, John Buke, John Ratte, William Brampton: the are atteinded for certayne. Howbeit ther was many gentlemen agaynst it, but it wold not be, for yt was the kings pleasure.[4]

Sir, here is much spech þat we shall have aschip agayne, & walchmen; & much spech is in the kyngs house & of his houshold men.[5] Sir, other tydings is none here as yett. Ther is much runyng [. . .][c] amongst þe lords, but no man wett what it is. It is sayd yt is not wele amongst them. Sir, I send your mastership a letter by Roger, Mr Mydeton man. Sir, if ther be any newer things, your mastership shall have word, if I can gitt it caryed from London. *In die [Sent][d] Lucie Virgi[n].*

Your Bedman Sir Tho: Betanson[e]

Endorsed (p. 91): To his speciall gud master Sir Robt Plompton kt deliuer these letter

[a] *Marginal note*: 1 H.7, 20 Decem.
[b] *MS* to.
[c] *A word deleted.*
[d] *MS* Sep.
[e] *Appended*: Copied þe 20 of Aprill 1613.

[1] 10 Dec. 1485. Parliament had assembled on 7 Nov., *RP*, vi, 276.
[2] Parliament was prorogued until 23 Jan. It did not reassemble, J.D. Mackie, *The Earlier Tudors 1485–1558* (Oxford, 1952), 65.
[3] The marriage took place on 18 Jan. 1485/6.
[4] *Crowland Chronicle Continuations*, 195.

43 *Thomas Betanson, priest, to Sir Robert Plumpton, 15 February [1485/6] (No. 147, p. 90)*

Sir, if it please your mastership, I haue made a letter vnto you afore Christenmas of such tydings as I know, but I was deceyved, for I went[a] your mastership had had it to within this ij dayes, & so ye shall have one other with it both. Sir, if yt please you, thes bene the tydings þat I know. The kyng hat resumyde by the Parliament into his hands all manner patayns, geftys, offyzs þat he dyd giffe from the ij day of August vnto the iij day of January,[1] & ther be many of his houshold in yt plesyde with yt. Also he hath resumyde all manner gyfts, patayns, offizs þat war gevon from the xxiij yere of King Herrie the vjth, by King Edward the iiijth, or by King Edward, his son, the vth, or by King Richard the iijth into his hands.[2] Also it is in actte in the Parlament þat all manner huntyng inparkes, chases, forest belonging to the kyng is made felony. Also, Sir, the king purposyse northward hastyly after the Parlament, & it is sayd he purposses to doe execution quickly ther on such as hath offended agynst him. Sir, other tyding I know none as yet. Sir, I besech you recomend me vnto both my gud ladis, & I send them [*p. 91*][b] a pauper of the rosary of our Lady of Coleyn, & I have regestered your name with both my ladis names, as þe pauper expresses, & ye be acopled as brethern & sisters.[3] Also, Sir, these lords and gentlemen þat was attaynted, they gytt no grace, as yt is sayd. No more, but I besech your mastership to be gud master vnto my father, & I shalbe your bedman, with Gods grace, who keepe you euermore in great ioy and felycyte. From London, *in crastino* St Valentin. Also, Sir, the king will come with great company, as it is sayd, with x hundred men in harnesse, & with him mo then v or six schore lords and knights. Also the duke of Bedford[4] goes into Wales to see þat country. Also it is inactt þat all manner of profyres is mayd felony. Sir, oder tydings I know none as yet, þat be certayne.

Your servant & bedman Sir Tho: Betanson[c]

Endorsed (p. 90): To his singular gud master Sir Robart Plompton kt deliuer these

[a] *Probably a scribal error: Stapleton suggests* weened, *p. 263*.
[b] *At the head of the page*: 15 Feb: 1 of H.7. *Followed by* either 1, 3, 4, 5 or 6 of Hen.7 *deleted*.
[c] *Appended*: Copied þe 20 of Apryll 1613.

[1] According to the Parliament Roll, 21 Aug. to 20 Jan.
[2] The Act of resumption put Henry in possession of all the crown lands held by Henry VI on 2 Oct.1455, *RP*, vi, 336–84.
[3] According to Richmond the attitude of the gentry towards religious fraternities was in reality somewhat superficial, 'The English Gentry and Religion c.1500', in C. Harper-Bill (ed.), *Religious Belief and Ecclesiastical Causes in Late Medieval England* (1991), 137; Marjorie K. McIntosh, 'Local Change and Community Control in England, 1455–1500', *Huntington Library Quarterly*, xlix (1986), 236.
[4] Jasper Tudor (d.1495), created duke of Bedford 27 Oct.1485, *GEC*.

44 *Edward Plumpton to Sir Robert Plumpton, 3 April [1486]* *(No. 207, p. 144)*

After most due recomendacions had, pleaseth your mastership in my most lowly wyse to recomend me vnto my singuler good lady. Sir, this day com William Plompton[1] to labor for Haveray Parke,[2] & brought to me nether byll, wrytting nor commandement by words, nor token for your mastership, & therof I marvell, considering þat at your instaunce I suffered him to occupie the same parke & office for þe tyme, & for þat cause I am not in certente whether ye be his good master or noe. Wherfore he hath not spedd as he myght haue done if your wrytting had com; notwithstanding yt is well. Sir, my lord[3] kept [*p. 145*] his Easter with my lord of Oxford[4] a[t] Laueham, & come to þe king vppon Fryday last, & comes with [the] king to Yorke; & my lord of Darby[5] departeth from Notingham into Lancashire. Sir, therle of Oxford, my lord chamberleyn,[6] with diuerse other estates, cometh to þe king to Notingham, & so forth to Yorke, as more at large þe brynger shall shew to you by mouth.

Sir, the first gift at my lady of Syon gave to me was a par of ienoper beads pardonet,[a] the which I have sent to you by þe bringer;[7] & if I had a better thing I wold haue sent yt with as good a will & harte. And any service that ye wyll comand me I am redy, as knoweth our Lord, who preserve you. At Lyncolne, the iij day of Apryll.[8]

Your servant Edward Plompton[b]

Endorsed (p. 144): To my singuler good master Sir Robt Plompton kt

[a] *Appended*: Copied þe VIth of May 1612.

[1] William Plumpton, of Kirkby Overblow, illegitimate son of Sir William (d.1480). A dispute between him and Sir Robert was settled 22 Nov. 1490, App. II, 53; **86**.

[2] Haverah Park, a royal chase in the liberty of Knaresborough, and parcel of the Duchy of Lancaster, of which the earl of Derby was seneschal of the North Parts, Stapleton, 51n.

[3] George, Lord Strange, **39**.

[4] John de Vere, earl of Oxford (d.1513), **16**.

[5] Thomas Stanley, earl of Derby, **39**.

[6] Sir William Stanley of Holt (exec.1495), younger brother of the earl of Derby, was lord chamberlain by Feb.1486, *CPR, 1485–94*, 69.

[7] Syon Abbey, a house dedicated to the Holy Saviour, St Mary the Virgin and St Brigitta, where it was the custom for pardons to be held on the feast day of the saint, 8 Oct., M.D. Knowles, *The Religious Orders in England* (3 vols), ii, 177–8; James Gairdner (ed.), *The Paston Letters* (6 vols, 1904), no. 827.

[8] The king kept Easter (26 March) at Lincoln, and afterwards travelled to Nottingham and York, *Collectanea*, iv, 185.

45 *Master Henry Hudson to Sir Robert Plumpton, 18 November [c.1486] (No. 165, p. 107)*

Reverend & my right trusty good master, due reuerence done, know ye I am at your comandment with prayer for you, my gode lady your wyfe, & mother, & your children. My lord[1] faryth well & recomends him vnto you, with harty thanks of your good & fast love, which he entendeth to content your mynd for. Sir, yt is so þat Sir Alexander[2] hat a *dedimus potestatem*[3] dyrect to thabot of St Mary in York,[4] Sir Richard Tunstall[5] & Sir John Hart,[6] for þe which matter my lord hath wrytten to thabot & Sir John Hart in recomendation of Sir Alexander. Wherfore, when expedient tyme shalbe apoynted, my lord wilbe glad & well content þat ye se the deling, and as ye vnderstand þat it will lest you, certyfie me by your wryting derected to me; & thus almyghty God preserve you. From Grenwich, þe xviij day of Nouember.

By your loving & due beadman Master Henry Hudson[a]

Endorsed: To my right worshipfull master Sir Robt Plompton kt

[a] *Appended*: Copied þe 27 of Aprill 1613.

[1] The earl of Northumberland.

[2] The writer was probably assistant priest at Spofforth under the rector, Alexander Lye, who was presented in 1481 by Northumberland, and resigned *c.*1499. Plumpton was in his parish, **110**.

[3] A writ commanding the taking of evidence.

[4] Probably William Senhouse (or Sever), **50**.

[5] Sir Richard Tunstall of Thurland, Lancs (d.1492), steward of the honor of Pontefract, CB, 548; App. III; **56**, **71**.

[6] Rector of the church of St Martin, Micklegate, York, 1476–1519, where the Plumptons held the advowson, *CIPM sive Escaetarum*, iv, 403; App. II, 2.

46 *Thomas Betanson, priest to Sir Robert Plumpton, [29 November 1486] (No. 146, p. 89)*

Right worshipfull & my singuler gud master, I recomend me vnto your mastershipe & vnto both my gud ladys & vnto all gud masters & frynds, your servants. If it please your mastership to here of me and where I abyde, I serve in the Sepultre church without Newgaytt. There is a woman was borne in Selby. I haue x marke & no charg, & the term <tymes> I haue meat & drynk of my Lord Beryan, cheife iudge of the common place;[1] & this Christenmas I goe with him into the country to his place, & comes agayn the next terme. Wherfore, if it wold please your mastership to send me a letter how <ye> & my ladys, with all your houshold, doth, for yt were to me great comforth; & if there be any thing here þat I can or may do, send me word & I shall indever me to do yt, as is my dewty.

Sir, as for tydings, here is but few. The king & quene lyeth at Grenwych; the Lord Perce[2] is at Wynchester; the earle of Oxford is in Essex; the earle of Darby & his son [*p. 90*] be with the king. Also here is but litle spech [...][a] of þe earle of Warwyke[3] now, but after Christenmas they say ther wylbe more spech of. Also ther be mayny enimies on the see, & dyvers schippes take, & ther be many take of the kyngs house for theues. Other tydings I know non. Also they begyn to dye in London;[4] ther is but few pariches free. At summer they die faster. Then I purpose to come into Yorkshire, with Gods grace, who kepe you & your lovers euermore. At London in vigil St Andrew appostle.

Your dayly bedman Tho: Betanson[b]

Endorsed (p. 89): To his worshipfull master Sir Robart Plompton kt this delyuer

[a] of the *deleted.*

[b] *Appended*: Copied þe 20 of Aprill 1613.

[1] Sir Thomas Brian (d.1500), justice of the bench from 1485, N.H. Nicholas (ed.), *Testamenta Vetusta* (2 vols, 1826), ii, 450; *CPR, 1485–94*, 1, 40 & *passim.*

[2] Henry Percy, eldest son of the 4th earl of Northumberland, who succeeded his father April 1489, **125.**

[3] Edward, earl of Warwick (exec.1499), son of George, duke of Clarence (exec.1478), was a prisoner in the Tower.

[4] Probably due to the 'old bubo-plague' which raged in York in 1485, and caused high mortality among the monks of Christ Church Priory, Canterbury, C. Creighton, *History of Epidemics in England* (2 vols, 1894), i, 282; J. Hatcher, 'Mortality in the Fifteenth Century', *Econ. HR*, 2nd ser., xxxix (1986), 29; *Crowland Chronicle Continuations*, 169.

47 *The earl of Northumberland to Sir William Ingilby, Sir Robert Plumpton, Sir William Beckwith, and John Gascoigne, esq., [?1487]*[1] *(No. 42, p. 28)*

Sir Randall Pygot, Sir William Stapleton, Sir Piers Middleton, Sir Christopher Ward, Sir Thomas Maliverer,[2] [. . .][a] John Hastings, John Rocliffe were comaunded to be ready vpon an ower warning.[3]
Endorsed: To my right hartely beloued cousins and frinds Sir William Inglebie, Sir Robart Plompton, Sir William Beckwith kts and John Gascoigne esquier

[a] Sir christopher Ward *repeated.*

[1] This summons may not refer to the meeting at Barnsdale in 1486, but to another occasion, perhaps Lincoln's invasion in June 1487, Hicks, *NH*, xiv, 99.
[2] Of the knights, all save Plumpton and Middleton had been closely associated with Gloucester; they were recruited by Northumberland between 1483 and 1489, Hicks, *loc.cit.*, 106–7.
[3] The esquires were John (later Sir John) Hastings, of Fenwick (d.1504), John (later Sir John) Rocliffe, of Cowthorpe (d.1531), and John Gascoigne, a kinsman of Sir William Gascoigne of Gawthorpe, App. III.

48 *Robert Greene*[1] *to Sir Robert Plumpton, [c.1486 × 1487]* *(No. 110, p. 66)*

Right worshipful Sir, in the most hartyest wyse I recomend me to you, thanking you of your tender mastership to me shewed in all causes. Please it your mastership to wyt þat I am some what in hevyness, for such sicknes as my wyfe hath, once or twyce at the least euery day, puts hir in ioperty of hir life with a swonnying, þat the morow next after the assise[a] I passe not from hir. Wherfore, Sir, I besech you to take no displeasure þat I se not you & my lady at Plompton no rather. And wherfore [blank] þat your mastership hath Robart Ward, clarke, in your ward at Knarsbrough. Sir, I purpasse to persew the law against him in þer names whomes cattell he heretofore helped to stele, now eftsonnes, entending the same to haue done forth of the lordship, if so be þat the awenness of the same cattell will mayntayne þer sute in þer name, at my cost. And in the meane tyme, I pray your mastership þat this pure woman, the bearer herof, beadwoman to your mastership, may haue suerty of peace of the same Robart, which I trust she will desire of your mastership of him. Written at Newby, the Wedensday next after our Lady Day in Lenten. And as for William Bulloke, I shall shortly send him to your mastership to know your gud aduice & counsell, & all causes concernyng me.

Your servant Robart Greene[b]

Endorsed: To his right worshipfull master Sir Robart Plompton kt deliuer these

[a] *MS* assiste.
[b] *Appended*: copied þe 9th day of Aprill 1613.

[1] Stapleton suggests the writer was the son of Richard and Elizabeth Greene, of Newby, and that he married Isabel, sister of William Tancred, bailiff of Knaresborough, Stapleton, 84n.; **51**, **55**; App. III.

49 *B. Roos*[1] *to Lady Plumpton, senior, [1480 × 1497]* *(No. 184, p. 121)*

Right reuerend Lady,[2] with due recomendacions, I haue wounder þat ye doe so vnkindly to me, but of great nede I wold not haue sent. I lent to my kynsman c marke, I haue yt not. They haue forfit cc marks, & for þe lake of þat I send more besily to you, praying you to send me iij*li* by this messenger, without delay, & than yt is but xl*s* owing, of þe which I shall suffer to Pasch; & Jhesu preserue you. Wrytten at Cristall in hast.

By your B. Roos[a]

Endorsed: To my worshipfull Lady Plompton the elder

[a] *Appended*: Copied þe ij day of May 1613.

[1] Possibly Brian Roos, priest (d.1529), rector of Kirk Deighton, near Wetherby, and brother of Thomas Roos of Ingmanthorpe. Described as 'Doctor of Decrees in the University of Valence', and as 'incorporated' at Oxford 3 Feb. 1510/11, *Test. Ebor.*, iv, 223–4.
[2] Joan, Lady Plumpton died between 19 Oct.1496, when she passed some copyhold land to Sir Robert, and the following year, when her son gave a twentieth part of a ducat to the rebuilding of the hospital of St James at Compostella, for prayers to be said for the soul of his mother, CB, 785.

50 *William Senhouse, abbot of St Mary's Abbey, York*[1] *to Sir Robert Plumpton [1485 × 1495]* *(No. 63, p. 37)*

Master Plompton, I recommend me vnto you, and thanke you for your letter. And it happyned Miles[2] went with me þat day, with whom I haue broken the matter. I felt him well disposed and even forthwith. I haue sent my mynd to Sir Thomas Maleverer,[3] þat he wilbe appliable to reason and doe wel. I shall in hast haue word againe from him. I pray you labor [*p. 38*] herin, and soe will I doe. And in conclusion, if other of them be obstynat & will not be counselled by frinds, the kings grace will be myscontent with him, whatsoeuer he be, and I & you.

Written in hast at my poor mannor of [...][a] Wreton.

Your owne William abbot of Yorke[b]

Endorsed (p. 37): To the right worshipfull Sir Robart Plompton knight

[a] *MS* Overton deleted.

[b] *Appended*: Copied þe 11 day of March 1612.

[1] William Senhouse (or Sever) elected abbot of the Benedictine abbey of St Mary, York in 1485, provided to the bishopric of Carlisle, 1495, translated to Durham 1502. He continued as titular abbot until 1502. Lieutenant in the North 1499–1502, R.R. Reid, *The King's Council in the North* (1921), 78, 84; A.B. Emden, *A Biographical Register of the University of Oxford to A.D. 1500* (3 vols, Oxford, 1957), iii, 1669; Lander, 23–4; *HBC*.

[2] Possibly Miles Wilstrop, **18**, **40**.

[3] Sir Thomas Mauleverer was dead by 1495. His son and heir, Richard, married Sir Robert's daughter Joan.

51 *Richard Greene[1] to Sir Robert Plumpton [possibly 8 February 1486/7] (No. 111, p. 67)*

My ful especial master, I recomende me to you. Please it you to wyte that this same day I haue deliuered mee a letter from my lord of Northumberland wherby his lordship hath streitly charged Mr Neuil[2] and al his seruants, and me, as to morow, to be at Toplyf, both there to see his woods, parke, and game, and furthwith by his seruants to be ascertayned in euery behalfe, acording to his said writing. For so it is, Sir, that ther are complaynts mad of the keepers of the game, wherin my lord is sore displeased withall, as I shall shew to you hereafter. Wherfor, Sir, I pray you to take noe displeasure for þat I am not with them at Knaresbrough as tomorow. Sir, I pray you to send me word by this bearer how my sayd lord and Mr Gascoygne[3] departed in all matters; and also what day Mr Gascoygne ridds up towards London from his place at Gaukthorp. And, Sir, I trust þat my servant, this bearer, shal find you his good master, as wel in the reports made to you of him, as in other matters for which he is bounde to you. And thus, Sir, it is not for you to forgeet þe matter þat I wrote to you in concernyng Sir John Wixeley;[4] so you her many askers of guds. And thus Jesu keepe you. Written in hast at Rippon, þe Thursday next after Candlemas.

Your servant Rich: Greene[a]

Endorsed: Unto his right worshipful master Sir Robart Plompton kt in hast

[a] *Appended*: copied þe 9 day of April 1613.

[1] Richard Greene, of Newby, had been implicated in the Plumptons' dispute with the Pierpoints, **5**, **48**, **55**; Apps II, 22; III.

[2] Ralph Neville, of Thornton Bridge, **138**.
[3] Sir Robert's nephew William Gascoigne of Gawthorpe (d.1551), knighted 25 Nov. 1487, the year of his father's death, **149**; App. III.
[4] Probably Sir Robert's chaplain, **34**.

52 *The earl of Northumberland to Sir Robert Plumpton, 23 June [1487] (No. 46, p. 29)*

Cousin Sir Robart, I commend me vnto you. And wher it is so that diuerse gentlemen and other commoners, being within your office at (this) tyme, hath rebelled against the king, as well in ther being at this last felde as in releving of them that were against the kings highnes. I, therefore, on the kings behalfe, straitly charge you, and on myne hartely pray you, for your owne discharge & myne, þat ye, incontinently after the sight hereof, take all such persons as be within your office, which this tyme hath offended agaynst the king. And in especiall, John Pullen[1] and Richard Knaresbrough.[2] And þat ye keepe them in the castell of Knaresbrough in suer keepeing to the tyme be ye know the kings pleasure in (that behalfe). And that this be not failed, (as ye love me; and to give credence [*p. 30*] unto this bearer), and God keep you. Written at Richmond the xxiij day (of Juyn). Se that ye faile not, as ye loue me, <within the time>, and as euer ye thinke (to have me) your good lord, & as euer I may trust you.

Your cousin Hen: Northumberland[a]

Endorsed (p. 29): To my right trusty and welbeloued cousin Sir Robart Plompton kt

[a] *Appended*: Copied the 25 day of February 1612.

[1] The battle of Stoke was fought on 16 June. John Pullein of Scotton received a pardon dated 22 Aug. 1487, *CPR*, 1485–94, 191.
[2] A former Gloucester retainer, Hicks *NH*, xiv, 97n.

53 *The earl of Northumberland to Sir Robert Plumpton, 26 June [?1487] (No. 41, p. 28)*

Right trusty and welbeloued cousin, I grete you hartely well. And if you haue suffered any person that was vnder your ward within the castell of Knaresbrough[1] to be deliuered at the desire of Sir Thomas Wortley, kt.[2] I lett you witt þat I am not therewith contented. Wherefor, cousin, see þat this be [...][a] <reformed>, and not to suffer any person within the said castell to depart thence vnto þat ye haue knowledg of the pleasure of the kings highnes, or from me, as my speciall trust is in you, whom God keepe. Written in thabbey of Funtayns þe xxvj day of Juyn.

Your cousin Hen: Northumberland[b]

Endorsed: To my right trusty and welbeloued cousin Sir Robart Plompton kt

[a] refused *deleted.*

[b] *Appended*: This letter hath a seale. Copied the 23 day of February 1612.

[1] The letter shows that Sir Robert had been granted the deputy stewardship etc. of Knaresborough; his predecessor in office, Sir William Gascoigne, died in March 1487, Wedgwood, 364; App. III.

[2] Sir Thomas Wortley, of Wortley (d.1514), knighted 1482. Knight of the body to Richard III; came to terms with the new régime and by Aug.1487 held the same office under Henry VII, *CPR, 1485–94*, 192.

54 *The earl of Northumberland to Sir Robert Plumpton, 28 June [1487 × 1488] (No. 38, p. 27)*

Right hartely beloued cousin, I recomend me vnto you, & desire & pray you to (caus) a buck of season (to) be taken within the forest of Knaresbrough vnder your rule, (to) be deliuered vnto this bearer to the behaufe of þe mawer of the cite of Yorke and his bredren; and this my wrytting shalbe your warrant. Wherefore I pray you that this be thankfully [...][a] <serued>, as my speciall trust is in you, whom (God) keepe. Written in my manor of Lekinfeild the xxviij day of Juyn.

Your cousin Hen: Northumberland[b]

Endorsed: To my right (hartely beloved) cousin Sir Robart Plompton kt

[a] *A word deleted.*

[b] *Appended*: This letter hath a seale. Copied the 22 day of February 1612.

55 *Elizabeth Greene to Sir Robert Plumpton,*[1] *[possibly 2 November 1487] (No. 126, p. 76)*

Right worshipfull Sir, I commend me to your mastership, certifying you þat I have shewed William Tankard[2] your comandment þat he shold have warned the tenaunts to pay no farme to William Aldburgh;[3] & he letting <them> pay farme to his mother, & wold not warne the tenaunts to pay none; & as for taking of William Aldburgh, he sayd he wold [*p.* 77] not take him, for ye let him alone & ye myght have taken him & ye wold, & may take him when ye wyll. <I> beseech you be so good master vnto me, & sett me & my husband tenaunts in rest of him, to God send my husband home, so þat I compleane no further for noe remedy, as my trust is in your mastership, as God knowes who preserve you to his pleasure. From Newby, on Munday after Salmesday.[4]

Your beadwoman Elizabeth Greene[a]

Endorsed (p. 76): Unto the right worshipfull Sir Robart Plompton kt deliver these

[a] *Appended*: Copied þe 14 day of Aprill 1613.

[1] Probably Elizabeth, wife of Richard Greene, of Newby, **48**, **51**.

[2] Son of William Tancred of Boroughbridge and Alice, sister of Sir William Plumpton's son-in-law Sir Richard Aldburgh (d.1476). The Tancreds were related to the Greenes of Newby, Somerville, 524–5; *Test.Ebor.*, vi, 191; Sir Thomas Lawson-Tancred, *Records of a Yorkshire Manor* (1937), 136; **36**.

[3] **65**.

[4] All Souls Day.

56 *Sir Richard Tunstall*[1] *to Sir Robert Plumpton, [?1487]* *(No. 117, p. 71)*

Right worshipfull cousin, I recomend me vnto you. And for as much as it is shewed to me þat ye doe make a pretence and claime to a man called William Wroes, dwelling within thoner of Pomfret, wher I am officer, premyssing þat he should be your bond man, wherin I haue sent his evydence of his manumission,[2] given by one of your ancestors called Sir Robart Plompton, with dyverse other wryttings þat byndes the sayd Sir Robart & his heires vnder a certayne payne which is expressed in ther sayd wrytinges, þat ther shall neuer no pretence nor clame be made by them, nor none of ther heires, for þe sayd bonde, but euermore perpetually to be at lyberty. Wherfore, cousin, inasmuch as the sayd William is dwelling within the honour wher I am officer, I nether can nor may see þat he be wronged, if it may lye in me to amend it. Therfore I will & pray you þat if ye intend to make any such pretence & clame, then þat ye wold send to me some of your counsell, so þat I may vnderstand wherby ye pretend your tytle; & if your tytle be good, ye shall haue such answere as of reason ye shalbe content with. I pray þat I may haue an answere in wrytting from you of these premysses.

Your cousin Richard Tunstall

Endorsed: To my right worshipfull cousin Sir Robart Plompton knyght

[1] Sir Richard Tunstall, of Thurland was granted the stewardship of Pontefract for life 12 Sept.1486, Somerville, 514; **71**, **45**; App. III.

[2] Manumissions provided landowners with 'an irregular but not inconsiderable income', e.g. on the estates of Edward, 3rd duke of Buckingham (d.1521) concealed bondmen were diligently sought out. A power of attorney granted by Sir William 10 April 1439 includes 'nativi et sequelae', C. Rawcliffe, *The Staffords, Earls of Stafford and Dukes of Buckingham, 1394–1521* (Cambridge, 1978), 60–1; K.B. McFarlane, *The Nobility of Later Medieval England*

(Oxford, 1972), 224–6; Eric Acheson, *A Gentry Community: Leicestershire in the Fifteenth Century, c.1422–c.1485* (Cambridge, 1992), 56; App. II, 9; **98**, **164**.

57 *The earl of Northumberland to Sir Robert Plumpton, 19 November [1486 × 1487] (No. 56, p. 34)*

Right trusty & welbeloued cousin, I gret you hartely well. And wheras I conceiue that ye prepared yourselfe to have ridden with me to this day of trewe,[1] I wele remembring that it wer not oonly to your great labor but also to your cost & great charg, therefore I take me oonly to your good wyll and thankfull disposicion, for the which I hartely thank you, and am right well content and pleased that ye remaine still at home. Written at Derham, the xix day of Nouember.

Your cousin Hen: Northumberland[a]

Endorsed: To my right hartely beloued cousin Sir Robart Plompton knight

[a] *Appended*: this letter hath a seale. Copied the 4 day of March 1612.

[1] Northumberland was restored to the wardenship of the Marches 3 Jan. 1485/6 on an annual basis; his contract was renewed 26 Feb. 1487/8. On the 30 Jan. 1485/6 he was appointed a commissioner to treat for peace with Scotland, a peace which was ratified 26 July 1486, *Rotuli Scotiae in Turri Londoninense et in Domo Capitulari Westmonasteriense Asservati* (2 vols, 1814, 1819), ii, 463–4, 470–1, 484–5.

58 *William Catton, canon of Newburgh, to Sir Robert Plumpton, 23 April [1487 × 1488] (No. 62, p. 37)*

Right honorable and my [. . .][a] <most trusty> good master. In as humble wyse as I can thinke or say, I commennd me to your sayd mastershipp. And, Sir, according to my dutie, I thank you of all gentle mastership vnto me shewed, and to my frinds, beseching you of contynuance. Morover, Sir, pleaseth you to vnderstand the affect of my desire at this tyme. It is so here by vs at Cukeswald the clarkship therof standeth avoyd, saffe it is observed be the meanes of 2 children, sons to the clarke, lait deceased. Wherin, good master, I besech you tenderly þat it wold please you to writ to Sir Robert Owtreth[1] that he wold, at request of your mastership, send wrytting to his tenants of the sayd towne, first to his keper, George Dayvell, Robart Cropwell, and John Barton, then all other in generall, that my brother, your trew servent, myght haue that service of the clarkship. Trustying to God he should please the parishoners according to his dutie. And I euermore your trew & faythfull priest & bedman, that knoweth almyght Jhesu, who you, my most trusty good master, preserue to his pleasure. At Newburgh, in hast, *in festo Sancti Georgij martiris*.

Your owne prest and bedman Sir William Catton, chanon of Newburgh[b]

Endorsed: To my most trusty good master Sir Robart Plompton knight

[a] mastership *deleted*.
[b] *Appended*: Copied the 10 of March 1612.

[1] Sir Robert Ughtred's will was proved 17 June 1488, Borthwick Institute of Historical Research, York, Prob. Reg., v, 333.

59 *Thomas Thorpe, priest, to Sir Robert Plumpton* (*No. 150, p. 93*)

Right worshipfull master, I recomend me vnto you, thanking you of your benyngne mastership shewed vnto me, for the which, Sir, without feyning I am, and shalbe, your trew & faythfull beadman. Beseching your mastership after the contemplation of this byll, þat it wyll please you to stand good master vnto the brynger herof in such matters as he shall shew vnto you. Sir, he hath bene with us & spoken with Sir Thomas Morwyn, and with Sir William his brother [and] with other dyuers of our brethren, þe which recomend tham vnto your mastership; & he hath shewed vnto them his intent & desire, þe which we intend, with Gods grace, to endeuer us to fulfill, if our power may so extend, in þe which we besech you to take no dyspleasure. Wherin ye shall bynd me, with all afore rehersed, to impend vnto your sayd mastership our prayer & service, according vnto our duety. By þe grace of Jesu, who preserve you euermore to his pleasure. At Newburght[1] in great hast this day.

Your chaplayn & bedman Sir Thom: Thorp chanon[a]

Endorsed: To the right worshipfull and specyall gud master Sir Robart Plompton knyght [deliuer these *deleted*] in hast

[a] *Appended*: Copied þe 20 day of Aprill 1613.

[1] Newburgh, an Augustinian priory near Coxwold.

60 *The Cellarer of Newburgh to Sir Robert Plumpton* (*No. 61, p. 36*)

Right worshipfull Sir & my especiall good master, I commend me to you, thanking you much for my veneson, for it did me great stead. I beseach God to encrease your veneson. Sir, there is certaine money owing to me in Follifait,[1] the which I besech you þat it wold please you to comannd them to pay it to the bringer of this byll, my servant; he shall shew you which they be þat owe the money. As touching the tenement in Pannall,[2] I let it to John Wilson, to the behalfe of another man, and the sayd John was his suertie the farm should be content; & I caused my servant [*p. 37*] to aske farme of this Wylson, and he sayd that they had discharged (him), that he should not occupie it, for they wold put in a tenant at your pleasure. Sir, if so be that he discharged him, suppose it will please you þat I be content þe ferm, or els remyt it to the sayd Wilson. It is run two yeares to the sume of 2 iiij*s*. As touching the matters he hard at the syse, I caused some to be thyn at this tyme, as God knowes, who preserue you euermore to his pleasure.

Your awne beadman Cellarer of Newburgh[a]

Endorsed (p. 36): To Sir Robart Plompton knight be these deliuered

[a] *Appended*: Copied the 10th of March 1612.

[1] Follifoot was within the lordship of Plumpton.
[2] Pannal, near Harrogate, was within the forest of Knaresborough.

61 *The Cellarer of Newburgh to Sir Robart Plompton* *(No. 60, p. 36)*

Right worshipful Sir, I recommend me to you. I thank you, Sir, of your labor and good will. Sir, it is so that I haue no more of the ferm content of þat at is owying, but xiiij*s*. Also Robert Goles [...][a] <brought> with him a byll of alowance for [...][b] <Aykton kilne>, and I haue answered him þat he shall haue as much as is our charge to do. Therfore it was sene by our tenants, & set to a valow what should be our charge to do, & þat shall he haue. I vnderstand it was either 25*s* or 27*s*. Also, Sir, as for as touching William Paver ferme, I am not content; I put it in respate til I come over, for he sayth at he hath payd for suyt of court at Spofforth ij yeare, and also fee ferme for one yeare; and he thinks to haue the farmhould for 2 vij*s* viij*d* in one yeare, but he shall not; and so I [...][c] <send him>. The bringer herof shall show you more credence herein. Sir, if it please you vpon Tewsday come a sennyt, I would haue your court at Follyfait, that i might make leuy of our fermes þat are behind. Sir, I say no more, but [...][d] <Jesus> haue you in his keping. Written at Newbrough this day, by your owne beadman, Cellarer of Newburgh[e]

Endorsed: To Sir Robart Plompton knight be thes deliuered

[a] brough *deleted.*
[b] xviij*s* *deleted.*
[c] should haue *deleted.*
[d] God *deleted.*
[e] *Appended*: This letter hath a seale. Copied the 10 of March 1612.

62 *William Calverley, the elder,*[1] *to Sir Robert Plumpton [1480 × 1489] (No. 124, p. 75)*

Right worshipfull cousin, after due recomendations I comend me vnto you, letting you wytt I am enformed þat ye are good master vnto my cousin John Baylton,[2] praying you of your gud contynuance therin for my sake. Sir, I vnderstand my cousin Sir Christofer Ward[3] hath put him ther to an occupation of the kyngs. Sir, if ther be any man that wold wrong him therin I desire you therin þat you will be his good master for my sake, as I may doe you any pleasure hereafter, which I shalbe redy. With grace of God at altymes with you, who have you in his keeping.

Be your owne William Callverley the elder[a]

Endorsed: To my right worshipfull cousin Sir Robart Plompton

[a] *Appended*: Copied the 14 of Aprill of 1613.

[1] William Calverley, of Calverley, Yorks (will pr.31 Jan. 1488/9), son of Sir Walter Calverley and Elizabeth, daughter of Sir Thomas Markenfield, Thoresby, *Ducatus*, 117; *Test. Ebor.*, ii, 281n.

[2] John Baildon, of Baildon, may have been a nephew of the writer, Thoresby, 117.

63 *The earl of Northumberland to Sir Robert Plumpton, 6 April [1486 × 1488] (No. 48, p. 30)*

Right hartely beloued cosin, I commend me vnto you. And for certaine considerations me mouying, I will and desire you that ye, incontynent after the sight hereof, cum hether vnto me, all excuses & delayes laid apart, as it be in nowise failed, as ye intend the pleasure of the kings highness & as ye loue me.[1] Written in my mannor of Lekingfeild the vi day of April.

Your cousin Hen. Northumberland[a]

Endorsed: To my right hartely beloued cousin, Sir Robart Plompton kt

[a] *Appended*: this letter hath a seale. copied the 26 day of February 1612.

[1] Northumberland had been appointed king's lieutenant in the North Parts, App. III.

64 *The earl of Northumberland to Sir Robert Plumpton, 31 July [?1488] (No. 54, p. 33)*

Right hartely beloued cousin, I commend me vnto you, thanking you for my servant, Richard Greene, and desire & pray you þat if Bastard Aldborgh,[1] Richard Leds, or such other as of late, as I am enformed, have made reuery and withdrawen goods, contrayrie to the kings lawes, within the lordshipp of Knaresborough, where as ye haue rule, can be come by, ye comitt them to ward [within] the castell of Knarsbrough, therin still to remayne vnto þat ye haue further knowledg of my pleasure in this behalfe. And [over] this, cousin, whereas I haue assigned my servant William Bullo<cke> to leuy & receiue such rents & farmes & also arrerages as are due & growen of the lands that late were William Aldburgs, wherin ye & I, with other, stand infeoffed, & to be reserved to that my pleasure therin be vnderstanden. I therefore desire & pray you if any person would interupt him in thexecution herof, ye will shew your good will in the lawfull defending therof, and also in the geting of all such hay as is vpon the sayd ground, not fayling herof, as my speciall trust is in you, whom God kepe. Written in my castell of Werkworth the xxxj day of July.

Your cousin Hen: Northumberland[a]

Endorsed: To my right hartely beloued cousin Sir Robart Plompton kt

[a] *Appended*: this letter hath a seale. Copied the 3 day of March 1612.

[1] William Aldburgh, son of Sir Richard Aldburgh's bastard son, also named William (d.1475), was indicted at York in late May 1489 for having, on 13 May, expelled Sir Robert Plumpton and Ralph Neville from certain lands, Hicks, in *Richard III and his Rivals*, 398; Lawson-Tancred, *Records*, 136.

65 *The Mayor, Robert Hancock,*[1] *and Aldermen of York to Sir Robert Plumpton, 11 September [1488]* *(No. 81, p. 45)*

Right worshipfull Sir, I recomend me vnto you. And wher ye haue shewed by [...][a] your curtace letter of late to me derect by one Robart Becke, your servant, berying date at Plompton the vj day of September, that your servants and lovers, John Persons & his brother, should be greatly vexed and trobled by Wylliam Whit[2] & his servants. Sir, as touching the same William, in the beginyng of the troble & variance betwixt the seruants of his & John Persons, his bretheren, and other, he was innocent, as fare as I, my bretheren aldermen, and other the common counsell of the cyttie of York, by any wayes and meanes can vnderstand. And the same Wylliam hath shewed vnto vs þat he at no tyme haue given cause to the sayd Person so to deale with his servants, as they tofore haue donn. And further, Sir, the said John Person & his brother bene fraunchised and sworne to þe kyng and maior of the citie of Yorke for tyme being, to be & deale according to the effect of their othes.[b] And if any variance or troble, tofore <this>, haue bene betwixt my cocitisons, þat they, according to ther duties, haue [...][c] <shewed> them in þe same to þe maior for tyme being, and for none other; and he to se amend betwyxt them and right wold, so þat no more inconvenient should fall by reason of the same. Sir, I am the man, I take God to record, without favor or partialite, to adoon the same in the premyses to the sayd John Person, & other in þe premyses, and they had shewed them in the same varience vnto me, as ther dutyes had bene. Wherfor, Sir, yf it like you, and by your advice the sayd John Person & his brother to come home, both my brethren & I shall endevor vs þat in þe said varyance & troble, to make a good and a loving end, and the better for your pleasure. And further, Sir, of my brethren behalfe & myne, we pray you to give credence to this bearer, & Jhesu preserue you. In hast from Yorke, the xi day of September.[d]

By your awne Robart Havock maior of Yorke and his bretheren aldermen[e]

Endorsed: To the right worshipfull Sir Robart Plompton kt be thes deliuered

[a] one of *deleted.*

[b] *MS* others.

[c] payne *deleted.*

[d] *Appended*: Copied the 18 day of March 1612.

[e] *At the foot of the letter, in a different hand*: His true loue, Dorety Straud.

[1] Robert Hancock (d.1495/6), grocer and freeman of York, MP York 1483, 1485–6, Wedgwood, 418; *Test. Ebor.*, iv, 274.

[2] William White was mayor of York 1491–94/5, A. Raine (ed.), *York Civic Records*, ii, (YASRS, ciii, 1941), 68, 114.

66 *Stephen Eyre, of Hassop,*[1] *to Sir Robert Plumpton [December 1482 × 1487] (No. 175, p. 114)*

Reuerent & worshipfull Sir & master, I recomend me vnto your mastership, beseching allmighty Jesu to preserue your worship & welfare to his pleasure & your harts comforth. Sir, please yt you to vnderstand my seruant, Thomas Coke, now late being with your mastership, hath shewed vnto me parte of your mynd & entent, by þe which I conceyve you wold I dyd your mastership a pleasure, & if I so myght or may it wold be to me comforth. Howbeyt my sayd servant shewed vnto me none of your mynd how or what tyme I shold be content þerof againe, if I myght so do. Wherfore, Sir, if yt wold either be pleasure, as I wylbe right glad to doe, if I shold therfore streame myselfe & my frinds also, & put me therfore to hurt, so þat will like your mastership to send me wrytting be þe bringer herof, what tyme þat will please to haue yt, & how & what tyme I shalbe content therof againe, & I shall put me in deuer to fullfill your intent & doe your pleasure in þat behalfe, or any other thing to your comandment, be þe grace of Jhesu, who euer preserue your mastership. At Hassopp, the Tuesday next afore St Thomas Day, the apostle.

By your tenant & servant Stephen Eyre of Hassopp[a]

Endorsed: To my right worshipfull master Sir Robt Plompton kt be these deliuered

[a] *Appended*: Copied the 29 of Aprill 1613.

[1] Stephen Eyre of Hassop, Derbys (d.1488), 10th son of Robert Eyre of Padley, established a collateral branch of the family as tenants of the Plumptons in Hassop from Michaelmas 1479, CB, 695, 751; App. III.

67 *The earl of Northumberland to Sir Robert Plumpton, 16 July [?1488] (No. 57, p. 34)*

Right hertely beloued cousin, I commend me vnto you. And wheras I conceiue that there is a grudge depending betwixt you & Sir William Beckwith, knight,[1] I, entending the peacifiying thereof, desire & pray you to forbere and contynue to doe anything in that behalfe against the said Sir William foresaid vnto my next comying into Yorkshire. And then I shall shew me in such wyse for the reformation therof, as I trust shall agre with right law & conscience. Wherefore I pray you to the accomplishment herof, as my very trust is in you. I haue wrytten in likwyse vnto sayd Sir William. That now God conserue you. Wrytten in my castell of Warkworth, the xvi day of July. Ouer this, cousin, ye shall understand that the sayd Sir William Beckwith will committ him vnto my rule in all behalues, & therefore I pray you to se the premysse performed.

Your cousin Hen: Northumberland[a]

Endorsed: To my right hartely beloued cousin Sir Robart Plompton kt

[a] *Appended*: this letter hath a seale. Copied the 4 day of March 1612.

[1] Husband of Sir Robert's step-sister, Elizabeth. Both protagonists were feed by Northumberland, Hicks, *NH*, xiv, 106; **6**; Stapleton, 6, 72n.

68 *Edward Plumpton to Sir Robert Plumpton, 11 January [1488/9] (No. 205, p. 142)*

[p. 143] In my most humble & faythfull wyse I recomend me vnto your mastership & to my singuler good lady. This day in þe mornying I spake with my master Gascoyne at Poynfrett, & he comended him to you & to my lady; and then I spake with Sir Rich. Tunstall, & had great commyng with him of pro & contra. Sir, I wold advyse your mastership to cause Wm Scargell[1] to take good regard to himselfe & not to vse his old walkes, for & he wylbe taken & brought to fynd such suerty for peace & othervyse as shalbe to him inconuenient. Notwithstanding, the sayd Master Tunstall gaue to me right curteouse words at my departing; but therto is no great trust. For þe tyme it is good to dreed þe worst, insomuch as þe land lyeth in his rule, in þe honor of Poymfrett.[2] Sir, afor such matters I had with Robt Leuthorp[3] he will giue me no perfitt answere vnto þe begining of þ terme. In þe meane tyme he will speake with a doctor & send to me a letter to London by one Watkinson of Poymfrett, atturney of þe common place, & than your mastership shalbe answered of þe premysses, with Gods grace, who euer þe same preserue in prosperouse felicitie long tyme to endure. Frome Poymfrett, þe xj day of January.

Your humble servant Edward Plompton[a]

Endorsed (p. 142): To my master Sir Robart Plompton kt

[a] *Appended*: Copied þe 10th day of May 1613.

[1] William Scargill (d.1497), of Thorpe Stapleton and Whitkirk, near the Duchy manor of Leeds, J.W. Kirby, *The Manor and Borough of Leeds, 1425–1662: An Edition of Documents* (P. Th.S., LVII, 1989), 280 & *passim*; **71**, **93**.

[2] **56**.

[3] Probably a scion of a major administrative family, with branches in Yorks and Herts. Nicholas Leventhorpe was receiver of Pontefract and Knaresborough at this time, Kirby, *Documents*, 21, 32; Horrox, *Richard III*, 41; Somerville, i, 400–1, 516–17, 526; **137**.

69 *Robert Eyre*[1] *to Sir Robert Plumpton [possibly 23 March 1488/9] (No. 104, p. 62)*

Right worshipfull Sir, I recomend me vnto your mastership. Please it you witt þat I vnderstand þat my cousin, Ralph Hawgh,[2] sendeth to your mastership for such dues as was granted to his mother & to him by my master your father & you, vnder your seales, þe which writting & your seales to come before men of worship & discretion. I am certayne, when ye se him, will not be denyed, for your seales be well knowne, & to show in money other matters <in> this contry, the which are of great charge. Wherwith, it please your mastership, þat after my poore advice, take a direction with him at this tyme, for it will els [...][a] <be proces>, turne to more cost, & þat wold I be right sory fore.[3] From Padley on Sunday next before St Mary Day in Lent.

From Yowres Robart Eyre[b]

Endorsed: To my right worshipfull master Sir Robart Plompton kt this bill be deliuered

[a] be past tyme *deleted*.

[b] *Appended*: Copied þe 4th day of Aprill 1613.

[1] Robert Eyre II, of Padley, Derbys (d.1498), elder brother of the writer of **67**, and head of the senior branch of the family, **139**; App. III.
[2] Of Elton, Derbys. There is no record of this grant in CB.
[3] The parties having agreed to submit to arbitration, Robert Eyre gave his award 1 June 1490, App. II, 51; **77**.

70 *Sir Richard Tunstall to Sir Robert Plumpton, [early 1489]* *(No. 116, p. 70)*

Right worshipfull cousin, I recomend me vnto you. And wheras I late wrote to you for one Skaggell[1] to haue come to me for a matter of causes betwixt him & [. . .][a] certayne other, with myne officer Thomas of Pomfret, wherin I understand by such an answer as I had from you since, þat he will not be aduertysed by you therein. Cousin, <I> eftsomes will desire & pray to advise him to come, for & he will not so doe, I intend to shew his obstynance to þe king & his counsell,[2] which if I so doe I think it will not be for his case; and also I intend, when I can finde a convenient time & place, to attach him if he thus contynew in his sayd obstynance.

Your cousin Rich: Tunstall[b]

Endorsed: To my right worshipfull cousin Sir Robart Plompton kt

[a] me *deleted*.
[b] *Appended*: Copied þe 10 day of April 1613.

[1] William Scargill, **69**.

71 *John Latoner, prior of Newburgh*[1] *to Sir Robert Plumpton* *(No. 59, p. 35)*

Right worshipfull Sir, I commend me to you, & am full sory þat ye should be displeased agaynst the writting which came last to you in my name. I comaunded the officer to write to you in my name, but I saw not the same after. Sir, ye haue alway bene good master to our house, and I pray you so contynue, & in any thing which ye are myscontent with, it shall be amended by the sight of your selfe; & I beseech you be good master to this bearer, for he is giltles in this matter. And as for our land, we pay our dymes therefore, and trust in you that ye will not ses none thereof, wherby we should haue cause to make further labor; for it is not the kings mynd to ses no dymeable land,[2] & we haue no suit land, but it is dymable, as God knoweth, who preserue you euermore.

Your louing frind the Prior of Newbrough[a]

Endorsed: To the right worshipfull knight Sir Robart Plompton

[a] *Appended*: This letter hath a seale. Copied the 8 day of March 1612.

[1] Newburgh Priory held lands in Spofforth. John Latoner was elected prior in 1483 and resigned in May/June 1518, *VCH, Yorks*, iii, 226, 230.

[2] Land subject to assessment for the tenth, *OED*.

72 *William Rowkshaw*[1] *to Sir Robert Plumpton 4 April [1484 × 1489] (No. 149, p. 92)*

Right reuerent & worshipfull and my specyall gud master, I hartely comend me vnto you, thanking your mastership of your tender & loving favour shewed to my poore kynsman, John Wynpenne, now late bryinging a letter from my lord to your mastership & me, & other moe. Beseching you to be his gud master touching his right according to conseyence, this holy tyme, vpon Wedensday at your [...][a] <court>. And wher your mastership wold þat I should wayt vpon you [*p. 93*] ther þat tyme, I wold haue bene bene right glad so to doe, but because þat I vnderstand þat Richard Danby,[2] to whom my lord hath wrytten, lyke as to other, cannot be ther as than. Wherfore I besech your mastership, at þe reverence of God, & be way of almes & charytie, to assigne a tyme & place wher the sayd Mr Danby, [...][b] Richard Grene,[3] [and I] myght awayte vpon you for the sayd matter, and I shalbe redy both for þat & to your service, by the grace of God, who euermore preserve & kepe your worship & good health. Wrytten the iiij day of Aprill, at Qatton.

By your loving servant William Rowkshaw prest[c]

Endorsed (p. 92): To the right reuerent & worshipfull & my especiall good <singuler> master Sir Robart Plompton knight

[a] Corte *deleted.*

[b] *MS* and I.

[c] *Appended*: Copied þe 20th day of Aprill 1613.

[1] Chaplain to the earl of Northumberland, who, in 1473 and 1484, respectively, presented him to the East Riding rectories of Lowthorpe, near Driffield, and Watton, near Leconfield, where there was a Gilbertine priory. He died 1504, *Test.Ebor.*, iv, 231–2; *VCH, Yorks*, iii, 254.

[2] Of Crayke (d.1504), lawyer, younger son of Sir Robert Danby, CJCP, of Farnley, near Leeds, and Thorpe Perrow, who died by suicide, 1472. Richard was filacer, 1485, Hastings, 85; J. Fisher, *History and Antiquities of Masham and Mashamshire* (1865), 249–51.

[3] **51**, **55**.

73 *The earl of Northumberland to Sir Robert Plumpton, 1 April [?1489] (No. 39, p. 27)*

Right trusty and welbeloued cousin, I commend me vnto you, and desire and [. . .][a] pray you that in such things as my right intierly beloued cousin, Mary Gascoigne, hath to doe with you as touching hir right of herytaunce,[1] that ye will giue vnto hir ayde and supportance, as right law & conscience will, as my speciall trust is in you, whom God keep. Written in my mannor of Seamer the first day of Aprill.

Your loving cousin Hen: Northumberland

Endorsed: To my right hartely beloued cousin Sir Robart Plompton kt

[a] *A word deleted.*

[b] *Appended*: this letter hath a seale. Copied the 22 day of February 1612.

[1] The matter relates to the house in Plumpton referred to by Sir William Gascoigne in **61** as belonging to his uncle, Ralph Gascoigne, of Burnby in the East Riding, 4th son of Sir William Gascoigne (d.1463/4), who died, 1488. In his will he mentions two unnamed daughters, *Test.Ebor.*, iv, 15; CB 747, 748.

74 *The earl of Northumberland[1] to Sir Robert Plumpton, 24 April [1489] (No. 40, p. 27)*

Right hartely beloued cousin, I comennd me vnto you. And for ryght weighty considerations [. . .][a] me mouing concerning the pleasure of the kings highnes, on the behalue of his grace, charge you and on my desire [. . .][b] pray you þat ye with such a company, and as many as ye may bring with you (with your) ease, such as ye trust, hauing bowes & arrowes & pryvy harnest, (cum with) my [. . .][c] nepvew Sir William Gascougne, so þat ye be with me vpon Munday (next comeing) at nyght in the towne of Thirske, not failong herof, as my (special) trust is in you, & as ye love me. Written in my mannor of Seemer,[2] the xxiij day of Aprill.[d]

(Your cousin Hen: Northumberland)

Endorsed: To my right hartely beloued cousin Sir Robart Plompton kt

[a] *One or two words deleted.*

[b] *A word deleted.*

[c] Cousin Gascougne *deleted.*

[d] *Appended*: Copied the xxiij day of Aprill 1612.

[1] This was probably the earl's last letter to Sir Robert, App. III.

[2] Michael Hicks suggests this was the 4th earl's only visit to Seamer, and that he was probably executing a commission to repair Scarborough castle, *NH*, xxii, 43.

75 *Thomas Wymbersley, abbot of Kirkstall*[1], *to Sir Robert Plumpton [before 1496]* (*No. 69, p. 40*)

Right worshipfull & my full trusty, enterley beloued gossep, after all herty recomendations as I can thinke, I pray you hartely to be good & tender master and lord to Thomas Hirst, my full speciall freind, in such matters as he hath to labor vnto you; & þe more tender at this my poore prayer & instaunce, & for the loue of my godson, to whom I besech almyghty God to give good grace to encrease in vertue; and you, with my lades, your mother[2] & your wyfe, my comedre, to preserve in worship & favor vnto his pleasure & harts ease. From Kyrkestall in haste, vpon Munday next before St Luke Day, evangelest.

Your poore gossep & true louer Thomas, abbot of Kirkestall[a]

Endorsed: To my right worshipfull and enterly beloued gossep Sir Robart Plompton knight

[a] *Appended*: Copied þe 12th day of March 1612.

[1] Thomas Wymbersley was confirmed in office at the Cistercian abbey of Kirkstall, 1468; his successor, Robert Killingbeck, was elected, 1499, *VCH, Yorks*, iii, 145.

[2] Joan, Lady Plumpton died soon after 19 Oct. 1496, **49**.

76 *John Darneton, abbot of Fountains*[1], *to Sir Robert Plumpton [before 1494]* (*No. 64, p. 38*)

Right worshipfull Sir, after dew recomenndations, pleaseth you to know þat, after as I am enformed, one John Bailton of Knaresbrough of layt bought & receiued of my kynsman, þe brynger, a ton of wyne, for the which he hath nought content. And noe for his offence all his goods standeth vnder arrest & in your will. I wold & hartely pray you that my sayd kynsman myght, for my sake, either haue his wyne againe, or els contentation therefore, after there comaunds; & ye therefore shalt have my good hart in any thing I may dooe for you. So knoweth our Lord, who haue you in his protection. From Fountayne, this same Tewsday.

Your awne John, abbot of Fount[ayne][a]

Endorsed: To my right worshipfull Sir in God, Sir Robart Plompton kt be this deliuered in hast

[a] *Appended*: Copied 11 day of March 1612.

[1] Elected abbot of the Cistercian abbey of St Mary of Fountains, near Ripon, in 1478, he appears to have ruled there until 1494, *VCH, Yorks*, iii, 138.

[2] Between 1446 and 1458 Sir William had been on terms of friendship with the abbey; Thomas Swynton (by 1471 Darneton's predecessor as abbot) conferred at length with

him on two occasions; his minstrel and players entertained there, and he was paid a fee of £3 6s 8d as feodary, J.T. Fowler (ed.), *Memorials of the Abbey of St Mary of Fountains*, iii (SS, CXXX, 1918), 18, 25, 31, 59, 74, 110.

77 *Robert Eyre to Sir Robert Plumpton, 4 August [?1489]* *(No. 103, p. 61)*

[p. 62] After all due recomendations had, please it youre mastership to witt þat Ralph Haugh, according to the agrement & award betwixt you & him made, hath deliuered into my hands all such evydence as he hath concernyng your mastership, endeferently to be kept vnto such tyme as a sufficyent & lawfull estate be made vnto the said Ralph of a yerly rent of v mark for terme of life of the sayd Ralph; þat is to say, a feoffament of trust indented made by your mastership vnto me & other of the manor of Darley with the appurtenances, & a letter of atturney according to the same; also ij obligations, one of ccc marke & another of x*li.* Wherfore I besech you to be good master, & to make him a lawfull estate acording to the award, at which tyme all the sayd evydence shalbe deliuered vnto your hands, or to your assigne;[1] and if there be any service or pleasure þat I may doe, it shalbe done at my power, by Gods grace, who ever preserve you, body and soule. Written at Padley, the iiij day of August last past.

Your owne Robart Eyre squire[a]

Endorsed (p. 61): To the right honorable and my speciall good master Sir Robart Plompton knight be this letter delivered

[a] *Appended*: Copied þe 3 day of Aprill 1613.

[1] On 12 July 1490, by deed witnessed by Robert Eyre, Sir Robert granted Ralph Haugh, of Darley, Derbys, an annuity of 5m out of the manor of Hassop, CB, 757; **70**.

78 *Sir Stephen Hammerton,*[1] *to Sir Robert Plumpton [1481 × 1500]* *(No. 80, p. 44)*

Right worshipfull brother <& syster>, I hartely recommend me vnto you. Where ye haue made a search, they for me thanke you hartely therefore, & I shall do service to you & I may therefore. I besech [you] to make a [. . .][a] throw search for my matter, as my trust is to you, & I wilbe ruled according to right, as my frynds, & ye in specyally, thinke þat I should be. No more at this tyme, but the Holy Trenite haue you in keeping. I pray you giue credence to the bringer of this byll.

Your loving brother Sir Stephen Hamerton[b]

Endorsed: To my right worshipfull brother Sir Robart of Plompton deliuer thes

[a] tryall *deleted.*
[b] *Appended*: Copied the 17 day of March 1612.

[1] Of Hammerton in Craven, he married Sir Robert's half-sister Isabel, and succeeded his father in 1480; knighted 1481; died 1500, Hicks, *NH*, xiv, 106; CB, 524.

79 *Henry VII to Sir Robert Plumpton, 13 October [1489] (WYASL, Acc 1731/6)*

Trusty and wellbeloved wee greet you well. And whereas wee understand by our squire Nicholas Kinston,[1] one of the ushers of our chamber, your true mind and faithful liegiance towards us, with your diligent acquitall for the reduceing of our people there to our subjection and obedience, to our singuler pleasure and your great deserts, wee hartily thanke you for the same, praying for your persevering continuance therein. Assureing you, that by this your demeaneing you have ministered unto us cause, as gaged to remember you in time to come in any thing that may bee to your preferment and advancement, as ever did any our progenitors to our nobles in those parties. And as any office of our gift ther falls voyd, wee shall reserve them unto such time as wee may bee informed of such men as in the said parties may bee meet and able for the same, praying that if there shall happen anie indisposition of our said people, ye will, as ye have begun, endeavour you from time to time for the speedy repressing thereof. And, furthermore, to give credence to oure squire aforesaid on such things as wee have commanded him at this time to shew unto you on our behalfe. Iven under our signet at our mannor of Sheene, the thirteenth day of October.

[1] Nicholas Kniveton, of Mercaston, Derbys, sheriff of Notts & Derbys 1489–90; his son, also Nicholas, was sheriff 1493–4. The king's esquire was probably the younger man, *List of Sheriffs*, 104; *CPR, 1494–1509*, 303. This letter is probably one of those missing from the Letter Book, Introd., above p. 18.

80 *Edward Plumpton to Sir Robert Plumpton, 17 December [1489] (No. 202, p. 139)*

[p. 140] Pleaseth your mastership, after all due recomendacon, to wyte þat this day was hanged at þe Tower Hill iiij servants of the kings,[1] wherfore þe brynger herof can shew to you by mouth. Other nowes as yet here is none. Sir, afore your indentures of Mr Chaunceler, he maketh none vnto Candlemasse next, & then he will haue a generall awdite, where ye & all other shall haue your lesses out;[2] & in þe meane tyme, euery man to ocupie ther owne farmes, notwithistanding þe premysses. Put ye no dout therin, for ye shalbe sure therof assone as any man of his. I haue spoken with Nicholas Leuthorpe[3] & fele him well dispossed toward you. Sir, if ye send therfore at Candlemasse, send to Mr Hemson,[4] by the token, I gat him a warrant for a doo of my lord in his parke of Hals yerely.[5] If it please you to assigne me, send me word what increse & approment ye wyl give, & I wyll applie my mynd & service to your pleasure & wele. Sir I purpose to se your mastership or to send this Cristinmasse, if I may goe home. This day my lord knoweth not whether he goeth home afore this tyme or noo. If we goe home I wyll send; if not, I pray you send to me afore Candlemasse. Remember Clement Simpson. Pleaseth your mastership to recomend me to my singuler gud lady. And your owne faythfull servant, as knoweth our Lord, who perserve you. Wrytten at London the xvij day of December.

Your humble servant Edward Plompton[a]

Endorsed (p. 139): To my master Sir Robt Plompton knight

[a] *Appended*: Copied the 20th day of May 1613.

[1] Edward Frank, Henry Davy, John Mayne and Christopher Swan, who conspired with John, abbot of Abingdon to aid the earl of Lincoln's rebellion. Stapleton points to an error in the printed Parliament Roll, which assigns the conspiracy to 20 Dec. 6 Hen.VII, whereas according to the date of their execution as revealed in this letter the date should be 10 Dec. 5 Hen.VII (1489), *RP*, vi, 436–7; Stapleton, 87n.

[2] The chancellor of the Duchy was at this time Sir Reginald Bray, appointed 15 Sept. 1485 for life. Sir Robert was seeking renewal of the leases granted to him by the late earl of Northumberland, after whose death Henry Wentworth was appointed steward of Knaresborough. Sir Robert seems to have continued for some time as deputy. His lease of the mills was renewed, Somerville, i, 392, 524; **87**, **122**; CB, 755.

[3] **69**.

[4] Richard Empson (exec.1510) was attorney general of the Duchy from 1485 to 1506, Somerville, i, 406.

[5] George, Lord Strange, **39**.

81 *Edward Plumpton to Joan, Lady Plumpton, [?1489/90] (No. 206, p. 143)*

Madame, in my most humble wyse I recomend me vnto your good ladyship, and let you wyt þat I have spoken with Master Receyuor;[1] iiij houres space tarryed me, & he is right lovingly disposed in euerything toward my master & all his, if he haue, or may have cause therto; & thus I haue left with him to be at Knarsbrough the Wedensday next after Saynt Eline Day;[2] & ther, or afore þat tyme, if they mete, to do his dutie to my master curtesly, and after þat, to be as favarable, & to shew his good wyll to my sayd master [*p. 144*] in euerything he may doe, as we wyll desire; & then I purpose, with Gods grace, to be ther; & afore þe langage þat Alan shold say, it is not so: he sayd none such langage. The mylner told Alan þat his farme was redy, & if yt so be, I pray you cause þe mylner to deliuer it to Benson, & if not, to make yt redy agaynst the receyver come thether, for this I haue promysed; & vnto þat tyme we mete, I besech you speake to my master þat no uncurtes dealing be had with none of his servants.

Also ther is a ax[3] at my master clameth þe keeping of; I pray you let them haue & occupie þe same vnto þe saime tyme, & then we shall take a dereccion in euery thing, as well the premysses as otherwyse, to my masters pleasure & entent. With Gods grace, who preserve you & him, both, & all yours. From Habberforth, this present Thursday.

Your most humble servant Ed: Plompton[a]

Endorsed (p. 143): To my lady, Dame Jane Plompton at Plompton

[a] *Appended*: Copied þe 11 day of May 1613.

[1] Sir Robert received a receipt, dated 8 March 1489/90, from Richard Harpur, receiver general of the Duchy, for the farm of the mills of Knaresborough, CB, 755.

[2] The feast of the Invention of the Holy Cross, 3 May, App. II, 31.

[3] Axle, *OED*.

82 *Edward Plumpton to Sir Robert Plumpton, 3 January [1489/90] (No. 197, p. 135)*

After þe most humble & due recomendation had, please yt your mastership þat in þe most humble lowly wyse I may be recomended vnto my singuler good ladies; praying you to haue me excused in þat I send no wyld fole to you afore this tyme, for in all Lancashire cold none be had for none money: the snaw & frost was so great, none was in þe country, but fled away to see, & þat cause me þat I sent not, as I promysed. Sir, Robt my seruant is a true seruant to me; neuerthelesse he is large to ryde afore my male, & euer weyghty for my horse, wherfore he hartely desireth me to wryte to your mastership for him. He is a true man of tongue & hands, & a kind & a good man. If þat it please your mastership to take him to your service, I besech you to be his good master, & the better at the instaunce of my especiall prayer.[a] Sir, I haue giuen to him the blacke horse þat bar him from the feild;[1] or if þer be any service þat ye will comand me I am redy, & wilbe, to my lives end, at your comandement, all other lordship & mastership layd aparte. My lord kepeth a great Cristimas as euer was in this countrey, & is my especiall good lord, as I trust in a short tyme your mastership shall know. My simple bedfelow, your bedwoman & seruant, in þe most humble wyse recomendeth hir vnto your mastership[2] & to my ladys good ladyship, & your seruants; as knoweth Jesu, who preserue you. Wrytten at Lathum, the iij day of January.

Your most humble seruant: Ed: Plompton sectory to my Lord Straung[b]

Endorsed: To þe most honorable my especyall good master Sir Robt Plompton kt

[a] *Marginal note*: Commendation of a seruant.
[b] *Appended*: Copied þe 8 of May 1613.

[1] Probably the field of Stoke, 16 June 1487, at which Lord Strange was present, whereas Sir Robert had probably been in the company of Northumberland, who had avoided Stoke by directing a diversionary attack on York, P.W. Fleming, 'Household Servants of the Yorkist and Early Tudor Gentry', in David Williams (ed.), *Early Tudor England* (Bury St Edmunds, 1989), 22n.; D. Hay (ed.), *The Anglica Historia of Polydore Vergil, A.D.1485–1537* (Camden Society, 3rd ser., lxxiv, 1950), 23, 27; Hicks, *NH*, xiv, 97.
[2] Stapleton suggests that Edward Plumpton's first wife was Agnes Griffith, sister of the correspondent, **90**, **121**; Stapleton, 99n.

83 *Thomas Darrell, of Sessay,[1] to Sir Robert Plumpton 4 January [?1489/90] (No. 114, p. 68)*

Right worshipfull uncle, I recomend mee unto you. Sir, it is so that my lord of Surrey[2] hath written to mee by the labor of Rich: Cholmley,[3] to be with him on Thursday next folowing in the matter depending betwixt mee & John Thorneton; [*p. 69*] wherfore, uncle, as my most especial trust is in you, praing you to be with mee at the day appointed, as I may deserue it to you in tyme to come. With grace of Jesu, who preserue you. From Sessay, 4 day of January.

Your louing cousin Thomas Darrel

Endorsed (p. 68): To my worshipful unkl Sir Robart Plompton kt

[1] Younger son of Sir George Darrell, App. III; **21**.
[2] Thomas Howard, earl of Surrey, appointed deputy warden-general of the Scottish Marches after the death of Northumberland 1489, Chrimes, 108; *GEC*.
[3] **110**.

84 *Edward Plumpton to Sir Robert Plumpton, 10 February [1489/90] (No. 195, p. 132)*

In my most humble & faythfull wyse I recomend me to your good mastership & to my especyall good ladyes. Sir, at my departing I rode, according to your co[m]andement, by my Lady Delphes,[1] a full trobleous way in þat great snaw. Notwithstanding, I cold not speed of your matters at þat tyme, but now she is at London & promyses me well, þe which I trust, as yet, shall [speed][a] afore your atturney came to London, within this vj dayes. He cometh euer at the last retorne, in þe end of þe terme; þat causeth me to haue more business than needeth. Your matters in the excheker is greuous: ther is iij wryttes agaynst you, wherof I haue a *dedimus potestatem* out þe escheker, & another out of þe chauncre, both [...][b] derected to Sir Guy Fayrfax,[2] to resayue your hothes & my ladyes; þe serch & your copy of þe wrytts out of one cort to another costeth much money, & the fees of them, & great [...][c] <soliciting>. If I had them now redy, I wold haue sent them to you: when they be, I pray God send to me a good messinger, or els I must nedes send my seruant. Afore þe iiijth wrytte for the entre into Wolfhountlands, [...][d] <all the> counsell þat I can gett can shew no way, as yet, necessary for you, saue onely I haue labored þe wrytt proceding [*p. 133*] agaynst you to be reteyned vnto [the][e] next terme, & in þe meanetyme to purvey our remedy.[3] Fech your pardon and my ladyes, & send them both, for without they will helpe us, I wote not well what to doe in the matter. Incontinent vpon þe comying here of Master Farfax, ye & my lady ride to his place with your wrytts, for so I am agreed with him, & as hastely as ye can <gett> down, send up þe sayd wrytts with his sertyficat, for then we must haue a *non molestando* out of þe chauncery to disharges.

The premysses maketh my purce light. To wryte partyclarly þe charges, I haue no tyme now. Bylby taketh to me no money. Neuerthelesse when <I haue, or> I may make any, your matters shall not slake, nor abate, vnto such tyme as your mastership send, as is aboue sayd. All other matters concernying you to þe kings grace & his counsell, I can send to you no word therof as yet. I trust in short space to do, with Gods grace, who preserue you. Wrytten in great hast, þe x day of Feb:

Your <most humble> seruant Ed: Plompton[f]

Endorsed (p. 132): To my master Sir Robt Plompton kt

[a] *MS* s<p>eep.
[b] *A word deleted.*
[c] charging *deleted.*
[d] no *deleted.*
[e] *MS* your.
[f] *Appended*: Copied þe 7 of May 1613.

[1] Ellen, Lady Delves, widow of Sir John Delves of Doddington slain at Tewkesbury 1471. His son James was executed after the battle, and attainted in the following Parliament. The reversal of the attainder in 1482 restored the heirs and feoffees to their original status, although with exemption to James Blount, for certain lands in Staffs. The matter at issue was Lady Delves's dower lands in the Notts manor of Crakemarsh in which Sir Robert had an interest, I. Rowney, 'Arbitration in Gentry Disputes in the Late Middle Ages', *History*, lxvii (1982), 102; *RP*, vi, 436; **92**; App. I, 4.

[2] The writ provided for the taking of evidence required in judicial proceedings in chancery.

[3] Robert Blackwall, attorney at the exchequer and Sir Robert's tenant in Flagg, Derbys, pleaded his landlord's cause in the matter of a bovate of land called Wolfhuntlands in Mansfield Woodhouse, so called because it was held by the service of winding a horn and chasing the wolves out of Sherwood Forest, *CPR, 1430–37*, 124; **85**, **147**; CB, 798; App. II, 67.

85 *Edward Plumpton to Sir Robert Plumpton, 20 February [1489/90] (No. 196, p. 133)*

In my most humble & faythfull <wyse> I recomend me vnto your good mastership & to my especyall good ladyes, certyfiing your mastership þat I deliuered to Sir Richard Thornton, prest, vpon Sunday last, to bryng to you a box sealed, and therin ij wrytts, one *dedimus potestatem* out of þe chauncere & another out of þe excheker, both derected to Sir Guy Fairfax, & my poore wrytting therwith, þe which was right simple, but I besech you haue me excused, though I wryte not at all tymes as my dutie is to do. Sir, I had neuer so great business as I haue now for your matters; I know not the causes, but much payne I had to avoyd your appearance in your proper person,[1] as ye shall more at larg know by mouth when I shall speak with you: þat shalbe at your comandement. [*p. 134*]

Hall demanded of me grene wax[a] þat I knew not of,[2] & I desired of him a byll, what he asked of you, & his bokes wanted: he cold giue me none, but I trust he wyll not be hasty vpon you therfore, & if he be, let Henry Fox speak with him in my name, & pray him to suffer vnto my comyng home. I made to him such chere as I cold at London. I haue found meanes to convey þe wryt shold goe to þe schereffe of Notinghamshire against you, vnto þe next terme. Then God send vs good speede therwith. Afore Easter, send vpp your pardons, wrytes of *dedimus* & escaptes of instruccion what plee we shall make for you in the excheker, of, & how, & wherby ye enter your lands & maketh clame;[3] the matter is litle, & ioyus, with Gods grace, I purpose to he euer <all> this vocacion, & unto þe next terme. I send to you a letter by Robt Beckwith, & more of euerything concerning you & your seruants your atturney can shew. I wold, if I might by wyshe, speak with you one houre, & yt pleased Jhesu, who preserue your <mastership> in prosperous long to endure. Wrytten at London þe xx day of February. My Lord Straunge came to þe kings grace vppon Munday last; my lord of Northumberland is in good health, [. . .][b] blessed be Jhesu. Please yt your mastership to commend me to my master Gascoyn. If I cold doe to his mastership any service in thes partes, I wold be glad. Robt Blackwall hath sent to you a patent to seale, as appereth by þe same, shewing to him your pleasure of vj*s* viij*d* by you, & that he toke to no regard:[4] the world is so couettus, I wott not what to say, nor nought I wyll, *paruum sapienti sufficyt.*

Your seruant Ed: Plompton[c]

Endorsed (p. 133): To my singuler good master Sir Robt Plompton kt

[a] *Marginal note*: grene wax.
[b] praysed *deleted.*
[c] *Appended*: Copied þe 8 of May 1613.

[1] It was necessary to be present in person to plead a pardon, Blatcher, *BIHR*, xiii, 148.
[2] The entreaty of fines, issues and amercements in the Exchequer under the court's seal made in green wax.
[3] Sir Robert's claim to Wolfhuntlands, **84**.
[4] Retainers paid by gentry clients were usually of the order of £1 13*s* 4*d*, or 10*s*. Thus the offer to Robert Blackwall, a master in chancery, was not appreciated; Plumpton later increased the fee to 10*s*, Ives, *CL*, 288; **84**; CB, 798 (dated 19 Sept. 1499).

86 *Edward Plumpton to Sir Robert Plumpton, 6 May [1490]* *(No. 200, p. 137)*

[*p. 138*] In my most humble & faythfull wyse I recomend me vnto your good mastership & to my especyall good ladys. Sir, the iij day of May I received your wrytting, & incontinent I labored to David[1] & spake with him according to your desire & ther is great labour made to him for to put you from Haueray parke, & offered to him x*li* by yere[a] & a reward of c*s*. Notwithstanding, I haue made such labor, & caused him to be agreable to let yt to you for vj yeare <viij*li*> [. . .][b] by yeare, & ye to send vj marke to him at Whytsonday next, to London, & then & ther ye to haue your indentures sealed & deliuered, & ye to enter & begine þe vj yeare to you & your assignes.

Sir, Dauid wrytteth to you in favour of William Plompton, bastard,[c] & for his excuse; & all is but a collor for dou[b]tles,[2] & I had not layd yt to David discretely by dyverse wayes, yt had bene gone from you, for I mad many meanes or he wold make to me any grant, & because your mastership wrote þat ye wold not for xx*li*, but ye had yt, according to my dutye I dilygently applyed it to accomplish your pleasure therin. Sir, afor þe arbage, dout yt not, for, Sir He[n]ry Wentforth,[3] nor yet none other, can haue <it>, nor nothinge þat belongeth to David. Sir, yt is well done ye remember to send his money & haue your indenturs in all hast possible; & if ther be anything þat I know not þat ye wold haue comprised within þe same indenture, send to me word. Sir, I marvell much of William Plompton, þat he sayth þat I am not true: I neuer did him harme, but at your comandement I haue done much for him. Yt is no marvell he þat is not naturall, þat cannot love & owe his service to you, though he loue not me. I trow he love all ill þat is faythfull & true to you. Sir, what soeuer any man say, I am, & wilbe to you & yours true & faythfull while I liue, with Gods grace, who preserue you. From Furnyswall, vj *die* May.

Your humble servant Edward Plompton[d]

Endorsed (p. 137): To þe right honorable & my [right worshipfull *deleted*] especyall good master Sir Robt Plompton kt

[a] *Marginal note*: Hauerey parke valued at 10 li.
[b] vij li *deleted*.
[c] *Marginal note*: William Plo: bastard.
[d] *Appended*: Copied þe 8th of May 1613.

[1] David ap Griffith, one of the earl of Derby's executors, was probably a member of the earl's household – possibly the writer's brother-in-law. He held the parkership of the earl as chief steward of the Duchy in the North Parts. Edward Plumpton's position as secretary to Lord Strange enabled him to importune Griffith in Sir Robert's interest, Stapleton 94n.; Horrox, *Richard III*, 207; Bennett, *Bosworth*, 87; **82**, **90**.
[2] William Plumpton, of Kirkby Overblow, the younger of the two illegitimate sons of Sir William Plumpton, **87**, **88**; App. II, 58.
[3] Sir Henry Wentworth, **87**.

87 *Edward Plumpton to Sir Robert Plumpton, [11 June 1490] (No. 204, p. 141)*

[*p. 142*] In my most humble wyse I recomend me vnto your mastership & to my singuler good ladys. Late ye wrote to me a letter, the which I receiued vpon Whitsonday at nyght, touching departing of Henry Wentworth,[1] & incontinent vpon þat I toke a bote & went to Grenewich & shewed the matters to my lord of Derby, & he appoynted me to attend vppon him vnto he spake with the king; & so I did, & þe kings grace will in no wyse þat Sir Henry Wentworth departe from your country, as more at larg I shall send you word in hast, when I haue more sure messinger.

Sir, I pray you shew to my [. . .][a] lady[s] þat Byrd of Knasbrough spake to me for certaine things to send them; & he cold cary none, for he went to Hales,[2] & many other pilgrimages. Wryte in a byll such things as they wold haue, & send to me.

Sir, ye haue a faythfull frynd & servant of Davy ap-i-Kriffith, but I marvell þat ye sent not þe mony at Pentycost. I am douted þat he wary from his grant, ther is so great l[a]bor[b] made to him [. . .][c] for Havarey. Notwithstanding his letter send to you in þe favor of Wm Plompton, I am through with him affor my lord of Derby, þat ye shall occupie, & put, & depute vnder you whosoeuer ye wyll at your pleasure, & so shall your indentures be made, ye observing all couenauntes. And euer your owne, to my pore power, as knoweth our Lord, who your good mastership & my good ladys, with all yours, preserue. From London, *crastino corporis*.

Your most humble servant Ed: Plompton[d]

Endorsed (p. 141): To the right honorable my singuler good master Sir Robart Plompton knight

[a] lords *deleted*.
[b] *MS* lober.
[c] find *deleted*.
[d] *Appended*: Copied þe 10th of May 1613.

[1] Sir Henry Wentworth, of Nettlestead, Suffolk (d. by 1499), sheriff of Yorks 1489–90. With Sir Richard Tunstall he was associated with the earl of Surrey in the lieutenancy of the North, *CPR, 1485–94*, 366; **105**, **107**; *List of Sheriffs*.
[2] The Cistercian abbey of Hales in Gloucs.

88 *Edward Plumpton to Sir Robert Plumpton, [28 June 1490]* *(No. 187, p. 123)*

In my most humble wyse I recomend me vnto your mastership & to my especyal good lades. Sir, I marvell much þat your mastership sendeth not þe iiij*li* for Dauid; he made to you a grant condicionally þat ye shold content & pay to him at London iiij*li* at Pentycost last past, whervppon ye put to me a byll þat [he][a] shold be payd at mydsomer; & to content his mynd I shewed to him your letter. What I shall say to him, or what excuse to make, I cannot tell. Sir, remember ye may haue his parke xl*s* yerly vnder þe price, by my labor, & if he change & let yt to another, blame not me: I haue done my duty.[1] William Plompton hath bene at London with Dauid, & made much labor agaynst you for his fee;[b] & otherwyse shewed to me a copy of a state & feftment, mad by my master your father to certain feofes, to his beofe, of lands & tenementes to þe value of x mark yerly for terme of his life, the remayndre to the right heire of William Plompton, knight.[2] Whervpon he intended to labor a preue seale to bring you before my lord chaunceler & þe kings Counsell, the which I haue stayed as yet. Sir, I pray you send me word in all hast possible of your mynd in this matter, & in especyall the money for Dauid; & our Lord preserue you. Wrytten in hele in great hast, vppon St Peter even. Sir, they begine to die in London, & then I must departe for the tyme & other men do. I wold make you sure of Awerrey, or I departe fro Dauid.

Your seruant Ed: Plompton[c] 1495[3]

Endorsed: To my master Sir Robt Plompton knight

[a] *MS* ye.
[b] *Marginal note*: William Plo: sueth Sir Rob:.
[c] *Appended*: Copied þe 4th of May 1613.

[1] Sir Robert obtained his indenture of lease of Haverah Park dated 26 Aug. 1490. A further payment is recorded 5 Oct. 1498, App. II, 52; CB, 795; **90**.

[2] In the Derbys manor of Ockbrook, conveyance of 7 Nov. 1475, CB, 600, 603; **150**.

[3] The date appears to be a copyist's error: by deed dated 1 Oct. 1490 William Plumpton submitted himself to the award of arbitrators, including Sir Robert Plumpton, in regard to all matters in dispute between them. The result was that William was to pay 50*s* for the herbage of Haverah, CB, 759. App. II, 58.

89 *Sir Randolph Pigott*[1] *to Sir Robert Plumpton [15 August 1490] (No. 122, p. 74)*

Cousin, after dew recomendations I comend me, & certify you, one my honesty, I payd my palesses of Auarey Parke durying the tyme I occupied, xxx*s*, dischargeng one of the palas[2] to the kings grace. Wrytten on our Lady Day Assumption.

Your cousin Randall Pyggott[a]

[a] *Appended*: Copied þe 12 of Aprill 1612.

[1] Of Clotherholme, Richmondshire (will pr.1503), one of Sir Robert's close friends and kinsmen (his grandmother was Sir William Plumpton's sister Margaret), cousin of sergeant Richard Pigott, *Test. Ebor.*, iv, 6–7, 213–15; **29**, **162**; App. III.

[2] Palessers were those who had the care of the palings in Haverah Park, Stapleton, 98n.

90 *Davy Hervy*[1] *to Sir Robert Plumpton, 31 August [1490] (No. 170, p. 110)*

Right worshipfull Sir, I comend me to you, and yt is so þat I am through with my brother Edward Plompton touching Haveray Parke,[a] and hath made a pare of indentures[2] betwixt you & me touching the same; & now at our Lady Day in Lent next comyng ther is to be payd due to me viij*li*, which I trust you comaund me, I am yours, as knowes God, who keepe you. At Waryngton, the last day of August.

Your Davy Hervy[b]

Endorsed: To þe right worshipfull & my good master Sir Robt Plompton kt

[a] *Marginal note*: Haveray parke in Edward Plo: hands.

[b] *Appended*: Copied þe 28 of Aprill 1613.

[1] David ap Griffith, **86**.
[2] **88**n.

91 *Edward Plumpton to Sir Robert Plumpton, 23 September [1490] (No. 186, p. 122)*

In my most humble wyse I recomend me vnto your good mastership [and] to my especyall good ladys. This day I haue spoken with Master Schereff,[1] &, Sir, I send Master Blakwall,[2] master of þe chancery, as the berer can shew to you more by mouth, & they both comend them to you. Master Schereffe hath & wyll doe as much in your matters as I can of reason desire him. At Nothingham vppon Munday come a senit must we fynd[a] a office for you. I haue bene with Thomas Horston, by þe advice of Master Schereffe, & pennyt ij inquisicions of diuerse ways: if one will not serue vs, the other shall. Sir [...][b] ye [...][c] <have> a simple tenant in Maunsfeld Woodhouse.[3] I wold haue sent him to Rich. Saxton for to mete with me at Master Schereffs, & he absent him. Any service ye wyll comannd me, send me word, & I am yours, as knoweth our Lord, who preserve you. Wrytten at Southwell, þe xxiij of September.

Your seruant Ed: Plompton[d]

Endorsed: To my master Sir Robt Plompton knight

[a] *MS* finyd.
[b] ther *deleted.*
[c] am *deleted.*
[d] *Appended*: Copied þe iij of May 1613.

[1] Nicholas Kniveton, the elder, of Mercaston, *List of Sheriffs*, 104; **79**.
[2] **147**.
[3] **84**, **147**; App. II, 44.

92 *Edward Plumpton to Sir Robert Plumpton, 4 November [1490] (No. 189, p. 124)*

In my most humble & lowly wyse I recomend me vnto your mastership & to my singular good lady. Sir, I sent to you late wryttings of all matters by Sir Edward Bothom, prest. I thinke long vnto I here word from you, whether they come to you in tyme or no, & of your welfare. Sir, I had no word seth I parted from Plompton, as many as hath comyn to London. I cannot gyt myne entent of my Lady Delphes,[1] wherfore I haue comyned with Masters Blunt & Shefeld[2] in this form: the say they will take yt in forme or els make yt exchaunce with you of <lands> lyeing in Yorkshire, or els pay to you redy money therfore. Which of these iij wayes ye wyll take, I pray you take good advise & send to me word as hastyly as ye can, for they will not tary here, & I will haue no further communycation therin tyll I know your pleasure & mynd, for they wyll take hold at a letle thing. <All> such newes as I here John Bell can shew ye by mouth, for he made so great hast I had no leasure to writt more at larg of al things at this tyme. I thinke long till I here from your mastership, þe which Jhesu preserue. At London, the iiij day of Nouember.

Your most humble servant Ed: Plompton[a]

Endorsed: To my master Sir Robt Plompton knyght

[a] *Appended*: Copied þe 3 iiij of May 1613.

[1] **84**, **93**.

[2] The heirs of James Delves (exec.1472) were his two daughters, Elizabeth, wife of James Blount, and Ellen, who married the lawyer Sir Robert Sheffield. The land in question was Ellen, Lady Delves's dower in Crakemarsh, Staffs, where the Plumptons held land, and upon which Blount and Sheffield were casting covetous eyes, **180**; App. III.

93 *Edward Plumpton to Sir Robert Plumpton, 27 November [1490] (No. 193, p. 129)*

"The replycacion of Margret Scargill[1] to þe answere of William Scargill. The same Margrett sayth þat þe byll put by hir agaynst þe sayd William is good & true in euery poynt, & þat þe same John Scargill, named in the sayd byll, made such wyll of þe same maner, lands, tenements & other premyses, & euery of them, as is [...][a] surmytted by the same byll; & ouer that, sayth althings as in þe sayd byll is surmytted. All which matters she is redy to prove as this court will award, & prayeth as in hir byll is desired."

In my right humble & tender wyse I recomend me vnto your good mastership & to my singuler good ladyes. Sir, I sent to you the copie of þe replycacion of Marg[aret] Scargill, whervpon my lord chaunceler[2] hath, at our speciall desire, comand a *dedimus potestatem* to Sir Guy Fayrfax to heare & examyn ther proves & ours both, in Yorkshire. Wherfore I wold aduyse your mastership to shew your copies of ther byll, our ansere & there replicacion to Mr William Fayrfax,[3] þat he may be perfitt by them, & your [*p. 130*] instruccion in þe matter, & to be for William Scargyll afore Master Sir Guy, at þat day of his sytting, with all other proves most necessary for him; & in any wyse se þat William S. agree with Watson, & bryng him vp with him to London to release his suerty for þe peace, or els he must goe to ward, or els loose c marke, & euery one of his[b] iiij ɪ marke, þe which God forbid shold be. Sir, afore your lands in Craken<marsh>, I can not deale with my Lady [...][c] <Delfs>: I find hir varyable in hir promyse. Wherfore I haue, according to your comandment, letten them in your name to Mr Blunt by indenture, as more at larg appereth by þe same,[4] the which I sent to you within this box inclosed vnder my seale; & ye to subscrybe your hand, & to send a seruant of yours with the same box & indenturs to thabbay of Dale,[5] & ther to se thabbot & conuent seale þe oblygation for suerty of your rent, as in them is specified, & to wryt his name down to deliuer one parte to Mr Blount, & retine another parte for you, with the obligation. All such matters as ye wrote for by George Croft, dout not for them: I haue & shall remember them to thaccomplishment of your mynd, with grace of Jhesu, who you & yours long preserue in prosperous felicite to endure. From London, the xxvij day of November.

Your <humble> seruant Ed: Plompton[d]

Endorsed (p. 129): To my master Sir Robt Plompton knyght

[a] surmytted *deleted.*
[b] *MS* hus.
[c] Delfe *deleted.*
[d] *Appended*: Copied þe 7 of May 1613.

[1] Margaret, widow of William Scargill (d.1484). Their eldest son, William (d.1497), had already been in trouble with the authorities at Pontefract. John Scargill was their deceased younger son, *Test.Ebor.*, iii, 256–7; **69**, **71**.
[2] John Morton, archbishop of Canterbury.
[3] William Fairfax (d.1514), son of Sir Guy Fairfax, **208**; App. II.
[4] **92**.
[5] Dale Abbey, often called Stanley Park, a house of Premonstratensian canons in Derbyshire; the rule of the current abbot, Richard Nottingham, ended in 1491, *VCH, Derby*, ed. Wm Page, ii (1907), 69, 75.

94 *David ap Griffith to Sir Robert Plumpton, 3 February [1491/2] (No. 138, p. 84)*

Right worshipfull Sir, I recomend me to your mastership; & it is so þat the kings grace hath appoynted my lord to wayt vpon his grace, now at his [...][a] noble vage into France. Wherfore I must take homely vpon your mastership, & desire you to helpe me with my fee for this yere, for I am distytute of money;[1] & this my wrytting shalbe your discharg & warrant to delyuer yt to the berer herof; & if yt may be done now, at this tyme, I am bounden to you to doe you any pleasure þat lyes in my power. With Gods mercy, who preserue you, my gud master, & I pray you to take credence to Rich: Shaw, this berer, in my behalfe. The iij day of[b] February.

Your owne servant David Griffith[c]

Endorsed: To my worshipfull master Sir Robart Plompton kt

[a] his *repeated.*
[b] *Appended*: Copied the 19 of Aprill 1613.
[c] D Graff *deleted.*

[1] On 8 Oct. 1492 Henry VII began the investment of Boulogne, and on 20 Oct. Geoffrey Towneley, servant to Sir Robert, paid over to the abbot of Whalley the rent for £8 for Haverah Park, Mackie, 107–8; CB, 766.

95 *William Markenfield*[1] *to Sir Robert Plumpton [after 1490]*[2] *(No. 77, p. 43)*

Right worshipfull cousin, I comennd me vnto you, letting you wyt þat ther is a neighbour of myne, this bearer, William Medley, nativ, which geysted with two of your servants[a] in Haywras × bests, Thomas Ward and Wylliam Thorp; and [...][b] <when> this poore man come at Michellms for his cattell, ther lacked one of the best, [...][c] which was delyuered him other cattel for his both, þat was fare fro <the> value <of> his. Wherfore, cousin, I hartely pray you to be his good master to this man, and þat ye wold call your said servants afore you, & þat he myght be payd for his best þat he lacks, as I may doe for you in like cause, which I shalbe glad to doe, as God knows, who euermore preserue you to his pleasure.

By your cousin William Merkinfeild[d]

Endorsed: To my cousin Sir Robart Plompton be thes deliuered

[a] *Marginal note*: a guist.
[b] A word *deleted.*
[c] A word *deleted.*
[d] *Appended*: Copied the 15 day of March 1612.

[1] William Markenfield, younger brother of Sir Thomas Markenfield, of Markenfield, near Ripon (d.1497), *Test.Ebor.*, v, 232–5.
[2] Sir Robert's lease of Haverah park commenced 26 Aug. 1490, **90**; App. II, 52.

96 *A tenant of Stanton*[1] *to Sir Robert Plumpton (No. 183, p. 120)*

Most & honorable & worshipfull master, of whom myne intellygence & service lyes vnto, with all due recomendations in þe most humylitywyse þat I can thinke, or may. I recomend me vnto your worthy estate, beseching you of this simple wryting & matter to giue audience &

intelleccyon, vnder what forme þe wrytting is made to you in preue. Please you to vnderstand, the cause of my writting is this: your lordship of Stanton,[a] wher þat I dwell, is made lesser of rent & halfe your valow, & yt may contynew so, & be suffered of you & yours, be the gressing of xx oxen be yere [...][b] for ther be such men dwelling in Stanton þat thus deale, þat will no other way but so; they will haue yt by ther [*p. 121*] seying be yt right or wrong; & yt please you to send your counsell over to hold a court, he shall haue such informacion be vs þat be your tenaunts, þat your lifflod shalbe saued & kept vnto you & yours, with þe grace of God, who haue you in his blessed keeping; & vppon this conclusion, & yt please you so to do, þat you seek up your evydence of a place is called Renald Riding, vnder what forme you haue yt, for except your euidence specyfie, you be lyke to goe without yt; & if yt please you þat these things here wryttin shalbe performed, I besech you þat I may haue answere fir to make your tenaunts perfect under what forme ye wold haue them demeaned, & they & I to be redy to do you a pleasure with our body & our goods, with þe grace of God, who defend you & yours, Amen.[c]
Endorsed: To my right worshipfull master Sir Robt Plompton kt

[a] *Marginal note*: Lordship Stanton.
[b] ther *deleted*.
[c] *Appended*: copied þe ij of May 1613.

[1] A Derbys property acquired by the Plumptons through the Foljambe inheritance, App. II, 11.

97 *Ralph Ryther,*[1] *to Sir Robert Plumpton [c.1490 × 1491]* *(No. 76, p. 43)*

Right worshipfull cousin, I comennd me vnto you, desiring to here of your well fare, praying you to giue me ij cople of conyes[a] to stocking of a little ground þat I make at Ryther, and I shall doe you as great a pleasure. I pray you þat I may be recommend to my lady your wyfe. We haue rest, & past this summer I wyll pray you to come and kill a bucke with me. I pray you, cousin, þat þe brynger herof, my servant, may haue the conyes; & Jhesu keepe you. At Ryther, this Fryday.

By your cousin Ralfe Ryther[b]

Endorsed: To my cousin Robert Plompton kt be these byll

[a] *Marginal note*: 2 cuple of conies.
[b] *Appended*: Copied the 15 day of March 1612.

[1] Younger son of Sir Wm. Ryther, of Ryther, near Harewood (d.1476). Succeeded to the family estate after the deaths of two elder brothers without issue. Knighted by the time he was sheriff, 1503. Will pr. 26 April 1520, *Test.Ebor.*, v, 125; **187**.

98 *Robert Warcop*[1] *to Sir Robert Plumpton* *(No. 118, p. 71)*

Right reuerend & worshipful cosin, I commend me unto you as hertyly as I kan, euermore desiring to heare of your welfare, the which I beseech Jesu to continew to his plesure & your herts desire. Cosin, please you witt that I ame enformed þat a poor man, somtyme belonging to mee, called Umfrey Bell,[2] hath trespased to a seruant of youres, which I am sory for. Wherfore, cosin, I desire & hartily pray you to take upp the matter into your own hands, for my sake, and rewle him as it please you. And therin you wil do as I may do that may be plesur to you, & my contry, [*p. 72*] the which I shalbe redy too, by the grace of God, who preserve you.

By your own kynsman Robert Warcopp of Warcopp[a]

Endorsed: To his worshipful cosin Sir Robert Plumpton kt

[a] *Appended*: Copied þe 11 day of Aprill 1613.

[1] Of Warcop, Westmorland. Kinsman of the Plumptons through inter-marriage with the Hammertons, W.H. Hylton and R. Longstaffe (eds), *Heraldic Visitation of the Northern Counties by Thomas Tonge, Norroy King of Arms, A.D.1530* (SS, xli 1863), 100; *Anglica Historia*, 100.

[2] Apparently a villein, **56**, **164**.

99 *John Swale of Stainley*[1] *to Sir Robert Plumpton* *(No. 168, p. 109)*

Right worshipfull Sir, after my duty I recomend me vnto your mastership, beseching you to be good master to Henry Gulles concerning one farmhold in Follifit,[a] which John Gullese now holdeth; þat if ye can git John Gullese goodwyll, þat ye wilbe so good master vnto Henry Gullese, þat he may have yt, & þe better master for my sake. No more at this tyme, but Jesu perserue you.

Your own to his power John [...][b] Swale of Staynley[c]

Endorsed: Vnto my right worshipfull master Sir Robt Plompton knight thes deliuered in hast

[a] *Marginal note*: Lands in Folifoott.

[b] Shaw *deleted.*

[c] *Appended*: Copied þe 27 of Aprill 1613.

[1] John Swale, of South Stainley in the North Riding, was a defendant in a case of trespass heard in Star Chamber c.1485, W. Brown (ed.), *Yorkshire Star Chamber Proceedings*, i (YASRS, xli, 1909), 5–8.

100 *Thomas Hawksworth*[1] *to Sir Robert Plumpton* *(No. 125, p. 76)*

Right worshipfull Sir, I oftymes comend me vnto your mastership, and for so much as ther is a matter betwixt John Marshall and his mother, I vnderstand, Sir, that his mother hath put hir matter to your mastership. Sir, and it be so, he shall byd your mastership in likewyse. Wherfore, Sir, I pray you hartely, and as euer I may do you service, for to be good master to John Marshall, & the better for this my prayer. For, Sir, I haue spoken of þat matter herbefore, and they sayd at they wold haue bydene my rule. Sir, I am well pleased þat ye haue a rule in þat matter, or another matter in this country; it pleases me well; for, Sir, I will take your part in any matter ye have here, or in any other place. Sir, I pray you harteley þat ye wold for my sake to let the matter rest, to þat I may speake with your mastership, for this my prayer. For, Sir, I am to you as I was to my master, your father, & so shall I be while I live, with grace of God, who kepe you. Morover, Sir, it is letten me wytt þat they have enformed your mastership þat John Marshall labors to a gentleman in this country. Sir, it is not so, and þat shall ye well know when I speak with you; & Jesu keepe you.

By your trew cousin and man Thomas Haksworth[a]

Endorsed: To my worshipfull master Sir Robart Plompton kt delyver these

[a] *Appended*: Copied the 14 of Aprill 1613.

[1] Of Hawksworth (*fl.*1492), one of the jurors at the Yorks IPM after the death of Sir William, App. II, 42.

101 *William Whitaker to Sir Robert Plumpton or Master William Plumpton* *(No. 112, p. 67)*

Right worshipfull [. . .][a] Master Plompton, as hartely as I can I recomend me vnto you, desirying you to be good master vnto this poore woman, þe bearer hereof. Sir, it is so þat a servant of yours hath gotten a child with hir, the which is lost for lacke of keeping, as God knowes. She hath kept it as long as she [. . .][b] may, whils she hath not a cloth to hir back but which I haue given hir since she came to my service. And if it wold please you to heare this poore woman speake, I trust to God ye wilbe good master [*p. 68*] to hir, and rather the better for my sake. And if I had not bene, she wold haue rune hir way; and all this wile[c] I keep the child of my owne proper cost, and will doe till I here some word from you, as knowes God, who preserve you.

Be your owne to his powr William Wittcars[d]

Endorsed (p. 67): To Sir Robart Plompton or to Master William his son

[a] Sir *deleted.*
[b] hath *deleted.*
[c] *MS* wilbe.
[d] *Appended*: Copied þe 9 day of Aprill 1613.

102 *John Walker to Sir Robert Plumpton, 27 May* (*No. 181, p. 119*)

Right worshipfull master, I recomend me vnto your mastership as hartely as I can, in my most lowliest maner. Sir, the cause of my wrytting to you at this tyme is this: þat it may pleas your sayd gud mastership to helpe my moder in hir right, as to get hir, by your good meanes, such small dutyes as is owne hir by such a person as she shall shew you þe name of; if þat your mastership, after þat you haue sent for him to your sayd mastership, & comon þe matter ripely with him; & if than þat ye can bring him to no reasonable end, then I besech your mastership to send me word by wrytting how he wilbe demeaned, & therafter I shall intreat him according; for if he will [*p. 120*] take none end with hir at your desire, I shall sharply sue him by þe comon law as shortly after as may conueniently. No more to you at this tyme, but Jesu perserue you. At London, the xxvij day of May.

By your seruant John Walker[a]

Endorsed (p. 119): To Sir Robt Plompton kt this be deliuered

[a] *Appended*: copied þe 20 of May 1613.

103 *Sir Edward Birtby, clerk, to Sir Robert Plumpton* (*No. 208, p. 145*)

Right reverent & worshipfull Sir, I recomend me vnto your mastership in the most lowly wyse, euermore glad to here of your prosperytie & welfare, which I besech almygty God to encrease to his pleasure & your harts desire. Letting your mastership vnderstand, the lowest price of the male which your mastership spake of is 2 iiij*s* viij*d* as the maker therof sayeth, & if yt please you to send for yt shortly, he shall kepe yt, or els he shall make one other when yt please your mastership to send [. . .][a] <him word> iij dayes before þe tyme þat it please you to have it. No more to your mastership at this tyme, but þe holy Trenite have you in his keping.

By your owne bedman Sir Edward Birtby[b]

Endorsed: To my worshipfull master Sir Robt Plompton knight be thes letter deliuered in hast

[a] for yt *deleted.*
[b] *Appended*: Copied þe 11th of May 1613.

104 *Robert Fitz John, abbot of Lilleshall,*[1] *to Sir Robert Plumpton [20 March 1491/2] (No. 67, p. 39)*

Right worshipfull Sir, I recomennd me vnto you, thanking you as hartely as I can for your great kyndnes & gentlenes shewed to me and to my poore tenaunts in Arkenden. And wheras ye haue written to me þat one Robert Walkinham[2] is iniuried & wronged of his tennor in Arkenden, contrarie to right & concience. Wherfore I purposse, sonne after Whitsontide next comying to send a brother of myne and other officers to Arkenden, and ther to haue a court to be houlden, & right to be had, according to reason & good concience, with the <grace> of God, who haue you in his gouernance. Written in hast on Tewsday in the ijd week of Lent.

Your good lover The Abbot of Lilleshill[a]

Endorsed: To the right worshipfull Sir Robart Plompton kt be thes letter deliuered

[a] *Appended*: This letter hath a seale. Copied 12 of March 1612.

[1] Elected abbot of the Augustinian abbey of St Mary, Lilleshall 1464, resigned 1499. The abbey held property in Arkendale, near Knaresborough and retained Sir Robert as steward, *VCH, Shropshire*, ed. A.T. Gaydon, ii (1973), 79: *CPR 1461–67*, 334; *ibid., 1494–1509*, 107.

105 *Thomas Howard, earl of Surrey, to Sir Robert Plumpton, 6 May [1492] (Stapleton, 96n)*[1]

Right worshipfull cousin, right hartelie I comend me unto you; and whearas I am enformed that a servant of yours had a gelding of myne, which I lost on the field;[2] I desyre and pray you that then ye will cause him to be delivered unto my said servant, as my singular trust is in you, whome our Lord have in his blessed safeguard. Written in the castle of Sheriff Hutton, the 6th day of Maye. Cosen, I have some proofs that your servant Robert Beck hath my gelding; one knoweth him well, told it me. I pray you, cosen, fail not to send me the geldinge with the hand.

Your loving cozen Thomas Surrey

[*No endorsement printed*]

[1] See Introd., above p. 19n.
[2] The skirmish at Ackworth took place April 1492. Surrey was under-warden of the

East and West Marches as deputy to Prince Arthur. The northern rebels objected to the levying of a benevolence, Reid, 80; **87**, **107**.

106 *Robert Fitz John, abbot of Lilleshall, to Sir Robert Plumpton, 28 May [1492]* *(No. 65, p. 38)*

Right worshipfull Sir, we recomennd us vnto you. And so it is that Dame Joyce Percy[1] hath shewed vnto the earle of Schrewesburie,[2] which is our very good lord and tender lord in all our rightfull causes, how ye enwrong hir of certayne lands lying within our lordship of Erkenden, were ye be our steward; [...][a] <wherein> the said lord hath made labour vnto vs for the sayd Dame Joyes, and desired vs that we wold she be not wronged in hir right. And considering how good lord he hath bene, & yet alwayes vnto us ys, and remembryng allso that we, being men of the holy Church, owe not to suffer any wrong to be done to any maner of persons within our lordship, may no lesse doo, but effectually tender the sayd lordes desire [*p. 39*] in that behalfe. Wherfore we desire you that ye will see the sayd Joyes to haue all þat which she of right ought to haue within our lordship of Erkenden foresayd, so as she find hir not greved, nor haue cause to make any more labor to the sayd lord for hir remedy therein. For and she doe, we must sett some other person in your rome þat will not wrong hir, soe we may in no wyse abyd the displeasur of the sayd lord. Tendering therefore this our desire, as we trust you. And our Lord haue you in his gouernance. From Lillishall the xxviij day of May.

Your good loving Abbot of Lileshull[b]

Endorsed (p. 38): To Sir Robart Plompton knight in Yorkshire be thes letter deliuered in good speed

[a] *A word deleted.*
[b] *Appended*: Copied þe 11 day of March 1612.

[1] Second wife of Sir Robert Percy, of Scotton, App. III.
[2] George Talbot, 4th earl of Shrewsbury (d.1538). His letter to Sir Robert includes a reference, presumably, to the field of Ackworth, which dates this letter to 1492. A competent estate administrator, he was chief steward of 11 monasteries, G.W. Bernard, *The Power of the Early Tudor Nobility: A Study of the Fourth and Fifth Earls of Shrewsbury* (1985), 148; **108**.

107 *Henry VII to Sir Robert Plumpton, 28 May 1492* *(Bodl.Lib., MS Dodsworth 148, fols 109r–v)*

Trusty & welbeliued wee greete you well, & as soone for the good & agreable seruice yee did vnto vs in this last commotion of our subjects

in our county of Yorke,[1] wee can giue you our full speciall thanks, & shall not forgite the good disposition yee haue been of in þat behalfe. And in as much as diuerse & many such commotions & insurrections haue beene heretofore committed in our said county, to thutter destruction of greate number of our subjects therein cause, wee would haue executed the just course of our lawes. We therefore, intendinge to prouide for the tyme to come & to haue the same our county in a restfullnes, both for the duty amongst God & vs, & alsoe for theire owne profites, will & desyre you þat forthwith & by as wyse wayes as yee can, yee put your selfe in a surety of your meniall seruants & tenants, & to knowe assuredly how many of them will take your parte in seruinge vs accordinge to your & theire duties foresaid. When yee shall haue demeaned [*fol. 109v*] the matter in this wise, which wee would yee did, as aboue, with all diligence, then wee pray you to certify our couzen the earle of Surrey of the number of such assured men as yee will bringe with you, to the intent hee may ascertayne vs by his wrytinge of the same.[a] Giuen vnder our signet at our manor of Shene the 28th day of May the seuenth yeare of our reigne.[b]
Endorsed (fol.109r): To our trustie & wellbeloued knight Sir Robart Plompton

[a] *Marginal note*: Letter 19.
[b] *Appended*: this was for his service against the rebells þat killed the earle of Northumberland at Thirske in the 4 yeare of H. þe 7 for yt was the last rebelliion afore 7 H.7 & 28th of May.

[1] A reference to the skirmish at Ackworth, **105**.

108 *George Talbot, earl of Shrewsbury, to Sir Robert Plumpton, 8 July [1492]* *(Bodl.Lib., MS Dodsworth 148, fols 114r–15r)*

Right welbeloued frend, I recommend me vnto you, ascertayninge you þat it is shewed vnto mee by my right welbeloued Dame Joyce Percy, now attendinge vpon my wife, how yee, contrary to right and conscience, haue interrupted the said Dame Joyce of certain land lying [*fol.114v*] within the lordship of Arkinden, and within þe county of Yorke, which land was purchased of one Robert Walkingham[1] by Sir Robert Pearcy, knight, her late husband, deceased, and by him granted vnto the said Dame Joyce as parcell of her joynture, yee now intendinge, by meane of a sinistre grant made vnto you of the said land by the said Robert, continually to keepe the same by extort power contrary to the law, as shee saith. Wherefore, if it bee soe, I greately marvell, willinge and desyreing you, therefore, þat vnto such tyme as this matter may be had in good and perfitt examination, [*yee*][a] will in noe wise further intromete or deale with the land, but suffer the seid Dame Joyce and her assignes peaceably to occupy the same, without any manner interruption to the contrary. And if yee, when the said examination shall bee had, shall haue any good euidence for your pretence and title in that behalfe þat yee of right are [*fol.115r*] to haue the said land, yee shall thereof haue possession and bee recompensed as right requireth. And ouer this, whereas I am enformed þat one Richard Nicoll, late tenant to the said Dame Joyce, was now in the field against the Kings good grace,[2] for the which cause yee haue seazed his goods, as it accordeth, I will and desyre you, consideringe the said Dame Joyce was innocent, and nothinge knowinge of his misdemeaninge, yee will see þat of his said goods such duties may bee contented as hee oweth vnto her by reason of any tenures or holdings, and that yee will tender her in these premisses the rather for my sake, soe as she haue not cause to make further suit for her remedy therein, as I trust you. From Ashby, the 8th day of July.[b]

Your frend, G. Shrewsbury.

Endorsed (fol.114r): To my right welbeloued frend Sir Robart Plompton knight

[a] *MS* wee.
[b] *Marginal note*: Letter 31.

[1] On 30 Jan. 1488/9 Robert Walkingham had sold 3 closes in the vill of Plumpton to Sir Robert and Dame Joan, his mother. It appears that the earl believed there was a conspiracy to defraud Dame Joyce, CB, 752; **104**; Introd., above p. 13.
[2] At Ackworth, **105**, **107**.

109 *David ap Griffith to Sir Robert Plumpton, 8 October [?1492]* *(No. 139, p. 85)*

Right worshipfull Sir, I comend me vnto your mastership. It is so I receiued of your chaplain in the New Castle under Lyne 8 pounds. And also I send to you my brother Midleton. And I pray you that ye wold content him of this yeare farme. And Christ keepe you. At Preston, the 8 day of October.

From your servant David Griffith[a]

Endorsed: To my right worshipfull master, Sir Robart Plumpton knight this bill be delyuered

[a] *Appended*: Copied 19 Aprill 1613.

110 *William Arthington to Sir Robert Plumpton 4 April [before 1494] (No. 166, p. 107)*

Right reuerent & worshipfull master, I recomend me to your mastership, certyfiing you þat John pullan & I meett this day at Castley, which John brought with him Harry Dickinson & John Tomlinson to support him & to testyfie his talke. Sir, þe dayes men canot agre vs, so Mr Mydleton make þe end. Wherfore I wold besech your said mastership þat yt wold please you to cause some of your servants to goe to þe sayd Mr Midleton, & þe bringer herof to goe [*p. 108*] with him, to whome I besech you giue credence, þat ye & the sayd Master Midleton wold assigne a day & a place, þat I may know the same & attend vpon him, beseching your sayd mastership þat it wold please you, if [...][a] ye so may, tobe at þe endmaking, or els I fere me we shall haue no end for myn avantag, & all by þe meanes of þe said John Tomlinson; for he seketh all þe meanes þat he can to put me from yt, as I am enformed, both to þe sayd Nichellas Midleton and also to my lord of Fountance. Sir, I shold haue comen to your mastership, but I must ned ride to Connesburgh for matters of my moders in law;[b] wherfore I besech your mastership to pardon me. Nomore at this tyme, but þe blessed Trenete preserue you in worship to his pleasure. Writtin at Arthington Hall the iiijth day of Apryll.

By your owne seruant William Arthington[c]

Endorsed (p. 107): To my right worshipfull master Sir Robt Plompton knight be thes deliuerd

[a] þat *deleted.*
[b] *Marginal note*: Arthington of Arthington. Plom. seruant.
[c] *Appended*: Copied þe 27 of Aprill 1613.

111 *Richard Cholmley*[1] *to Sir Robert Plumpton 16 June [1493] (No. 123, p. 74)*

Right worshipfull Sir, after all due recomendations, please it you to know I haue latly bene in the byshopryk of Durham, by the kings comandement, for leveing of such arrerages and other dutyes as were [...][a] due to the late byshop, decessed,[2] whose sole God pardon. And then it was shewed vnto me by certayn frinds of Mr Alex Lees,[3] and also by his old servant Lawrence Canwick, who ye know, þat ye without your duty belonging to þe sayed Mr Lee, wherwith all the kings comyssioners and I marvelled þat ye wold, so doe. Whervpon, the sayd Lawrence, with other his master frynds, wer in mynd & fully determyned to haue made complaynt of you vnto the kings grace in þat behalfe; &

then, Sir, in avoyding of such inconuenients as myght have ensued to you by reason of the same, & also for such speciall [*p. 75*] favour as I owe vnto you, I caused them to surcease ther purposse vnto the tyme I had wrytten to you & known your mynd in þat partie. Wherfore, Sir, I pray you, according to the kings comandements, which I haue sene, and also for your singuler wele, þat ye will see the <said> Lawrence content of parte of the sayd duty at this tyme, & so to finde him suffycyent suerty for the residue as ye & he an agre. And, Sir, if ye endeuer not yourselfe for the accomplessment of þe premysses, I haue promysed them to wryte to the kings grace for the contentation of the same, which I wold be loth to doe.[4] Sir, I doubt not so ye will deale herin þat it shall not miscare. And, Sir, of your toward mynd herin, I pray you if I may be answerd by my servant, this bearer, to whom, I pray you, give credence. And I am yours. At Cotingham, the xvi day of June.

Your owne Rich: Coverley[b]

Endorsed (p. 74): To the right worshipfull Sir Robart Plompton kt at Plompton

[a] late *deleted.*
[b] *Appended*: Copied þe 12 of Aprill 1613.

[1] As suggested by Stapleton, the subscription is a scribal error. The writer was Richard Cholmley, of Braham Hall, near Plumpton, whose appointment as receiver and surveyor of the temporalities of the see of Durham is dated 1 March 1493, *CPR, 1485–94*, 418; Stapleton, v; App. III.
[2] John Sherwood, died 12 Jan.1493/4, *HBC*, 221.
[3] Alexander Lye, instituted rector of Spofforth 25 Dec.1481, **45**.
[4] The warning had its effect, for Sir Robert paid his tithe 1 Feb.1494, CB, 770.

112 *Edward Plumpton to Sir Robert Plumpton, 26 October 1495* *(No. 199, p. 136)*

[*p. 137*] In my right humble wyse I recomend me vnto your good mastership. I haue receyved your wrytting & the credaunce of your servant; & in stopping & letting of your prevey seale at the instance & especyall labor of my master Gascoyne, my lord prevy seale[1] hath done þat he myght with reason, in so much þat he lettyt yt, & comaunded Mr Bele, clerk therof, þat none shold passe vnto such tyme as all þe lords of þe kings Counsell comanded yt to passe, vppon his surmyse & complaynt, wherof I sent to you a copye; & when we sought no remedy we found the meanes þat Ch. Kilborne,[2] & suffitient suertyes with [. . .][a] him, shold be bonden in a reconusaunce of x*li* to content & pay your cost & charg, if his surmyse & bill of complaint be founded insufficyent & not true. My <sayd> Master Gascoygne hath dyligently applyed your matter as much as is possible for to doe, as your servant Geffray[3] can shew vnto you more at large euerything by mouth, & as yet he can get no surtyes. Wherfore my lord abbot of St Mary Abbay[4] shewed to me <þat his servant Kilborne wold haue a writ, subpena. Sir, for þat I haue lade good watch. Also my lord abott told me> this day þat Edmound Thawites[5] hath sene his evedence & sath þat your mylne standeth vppon his ground & more, & þat he is not your ward. Wherby I perceive by well, he haught a favor & good lordship to his servant Kilborne. He desired þe matters to be put vpon my lord of Surry & him, & I answered þat your matters concerned your inherytance & matters of land, þe which cold <in> no wyse be rightfully determyned without learned counsell.[6] Sir, I trust we shall so provide for him here þat he shal not haue all his intent. With Gods grace, who preserue your good mastership & my singuler good ladys & all yours long tyme to endure, with encrease of greate & honor. From Furnyvalls Inne, þe xxvj of October 1495.

Your humble servant Ed: Plompton[b]

Endorsed (p. 136): To my master Sir Robart Plompton knight

[a] them *deleted*.
[b] *Appended*: Copied þe 8 of May 1613.

[1] Richard Fox, bishop of Durham from 1494 to 1501 when he was translated to Winchester. He remained in office as keeper of the Privy Seal until 1516, *HBC*, 93; Kirby, *NH*, xxv, 119; **116**.
[2] Christopher Kilborne, **113**, **115**, **124**.
[3] Possibly Geoffrey Towneley, **163**.
[4] William Senhouse, **50**.
[5] Edmund Thwaites of Lund, near Beverley (d.1500), succeeded William Elland as recorder of Hull in 1486/7, a post he occupied until 1489/90. Retained by Northumberland, who appointed him an executor, *Test. Ebor.*, iii, 304–10; Pauline Sheppard Routh, 'The Thwaites Family and Two Effigies at Lund, East Riding', *YAJ*, lxi (1989), 89–90; *VCH, York, North Riding: City of Hull*, ed. K.J. Allison (1969), 34.
[6] The case had been referred by Star Chamber, Reid, 80.

113 *Edward Plumpton to Sir Robert Plumpton, [14 January 1495/6] (No. 188, p. 123)*

In my ryght humble wyse I recomend me vnto your good mastership, & to my singuler good lady. Afore my lord of Carlel[1] hath passed <so> by the way at his lodging at Poumfret & Scroby, þat as yet I spake not with his lordship. I spake with his seruants, & they shewed to me Ch. Kilborn rideth not vp with him. Yt was shewed me þat vppon Thursday last ther was a great iustice sat at Wentbrig; [*p. 124*] I wold fayne know what was done there, & afore þat in such matters as concerned you.

Master Tailbose[2] was at Colliweston[3] vppon Tuesday, Wedensday & Thursday last, as the bringer can shew, els I wold haue written much more. My lord of Darby departith towards London vpon Munday come a senit. Davy[4] recomend him to your mastership, & when we come to London ye shall haue a strayt restreynt for Haueray. Our Lord preserue you & yours. At Stampforth, *crastino hallarij*.

Your humble seruant Ed: Plompton[a]

Endorsed (p. 123): To my singuler good master Sir Robt Plompton knight

[a] *Appended*: Copied þe 4 day of May 1613.

[1] William Senhouse, **50**, **112**.

[2] Sir George Tailbois, of Kyme, Lincs, JP Lincs, later made knight of the body, *CPR, 1494–1509*, 611, 647–9.

[3] Collyweston near Stamford, the residence of Margaret, countess of Richmond and Derby, the king's mother, wife of Thomas Stanley, 1st earl of Derby, M.K. Jones, 'Collyweston – an Early Tudor Palace', in D. Williams (ed.), *England in the Fifteenth Century: Proceedings of the 1986 Harlaxton Symposium* (1987), 134–36; **39**.

[4] David ap Griffiths, **94**, **109**.

114 *Edward Barlow[1] to Sir Robert Plumpton 4 February 1495/6 (No. 177, p. 115)*

Right reuerent & my singuler good master, I comend me to your good mastership, to my gode lady your mother & my lady your wyffe. Please yt your mastership to know þat I haue receiued your letters sent to me by Robart Benson, & hath hard his commyng from you. And I haue bene & labored to þe clarkes of þe privie signit dyuers tymes afore þe making herof, & to my lord [. . .][a] <presedent>,[2] after thentent of your wrytting; & the day of the delyuerie of this wrytting by the sayd Robt Benson, Percyvall Lanton[3] & I went to þe Tower to speak with my lord pryuey seale,[4] as þe clark of þe kings signet aduised vs, thynking þat to be our next way, if so were þat we wold not aduise you to com not vp by the pryvie seale. For ther was a byll put into þe Parliament a litle before Christynmas þat no privie seale shold go against no man, but if þe suer therof wold find surety to yeld the parties defendants ther damages;[5] & after þe intent yt is sayd þat þe lords of þe Counsell behaue them selfe;[6] & þe most dylygent labor & way þat the sayd Percyvall & I can doe our [*p. 116*] good master in his behalfe, we shall endeuer our selfs.

For to the sayd Percyvall for both his labour at the last terme, & this terme ye be much beholden vnto; & þe sayd Lanton is generall atturney to my said lord privey seale; & as for Edward Plompton,[b] he is not commyn to London at the making of this simple wrytting. Also Sir Robt Blawall, your atturney in the kings escheker,[7] hath shewed me þat Edward Plompton[c] hath not payed þe money for respityng of your homage in þe sayd escheker, as he promysed me & your menyall seruant Goffray Tounley[d] the last terme; & by great labour of the sayd Blakwall he hath saved your issues to this terme; & he will lay down no penny; & it is so þat I haue promysed payment or I come home, & with þe grace of God, so shall I make payement; & at my commyng home I shall shew to your mastership al things more clerely, praying your sayd mastership be not displeased with my homely wrytting. Written in þe even & in great hast, for parte of your matters I haue spede, & parte of my ladies matters also; & as touching the remnent of your matters, I shall indeuer me for you as farre as I can. With the grace of God, who preserue you <& all yours> to his pleasure. Wrytten þe Thursday next <after> [...][e] þe Puryfication of our Lady þe <Virgin> last past. *Anno* xi H. VII.

Your seruant Edw: Barlow[f]

Endorsed (p. 115): Vnto my singuler good master Sir Robt Plompton kt be thes <letter> deliuered in goodly hast

[a] *A word deleted.*
[b] *Marginal note*: Edw: plo:.
[c] *Marginal note*: Ed: Plo: vidz.
[d] *Marginal note*: Geffray Townley, Sir Rob: Plo: seruant.
[e] A word *deleted.*
[f] *Appended*: Copied 30 of Apryll 1613.

[1] Probably an attorney; perhaps the Owen Barley mentioned in **115**.
[2] Sir Thomas Lovell (d.1520). Of recent origin, the presidency of the Council, as implied in this letter, controlled the office of the signet, *Select Cases*, p. xxxix.
[3] Percival Lambton, lawyer, son of Richard Lambton, of Harrogate. Ives calls him 'an apparently insignificant' member of Lincoln's Inn. Attorney-general of the Palatinate of Durham 1492–1501, E.W. Ives, 'Promotion in the Legal Profession of Yorkist and Early Tudor England', *Law Quarterly Review*, lxxv (1959), 303; **106**, **115**, **116**.
[4] Richard Fox, **112**.
[5] Parliament sat from 14 Oct. 1495 until just before Christmas, but the bill is not mentioned in *RP*. An Act was passed against similar abuses in the county courts, *Statutes of the Realm* (11 vols, HMSO, 1810–28), ii, 579; *RP*, vi, 458–508.
[6] Probably a reference to the unscrupulous methods of Empson and Dudley, A.F. Pollard (ed.), *The Reign of Henry VII from Contemporary Sources* (3 vols, 1913), ii, 123n.
[7] **147**, **91**, **85**. On legal managers who put up money for their clients' costs, see Ives, *CL*, 142; **116**.

115 *Percival Lambton to Sir Robert Plumpton, 9 February [1495/6] (No. 171, p. 110)*

[*p. 111*] Please yt your good mastership to vnderstand, your seruant & atturney, Mr Owen Barley,[1] desired mee to labor to my lord of Duresm[2] that sum meanes might bee found to excuse your appearance if the priuy seale were deliuered unto you, which one Kilburn[3] labored against you this last term; and according to his desire I haue labored at diuerse tymes. My lord shewed me dyuerse things which was shewed him in þat matter, as I shall shew your mastership at lasor; & in conclusion this is his mynd: if the privie seale be deliuered you afore his comyng home into þat country, which I trust wilbe about þe iiijth weeke of Lente, thin he wold ye shold set seale your selfe & send a seruant to me as shortly as ye can, & he & I shall purvey a remedy þat ye shall take no hurt therby; & if ye privie seale be not deliuered afore my lords comyng home, than he sayeth þat he will send for þe partie, & cause þe matter be exomyned endefferently; & thus he was content þat I shold wryt vnto your mastership. [4] And therfore dowt not in this matter, but take your ease & in no wyse charg yourselfe with comyng upp for this matter, thoffe the privie seale be deliuered vnto you. Herin, I assure you, I shall giue as great delygence as the matter were myne owne, & thus our lord God preserue your mastership to your most comforth. At Lyncolnes Inn, the xith day of February. By þe hand of

Your seruant Percivall Lambton[a]

Endorsed (p. 110): To my good master Sir Robt Plompton knight at Plompton in hast

[a] *Appended*: Copied þe 28 of Aprill 1613.

[1] Surely the writer of **114**.
[2] Richard Fox, translated from Durham to Winchester Aug. 1501, *HBC*, 221.
[3] **112**.
[4] Bishop Fox as lord privy seal was here 'privately rendering nugatory his official acts', Pollard, *Reign of Henry VII*, ii, 124.

116 *Edward Plumpton to Sir Robert Plumpton, 13 February 1495/6 (No. 185, p. 121)*

In my right humble & harty wise I recomend me vnto your good mastership & to my singuler good lady, þe ix day of February I receiued your wryting, the which was to me great comforth. The contents therof was moved to my lord priue seal afore þat by Percyvall Lambton, as ye shewed to me, & as he hath wrytten to you the scanty in euerything of my lords [*p. 122*] mynd in þat behalfe; the which me semeth right good & necessary for you. And yt pleaseth you when my lord cometh into your country, to se him & ride a myle or ij with him & wellcome him to [the] country, yt will doe good many wayes. Sir, afore credance of [. . .][a] Ewene Barle he gaue none to me but for these premyses, & þat, I thinke, nedeth no more labor nor cost. For when my sayd lord had ansered reasonable therin, yt sufficeth for þe same.

Also I send herin a byll of discharg for your fine, & I wold I myght haue content þe same fyne at the last terme, but I spared for þe more aduauntage, for ye payd none syth trenetie term vnto now; & your owne & euer wylbe, to my power, as knoweth our Lord, who euer preserue you <& yours in prosperous long tyme to endure>. From Furnyvalls Inn the xiij of Februray.

Your humble seruant Ed: Plompton[b] 1495.

Endorsed (p. 121): To my master Sir Robt Plompton knight at Plompton

[a] *Appended*: Copied þe iijth of May 1613.

117 *Sir John Kendal, prior of St John,*[1] *to Sir Robert Plumpton 3 September [before 1501] (No. 143, p. 87)*

Right worshipfull Sir, I comend me vnto you with all my hart, thanking you of þe great love & favour þat ye have shewed vnto my nephew, the comander of Rybston;[2] & not only vnto him, but as well vnto his servants & tenaunts in these partyes, as well in his absence as in his presence, praying you so to contynew; & ye may be assured if ther be any thing þat I may doe for you or for any of yours, ye shall alway find me redy, to my power. John Trongton, the brynger herof, shall shew vnto you in what case the matter standeth in that is betwyxt my nephew & John of Rocliffe,[3] & I pray you give credence to the sayd brynger of herof; & Jesu keepe you. Wrytten at St Johns þe iij day of September.

Your owne Sir John Kendal, prior of St John[a]

Endorsed: To the right worshipful <and my right hartely beloved friend> Sir Robart Plompton knight

[a] *Appended*: Copied þe 19 day of Aprill 1613.

[1] John Kendal (d.1501), Grand Prior of England of the Order of St John of Rhodes, *VCH, Middlesex*, ed. R.B. Pugh, i (1969), 200.

[2] John Tong, **118**.

[3] John Rocliffe, App. III.

118 *Sir John Tong to Sir Robert Plumpton, 11 March [?1495/6] (No. 211, p. 148)*

Right worshipfull & my right entyrely beloved Sir and father,[1] I recomend me vnto you, & thanks the same for your loving dealing in myne absence, shewed to my tenaunts & servants, & especiall to my servant Tromton, this bringer, for the good mastership shewed to him at Yorke, to your cost & charge. My sayd servant shall shew you my further mynd, to whom it will please you to give credence; & also þat I may be recomended to my good lady & mother, your wyfe. Jhesu preserve you. At London þe xith day of March.[2]

Your owne son Sir John Tong commander of Rybston & Mownt S. Johns[a]

Endorsed: To my right worshipfull & my right hartly welbeloved neghbor & fadyr Sir Robt Plompton knight

[a] *Appended*: Copied the 12th day of May 1613.

[1] Sir Robert and Dame Agnes stood sponsors at the birth of the writer, Stapleton, 120n.

[2] After the suppression of the Templars in 1312, Great Ribston, near Plumpton, was the only one of their seven Yorkshire preceptories to retain an independent position, *VCH, Yorks*, iii, 262.

119 *Edward Plumpton to Sir Robert Plumpton, 3 February 1496/7 (No. 203, p. 140)*

[*p. 141*] In my right humble wyse I recomend me vnto your good mastership & to my singuler good lady, acertaynyng you þat ther is in thes partes a great talking of those þat belong & medle with Mr Hemson, þat he intendeth to attempte matters agaynst you[1] in þe title of þe heire of John Suttell,[2] wherin he moved & brake the same vnto Mr Gascoyne,[3] of whom he had a discret & good answere, as thus: he desired my sayd Mr Gascoyne to be favorable to him in þe premysses, & he answered to him & sayd thus: "If your matter were against any man in England except my vncle, I wold take your parte, but in this ye must have me excused," with dyvers words more concerning your honor & wele.

Sir, the sayd Mr Hemson moved this matter greatly & maketh his frinds, & diuers þat he hath broken his hart & mynd too hath told me þe same, & his saying afore, as they knew. If yt please your mastership, to [. . .][a] <cause> your loving frinds & servants to haue knowledg therof. Sir, I shewed to a gentleman þat is of counsell & fee with Master Hemson, & a companyon of myne, how þat King Richard, in his most best tyme, & the first yere of his reigne,[b] having you not in þe favor of his grace, but vtterly against you, caused them to haue a parte of þe lands by his award and ryall power, contrary to your agrement & all ryght conscience;[4] the which I trust to god wylbe called againe. Sir, ye haue many good frinds & servants, & moe, with Gods <grace>, shall have. This is þe matter I thinke no dout yn. Ye haue a great treasour of Mr Gascoyn. If ther be any seruice your mastership wyll comand me, yt shalbe done to þe uttermost of my power, as knoweth our Lord, who preserue you. Written in Furnyvalls Inne, þe iij day of Feb. 1496.

Your humble servant Ed: plompton[c]

Endorsed (p. 140): To my singuler good master Sir Robt Plompton knight

[a] call *deleted*.
[b] *Marginal note*: King Ric: not frendly in is award.
[c] *Appended*: Copied þe 20th day of May 1613.

[1] This is the first intimation of Richard Empson's intention to oust Sir Robert from the lands secured to him by Richard III's arbitration of 16 Sept.1483, App. II, 48.
[2] Husband of Elizabeth Plumpton.
[3] Sir William Gascoigne (d.1551), Sir Robert's nephew, App. III.
[4] The rule applying to most land held by free tenure was that the daughters of a dead eldest son excluded a younger son, Sir F. Pollock and F.W. Maitland, *The History of English Law* (2nd edn of 1898, Cambridge, 1968), 260; Introd., above p. 8.

120 *Richard Empson*[1] *to Sir William Gascoigne, 7 September [possibly 1497] (No. 79, p. 44)*

Master Gascoygne, after most harty comenndations, pleaseth you to wyt that Richard Falbarne,[2] late clarke to Bryan Rowclife, according to the trust put in him, hath made astate of dyuers maners, lands and tenements, late Sir William Plompton in the county of Yorke,[3] wherwith, as it is sayd, Sir Robart Plompton taketh dyspleasure, and his servants speake such words & so to demeane them selfes that the poor man for dread dare not apply his busines. Sir, I heare þat ye be frend to þe sayd Sir Robart; I pray you move him þat the pore man may passe his busines in Gods peace and the kyngs, the rather at this my motion, ore þat ye wyll please to send me word of his disposition, to thentent I may further do & provide that best may before the poore mans suerty in this partie, and þat I may know the sayd Sir Robart is disposition by you herin; whereby ye shall bynd me to do your good pleasures, if it be in me. So knoweth our lord God, who preserue you. Fro Gascoyn,[a] in vj day of September.

By yours verely Rich: Empson[b]

Endorsed: To the right worshipfull Sir William Gascoygne kt deliuer these

[a] *A copyist's error: Stapleton suggests 'Easton', Richard Empson's house in Northants, p. 123n.*
[b] Gascoyn *deleted*.
[c] *Appended*: Copied the 17 day of March 1612.

[1] Empson was at this time attorney-general of the Duchy, Somerville, i, 392–3.
[2] Richard Fawberg, Introd., above p. 14.
[3] Fawberg was the surviving feoffee for the midlands estates, App. II, 29.

121 *Edward Plumpton to Sir Robert Plumpton, 2 March [1496/7] (No. 194, p. 120)*

In my right humble & most hartyest wyse I recomend me vnto your good mastership & to my singuler goode lady. Sir, yt is so þat certaine lovers & frinds of myne in London hath brought me vnto the sight of a [*p. 131*] gentlewoman, a wedow of xl yeres & more,[a] & of good substance. First, she is goodly & beautyfull, womanly and wyse, as euer I knew any, none other dispraysed, of a good stocke & worshipfull; hir name is Agnes. She hath in charge but one gentlewoman to her daughter, of xij yer age. She hath xx mark of good land within iij myle of London, & a ryall[1] maner buyld [...][b] thervpon, to giue or sell at hir pleasure. She hath in coyne in old nobles cl, in ryalls – cl,[2] in debts xl*li*, in plate cx*li*, with other goods of great valour; she is called worth iij*li* beside her land.

Sir, I am bold vpon yor good mastership, as I haue euer bene, & if yt please God & you þat this matter take effect, I shalbe able to deserue althings done & past. She & I are agreed in onn mynd & all one, but her frinds þat she is ruled by desireth of me xx marke iointor more than my lands come to, & thus I answeered them, saying þat your mastership is so good master to me þat ye gaue to my other wyfe xij marke for hir ioyntor, in Studley Roger,[3] & now, þat it wyll please your sayd mastership to indue this woman in some lordship of yours of xx marke duryng her life, such as they shalbe pleased with; & for this, my sayd frinds offer to be bonden in M*li*. Sir, vpon this they intend to know your pleasure and mynd preuely, I not knowing. Wherfore I humbly besech your <good mastership>, as my especiall trust is & euer hath bene aboue all earthly creators, now, for my great promotion & harts desire, to answere to your pleasure & [...][c] my well & poore honesty; & I trust, or yt come to pass, to put you suertie to be discharged without any charg. For now your good and discret answere may be my making, for & she & I fortune, by God & your meanes, togyther our too goods & substance wyll make me able to doe you good service, the which good seruice & I, now & at all tymes, is & shalbe yours, to ioperde my life & them both. Sir, I besech your good mastership [*p. 131*] to wryte to me an answere in all hast possible, and after þat ye shall here more, with Gods grace, who preserue you & yours in prosperous felicyte long tyme to endure. Wrytten in Furnywall Inne in Oldborn, the ij day of March 1496.

Your humble seruant Ed: Plompton[d]

Endorsed (p. 130): To my master Sir Robt Plompton kt

[a] *Marginal note*: Ed: Plo: is to be married to a weadow.
[b] dig *deleted*.

[c] hart *deleted.*
[d] *Appended*: Copied the 7 of May 1613.

[1] Sufficient.
[2] The ryall, first minted in 1463, was valued at 10s. It replaced the noble, valued at 6s 8d, *Three Fifteenth-Century Chronicles*, 80.
[3] On 10 Dec. 1483 Edward Plumpton entered into a bond to release a rent out of Nether Studley granted to him and his first wife, Agnes, CB, 728.

122 *Edward Plumpton to Sir Robert Plumpton, 10 March 1496/7 (No. 201, p. 139)*

In my right[a] [...][b] humble wyse I recomende me vnto your good mastership & to my singuler good lady your wyfe; & wher it hath pleased almyghty Jhesu of his grace, by meanes of my lovers & frinds, to bryng me to þe sight & acquantance of a gentlewoman in London, whose name is Agnes, late wife of Robt Drayate, gent., who is a woman þat God hath indued with great grace & vertue. She is wyse & goodly & of great substance, & able for a better man then I am. Notwithstanding it pleaseth so þat I myght content hir frinds mynds, for hir [...][c] <iointor> is xx marke by yere þat they demand of me. My answare is to them þat I haue no lands but in reuersion, & þat yt pleaseth your good mastership to giue my last wyfe xij marke by yeare out of your lands;[d] & my especyall trust is þat it will please your mastership, for my promoton, & in especyall for my harts desir & wele, þat faythfull is set vpon this sayd gentlewoman, to grant & make sure to hir a ioyntor of xx marke yerely ouer all reprises during hir life, & I besech you [so] to do, & þat þe [...][e] <berer> hereof may be certayne of your mynd in the premysses, and also answere to them by your wrytting of þe same. This don, incontinent after Easter, I trust in Jhesu to fynysh this matter, for they demaund of me certayne lands & goods, as more at larg appereth within a byll here inclosed, the which I obserued in euery poynt to thaccomplishment of ther pleasures. Sir, you know I haue no lands nor lyving in substaunce, but onely of you; & this hapen, I shalbe more able to do your mastership service. From London, in my sayd master lodging, þe x of March 1496.

Your humble servant Ed: Plompton[f]

John Chasser of Lyncolnes
Sir William Chamber, chaplaine
Edward Chesseman

Endorsed: To my singuler good master Sir Robart Plompton kt

[a] *Marginal note*: 11 H.7 M.10.
[b] honorable *deleted.*
[c] 2 words *deleted.*

[d] *Marginal note*: Edward Plo: a suter in Midlesex. *Below*: non nuptia 10 m.1496. 11 H.7. *Below*: obiit 9 Aug. 1499 [*illeg.*].

[e] better *deleted.*

[f] *Appended*: Copied the 10 day of May 1613.

123 *Edward Plumpton to Sir Robert Plumpton, 19 March 1496/7 (No. 190, p. 125)*

In my most humble wise I recomend me vnto your good mastership & to my specyall good lady. Sir, I sent a letter this last weke to you by James Colton, seruant to Master Gascoyne, to shew to your mastership my fortune at this tyme, if your mastership be – as I dout no other in my mynd, nor with my words to noble men of worship, but that ye be - my good master, the which hath & euer shalbe to your honour & profitt. Though I haue afore this been chargable <to> you, now, I trust in God as true & as profitable to be, as euer I was, & much more, & [. . .][a] <able> to restore & amends make of all cost done to me afore tyme.[1] Sir, I besech you, after your most discret mynd & wysdome, to answere this messenger þat shall come to you for this iointer of xx marke, both in words & in your wrytting, so þat yt be to your honor & my poore honestie & truth & making in this world; for vppon þat answere lyeth my great wele, & if yt were otherwyse, my vtter vndoing for euer, the which God forbyde.[b] Yt shall cost your mastership no penny more, nor charge to you, for if your mastership say to him þat ye are content, & wold grant & make to him this ioynture incontinent after our marriage, when we two shall come to you, & shew yt louingly to þe sayd messenger, & in your wrytting to them agayne, & then all is done; for when I am maryed to hir thes men þat now are counsellers shall bere but little roome, & therfore this is a matter of no charg, & to me great promoton all manner of wayes.

She is amyable & good, with great wysdome & womanhood, & worth in land yerly xx marke & more to you at hir wyll, the which, I trust in God, shalbe loving for you & yours in tyme to come for euer. Also in gold & [. . .][c] siluer, coyned & vncoyned, D*li*, I thinke verily, as I perceyue by hir. Beside hir lands, in all she is worth X*li* marke & more. She hath refused for my sake many worshipfull men & of great lands, some of them hath offered to hir xl*li* ioynter within London. Notwithstanding, she is to me singuler good mystres, as after this your mastership shall know. This same day she gaue to [*p. 126*] me a chayne of gold with a crosse set with a ruby & pearles, worth xx*li* & more; & because þat [. . .][d] <ther> messinger shall bryng my letter with him <þat they se, for I clossed yt> afore to shew your mastership my mynd, I besech your mastership to cause him þat shall come with these letters from my mystres & hir counsellors, to haue good chere, þat I trust to deserue, & to send to me <a bill> by the same, as yt shall please you.

Sir, I haue sent to you iiij yerds of whit damaske for a cowrenet, as good as I cold bye any, & I wold haue sent much more things, saue only my business is great. Also I haue payd your fyne in the excheker, but I take not out a discharge vnto the next terme because I purpose to get a grant more. Also I besech your mastership to shew þe sayd messinger þat ye had no word from me this vj weeke, & no man in your place to know from whence this berer come, lest þat ther messinger shold vnderstand of my sending. Please yt your mastership to giue credence vnto this beror & let him departe or the other man come with the letters; & all such service as yt pleaseth you to comand me, yt shalbe done, with Gods grace, who euermore preserue you & yours in health & honor. Wrytten in Furnyualls Inne, the [...][e] <19> day of March 1496.

I humbly pray your mastership to cause the messinger to speake with my lady, & if hir ladyship wold send by him a token[f] to my master, yt shall avale hir another of xx tymes the valor. Now, & my good lady wold of hir great gentlenes and noble myne send a token as is within wrytten, [*p. 127*] I cold neuer deserue yt to hir, for yt shold be to me great honesty & the greatest þat euer I had, for by your mastership & hir I am put to more worship than euer I shold haue comyn to. Sir, <as I wrote in,> I was purposed to haue sent a fellow of myne to your mastership, but now I send this my wrytting by Preston, seruant with my Master Gascoigne. Pleaseth your mastership to kepe this byll; & whatsoeuer you doe for me in word, cost & wrytting, yt shalbe mine, when we be maryed, to relesse & vnbind; & so I will. Sir, I besech you pray my lady to make þe messinger that shall come from my mistres good chere. I know not at yet what shall come, but as I am informed, a gent of Clementts Inne. I besech your mastership & good lady both, to take no displeasure with my simple wrytting this tyme, for my mynd is set so much otherwise þat I cannot perfictly do my duty.[2] Our Lord preserue you.

Your seruant Edw: Plompton[g]

Endorsed (p. 125): To my singuler good master Sir Robt Plom Plompton kt

[a] about *deleted*.
[b] *Marginal note*: Edward Plo: is to be married what [...].
[c] *Misspelling deleted*.
[d] my *deleted*.
[e] xx *deleted*.
[f] *MS* taken.
[g] *Appended*: copied the 6 of May 1613.

[1] **38n**.

[2] Edward and Agnes were married but their union was to be short. Less than four years later she appealed one Robert Tykhull of the murder of her husband, *CPR, 1496–1509*, 233.

124 *Edward Plumpton to Sir Robert Plumpton, 16 February [?1497/8] (No. 198, p. 135)*

[*p. 136*] In my most humble wyse I recomend me vnto your good mastership & to my singuler good lady. Sir, I haue bene at Sacombe[1] & had [...][a] <theder> with me from Ware, William Barlow, goodman of Christofer & William Waman, now for þe tyme baly; & of thos I haue bylls, of þe which I sent to your master the copies, of such woods as is sold later. The maner goeth downe & decayeth, & all þe houses about yt; the woods are clene destroyed & ligly to be in hast. I haue giuen & done as fare as I myght in comandment & charge for further felling & carying such as are felled & remane ther. Necessary yt were, me seames, þat ye made a bargain with Master Hastyngs, & it wold be. It is a fayre lordship & yt were well gidded, it is ix myle compasse about. Sir, I haue done good ther & avantaged much wood & tymber, both as were felled as not felled, & my doings wyll stand. I haue put byers in great fere. I pray you, master, in all hast possible, send to me word of your mynd in þe premysses & all other, & a byll of such lands as ye are [...][b] content to departe with to Kilborne[2] in exchange, & if ye will haue þe surcrortr.[3] Our lord Jhesu preserue you & all yours. From London þe xvi of February.[4]

Your humble seruant Edward Plompton[c]

Endorsed (p. 135): To my singuler good master Sir Robt Plompton kt deliuer these

[a] þe der *deleted*.
[b] *A word blotted*.
[c] *Appended*: Copied þe 8 of May 1613.

[1] The manor of Sacombe in Hertfordshire had descended to Isabel, wife of William Plumpton. At this date Sir John Hastings (d.1504) held the manor by courtesy of England, Introd., above p. 16, **126**; App. II, 63.

[2] On 28 Jan. 1501/2 Thomas Kilborne sold property in Plumpton to Sir Robert and his son and heir William, CB, 806.

[3] Surplus, excess.

[4] This is Edward Plumpton's last surviving letter.

125 *Henry Percy, 5th earl of Northumberland,*[1] *to Sir Robert Plumpton 20 January [?1498/9] (No. 47, p. 30)*

Right hartely beloued freind, I commend me vnto you, and pray you to apply your comyng vnto me according unto such order as was taken of late tofore your departure from me, and þat ye faile not herof, as my very trust is in you. Written in my castell of Wresull, the xx day of Januarie.

Yore cousin Hen: Northumberland[a]

Endorsed: To my right hartely beloued cousin Sir Robart Plompton kt

[a] *Appended*: This letter hath a seale. Copied the 25 day of February 1612.

[1] The writer of this and subsequent letters was probably Henry Percy, 5th earl of Northumberland (1478–1527), who achieved his majority in 1499, but was given livery of his lands 14 May 1498, App. III.

126 *John Pullein*[1] *to Richard Plumpton, clerk, [23 January 1498/9] (No. 213, p. 149)*

Sir, as hartylie as I can I commaund me vnto you; & within a box to my lady, to whom I pray you I may be recommended as hir servant, is the fest[a] of *Nomen Jhesu* with vtas,[2] & also the fest of the Transfiguration, that ye desired me to send to you. As for the price of them, ye & I shal agree at our next cominge togither. I doubt not ye know þat the *venire facias*[3] againe Ellis of York[4] com not according to our comunicacion; I wold it com vp servid [*p. 150*] any wyse this terme.

Sir, with Bryan Pullen [...][b] of Gawkthorpe I send a letter to my master & yours of all the [...][c] about the matter here at London againe Babthorpe,[5] as that none other way wold be in any wyse; but the *venire facias* com in served by one Thomas Rokeby,[6] servant to Mr Constable the servant.[7] The copie of the retorne & panell I send to you inclosed herin for more surtie, as tother letter is deliuered. Sir, to speake of the labor I maide to the contrary, I haue written the circumstance therof in my master letter, & surelye it was to þe vttermost of all my power. It is so now, I vnderstand, they will haue a *habeas corpora*[8] againe the iurrors retornable *Octabis trinitate*, so þat they may haue a distres with a *nisi prius*[9] againe Lammas assise. Therfore, Sir, between you & my lady ye must cause speciall labor be made, so it be downe preuely to such of iurrers as ye trust wilbe made frindly in the cause.

Sir, in the box is a bonet of velvet for [...][d] Mawleuery,[10] according to my ladies infirmacion; the price therof is x*s* viij*d*, so that I layd down xx*d* more than my lady toke to me for brying therof. Also trussed to the same box is a dagger to Master Pole,[11] according to his mynd; I pray you shew [it] to him, it cost viij*d* more then his money. As for the subpena, with all other matters that longeth to my master & you, they shalbe send with the next trusty messinger thet cometh home; & thus Jhesu be your preseruer. From Lyncolns Inne at London this Munday next afore Candlemas Day.

Servant John Pullen[e]

Endorsed (p. 149): To Sir [Robt *deleted*] Richard Plompton chapleyn at Idell

[a] *MS* fist.
[b] *Misspelling deleted.*
[c] *Blank.*
[d] *Blank.*
[e] *Appended*: Copied the xxth of December 1613.

[1] Probably succeeded Edward Plumpton as Sir Robert's principal man of affairs, App. III.
[2] Octave.
[3] Writ to summon a defendant against whom an indictment for a misdemeanour had been found.
[4] **127**, **128**.
[5] Introd., above p. 16; **124**; Apps II 56; III.
[6] **225**n.
[7] **153**; App. III.
[8] Writ commanding the sheriff to have before the court at Westminster, or before the judges of assise at *nisi prius*, the bodies of the jurors named in the panel to the writ.
[9] Writs of *nisi prius* empowered the king's justices to come into the country to receive jury verdicts there, for transmission to the bench on their return. Under *nisi prius* they had no original jurisdiction, but merely the power to proceed on issues referred to them for convenience out of one of the benches, Baker, *Introduction*, 19–20.
[10] Joan, daughter of Sir Robert Plumpton, married Sir Richard Mauleverer, CB, 799; App. III.
[11] Probably German Pole, **138**.

127 *John Pullein to Sir Robert Plumpton, [29 January 1498/9] (No. 151, p. 93)*

[*p. 94*] Sir, please yt your mastership to vnderstand þat I sent a letter to you with Bryan Pullan of Gawkthorp of all the cyrcumstances of þe matter betwene my master & your son & his wyfe, & William Babbthorp;[1] & as þat none ther wold be. But the *venyre facias* com in servid.[2] Sir, so yt is now pat surely they intend to haue a *habeas corpora* agayn the iurrours, with a *nisi prius* this next assise in Lent, at Yorke. Therfore, Sir, ye must make speciall frynds to the iurrours, þat they may be labored specially to such as ye trust wylbe made frindly in the cause.[3]

Sir, I have letton Mr Kyngesmell[4] see þe dede of gift of þe chaunchry of Elton,[5] & shewed to him as your mastership presented in after þe deith of þe last incumbent, which presentee was in by þe space if iiij or v dayes, at the least, & desired of hym to have his best counsell; & he answered to me thus: at *subpena* lay not properly in þe case, but þe best remedie for your incumbent was to haue assise at þe comon law, if any land belonged to þe sayd chaunchre; & if he had no land, then to have a spoliacion[6] in þe spirituall court agaynst þe preyst that now occupyeth, because he is one disturber, or els to suy a *quare impedit*[7] at þe comon law. And so is to take no *subpena*; & for these causes I rest to I know your pleasure [or] wryting. Sir, as for þe subpena agaynst Sir John Hastyngs, I shall remember it; þat accion of wast agaynst Sir John Hastings goeth forward as fast as þe law wyll serve.[8] And if þer be any other service to doe, it shalbe done to all my power, with Gods grace, who be your preserver. From Lyncolns Inn at London, this Tuesday next Candlemas Day.

Your servant and bedman John Pullan[a]

Endorsed (p. 93): To his especyall good master Sir Robt Plompton knight at Idell in hast

[a] *Appended*: Copied þe 21 day of Aprill 1613.

[1] **126**n.

[2] Against John Ellis, of York, **126**, **128**.

[3] In a case of novel disseisin the jurors were required to inspect the lands in question before coming into court ready with their verdict, Donald W. Sutherland, *The Assize of Novel Disseisin* (Oxford, 1973), 1, 18.

[4] **129**.

[5] The Derbys manor of Elton with the advowson of a chantry in the chapel of St Margaret in the parish church was conveyed by Sir William to Dean Andrews of York and his co-feoffees in 1475, although it was then the subject of a dispute with Thomas Foljambe of Walton, who claimed it as heir of Sir Edward Foljambe (d. before 1464). On 2 Nov. 1479 Sir Edward's widow conveyed the right of seisin to Sir William, but it was excluded from Richard III's award 16 Sept. 1483 because the title was still in question, CB, 598, 693; App. II 40, 48.

[6] Writ for the purchaser against the disturber where no right of patronage was in dispute.

[7] Writ for the recovery of an advowson.

[8] **124**n.

128 *Thomas Lyster to Sir Robert Plumpton, [4 February 1498/9] (No. 164, p. 106)*

After due recomendations, please yt your mastership to vnderstand þat of late I was at Yorke, wher I vnderstand ye haue an accon hanging against myne host John Ellis of Yorke, wherof I am right sory, for the good hart I bere to him, þat he shold myscontent your mastership &

giue you cause of accon. Neuerthelesse, Sir, I haue broken my mynd, & he is not þat man þat wold displease your mastership in no wyse, nor troble you in any matter; & for any fault, whatsoeuer yt be, abyde your owne iudgment & award in euery poynt, & be corrected in all causes after your owne mynd, if yt please your mastership so to take him. And ouer this, he shall come to your mastership & submyt him selfe acording to his duety, as yt is aboue sayd; &, Sir, if your mastership be thus content, I trust ye will se him have fre lyberty in comyng & goying; & if yt please your mastership to be thus content, & þat I [*p. 107*] come with him to you, I trust to God he shall so deserve at his departure, ye shall haue cause to be his good master; & so as I may besech you to be, vpon this humble submyssion, for I have advysed him so to doe, þe which he is right glad and aplyable; & thus our blessed Lord euer preserue you. Wrytten at Harwood the Sunday after Candlemasse Day; & by this bringer I besech your mastership I may know your good mynd.

Your louing servant Thomas Lyster[a]

Endorsed (p. 106): To my worshipfull master Sir Robt Plompton kt

[a] *Appended*: Copied þe 27 of Aprill 1613.

129 *William Elleson*[1] *to Sir Robert Plumpton 12 February [1498/9] (No. 140, p. 85)*

Right worshipful Sir, I recomend me to you. By your letter I understand William Babthorp will haue a *nisi prius* at this next assizes.[2] Sir, it is necessary for you to get a copy of the panel, & then to enquire if any of them, or if their wyfes be sybb or allied to William Babthorp, and yf any cause in them bee wherby they may be challenged. And also to make labor to them that they appeare not, or els to be faourable to you, according to right, & enform them of the matter as wel as ye can for their consciences. Sir, for Mr Kingsmel,[3] it were wel doon that he were with you, for his auctority & worship, for he may speke more plainly in the matter then any counsel in this country will, for he knowes the crafty labor that hath been made in this matter; & also he will not let for no maugre. And yf the enquest passe against you, he may shew you summ comfortable remedy. For I suppose with good counsel you may haue remedy. But, Sir, his comming wilbe costly to you.[4] Sir, I purpose, with the grace of God, to be at Knaresburg upon Tewsday next coming, & if ye be there, or any for you, I shall shew you more of my mind. No more, but God perserue you & further treweth. Written the 12 day of Februar.

By your servant at his litle power William Eleson[a]

Endorsed: To his right worshipful master Sir Robart Plompton kt be this deliuered

[a] *Appended*: Copied 19 April Munday 1613.

[1] Possibly an older half-brother of Sir Robert's daughter-in-law, Isabel, née Babthorpe. He and Sir William Gascoigne were nominated by Sir Robert to treat for him during the trial of Bubwith & Burgh v. Plumpton at York assizes in Sept. 1502, Stapleton, 218n; **250**; CB, 824; App. II, 64.

[2] The case appears to have been heard at York assizes in the Michaelmas term, 1499, BL, Add. MS 32,113, fols 230–234v; **142**.

[3] John Kingsmill (d.1508), called sergeant 1495, king's sergeant 1497, JCP 1508. Noted for his high fees, E.W. Ives, 'The Reputation of the Common Lawyers in English Society, 1450–1550', *University of Birmingham Journal*, *vii* (1960), 152; Idem, *CL*, 123, 467; Idem, 'The Common Lawyers of Pre-Reformation England', *TRHS*, 5th ser., xviii (1968), 145, 157.

[4] There were several challenges to proposed members of the jury on the ground of consanguinity, BL, Add. MS 32,113, fols 233–233v.

130 *William Elleson to Sir Robert Plumpton [1498/9]* *(No. 141, p. 86)*

Right worshipfull Sir, I comend me to you. Sir, this day I receyued your letter, by the which ye desyred me to be at Helagh[1] vpon Myghellmas even. Sir, þat day I may not keepe, for I must then be at Malton for my Lord Clifford, for keeping of his court.[2] But if it please you to send to Master [...][a] Babthorppe, which is yet at Dighton,[3] to appoynt Fryday or Satterday before Myghellmas Day, or Fryday or Satterday next after Myghellmas, I shall then attend of you, with the grace of God; & of the day that ye appoynt, I pray you send me word by my servant. Sir, I pray you [...][b] hold me excused of the breaking of my promyse, for I was vij nyghts from home more then I went I should haue bene when I rodde forth; & thus God preserve you. Wrytten at Selby this Wedensday.

By your servant William Eleson[c]

Endorsed: To his right worshipfull master Sir Robart Plompton kt

[a] Which is y *deleted*.

[b] send me word *deleted*.

[c] *Appended*: Copied the 19 of Aprill 1613.

[1] In CB, fols 159–62 are extracts from the Coucher Book of the Augustinian priory of St John the Evangelist, Healaugh Park, near Wetherby, recording grants made by Peter de Plumpton and others.

[2] Henry, 10th Lord Clifford, later 1st earl of Cumberland (d.1542). Elleson was apparently his steward at Malton.

[3] Kirk Deighton, near Plumpton.

131 *John Taylor to Sir Robert Plumpton, [20 March 1499]* *(No. 172, p. 111)*

Right honorable Sir, I humbly recomend me vnto [your] mastership. Please yt your mastership, I wold be right glad þat ye wold haue a commynyng with my master in such matters as in parte I haue shewed you, Sir. Sir, I have so spoken to my master, if ye please to be at Poumfrett on Munday, ther & then my master will meet you, [*p. 112*] and ther your mastership to know in thosse ye wilbe content; and or els your mastership will pardon me þe reuersion of Kirkbey,[1] & <I> wyll abyde with my master Sir John Hastynygs. Sir, I thinke, if yt please your mastership, I haue desarved[a] a dobellett in laboring him to showe your mastership a pleasure.[b] No more at this tyme, but Jhesu haue you in his protecion. Wrytten at Watterton on Wedensday after St Edward Day.[c]

By your servant John Tayler

Endorsed (p. 111): To my right worshipfull master Sir Robt Plompton kt

[a] *MS* resarved.
[b] *Marginal note*: John Tailoir.
[c] *Appended*: Copied the 29 of Aprill 1613.

[1] Kirkby Wharfe, near Tadcaster, part of the Babthorpe inheritance, App. I, 5.

132 *The earl of Northumberland to Sir Robert Plumpton, 27 March [?1499]* *(No. 49, p. 30)*

Right hartely beloued cousin, I commend me vnto you. And whereas I of late hath had in ward two servants of Thomas Myddleton[1] for hunting within my parke of Spofford, which I send vnto you by my servant, Richard Saxton, praying you, therefore, to take an obligation of them, and two sufficient men bounden with them in the (sume of xx*li* to be) of good bearing, and in law themselves [*p. 31*] vppon viij dayes warning whensoever I send for them. Not failing, as my singuler trust is in you, whom God keepe. Written in my mannor of Semar, the xxvij day of March. Over this, cousin, I hartely thanke you in executing my commaundment.

Your cousin Hen: Northumberland

Endorsed (p. 30): To my right hartely beloued cousin Sir Robart Plompton kt

[a] *Appended*: this letter hath a seale. Copied the 27 day of February 1612.

[1] **14**; App. III.

133 *The earl of Northumberland to Sir Robert Plumpton, 2 April [?1499] (No. 44, p. 29)*

Right hartely beloued cousin, I commennd me vnto you, (and desire and) pray you to cause suer search to be made what horse & cattaille (there be) that goes in my spring within my parke at Spofford, and such as can (be found) their, I pray you to se them dryven & voyded out therof, & also henceforth þat ye will se neither horse nor cattell goe not into my said spring, as my speciall trust is in you, whom God preserue. Written in my mannor of Semar, the ij day of Aprill. Ouer this, cousin, I hartely pray you to se my said parke vewed, & <þat> the dere within the same may be easily delt withall, & what remains within the same, I pray you to certifie me after the said vew be taken.

Your louing cousin Hen: Northumberland[a]

Endorsed: To my right hartely beloued cousin Sir Robart Plompton kt

[a] *Appended*: this letter hath a seale at [the copying]. Copied the 23 day of February 1612.

134 *Geoffrey Beyton, abbot of Lilleshall,[1] to Sir Robert Plumpton 26 May [?1499] (No. 66, p. 39)*

Right worshipfull Sir, I comand me to you, beyng glad to here of your welfaire. Sir, I hartely thank you for my tennaunts of Arkenden, praying you of good contynuance, and also for your wryting, the which ye send vnto me towching to the lands of myne in Arkenden. Sir, I haue sent to you by my servant, Thomas Morton, the copis of my evydents of the ix acres of land, the which they clame intrest for the king, and I trust þat I haue sent to you such wrytting as shall dyscharg that matter. Sir, I pray you þat ye will shew my matters according to right & after your good mynd, for I remytt all vnto your good wysdome. Sir, it is so þat I am a yong beginner of the world in my office, & Sir, for your good will and counsell I will þat my officer reward to you yearly vj*s* viij*d* as was rewarded to other men afor tyme, praying you of your good contynuance; and anything as I can, [I will,] as God [knoweth,] who have you in his blessed keeping. Amen. Written at Lilleshull, the xxvj day of May.

Your loving frind the Abbot of Lilleshull[a]

Endorsed: To the worshipfull in God, Sir Robart Plompton knight these letters be deliuered in hast

[a] *Appended*: Copied the 11 day of March 1612.

[1] Elected 1499, in office 1516. Presumably Sir Robert's stewardship would require confirmation by a new abbot, **104**n.

135 *John St Andrew of Gotham*[1] *to Sir Robert Plumpton* *(No. 113, p. 68)*

Right worshipfull Sir, in my best manner I lowly recomend me to you, hartely desiring your welfare, thanking you of þe patience þat ye sufferred at my poore place, I being from home. God giue me grace once to see you ther againe, þat I may make you better chere & doe you sume pleasure. Moreover, Sir, it pleased you to write to me of a gentlewoman for my son. Sir, God giue me grace to deserve it, and I thanke you hartely þat it pleased you so louyngly to remember both him & me. Sir, her[a] frinds bene worshipfull, and I am a poore gentleman. Well I wotte they will learne, whosoeuer they medle withall, what landes and substance he is of. I am willing to depart with him in lands and in goods, as he may lyve, so þat I may haue, according to reason, money or els lands, and to giue money. And, Sir, I am moued in a place of worship and haue made promyse to see a gentlewoman. Howbeit, lyke as I doe, ye shall haue knowledg, & I shalbe glad to be moved and counseld by you, trystyng ye wilbe gud master and lover to me. And thus Jesu preserue you. At Gotham in hast. Scribled with the hand of your owne, at my litle poore.

John Saint Andrew[b]

Endorsed: To the right worshipfull Sir Robart Plompton kt delyver these

[a] *MS* ther.
[b] *Appended*: Copied þe 10 day of Aprill 1613.

[1] A Notts gentry family which claimed a distinguished ancestry, but had failed to augment its fortunes by marriage, Payling, 73–4, 245; **147**.

136 *The earl of Northumberland to Sir Robert Plumpton, 15 June [?1499]* *(No. 58, p. 34)*

[*p. 35*] Right hartely beloued cousin, I commend me vnto you. And wheras variance and discord is depending betwixt my servant Thomas Saxston and Richard Ampleford,[1] of my lordshipe of Spofford, the cause wherof, as I am enformed, hath bene, or this, shewed vnto you, and if it hath not, I desire & pray you reply to examen it, and therevpon to shew your louyng diligence, not onely to se the peace kept in this behalfe, but also to sett the sayd parties at agreement, so that this matter may be pacefied. And for as much as ye have the rule ther vnder me, I pray you to shew you of semblable disposicion if any matter of varience hereafter happen within your sayd rule, so that the parties sue not to me, if ye by your discret wysdome can reforme it, as my very trust is in you. And in this doyng ye shall shew vnto me thankfull pleasure, that knoweth God, who preserue you. Written in my castill of Wrekworth, the xv day of June. Cousin, I pray you to se this matter pacefied, that there be no more calling vpon me therfore, as my very trust in in you.

Your cousin Hen: Northumberland[a]

Endorsed (p. 34): To my right hartely beloued cousin Sir Robart Plompton knight

[a] *Appended*: this letter hath a seal. Copied the 6 day of March 1612.

[1] A Richard Ampleforth witnessed the will of Sir Robert's eldest son William who died 1 July 1547, *Test.Ebor.*, vi, 260.

137 *Robert Leventhorpe*[1] *to Sir Robert Plumpton [14 September 1499] (No. 163, p. 105)*

[*p. 106*] After due recomendations to your good mastership & hartely desire of your welfare, for which, of duty, I am euer bound to pray for. And sithe I hard say þat a servant of yours as decesed of the sicknes which hath bene to your disease,[2] I am right sorey therfore. Wherfore I wold aduise your mastership, my lady & all your houshold many from hencforth to make promyse, & keepe yt, to fast the euen of St Oswald [...][a] king & marter,[b] yerly;[3] and þat promyse truly entended to be performed, I trust verely ye shalbe no more vexed with þat sicknes, & thus the Most Myghty preserve you & yours, this fest of Exaltacon of þe Holy [Cross][c].

Your servant Rob[ert] Leventhorp[d]

Endorsed (p. 105): To my right worshipfull master Sir Robt Plompton kt

[a] & kepe yt *deleted*.
[b] *Marginal note*: A remindir for preventing of þe plage.
[c] *MS* ghost.
[d] *Appended*: Copied þe 27 of Aprill 1613.

[1] **69**.
[2] London and Oxford suffered heavily from an outbreak in 1499–1500. Among the local victims was the archbishop of York, Thomas Rotherham, at Cawood, Creighton, 287; F. Drake, *Eboracum* (1736), 447; D.M. Palliser, 'Epidemics in Tudor York', *NH*, viii (1973), 47.
[3] 5 Aug. Lady Margaret Beaufort acquired a manuscript book (*c.*1500) that included a list of prayers and anthems for use by those seeking protection against the pestilence, Jones, *King's Mother*, 147.

138 *German de la Pole*[1] *to Sir Robert Plumpton [c.1499]* *(No. 98, p. 57)*

[*p. 58*] Right <honorable> & worshipfull father & mother, in þe most lowliest wyse þat I can, I mekely recomend me vnto you, desiring to here of your welfare & prosperitie, the which I pray almyghty Jhesu long to continew, to his pleasure & to your most ioy & comforth and harts ease. Also, father, my brother William[2] hartely & mekely recomendeth him vnto you, and vnto my lady my mother, desiring you of your dayly blessing; and I also pray you of your dayly blessing, the which is as glad vnto me as vnto any child þat you haue, <for I haue> no other father but you, nor no other mother but my lady, for my speciall trust is in you. Therfore I pray you take me as your poore son; a beadman for my prayer you shall wyt I life. Sir, if it pleaseth you to know þat a Munday my brother was at Thornton Brygge and I were; all, blessed be almyghty Jesu, be in gud health; & my sister Margett, & my wife, & my sister Elinor lowly comend them vnto you and vnto my lady,[3] praying you of your daily blessing, the which is better vnto them then any worldly goods. Veryly, Sir, Master Nevele nor Mistress Nevele,[4] neither of them, was at home, but his brother[5] was at home, & he made us very great chere as myght be.

Also, Sir, I am very sory þat the death seaseth not at Plompton, but I trust to almyghty Jhesu that his great mercy & grace [...][a] send to my lady hir ioy & comforth, & to all your frinds, as my daly prayer shalbe therfore. Sir, the cause of my wrytinge is but to heare of your gud welfare, the which is to me great ioy & comforth. And, Sir, I lowly pray you & my lady my mother to take this letter in gud parte, for it is wrytten hastyly with my own hand & without the vise of any other body; for I trow you had rather haue it of my own hand then of another bodyes. Also Sir John Tynderley recomendeth him vnto you, & vnto my lady my mother, gladly willing to heare of your welfare. No more vnto you, gud father, nor mother, at this tyme, but pray þe holy Trenytie to haue you in his blessed keeping.

Your good son & beadchild German Pole[b]

Endorsed (p. 57): To his right worshipfull father Sir Robart Plompton kt be these letters deliuered in most godly hast

[a] *Blank.*

[b] *Appended*: Copied þe 29 day of March 1613.

[1] Son of John de la Pole, of Radburne, Derbys, deceased, and grandson of Elizabeth (**159**), now aged about 16, App. III.

[2] Sir Robert's son and heir, William Plumpton.

[3] Sir Robert may have sent his daughters Margaret and Eleanor away from plague-stricken Spofforth, **137**.

[4] Ralph Neville and his wife, Anne, daughter of Sir Christopher Ward of Givendale, **51**, **149**.
[5] John Neville.

139 *Robert Eyre III*[1] *to Sir Robert Plumpton [15 October 1499]* *(No. 107, p. 64)*

Right worshipfull brother, I recomend me vnto you & to my lady, & also to my daughter[2] & yours, with all my other yong cousins, desiryng hartely to here of your welfaire & theres both, which I besech Jesu preserve vnto his pleasure & your harts comforth, ever thanking you & my lady, both, of þe great worshipe & gud chere þat I & my frinds had at my last beyng with you. Brother, it is so þat your farward, Christopher Law, is departed of this word & hath left behind him a wyfe & vij smale children; wherfor I hartely pray you to be gud master vnto hir, so þat she might haue hir farme, & the rather for my prayer; & if it please you, when your servants come over into this country, þat they will haue my mynd in the letting of the sayd house; & I trust to take such wayes therin as shalbe for your worship & profit both, as Jesu knoweth, who ever preserue you. At Padley, the Tewsday next afore St Luke Day in hast.

Your loving brother Robert Eyre[a]

Endorsed: To my right worshipfull brother Sir Robart Plompton kt this byll be deliuered

[a] *Appended*: Copied þe 7 of Aprill 1613.

[1] Son or younger brother of Robert II, **69**; App. III.
[2] Sir Robert's daughter Margaret, wife of the writer's son Arthur Eyre.

140 *The earl of Northumberland to Sir Robert Plumpton, 29 October [?1499]* *(No. 43, p. 28)*

Right hartely beloued cousin, I comaund me vnto you. And for as much as I am destetute of running hounds, I desire & pray you to send me a copple with my servant, this bringer. And of thing like I have fore your pleasure, it shalbe redy. Written in my lodging at Spetell of the Street,[1] the xxix day of October. Ouer this, cousin, I pray you send me your tame haert, for myne dere ar dead.

Your cousin Hen: Northumberland

Endorsed: To my right hartely beloued cousin Sir Robart Plompton kt

[1] Spital-in-the-Street, Lincs.

141 *John Morre to Sir Robert Plumpton* (*No. 167, p. 108*)

Right worshipfull & my especiall good master, I recomend me vnto your mastership, thanking your mastership hartyly of your kindly & hartely mastership shewed vnto me, vndeserued of my partie as yet. I besech almyghty Jhesu þat I myght doe þat thing <myght> be pleasure to your mastership: ye shall haue my seruice. I haue many things to thanke your mastership for, & especially for Richard Ampleforth, the which I besech your mastership to be good master to helpe, ayd & assist him in his necessitie; & wher he thinks that he offendeth to your mastership in any behalfe, he shall amend it at your pleasure. Your mastership shall vnderstand his wyffs confescion, as she hath shewed vnto me.[1] She besecheth your mastership to be [*p. 109*] hir good master & to helpe hir & sucker hir in hir great necesity, & to set hir in rest & peace anente Thomas Saxton; for without your mastership wilbe good master to hir husband & to hir, she shall neuer be in rest & peace; & if she wilbe a good woman, it is a good and gracious dede to your mastership to help hir; & if I know þat she wold be a miskidyd woman, I shold neuer speake word to your mastership for hir, nor to no other also.

I besech your mastership to be good master to John Myming, your owne servant. I trust veryly þat you haue a trew seruant of him, to his power, to whome I pray your mastership to give credence. I beseech God thank your mastership of þe great reward þat you gaue the sayd John Myming, whom you sent into Bishopprike[2] to me. No more at this tyme, but I am your seruant, as God knowes, who your mastership preserve to his pleasure. At Knaresbrough in hast.

Your servant John Morre[a]

Endorsed (p. 108): To my most speciall good master Sir Robt Plompton knight be this deliuered in hast

[a] *Appended*: Copied þe 27 of Aprill 1613.

[1] **136**.
[2] County Durham.

142 *John Pullein to Sir Robert Plumpton, 21 November [1499]* (*No. 155, p. 97*)

Right worshipfull Sir, I recomend me vnto your mastership. Sir, laytly I sent wryting to my father[1] to convey to you, which I trust becomes to your hands afore this tyme, in which wrytinge is conteyned how the iustices of the common place [*p. 98*] awarded a new *venire facias* betwyxt my master your son and William Babthorpp;[2] and also in a lytle byll therin is contayned all the names of such persones as the sayd William Babthorpp entended to haue had reconnyd in the first *venire facias*. I wold your mastership made specyall labor to haue one indefferent pannell of þer coroners; they must be labored by sum frynd of yours. Sir, the proces in thaccion of West goeth forward as fast as the law wyll serue. Sir, I receued two letters from you with xxvj*s* viij*d*, and all such copies as was conteyned in your wryting.

Sir, so yt was þat Parkin Warbek & other iij were arreyned Satterday next before þe making herof[3] in þe Whithall at Westmynster for ther offences, afore Sir John Sygly, knight marshall,[4] & Sir John Trobilfeild,[5] and ther they all were attended, & iudgment given þat they shold be drawn on hirdills from þe Tower, throwout London to þe Tyburne, & ther to be hanged & cutt down quicke, & ther bowells to be taken out & burned; ther heads to be stricke of, & [...][a] quartred, ther heads & quarters to be disposed at the kings pleasure; & on Munday next after at þe Gildalle in London, wher þe iudges & many other knyghts commysioners to inquer and determayn all offences and tresspasses; & theder from the Tower was brought viij persones which were indited, & parte of them confessed themselfe gyltie, & other parte were arreyned, & as yet they be not iuged.[6] I thinke the shall haue iudgement this next Fryday. Sir, this present day was new barresses made in Westmynster Hall, & thether was broguht therle of Warwik & arrened afore therle of Oxford,[7] being the kings greate comyssioner, & afore other lords, [*p. 99*] bycause he is a pere of the realme, whos names followeth: the duke of Bokingham, therle of Northumberland, therle of Kent, therle of Surrey, therle of Essex; the Lord Burgenny, Lord Ormond, Lord Beyngham, Lord Broke, Lord of Saynt Johns,[8] Lord Latymer, Lord de la Warre, Lord Mountioy, Lord Daubeney, Lord Hastings, Lord Barns, Lord Zowch, Lord Sentmound,[9] Lord Willoughby, Lord Grey of Wylton and Lord Dacre; & ther therle of Warwek confessed thenditments that were layd to his charge, and like iudgment was given of him as is afore rehersed. When thes persones shalbe put in execution I intend to shew to your mastership right shortly. And give credence vnto this berrer. From Lyncolns Inn at London this xxj day of November.

By your servant and bedman John Pullan[b]

Endorsed (p. 97): To his especyall gud master Sir Robart Plompton knight

[a] burne *deleted*.
[b] *Appended*: Copied þe 23 of Aprill 1613.

[1] Probably Richard Pullein of Kirby Hall and Killinghall, near Knaresborough, Somerville, i, 179.

[2] **148**; Introd., p. 16.

[3] John Atwater (mayor of Cork), his son, and John Taylor, arraigned 16 Nov. 1499, Robert Fabyan, *The New Chronicles of England and France, in Two Parts*, ed. Sir Henry Ellis (1811), 687.

[4] Sir John Sely.

[5] Sir John Turbervile of 'Suthwerk', Surrey, marshal of the Marshalsea, steward and constable of Corfe, treasurer of Calais, *CPR, 1494–1509*, 365, 367; *RP*, vi, 367.

[6] They were found guilty of a plot to slay the marshal of the Tower and release the earl of Warwick 18 Nov. R.L. Storey believes the whole episode was engineered by the king, *The Reign of Henry VII* (1968), 87.

[7] Arraigned 19 Nov., executed 29 Nov., Sir Henry Ellis (ed.), *Original Letters Illustrative of English History* (3 vols, 1824), i, 34–8; *Anglica Historia*, 116–19.

[8] Stapleton suggests this was the Prior of St John's Clerkenwell, 143n.

[9] Richard Beauchamp, Lord St Amand (d.1508), attainted 1483/4 but soon pardoned, *GEC*.

143 *Robert Eyre III to Sir Robert Plumpton, 14 February [1499/1500] (No. 102, p. 61)*

Right worshipfull brother, I recomend me vnto you, & to <my> lady your wyfe, and to my daughter & yours, with all my other cousins your childred, desiring to heare of your welfaire & thers both, which I besech Jesu preserve vnto your most harts comforth, evermore thanking you & my gud lady your wyfe of the great & worsipfull chere þat I & my kynsmen had with you. Brother, ye be remembred how the writings of the couenaunte of marrage of my son & your daughter, as it be not made vpp by the [...][a] <vise of learned> counsell; wherfore, if it please you to apoynt any day, & please about þe beginyng of <Lenten>, when þat I might wayt vppon you, I wilbe glad to wayt vpon you & a learned man with me; & all such promyse as I haue made on my part shalbe well & trewly performed,[1] with the grace of Jesu, for ye shall find me ever one man. Also, brother, I pray you þat ye wold send me by my servant William Bewott, this bringer, the payment which I shold haue of you att Candlemas last past, for I haue put my selfe vnto more charge since I was with you then I had before, for I haue maryed another of my daughters, & I haue begon to make a wall about my parke þat I shewed you I was mynded to do, which, I trust, when ye se it, ye will like it well [...][b] <Praying you not to fale herin,> as my trust is in you, & to giue credence to this bringer. No more, but Jesu preserve you. Written at Padley on St Valantyne Day, with the hand of your brother

Robart Eyr[c]

Endorsed: To my right worshipfull brother Sir Robart Plumpton kt these be deliuered

[a] veyse of lurnd *deleted*.

[b] fale ye not to seytt *deleted.*
[c] *Appended*: copied the 3 day of Aprill 1613.

[1] A receipt dated 4 Aug. 1500 for 20m was received by Sir Robert in acknowledgement of an instalment on 250m covenanted for the marriage of his daughter Margaret with the writer's eldest son, the future Sir Arthur Eyre. For her keep 50*s* was to be allowed out of each instalment, CB, 800; **139**, **218**.

144 *George Emerson*[1] *to Sir Robert Plumpton 1 May [1500]* *(No. 160, p. 103)*

Right worshipfull Sir, & my especiall good master, after due recomendations I hartyly thanke your mastership for many great things done for me afore this, beseching allmyghty God þat I may doe your mastership some service therfore. I receyued your letter by George Crose, and as for all your great matters, as yet nothing sayd. Yet yt is shewed me þat they purpose suerly to haue an assise this somer.[2] Wherfore I trust your mastership doth provide for þe best remedy, which after my mynd is to make many frinds & of the best. I send vnto your mastership, closed in this box, the sawar for the inditement, according to your comandement, which is retornabile xv *Trinitatis*; & thus almyhgty Jesu preserue your mastership & all yours to his pleasure. From London the first day of May, with one of your servant, to his power.

George Emerson[a]

Endorsed: To the worshipfull Sir Robart Plompton kt deliuer thes

[a] *Appended*: Copied the 24 of Aprill 1613.

[1] **146**.
[2] **119**.

145 *Robert Hastings*[1] *to Sir Robert Plumpton 30 August* *(No. 137, p. 84)*

Right worshipfull cousin, I hartyly recomend me vnto you desiring you to send me my letter John Talloyr delyvered you. Please yt you to doe so much for me in this terme, to leyn me & send vnto me by this berrer, James Potsay, v marke. I by this my wrytting fathfully I promyse you to content & pay you the sayd v markes by the date of this my byll at Mighellmas the next, & for þat defalt, I hearby dyscharg me, & ye to have all my lands & rents at Kyrby uppone Wharfe for ever.[2] And also I desire you to take credence unto this berer which knowes my mynd; & also this letter may recomend me vnto [. . .][a] my lady your wyfe; & euermore fare ye well, the xxx day of August.

Your cousin Robert Hastings[b]

Endorsed: To my right worshipfull cousin Sir Robart Plumpton knight

[a] your *deleted.*
[b] *Appended*: Copied the 19 of Aprill 1613.

[1] Probably a younger brother of Sir John Hastings, **124**, **127**, **148**.
[2] **131**.

146 *George Emerson*[1] *to Sir Robert Plumpton 10 November [1500] (No. 162, p. 104)*

Right wyrshipful Sir & my special good mastre, after dew recommendations had, I hartely thank your good mastership that it wold please you to cause mee to bee praied for. I beseeche almighty God that I may liue to do you such seruice therfore as may contente your mastership. I receiued your letter by Mr Sygskyke, clerk, & 2 ryals closed therin; and acording to your commandement I haue retained in the exchequer, by the aduice of Mr Blakewall, Mr Denny;[2] in the chauncry, Porter,[3] & giuen vnto them ther fees. I have deliuered all your letters, and from Mr Blakwall I trust ye haue answer by on of Mr Gascoygne servants; & also for all things compresed in your first letter þat I receiued by John Wadd, as touching any accion to be taken against [*p. 105*] you, or any *diem clausit extremum* for any office to be found, I shall doe therin as much as lyeth in my power, þat your mastership may haue knowledg therof. If ther be any such wryt made, yt must be in Porters office, & he hath promysed me þat ther shall none passe but he shall giue me knowledg therof; & if ther come an *inquisicio virtute officij*, yt must come into the office, wherat[a] Mr Deene is dayly. Wherfore I trust to God þat your mastership shall have knowledg if any such things fortune. They haue made search in the escheker for the perdon þat was pledet, suppose the title had bene made therin as here to Sir William, & when they saw þat it was by feffment they were not well content.

The names at are in the byll for to be schereff: Not[inghamshire] & Derb[yshire], Sir Ralfe Langford,[4] Ormond[5] & Such;[6] Yorkshire, Sir William Bulmer,[7] Sir William Engelby[8] & Sir W[alter] Griffith;[9] Sir Humfrey Stanley[10] laborers to be schereff in Staffordshire. Herof I shall acertan you as sonne as the byll cometh from the king. I haue receyued from your mastership xl*s*; at the end of this terme I shall send you a byll of all the matters of this terme; & as for the accon which procedeth against Sir John Hastyngs,[11] I shall contynue yt to the next terme, by þe grace of God who euer kepe you & yours. From London with the hand of your servant, the x day of November.

George Emerson

Sir, also yt was shewed vnto me by one Mr Newdigate[12] þat thes names for Not[tinghamshire] & Derb[yshire] were put in þe byll by þe labor of the sayd Mr Newdigate, at the request & desire of Sir William Meryngs heire;[13] & yt please your mastership, me semes yt were well done to send vnto Mr Meryng to know wheder he wilbe frindly in thes matters or no, & if he may doe anything with the aboue named personnes.[b]

Endorsed (p. 104): To the right wyrshipful Sir Robert Plompton kt in hast

[a] *MS* wheras.
[b] *Appended*: Copied the 26 of April 1613.

[1] The Lincoln's Inn accounts for 1500–1 record the receipt of 26*s* 8*d* from John Pullein and George Emerson for pensions, and their assignment to Newdigate's chambers, J.R. Walker and W.P. Baildon (eds), *Records of the Society of Lincoln's Inn: the Black Books* (4 vols, 1897–1901), i, 122.
[2] Edmund Denny, a clerk in the Exchequer, later appointed 4th baron, *CPR, 1494–1509*, 420, 436.
[3] William Porter, granted the office of clerk of the chancery for life, 12 Nov. 1504, *CPR, 1494–1509*, 401.
[4] Of Longford, Derbys, pricked, *List of Sheriffs*, 104; **147**.
[5] John Ormond, of Alfreton, Derbys (d.1503).
[6] William Zouche, of Morley, Derbys.
[7] Of Wilton, Yorks (d.1531).
[8] Sir William Ingilby, of Ripley, Yorks.
[9] Sir Walter Griffith, of Burton Agnes, Yorks (d.1531) was pricked, *List of Sheriffs*, 163.
[10] Sir Humphrey Stanley (d.1505), younger son of Thomas Stanley, earl of Derby.
[11] For detention of deeds, BL, Add. MS. 32,113, fol. 224v.
[12] John Newdigate called Sergeant, *DNB*.
[13] Sir William Mering, of Mering, Notts. His family's long-standing quarrel with the Stanhopes of Rempston, the latter now backed by Richard Empson, erupted into violence in 1501, when Sir William was set-upon and wounded by Sir Edward Stanhope, so that he was unable to attend the Notts quarter sessions. The Stanhopes and their allies, the Cliftons and Willoughbys, supported Empson against the Plumptons at York assizes, 1502, Payling, 192; Cameron, 29; **157**.

147 *Robert Blackwall*[1] *to Sir Robert Plumpton 16 November [1500]* *(No. 178, p. 116)*

[*p. 117*] Right worshipfull Sir and my especial good master, with due recomendation please yt your mastership to vnderstand þat Master Gryffith is schereffe of Yorkshir, Sir Ralfe Longford of Not[tinghamshire] & Derby[shire], & John Caston[2] of Staufordshire. And as for þe eshetours in Staffordshire, as yet, as fare as I know, is non. Ralfe Saucheuereth of Hopwell[3] is eschetour of Nottinghamshire, & Derby[shire], & as farre as I vnderstand William Crowch, þat was custymer of Hull, is eschetor of Yorkshire.[4] My lord of Carlile[5] hath athorytie to make eschetor ther, & as fare as I know or can learne þe sayd Crowch occupieth still ther; & as yet, as fare as I can vnderstand, ther is noe office found, nor as yet reconed, nether into þe chaunchry nor yet into þe eschetor after þe death of my master your father. I shall lye in awayte as much as I can therfore.

I pled for your mastership yere agoo a pardon[6] for Wolfehuntlands about Maunsfeild in Shirwood, by which plee ye clamed þe land by fefement of my master yore father.[7] A gentilman þat is of counsell with Master Empson enquered for the same plee, & saw yt, & was sory þat ye had not clamed þe saide land as son & heire.[8] Other tydings there be none, but þat make you redy, for surely, as farre as I kow, Mr Emson will in hand with you this yere, & as farre as I can know by <assise>.[9] I besech you þat I may be recomended to my good lady, my lady your wyfe, with Master Pole & my mystres his wyfe. My master recomendeth him to you & prayeth you to remember his I marc now, for he sath þat he hath nede therof.[10] And Jesu preserue you. From London in great hast <as apeareth> the xvj day of Nouember.[a]

Your seruant Robt Blakwell[b]

Endorsed (p. 116): To his right worshipfull & especiall good master Sir Robt Plompton knight be these deliuered in hast

[a] *Marginal note*: 15 H.7.
[b] *Appended*: Copied þe 30 of Aprill 1613.

[1] Clerk, of Blackwell, Derbys, master in chancery and attorney in the exchequer. A pluralist, he held numerous vicarages, including Mansfield, CB, 789; **85**, **91**.
[2] John Aston of Tixall, Staffs, J. Wedgwood, 'Sheriffs of Staffordshire', *Historical Collections of Staffordshire* (1921), 283; *List of Sheriffs*, 128.
[3] Ralph Sacheverell was probably a younger son of John Sacheverell, of Morley, Derbys, and younger brother of Sir Henry (d.1536), G.M. Marshall (ed.), *The Visitation of Nottinghamshire in 1569 and 1614* (Harleian Society, iv, 1871), 163.
[4] William Crouch was appointed escheator for Yorks 5 Nov. 1498, and held the office until 1506, *List of Escheators*, 72; *CPR, 1494–1509*, 504.
[5] William Senhouse, **45**, **50**.
[6] **84**.
[7] The feoffment was made by Sir William 6 Nov. 1475, CB, 598.
[8] It appears that the estates were not entailed to the heir male, but that Sir Robert held them as heir special, **146**, **152**; Stapleton, 147n, 131n; App. II, 35, 36.
[9] **119**.
[10] Sir Robert Lytton (d.1505), under-treasurer of England, who had a pecuniary interest in the marriage of German de la Pole, *CPR, 1494–1509*, 10; *Anglica Historia*, 52, 94.

148 *John Gascoigne*[1] *to Sir Robert Plumpton* *(No. 129, p. 78)*

Brother, I recomend me vnto <you>. This Sunday my nephew Sir William Gascoygne is ryden from home towards Colyweston,[2] & whether further or nay I know not. Howbeit I trow better he had not. Brother, he desired me to wrytt vnto you [. . .][a] praying þat ye wille content vnto this bringer, my cousin Robart Hastings[3] iiij markes and xx*d* now dew vnto him at this Martynmasse last, which is right gredy therupon, & gladly my nephew wold he were content. If ye wold any thing to London, send me word, þat I can; for I thinke I send one right shortly after my nephew. Thus farewell. At Gaukthorpe, this Sunday.

Your owne at his power John Gascon[b]

Endorsed: To my hartyly beloved brother Sir Robart Plompton knight

[a] wilbe *deleted.*
[b] *Appended*: Copied the 16 of Aprill 1613.

[1] Younger son of Sir William Gascoigne of Gawthorpe (d.1460), and Sir Robert's brother-in-law.
[2] **113**.
[3] **157**.

149 *Sir William Gascoigne to Sir Robert Plumpton* *(No. 71, p. 41)*

Vncle Plompton, I comend me unto you. And where I should haue bene with you tomorow at Selbie, in good fayth it is so þat I was yesterday so crased and sicke þat I kept my bedd all day, and this day I am not of power to goe, nor ride as yet. And also there is with me my vncle Ward,[1] Thomas Lawrance,[2] Ralfe Nevell,[3] & others; but þat notwithstanding, if I had my health I should be with you. And if ye cannot conclud tomorow, appoynt a new day, & I shalbe glad to be with you, with the grace of Jesu, who euermore keepe you. Scribled at Gaukthorp, this Fryday, in hast.

Your nepho William Gascoygne kt[a]

Endorsed: To my vncle Plompton be thes deliuered

[a] *Appended*: Copied the 13 of March 1612.

[1] Sir Christopher Warde of Givendale, whose wife, Margaret, was Dame Agnes Plumpton's sister, **168**.
[2] Of Ashton, near Lancaster, he married Sir Christopher Warde's daughter Margaret. In May 1490 he was commissioned to purvey capons, swans, pullets, pigeons and other fowl for the royal household, *CPR, 1485–94*, 304.
[3] **51**, **138**.

150 *Robert Plumpton*[1] *to Sir Robert Plumpton 12 January [1500/1] (No. 157, p. 100)*

After lowly & all due recomendations, I recomend me vnto your good mastership & good brotherhode, praying the same þat it will please you to send me by this berer the Martynmese farme for such lands & tenementes as ye haue by lease made betwext you & me; &, Sir, as I suppose, insomuch as ye pleased not to content me at þe vntermost day limytted in þe sayd lease, ye wylbe agreable þat I enter to þe sayd lands & tenements.[2] Wherfore, so I pray you to send me word in a byll by this berer, whether ye will þat I enter to the same lands & tenements, or þat ye will hold them still, & content according to the sayd lease; &, Sir, in so much as this is the first day of breach of your payment, I wyll nothing attempt therin to I haue word from you by this bearer, if it may please you. And almyghty Jesu preserve you in prosperouse lyffe, long to endure. From Yorke, the xij day of January.

Your servant Robt Plompton of Yorke[a]

Endorsed: To my right worshipfull master and brother Sir Robart Plompton knight

[a] *Appended*: copied þe 24 of Aprill 1613.

[1] 'Robinet', **26**, **154**.

[2] The property comprised parcels of land in the Derbys manor of Ockbrook, the reversion of which was granted by Sir William to his bastard sons Robert and William for life, CB, 600, 603; **88**.

151 *Henry Columbell*[1] *to Sir Robert Plumpton 6 March [1500/1] (No. 176, p. 114)*

[*p. 115*] Right worshipfull Sir, I recomend me vnto you, desiring to here of your welfayre. Certyfiing you I haue receyued your letter and hath spoken with Sir Edmond Batmon, & he is right glad of the mocion, and wyll abyde by yt for his dede, & by all things þat his attorney doth in his name, & so will shew to all men þat spurns[2] him any wher. But he is feard lest they wyll not appeare without a suppena; & if ther be any thing þat ether he or I can doe you seruice or plesure, we are you. No more at this tyme, but Jhesu preserue you. Wrytten at Darley in þe Peke, the vj day of March

By your lover & seruant Herrie Cullumbell[a]

Endorsed (p. 114): Vnto Sir Robt Plompton knight be this letter deliuered in hast

[a] *Appended*: Copied þe 29 of Aprill 1613.

[1] The Columbells were probably tenants of the Plumptons in the Derbys manor of Darley.

[2] Spur = to seek out, ask, J. Wright (ed.), *The English Dialect Dictionary* (6 vols, Oxford, 1898–1905).

152 *John Pullein to Sir Robert Plumpton, [18 May 1501]* *(No. 158, p. 95)*

Right worshipfull Sir, I recomend me vnto your mastership, letting you vnderstand þat laytly I wrott to you a letter of your matters, where was þat the great man E.[1] as [far as][a] vndoubted <as> I can know, intendeth to have assyses agaynst you. Wherfore tyme is to labor as well the schereffes as all your frynds, & euery country where your land lieth. It is soe þat the same great man E., with other of the kings counsell, sitting for assessyng of fynes for knyghts[2] [...][b] which may doe hym pleasure, he is intreated scetretly to [...][c] <owe> his god will. Ye may <haue trial> by lyklyhed what ther anyswere shalbe.[d] Thus he vndermyneth. But let you for no labour. All such copies of your matters resteth in my keeping; & this was <your lawiers> conclusion: þat your mastership should take a sure frynd[e] to se all your evydence, which I thynke after my mynd must be Mr Eleson,[3] to this entent: þat your sayd counsell may have all the estayts made by your graunser & father, as well vppon marrage lesses, as other wayes, & in lykwyse, how all the sayd estates come home agayne, wrytten verbatim in paper; & to have all your newe evidence by your father to John Norton & others,[4] & estates made to have to your father for terme of lyfe; & to send copies of all matters proving matrymony betwixt my sayd master your father, & my lady your mother;[5] & further prove which of the sayd feffees was present at possession. Like <they> be at London the beginning of thes next terme, w[ith] xl*li* [...][f] <Sir Rich:>[6] [and] ij men & the sayd copies. If Mr Eleson can fynd any of your lands talled to the here male, send copies therof. I think none be; & thus the holy Trenety send good speed to yours. From Lyncolnes Inn at London this Tuesday in the Crosse Dayes.[7]

Your servant John Pullan[g]

Endorsed: To the right worshipfull & his specyall gud master Sir Robart Plumpton kt deliuer these

[a] *MS* as for us.

[b] *Several illegible words.*

[c] note *deleted.*

[d] *Marginal note*: Assessing of fines for knights.

[e] *Marginal note*: I find no sure frends in all cause but George Emerson. Yaxley and Frowyk serieants and Brook and Edgar are your counselors.

[f] *MS Several words appear to be missing.*

[g] *Appended*: Much is omitted becaus it is riuen. copied þe 21 of Aprill 1613.

[1] Richard Empson.

[2] Fines for distraint of knighthood, Kirby, *NH*, xxv, 117.

[3] William Elleson of Selby. Sir Robert was being advised to 'prime his lawyer', Ives, *CL*, 298; **129**, **130**, **164**, App. II, 64.

[4] Sir John Norton of Norton Conyers was one of Sir William's feoffees for the conveyances of 1475, Introd., p. 4; **208**; CB, 586–603; Apps. II 35; III.

[5] Sir Robert's mother, Joan Wintringham, was dead by this time, **119**.

[6] Probably Sir Richard Plumpton, cler., **157**.

[7] Monday, Tuesday and Wednesday before Ascension Day, Stapleton 152n.

153 *John Pullein to Sir Robert Plumpton, [31 May 1501]* *(No. 154, p. 97)*

Right worshipfull Sir, I recomend me vnto your mastership, letting you vnderstand þat latly I sent dyvers letters to you, thaffect of which letters was þat your aduersaries intendeth suerly to attempt þe law against you. Therfore I can wryt no other thing to your mastership, but oftymes remember my wryting: it toucheth your worship & welle. Therfore make your frynds to take your part as frynds shold doe, as well in Nott[inghamshire], Derb[shire], as Yorkshire, and God, I trust, shalbe steresman in every ryghtwyse cause. Master Robt Constable, servant,[1] shalbe iustice of assise in Cornewall, Devenshir, and other west countryes, with Master Frowike,[2] so þat I trust he shal not be at this assise. Such pronunstications as a speciall freind let to me, I copied them, as your worship shall see & receiue herwithall, closed. As for all other causes, this bringer can shew to you by word as larg as I can wryte, as Jesu knoweth, who preserve you. From Lyncolns Inne at London, this Witsonemunday.

Your seruant and beadman John Pullan[a]

Endorsed: To the right worshipfull & his especiall good master Sir Robart Plompton knight

[a] *Appended*: Copied þe 23 of Aprill 1613.

[1] **126**.

[2] **152** (marginal note); App. III.

154 *Robert Plumpton and others to Sir Robert Plumpton, [1501]* *(No. 159, p. 101)*

[*p. 102*] After most lowly & all due recomendations, we lowly recomend us vnto your good mastership, certyfying you þat as fare as we can vnderstand or know, John Rocliffe & John Sotell[1] ar come to Knyreston Place,[2] & ther purpose to tary & abyde to such tyme as they thinke tyme convenient for to enter into your liflods in this country, & toke distor;[3] & we have bene at dyverse places of your liflods & finds your tenants well disposed toward you, & [...][a] sithen the most part of gentlemen in this country, & especyally þe Eyres, so þat ye wold come yourselfe & be sene amongst [...][b] your tenants & frynds, the which were to them a singler pleasure & comforth, & to yourselfe a great strength; & to bring with you not ouer the number of xx horse at þe most, & such as may have your aduise & counsell to take derection, the which may be to the suerty of your lyflod & tenants; & if ye can gett Master Mydleton[4] & bryng him with you, or Richard Grene,[5] or some other, & come to Hassop, for we haue deseuered us & some departed tham; & with the grace of Jesu, & ye come betwixt this & Tuesday, þat all things shalbe to your harts comforth in tyme to come. But Sir, they haue bene here diuerse tymes doing for your wele & pleasure, & thinkes ye will or dar not put you in iopartie for your owne. For & ye come they will put them in deuer to do any thing þat may be to the well of your liflod & tenants; &, Sir, bryng with you money convenient for your expenses, for as yet [*blank*] here be now rent teyned. Now ouer to you at this tyme, who the holy Trenety haue you in his keping.

By your servant Robinit Plompton with other moe[c]

Endorsed (p. 201): To our right worshipfull master Sir Robart Plompton kt be this letter deliuered in hast

[a] since *deleted.*

[b] them *deleted.*

[c] *Appended*: Copied the 25 of Aprill 1613.

[1] Sir John Sotehill, husband of Elizabeth Plumpton, having died in 1494 the writers are in error. The legal estate was by now vested in Robert Bubwith and Richard Burgh, Kirby, *NH*, xxv, 117; **120**; App. II, 58.

[2] Kinston Place, home of the Babingtons, Stapleton, 156n; **157**.

[3] The tenants of lands in contention were in an unenviable position, cf. Gairdner (ed.), *The Paston Letters*, nos 485–7, 579, 587.

[4] The lawyer Thomas Middleton, **14**, **132**; App. III.

[5] **51**.

155 *William Sanderson*[1] *to Sir Robert Plumpton, [1501]* *(No. 179, p. 117)*

After my duety, please yt your good mastership to wyt þat Sir John Rocliffe & Master Antony Clifford[2] [...][a] send for me to Notingam, & when I came þither they asked me whether I had brought money, and I shewed them ye herd receiued it alredy, & then they were very angree, with many sore words. I was neuer so werie & soferd of my life since I was borne; & they wrote euery word I sayd & more; & I trow, but þat they were in troble before, I shold neuer have escaped them; & all ther seruant beated me one after another. I trust I shall hold me at home if they send for me; & euer they thratte me þat I shold goe to London, & if I wold come up vnsent for yt shold be þe better for me; & if I taryed tyll I were sent fore I shold be vndone. Wherfore, Sir, I pray you let yt be loked to if they wold take out any accon against me. I bere me much of Master Sacheuerell, which is your stuard;[3] but they had me in þat case, whatsoeuer they sayd I durst not say nay, nor I wist not what I sayd nor what I did.

Your bayley & seruant William Sanderson[b]

Endorsed (p. 117): To my right worshipfull master Sir Robart Plompton knight

[a] said *deleted.*

[b] *Appended*: Copied þe 30 of Apryll 1613.

[1] On 2 July 1500 Robert Bubwith and Richard Burgh appointed William Sanderson and William Sacheverell their attornies to take seisin of the Derbys manors of Edensor, Stainton, Pilsley and Darley, of which the last-named had been awarded to the Plumptons in 1483, **120**; App. II, 58.

[2] Apparently Elizabeth Sotehill's attorney.

[3] By charter dated 7 March 1501 Thomas Sotehill, son and heir of John Sotehill enfeoffed Bubwith and Burgh in his manors of Ockbrook, Spondon, Chaddesden, and Hassop, of which the last-named was still in Plumpton hands, and appointed William Sanderson and Edmund Lenton his attornies therein, WYASYAS, MS. 650, p. 351.

156 *Robert Eyre III to Sir Robert Plumpton, [20 June 1501]* *(No. 105, p. 63)*

Right worshipfull brother, I recomend me vnto you. Brother, I haue receiued your letter, be the which I perceived ye be mynded to be with my lord of Schrewsbury[1] on Munday next, be noune of the day, & þat ye wold haue me to meet you by the way. Brother, my lord is at Wynfeld & my lady both, & I wilbe glad to wayte vpon you at Hegham, a myle from Wynfeld, or els at Chesterfeld, whether it please you. Brother, I am afrad lese this labour be vayne, for in certayne I caused all þe labur to be made possible at this tyme, both to my lord & to my lady, & he wold not be turned, for he myght not, & keepe his truth & promyse made afore. Notwithstanding, sithe ye be comyng on your way, I thinke it is well done, ye to speake with my lord yourselfe, as prevely as ye can, & thus Jesu kepe you. At Padley, the Sunday next afore the feast of St John Baptise.

Your loving brother Robart Eyre esquire[a]

Endorsed: To my right worshipfull brother Sir Robart Plompton kt these be deliuered

[a] *Appended*: Copied the 7th day of Aprill 1613.

[1] The writer was steward of the Derbys estates of George Talbot, 4th earl of Shrewsbury (d.1538), whose wife, Anne, was a daughter of William, Lord Hastings (d.1483). As the Eyres had been Hastings retainers, Sir Robert must have hoped the writer would prove an effective suppliant on his behalf, Wright, 62, 79; **70**, **77**, **106**, **143**.

157 *Richard Plumpton, priest,*[1] *to Sir Robert Plumpton [27 June 1501] (No. 145, p. 87)*

[*p. 88*] In my most humble wyse,[a] Sir, I recomend me vnto you & to my lady. Also, Sir, it is so, according to your wrytting þat ye send me by Robart Smyth, I sent a letter in your name to William Rossell,[2] & he sent me a copie of the inpanell that Rocliffe & Suttell intend shall passe agaynst you for the manner of Kenalton & the towne also,[3] which inpanell the sayd William Rossell had of þe under schereffe of Nottingham, & he gave him therfore ij*s*; which inpanell is so [...][b] favourable mayd, so I vnderstand by dyvers of your frynds now of layt, wylbe great hurt to your worship, & [...][c] except the great mercy of God & great labor & cost.[4] Also, Sir, I have spoken with the baylay of Byngham vapentake, & he will [...][d] <owe> you as mekell fauour as is in him doo, for hes master Beron[5] servant, & his name is Ednund Mylnes; & so I vnderstand by him his master wold doe also, if he were labord.

Sir, I have teryed at Kenalton this Satterday for the cause I cannot haue my money þat I should haue had of him,[6] & my horse wold bere me no further; & this Satterday I haue bought another horse of Robart Towyll of Nottyngham, for which I haue payd him v nobles, of which sume Thomas Haym of Kenalton hath lent me for your sake & my ladys xx*s*, which I have promysed in your name shalbe payd vnto him agayne, with the grace of God. Sir, I send vnto you a copie of þe inpanell that William Rossell sent vnto me, & all these þat is at þe end of the names ar hundrythars, as I vnderstand by the baylife of the waypentake of Byngham & other of your frynds and lovers; [*p. 89*] & also, Sir, Robart Smyth xx*s* & John Roger x*s* hath lent me xxx*s* for your sake and <my ladyes>. As for John Wellemett hath payd me iiij*li*. As for William Tusell[7] hath maryed Mr Beron syster; & as I vnderstand, Mr Berron may cause him & other of the inpannel. Therfore I thinke, by my simple advice, þat ye caused Mr Beron to be spoken withall, for if I myght haue had space I shold haue labored him in that matter. Sir, Thomas Babington[8] & a lerned man called William Wyneswold[9] is greatest laboures agaynst you in this matter, as is shewed me by your lovers; & as for Richard Trumyll, he is houshold servant vnto Sir Henry Wyllowby;[10] & thus I betake you to the keping of the holy Trenete.

From Kenalton, the Sunday next after Natyvytie of St John Baptest.

By your beadman & servant Sir Richard Plompton prest[e]

Endorsed (p. 87): To my worshipfull master Sir Robart Plompton knight be these deliuered

[a] *Marginal note*: 16 Hen.7, Sunday after the 4 of June.
[b] favorabell *deleted.*
[c] profett *deleted.*
[d] have *deleted.*
[e] *Appended*: Copied the 19 of Aprill 1613.

[1] Son of Sir Wm. Plumpton's younger brother Godfrey and his wife Alice Wintringham, whose sister became Sir William's second wife. Richard's will was proved 15 March 1524, Francis Collins (ed.), *Wills and Administrations for the Knaresborough Court Rolls*, i (SS, civ, 1902), 18.

[2] Perhaps a younger brother of John Rossall of Radcliffe, Notts, Sir Thomas Babington's brother-in-law, Wright, 211; Stapleton, 159n.

[3] **120**; App. I, 6.

[4] The writ *decies tantum* was the remedy against jurors who accepted bribes, but the most effective way of influencing a jury was through the influence of some great lord: Plumpton had failed to secure Shrewsbury's protection, and Northumberland lacked influence at court, Hastings, 220–22; **156**.

[5] Sir Nicholas Byron, of Over Colwick, Notts may have been a kinsman of Sir Robert through his wife Alice Botiller, a great-great granddaughter of Sir William Plumpton (exec.1405), whose daughter Alice married Sir John Botiller, of Warrington, Roskell, *Knights*, 18, 152–5; Payling, 166; Bennett, *Bosworth*, 112.

[6] Sir Robert leased Kinoulton in 1486, App. II, 50.

[7] William Turvile, of West Leke, Notts, Wright, 243.

[8] Of the Inner Temple, son and heir of Sir John Babington, of Kinston, Notts (d.1485). Recorder of Nottingham 1492 to his death in 1519; feoffee of Elizabeth de la Pole, 1492, Wright, 204, 211, 243; *Collectanea*, viii, 324; S.T. Bindoff (ed.), *The House of Commons 1509–1558* (4 vols History of Parliament Trust, 1982), i, 356.

[9] William Wymondeswold, of Southwell (d.1520), lawyer and member of Sir Henry Willoughby's household, *Visitation of Notts*, 114; A. Cameron, 'Sir Henry Willoughby of Wollaton', *Transactions of the Thoroton Society*, lxxiv (1970), 17.

158 *Robert Eyre III to Sir Robert Plumpton, [September 1501] (No. 106, p. 63)*

Right worshipfull brother, I recomend me vnto you, & to my lady your wiffe, & to my daughter Margaret. Brother, I spake with Frowick[1] on Satterday next after St Bartelmew Day,[2] & I enquired of him whether the assisse held at Nottingham & Darby or not; & he answered & sayd þat he cold not tell, nor man els, vnto Munday next after, for þat day the kings grace had comaunded all the iudges & servants to be with him at Richmond; & whether he wold command them to keepe your servants, or to tarry for other besines at þat tyme,[3] he west neuer. Also, brother, as for your parte of your pannell, I am promysed suerty they will appere, whose names ar closed in a byll; but as to the attachment of your proces for your sute,[4] is not yet, as fare as I vnderstand. But I send about it vnto þe shereffe as sone as Hare Harlad com from you, for sume remedy ther, if he myspede. I haue sent you part the names of þe enpannell for Suttell & Rocliffe, which be in the end of the Hye Peyke, of þe which diuers haue promysed me not to appere, & moe I trust for to stoppe. Marveling ye send nobody to Darby for to take you lodging, for Empson hath taken much lodging for him, as I am enformed. Also, I shall wate one you at Nottingham one Sunday next, except ye comand me contrary. Praying you to send me answer shortly.

Your loving brother Robart Eyre esquire[a]

Endorsed: To my right worshipfull brother Sir Robart Plompton kt deliuer these

[a] *Appended*: Copied þe 7th of Aprill 1613.

[1] **152**, Marginal note.

[2] Saturday, 24 Aug. 1501. On 4 Aug. writs had been issued to the four justices specially appointed for the trials at Nottingham and York. **181**; Kirby, *NH*, xxv, 118; App. II, 61.

[3] Until the judges and sergeants had received their instructions from the king in person the holding of the assize v. Plumpton could have been delayed.

159 *Dame Elizabeth de la Pole*[1] *to Sir Robert Plumpton [26 November 1501] (No. 109, p. 65)*

Right reverent and worshipfull & my singuler gud master, in the most humble & lowly manner þat I can, I recomend me vnto you & vnto my gud lady your wyfe, desiryng to have knowledg of your prosperous helth, worship & welfayre, which I besech almighty Jesus long to contynue, to his pleasure & your most comforth. Hartely beseching the gud Lord that redemed me & all mankind vpon the holy Crosse, þat he will of his benigne mercy vouchsafe to be your helper, & give you power to resist & withstand the vtter & malicius enmity & false craft of Master Empson, & such others your adverseries, which, as all the great part of England knoweth, hath done to you & yours the most injury & wrong þat euer was done, or wrought, to any man of worship in this land of peace;[2] & no more sory, therfore, then I my self is. If it were, or myght be in my poore power to remedy the matter, or any parcell of the matter, in any manner, condition, or dede, & wheras I may doe no more, my dayly <prayers> shalbe, & haue bene ever redy, with the prayers of Jhesu.

And wher it is so þat I am bounden to pay to your mastership, or to your assignes, certayne money by yere to þe sume of x*li*, at ij tymes, for such lands as be assigned in ioynter to my nephew, Germayne

Pole, & my cousin, his wyfe & your daughter, I have deliuered & payd to his hands for this last [*p. 66*] past Martynmas rent v*li*, trustyng þat your mastership is contented therwith. What parte, or how much therof my sayd nevew, Germayne, hath sent to your mastership, I am ignorant, saving þat he shewed me þat he sendeth you but x*li* towards the exibicions of my nese, his wyfe. I required you, as my singuler trust is in you, to send me acquitaunce for my discharg for þe payment of this sayd v*li*; & morover I besech you to send me word in writting, by the bringer herof, how I shall pay my rent from henceforward, & to whom I shall pay it. And as it pleaseth you, by yore owne writting to comand me, I shalbe redy to performe it by the grace of Jhesu, who euer preserve your gud mastership. Wrytten at Rodburne, in hast, the morow next after St Kathren Day.

Your true & faythfull beadwoman to hir power Elizabeth de Pole[a]

Endorsed (*p. 65*): To the right worshipfull my full singuler good master Sir Robart Plompton knight this letter be deliuered in hast

[a] *Appended*: Copied þe 8th day of Aprill 1613.

[1] Widow of Ralph de la Pole, of Radburn, Derbys (d.1492), whose heir was his grandson, German (d.1551/2), Sir Robert's son-in-law, whose custody was granted in survivorship to his grandmother and Thomas de la Pole his uncle, 10 Aug. 1493. On 28 Aug. 1499 Elizabeth had given bond to Sir Robert for the assignment to the couple of lands in jointure, *CPR, 1485–94*, 431; CB, 797; **193**; App. III.

[2] The verdict at the Nottingham assizes had recently gone against Sir Robert.

160 *Sir William Gascoigne to Sir Robert Plumpton* *(No. 73, p. 42)*

Right worshipfull Vncle, I comennd me unto you, praying you to send me all evidence as ye haue concernyng any lands or tenements in Tokwith, so þat I may haue them at Tadcaster this nyght, for the matter is in communication there; and the sayd evidence shalbe safly kept for you, as knoweth almyghtie Jesu, who euermore preserve you. Written at Tadcaster this Fryday.

Your nephew William Gascoygne[a]

Endorsed: To his [right *deleted*] worshipfull vncle Sir Robart Plompton kt deliuer these

[a] *Appended*: Copied the 13th day of March 1612.

161 *Sir William Gascoigne to Sir Robert Plumpton, [19 March 1501/2]*[1] *(No. 72, p. 21)*

Vncle Plompton, I recomannd me unto you as hartely as I can, shewing you þat my lord Archbishop hath sent a letter to my cousin William, your son, & a byll closed therin, which byll & letter I wold ye gaue good heed to, & vnderstand whether it be kings comanndement or nay. And also John Vavasour of Newton is departed to mercy of God sence ye departed from home, & I haue inquered of the age of his son and heire, which shalbe at ful age within a moneth, & then I am in a suerte to haue the release of him. Also there is a mariage moved betwixt the sone of Sir John Roklife and Jane Ughtred, sister to Henry Ughtred,[2] and great labor haue they made to my lord of Northumberland for þe same, which I have stoped, as yet, & thus þe sayd Sir John Rokclife, Henry Ughtred, and Anthony[3] draweth all one way; & I vnderstand they will make more labor to my sayd lord hastely, for which cause I will goe to Lekinfeld the next weke, where I shall know further herein of my lords pleasure, which I know is your especiall good lord. And as I can know further I shall send you wrytting shortly.

And also, as I vnderstand, your aduersaries will lay a fine against you,[4] which fine is parcell of William Midletons evidence,[a] & is the fine of the house in Plompton þat was my vncle Ralfe Gascoygne.[5] I pray you to send me some good tydings as sonne as ye can, of your good speed in your matters, which I besech Gode may be to his pleasure & your comforth & myne; & thus our Lord kepe you. At Gaukthorpe, in hast, the second Sunday in Lenten.

Your nephew William Gascon[b]

Endorsed: To my vncle Sir Robart Plompton kt be this byll deliuered in hast

[a] *Marginal note*: A fine of all of W. Midletons euidence in Plo. Raf. Gascoing.

[b] *Appended*: This letter hath a seale. Copied the 13th day of March 1612.

[1] The dating of this letter presents a problem: the fine (note 4, below) was later produced as evidence at the York assizes, Sept. 1502, suggesting a date prior to that event, but the king's precept to the archbishop was sent some time after the trial, **174**, **175**. A John Vavasour of Newton signed a release to Sir Robert's son William in Aug. 1503, CB, 821; App. II, 64.

[2] Afterwards Sir Henry Ughtred of Kexby (d.1510). The marriage does not appear to have taken place, Borthwick Inst., Prob. Reg., VIII, 333; **16**, **58**.

[3] Anthony Ughtred, made banneret at the battle of the Spurs, Aug. 1513, G.R. Elton, *England under the Tudors* (3rd edn., 1991), 73.

[4] The fine was produced by John Vavasour JCP as clerk of assize, claiming that it granted reversion of Sir William Plumpton's Yorks estates to the heirs general, CB, 824; Introd., p. 15; App. III.

[5] **43**.

162 *Sir Robert to Dame Agnes Plumpton, [9 September 1502] (Bodl.Lib., MS Dodsworth 148, fol. 62)*[a]

My deare [. . .][b] hart, in my most hartily wyse I recommend mee vnto you, hartily prayinge you, all thinges laid apart, þat you see þat þe manor & the place of Plumpton bee surely & Stedfastly kept;[1] & all soe þat I haue this Tuesday at euen vj muttons seene to be ordained for the supper the said Tuesday at night; & also þat yee cause this said Tuesday a beast to be killed, þat if neede bee þat I may haue it right shortly. As for my nephew Gascoigne & my couzen Pygot,[2] my brother Ward, Ralph Neuill, Ninne Markinfeld,[3] Thomas Fairfax,[4] Nicholas Girlington,[5] with many other frends & louers were with mee at supper this night.

And thus I betake you to þe keepeinge of the Holy Trinity, who preserue you euermore to His pleasure. From Yorke this Tuesday the morrowe next after the Natiuity of Our Lady.

By your owne louer Rob: Plompton

Endorsed: To my entyrely and most hartily beloued wife Agnes Plumpton be this letter deliuered

[a] *The folio is headed*: In Sir Edward Plumpton's book of letters.
[b] *MS* heare.

[1] The trial at York assizes, in which the verdict had gone against Sir Robert, had recently taken place, Introd., p. 15.
[2] Sir Randolph Pigott, **89**.
[3] Sir Ninian Markenfield of Markenfield (d. March 1572/3), Sir William Gascoigne's brother-in-law, R.W. Hoyle, 'The First Earl of Cumberland: a Reputation Re-assessed', *NH*, xxii (1985), 72.
[4] Probably Thomas Fairfax, of Walton (d.1520) also Sir William Gascoigne's brother-in-law.
[5] **250**; App. II, 68.

163 *Sir John Towneley*[1] *to Sir Robert Plumpton [2 November 1502] (No. 78, p. 43)*

Right worshipfull Cousin, I recomend me vnto you, desiryng to here of your well fayre. Cousin, I vnderstand there was a servant of yours, & a kynsman of myne, was myschevously made <away> with,[2] which I am sory fore.[a] Cousin, I desire & pray you to be good master to Nycholas Lee my lyaufe,[3] as touching his goods, & the better at the instance of this my wrytting. And if there by any thinge þat I may doe for you, yt shalbe redy to you, as euer was any of my ansitors to yours, which I enderstand they wold haue bene glad to do any pleasure <to>. Written at Townley on Salmes Day last past.

John Townley kt[b]

Endorsed: To my right worshipfull cousin Robart Plompton kt be these deliuered

[a] *Marginal note*: Sir J. Townley. Nic: Lee.
[b] *Appended*: Copied the 17 day of March 1612.

[1] Sir John Towneley of Towneley, Lancs (d.1539), App. III.
[2] Probably Sir Robert's servant Geoffrey Towneley, who may have lost his life in a fight for the defence of Plumpton. Although forcible entry by claimants to disputed land was common, it was unusual by the 15th century for fatalities to occur, J.G. Bellamy, *Criminal Law and Society in Late Medieval and Tudor England* (Gloucester, 1984), 69–70.
[3] Possibly 'neif', a bondman *OED*; **56**, **98**.

164 *William Elleson to Sir Robert Plumpton, [November 1502]* *(No. 142, p. 86)*

Right worshipfull Sir, in my lowlyest wyse I comend me to you. Sir, I purpose, with the grace of God, to be with you or Martynmas, if I may. This day I must ryde to Yorke, & how long I shall tary ther I cannot shew you; & as for compleanyng to my lord Archbyshop of any ryott,[1] the tyme is not now; and when I speake with you, i shall shew you more of my mynd. With the grace of Jesu, who I besech preserve you, &c.

Your servant William Eleson[a]

Endorsed: To his worshipfull master Sir Robart Plompton kt

[a] *Appended*: copied the 19 of Aprill 1613.

[1] There had been violence at Plumpton following attempts to distrain the goods of tenants refusing to pay their rents, **168**.

165 *John Pullein to Sir Robert Plumpton, [6 November 1502]* *(No. 153, p. 95)*

[*p. 96*] Sir, after my duety remembred vnto your mastership, please it you the same to know þat by instant labour I have gotte a copie of the wryt of thassisse & playnt agaynst you, to þe intent therby to haue a wryt of error,[1] which wryt, by the advise of your counsell, which I had togither, is put to making; and for the expedition therof it shall want no dyligence nor calling vppon. For þe costs & expences about thes busines wilbe great.[2] Therfore I wold ye prepared money to send vppon all goodly hast; & your learned counsell thinketh verily, if the law maybe indefferently hard, þat þe proceeding in the sayd assies is error.

It is so þat Mr Frawyke is made cheife iustice of the common place, and therfor ye must myse his counsell; & þat I forthynke. Sir, I haue deliuered your letters, as well to Mr Under Tresorer[3] as to Blackwall; & Mr Tresorer[4] shewed me aparte how your wryting was, & [I] desired him, seeing your great troble & cost, to spare the payment þat ye owed him for a season; & þat he sayd he myght not doe in no wyse, because he had appoynted such summes of money as ye owe him to pay it to [other][a] persons. And further sayd þat he could not do no other wayes but attempt the law against you & your suerty if ye pay not according to your wrytting. I intreated him as specially as I could to spare you for a season, but it wyll not be. Therfore make schift to pay him, or els you & your surty wilbe sued. Euer after this as I may have knowledg in all your [matters][b] to your comforth, I shall wryt [*p. 97*] to your mastership, with the grace of almyghty God, who send you & all yours ther healths also. From Lyncolnes Inn, this Sunday next after All Saints Day. Sir, for all other matters this berer can shew you at large, for a proteccon & what your lerned counsell sayd therin.

Your beadman John Pullan[c]

Frynds þe bishop of Rochester[5] & Doctor Wargham[6]

Endorsed (*p. 95*): To the right worshipfull Sir Robart Plompton knight

[a] *MS* your.
[b] *MS* knowledg.
[c] *Appended*: Copied the 23 of Aprill 1613.

[1] An error in the wording of a writ might be sufficient cause for the reversal of a verdict, Hastings, 158n.
[2] The greater proportion of legal fees was for administrative costs. Though fees for consultations and court appearances were not high, they were paid frequently: 'Even with prominent counsel little and often was the rule', Hastings, 108; Ives, *CL*, 306.
[3] Sir Robert Lytton, **147**.
[4] Thomas Howard, earl of Surrey, *HBC*, 103.
[5] Richard Fitzjames, bishop of Rochester, *ibid.*, 240.
[6] William Warham, provided to the bishopric of London 1501, *ibid.*, 240.

166 *Sir Robert Plumpton to Henry VII, [1502 × 1503] (WYASL, Acc 1731/9-M15; Stapleton, cxi)*

In most lamentable and piteous wise sheweth and complaineth vnto your most gratious highnes, your daylye orator and [*blank*], Robert Plompton, knt, how that Sir John Rocliffe, Dame Margaret his wife, and Elizabeth Sothill, through the great [*blank*] mantenance and supportation of Richard Empson &c., haue recovered by assize lands of the vallue of 500*li*, whereof your orator and ancestors haue beene seased aboue 300 yeares &c. And the said Sir John and Richard, not regarding the displeasure of God, nor of your Grace, intend to attach and cast in prison the body of your beseecher &c. Wherefore the said orator hath, and ever shall bee, best content to put his said whole lands to the judgement and award of your most noble Grace and Councell, or vpon any two judges.[1] And wherefore, most gracious soveraigne Lord, your said poore orator, at the reverence of allmighty God, humbly beseecheth your Grace that hee may haue protection [*blank*] for a whole yeare &c., and shew the same how craftily, and by maintenance hee is disherited of all his fair lands, which without onely the helpe of your Grace he can never recover.[2]

[1] The king appointed Sir Robert a knight of the body and ordered an examination of the case before the archbishop of Canterbury and the two chief justices. On 17 July 1504 Sir Robert bound himself in an obligation of £200 to the king to observe the judgement given by the king's council on 6 Dec. 1504, J. Lister (ed.), *Yorkshire Star Chamber Proceedings*, iv (YASRS, lxx, 1927), 26; *CCR, 1500–1509*, 104–5; **169**, **175**n, **177**, **182**, **206**; WYASL, Acc. 1731/9-M 15, 18. This letter is probably one of those missing from the Letter Book, Introd., p. 18.

[2] In reply, John Rocliffe deposed that all had been done by due process of law, but that the Plumptons had fortified and stocked the manor with weapons, and were in a state of war, **177**; WYASL, Acc. 1731/9-M 16 (transcript in Stapleton, cxi).

167 *German de la Pole to Sir Robert Plumpton, 8 November [1502] (No. 99, p. 58)*

[*p. 59*] Right worshipfull father, in the most humble & lowly wyse þat I can or may, desiryng to here of your prosperous health, worship and welfaire, which I hartely besech almighty Jesus encrease & contynew, to his pleasure & your most comforth. Father, I am very desirous to here from you & to know how you doe in your matters. I can noe more doe therin, but hartely pray to God to helpe you in your right, & send you gud speede. And I pray you let my wyfe haue some word from you, by this next carryer, how you doe in your sayd matters; & [she and] my sister Ellynor hartely recomend them vnto you, & pray you of your dayly blessing; & both they & I pray you þat we may be recommended vnto my brother William Plompton & all your folkes, and we rehearsed them by name. And thus the Holy Ghost guid you & all the matters þat you labor about. Scribled in hast the viij day of November. Father, I can not yet tell whether I come to London my selfe on this side of Christenmas or not, my servent, the brynger herof, shall shew as sone as he hath the certenty, whether I shall come or be at home.

Your loving son to his smale poore Germayn Pole[a]

Endorsed (*p. 58*): To his right worshipfull father Sir Robart Plompton kt deliuer thes

[a] *Appended*: Copied þe 2 day of Aprill 1613.

168 *Dame Agnes Plumpton*[1] *to Sir Robert Plumpton, 16 November [1502]* *(No. 88, p. 48)*

[*p. 49*] Sir, In my most hartiest wyse I recommend me vnto you, desiring to heare of your prosperitie & welfaire, & of your good spede in your matters; certyfing þat I & my sone William with all your children are in good health, blessed be Jesu, with all your servants. Sir, ye & I and my sone was content, at your departing, þat my sone shold take þe farmes at Martinmas of his tenants, or els cast them forth & prayse [their] goods, & so my sone hath done with some of them; & here are the names of them þat hath payd me: Robert Wood, Peter Cott, John Gloster, Robert Taler, William Bentham. Sir, it ys to let vs vnderstand þat thers other tenauntes þat are cast forth each bene att Cothorpe,[2] and make one ragman to compleane on my sone & you, þat ye take their goods from them;[3] & it is not soe, for my sone hath sent for þe neighbours of Knaresbrough & Harrogate & Spofforth to set pryse on ther comon & cattell, after ther consience, & my sone hath set streyes some in ther layes, for there is some þat will not apply to his mynd, & they purpose to get on descharge for my sonne þat they may be set in again, & he not to occupie.[4] Therefore, I pray you to take good heed þervpon & they haue set these names in the ragman þat hath payd my sone, þat they know not of, nor will not be consellled thereto.

Also Sir Richard Goldsbrough[5] hath taken an ox of William Bentham þat was dryven over the water with ther cattell of the toune of Plompton, þat be caused to be put over for þe sayfgard of ther cattell; and when he came for his ox, he answered him & sayd: Sir George Ratclife had wrytten for certayne tenauntes to be so taryed by him, & spirred him whose tenaunt he was, & he shewed him whos he was, & he will not let him haue them without a replevie; and I trow he will dye in the fold, for I sent William Skargell[6] & William Croft & they cannot get him without a replevie; & therfor if ye can find any remedie I pray you for. And also I pray you to send me some word, as ye may, of your good speed. No more at this tyme, but I betake you to the keping of the Trenetie. From Plompton in hast, the xvj day *Nouembris*.

By your wife Dame Agnes Plompton[a]

Endorsed (p. 48): To the worshipfull Sir Robart Plompton kt be thes deliuered in hast

[a] *Appended*: Coppied the 21 day of March; 1612.

[1] Sir Robert's first wife, Introd., pp. 8–9, App. II, 37.
[2] Cowthorpe near Wetherby where the Plumptons and Rocliffes held land.
[3] Ragman = catalogue of complaints, *OED*. See also the Statute of Rageman (1276), *Statutes of the Realm*, i, 44.
[4] The taking of the cattle of tenants refusing to pay dues and rent to a claimant 'may be adduced as evidence to prove seisin in court at a later time', Bellamy, *Criminal Law and Society*, 70.
[5] Sir Richard Goldsburgh of Goldsburgh (d.1504), a near neighbour and kinsman of the Plumptons, **8**.
[6] William Scargill, possibly a scion of the Scargill family of Thorpe Stapleton, was in service with Sir Robert, **69**n.

169 *Thomas Savage, archbishop of York,*[1] *to William Plumpton, 25 November [1502] (No. 20, p. 199)*

Trustie and welbeloued[a] I greate you well, and let you wit that on the behalfe of Dame Elizabeth Sutell and other the inhabitants dwelling in the lordship of Plompton, I am informed that wheras acording to the kings lawes theare hath bene exhibite a repleue for such cattel as ye latle hau taken for a distres within the said lordship; yet not onely will not obey the same, but continueth in maner contrary to the kings laws, right, and good consiences, as well in taking their cattell as other houshold stuf; if it so be, to their vtter vndowing, if ye that should be sufred, as by their lamentable complaints mad at large I am informed. Wherfore, the premeses considred, I desire you, and in the kings name commaund you, imeadetly and furthwith, vpon the deliuery of this repleuie, that ye obay the preceps of the same, acording to law.[2] And els, vpon the sight of this my writting, that ye, or your councell learned in your name, dres you to appear afore me, thear to shew me som reasonable cause what so to doe ye make refusall. And of this faill not, as ye will answer at your perrill. At my castell of Cawood, the xxv day of November.

Yors Th: Eborum[b]

Endorsed: To my trustie and wellbeloued William Plompton esquire to this deliuered

[a] *Marginal note*: 20 letter by Thos Eborum.
[b] *Marginal note*: Copied the 9 June 1626, Friday.

[1] Thomas Savage, archbishop of York 1501–7, younger son of Sir John Savage of Clifton, Macclesfield (d.1497), succeeded William Senhouse, bishop of Carlisle, as lieutenant in the North in 1502, the year of the latter's translation to Durham, Reid, 86, *Test.Ebor.*, iii, 308–23.
[2] After complaints that the Plumptons were felling timber at Plumpton the king directed letters to the archbishop of York giving him authority to enforce a previous order by the chancellor, John Morton, requiring them to desist, pending the verdict of a royal

commission of enquiry into the verdict of the York assize court, *Yorkshire Star Chamber Proceedings*, iv, 26–7; **166**n.

170 *Dame Agnes Plumpton to Sir Robert Plumpton, [27 November 1502] (No. 87, p. 48)*

Right worshipfull Sir, in my most harty wise I recommend me vnto you, desiring to witt your prosperytie & well fayre; letting you vnderstand þat I & all your children is in good health, blessed be Jesu, with all your servants. Lettyng you to vnderstand þat my lord Archbishop sent one servant of his vnto my son William, chardging him in the kyngs name to sette in the tenaunts <agayne>, & if he wold not, he wold send to the schereffe & cause him to poynt them in agayne; & so I sent one servant to the schereffe, & the schereffe shewed my servant þat my lord had wrytten vnto him for to poynt them on agayne; but my sone kepes them furth as yet, & therfore I trow my lord Archbyshop will compleane of my son & you, & sath þat he will indyte them þat was at castyng out of yam.

And, Sir, I pray you þat you be not myscontent þat I sent not to you, for indeed I make þe labor that is possible for me to make, and as yet I cannot speed, but as shortly as I can I shall spede the matter. No more at this tyme, but the Trenytie haue you in his keeping. Scribled in hast at Plompton, this Sunday next after St Katheryne Day.

By your wiffe Dame Agnes Plompton[a]

Endorsed: To the worshipfull Sir Robart Plompton kt be thes deliuered in hast

[a] *Appended*: Copied þe 20 day of March 1612.

171 *Dame Agnes Plumpton to Sir Robert Plumpton, [21 December 1502] (No. 83, p. 46)*

Right worshipfull Sir, in my most hartie wyse I recommennd me vnto you, desiring to here of your welfare & good speed in your matters. I & all your children is in good health, blessed be Jesu. And, Sir, so it is, as God knowes, þat I have mayd as great labor as was possible for me to make to content your mynd in all causes; & now I haue mayd the usance of xx*li* & sent you with Thomas Bekerdike[1] to content where ye know; & I pray you to send some wrytting to Thomas Meryng[2] for the repayment of the money & your discharg. Sir, it is so þat my lord Archbyshop hath indyt my sone William & xvj of his servants an Tewsday was a senit. But Anthony Cliforth gaue in the byll of dytement against my sone & his servants, but the quest[3] would not endyte them. But my lord Archbyship caused them, or els he bad them, tell him who wold not, & he should ponishe them, þat all oder should take insample; & I cannot get the copie of the indytement, for my lord hath it in his hand. No more at this tyme. The Lord perserue you. From Plompton in hast, this St Thomas Day.

By your wyfe Dame Agnes Plompton[a]

Endorsed: To the [right *deleted*] worshipfull Robart Plompton knight be this byll deliuered in hast

[a] *Appended*: Copied þe 19 of March 1612.

[1] Thomas Bickerdyke, yeoman, one of the Plumpton servants accused by Thomas Babthorpe of invading the manor of Babthorpe and stealing 5 horses, c.1506/7, App. II, 69.

[2] A receipt from Thomas Meering, dated 18 Oct. 1512, for 21s payable by the vill of Plumpton for the tenth granted to king, is extant, CB, 837.

[3] Jury of inquest.

172 *Dame Agnes Plumpton to Thomas Everingham,*[1] *[15 January 1502/3] (No. 86, p. 47)*

[*p. 48*] Cousin Thomas Everyngam, I recomennd me vnto [you], thanking you of your good mynd & will at all tymes, praying you þat ye will take þe labor & payne vpon you to come & speak with me betwyxt this & Tewsday next, as my speciall trust is in you; & þat ye faylle not therof, as I may dow for you as much in tyme to come. No more at this tyme, but the Trenytie kepe you. From Plompton in hast, this Sant Maury Day.

By yours at my power Dame Agnes Plompton

Endorsed (p. 47): To Master Thomas Eueringam be this bill deliuered in hast

[1] The letter implies that the recipient, possibly a cleric, was an employee of the Plumptons. He was a younger son of Sir John Everingham, of Birkin, near Selby, who died in 1528, *Test.Ebor.*, iv, 171; *ibid.*, v, 9.

173 *Robert Plumpton to Sir Robert Plumpton, 6 February [1502/3] (No. 158, p. 100)*

[*p. 101*] After most harty and due recomendations, I recomend me vnto your mastership & brotherhode, and to my lady your wyfe, beseching allmyghty God euermore to preserve & prosper you. Sir, on Munday last come a seruant of Sir John Roclyfs frome <Mr> Emson to Brian

Palmes,[1] & caused him forthwith to take his waye toward London, & as I am enformed, the sayd servant shewed that at the comyng up of [...][a] Bryan Palmes, thei shold haue an end with you, and if ye had any land, þat ye shold be charged with my brother William and me.[2] Therfore, Sir, if ye & thei drawd to an end, as I besech allmyghty Jesu to send you a good end after your pleasure & mynd, see how ye shall stand charged anenst us, & whether ye shalbe charged with þe one or with both; &, Sir, wher ye sent me word by George Barbor to search for the call of the *exigent*[3] in the castell of Yorke agayn you, my cousin your son, or any other of your name or servant. Sir, on Tewsday last was þe court in the castell, & then was ther none *exegent* called agaynst you, none of your servants, nor of your name, but ther are ix playnts by *replegiare*[4] by ix of your tenaunts against you, my cousin your son, Sir Richard Plompton,[5] & dyuerse of your servants. But how many playnts & how many defendants, as yet I can not get any knowledg, for the schereffs clarek sayth his master hath all the records & notes, and the playntyffs þat day was essoined; & thus almyghty Jesu, our Lady Saint Mary Virgin, Mary Magdalene, with all the saints in heaven, as I shall dayly besech, prosper & spede you in all your great besines. Scrybled in hast the vth day of February.

Yours at prayer and power Robt Plompton of Yorke[b]

Endorsed (p. 100): To Sir Robart Plompton knight, being lodged at the Angell behind St Clement kirk without the Temple Barr at London be thes deliuered

[a] Bria *deleted.*

[b] *Appended*: Sir Thomas Granger of Yorke deliuered this letter. Copied the 24 of Aprill 1613.

[1] Brian Palmes of Naburn (d.1529), son of Guy Palmes, sergeant-at-law (d.1516), who had been sponsored at the Middle Temple by his uncle Brian Rocliffe. Called sergeant 1510. The family were also kinsmen of Sir William Babthorpe, *Test.Ebor.*, iv, 105; **38**, **209**; App. III.

[2] Lands in Ockbrook, **150**.

[3] Writ requiring appearance in person upon pain of outlawry, Pollard, *Reign of Henry VII*, 140n.

[4] Order for the restitution of cattle and goods distrained, the plaintiff giving surety to prosecute for wrongful distraint, *ibid.*

[5] Sir Richard Plumpton, clerk, **157**.

174 *Thomas Savage, archbishop of York to William Plumpton 16 February [1502/3] (No. 21, p. 200)*

Right trusty and welbeloued,[a] I commend me vnto you, and trust that such derrection as was of late taken by me, and by your assent, for matter in varrience betwene you and Sir John Rocclife be vnto the first Monday in Cleane Lent.[1] I vnderstand that not withstanding ye vse your selfe, as it is to me complayned, contrary to that agrement, as in felling down ashes and other woods in soundry maner. Wherfore I will eftsones dessire you that ye withdraw your selfe from so doing vnto such time that we heare from your father, which is now at London; & thus far you well. Written at Ribston, the xvj day of Febuary.

Yours Tho: Eborum[b]

Endorsed: To my right trusty and welbeloued Wm Plomp<ton>

[a] *Marginal note*: 21 letter by Tho: Eborum.
[b] *Marginal note*: Copied the 10 of June, Saterday.

[1] Quadragesima Sunday, 5 March 1502/3, Stapleton, 173n.

175 *Thomas Savage, archbishop of York, to William Plumpton, 24 February [1502/3]* *(No. 19, p. 198)*

Right trusty and welbeloued[a] I greet you well, and greatly marvill that ye, not withstanding my oft wryting vnto you for reformation of dooing contrary to the apoyntement taken for the matter in varience betwene you and Sir John Rocelif, to be determined by the first Sonday in Lent, vse your selfe in senestor maner: as wher it was agred, in the mean time, ye to haue your fewell nesesary of such bowes of trees that best might be spared, not hurting the bodyes of the same, and as I vnderstand, ye take both bodyes and bowes, and fell them downe by the rowts, [and] that [contrary] to your said apoyntment. But, Sir, I wold advise you to doo otherwise.[b] If ye will not be reformd, I acertaine you that the said Sir John shall be <for me> at liberty to take his most avantage. And wheras it hath pleased the kings highnes to grant vnto your father his letter of protexion,[1] which, vsed as ye vse them, shold be contrary to his lawes, and occation to the breach of his [peace], wherin I know his highnes pleasure by his letters latley derected vnto me, not intending to haue his grant derogatorie vnto iustice, whervnto I will, and neds must haue respect. And thus far ye well. Written at my castle at Cawod the xxiiij day of Febuary.

Thomas Eborum[c]

Endorsed: To my trusty and welbeloued William Plompton

[a] *Marginal note*: 19 by Thomas Eborum.
[b] *Marginal note*: This Williams father had a protection.
[c] *Marginal note*: Copied the 9 June 1626, Friday.

[1] Sir Robert's appointment as a knight of the body, **166**.

176 *William Plumpton to Sir Robert Plumpton [21 March 1502/3] (No. 92, p. 52)*

Right worshipfull father & mother I recomend me unto you, praying you of your dayly blessing, & all my bretheren & systers is in good health, blessed be Jesu, & prays you of your dayly blessing, & my lady mother also. Sir, I marvell greatly þat I haue no word from you, and my cousin Gascoygne[1] also, vnder what condition I shalld behaue me & my servants. Sir, it is sayd þat Sir John Roclife will ploue, but we are not certayne, & þat they come, my cousin Gascoyn saith well therin, for he will see yam on þat mannor þat they will not like, & bytts me & my servants kep house, & he will send vs x bowes & vs ned. Sir, your frinds trowes ye beleve fayr words & fayr heightes, & labors not your matters, for they trow þat þis is not the kings mynd nor knowes not of ther [...][a] dealings, þat they indyte you & me & your servants, as ye may se be the iudgment herof.

Sir, I haue sent you ij letters derected from my lord Archbishops, the which I haue answered him þat I will keepe the kings peace; & also I meane sent him word whether the tenants should occupy or no. And it is my cousin Gascoyns mynd þat they shalt occupy for the tyme, & therfor I besech you send me word how I shold do in euery case, & my servants also. Sir, your frinds thinkes þat thes indytements ar for you, and it be shewed to þe king of his counsell. Both my cousin Gascon and my brother Elson,[2] as your counsell, gives you so to doe. And also I besech you send me word as shortly as ye may possibly. No more at this tyme, but the Trenetie kepe you. From Plompton on Saint Benedict Day.

By your son William Plompton esquer[b]

Endorsed: To the worshipfull Sir Robart Plompton kt be thes deliuered in hast

[a] king *deleted.*
[b] *Appended*: Copied þe 24 of March 1612.

[1] Sir William Gascoigne, App. III.
[2] William Elleson, **129**, **164**.

177 *George Emerson to Sir Robert Plumpton, [1502 × 1503] (No. 161, p. 103)*

Right worshipfull Sir, After due recomendations had ecra, I vnderstand by my lady þat your mastership hath spoken with the kyngs grace, wherof I am very glad. Sir, I wold auise your mastership þat if the king command your mastership to nayme any of his Counsell which ye wold shold haue examination of your matters, þat ye refare þat matter vnto his grace, & your mastership name none; for if your mastership whold name any, peraduenture the king wold thinke parcialty in them, & also your frinds shold be knowne. If yt like your mastership, yt were best for to shew þe kyngs grace þat ye wold refuse none of his Counsell except Mr Bray,[1] Mr Mordaunt,[2] & such other as are belonging to Mr Bray. Sir, at the reuerence [of] God, keepe your frynds secret to yourselfe, for fere þat ye [*p. 104*] <leese> them. I remit all these matters to your wisdom; and thus I beseech almighty Jesu send your mastership good speed. At London, with the hand of your seruant[3]

George Emerson[a]

Endorsed (p. 103): To the right worshipfull Sir Robart Plompton knight this byl be deliuered

[a] *Appended*: Copied 25 of April 1613, Sunday.

[1] Sir Reginald Bray of Eaton Bray (d.1503), a member of Henry VII's Council Learned in the Law etc. Empson was one of his executors, N.H. Nicolas (ed.), *Testamenta Vetusta* (2 vols, 1826), ii, 446.

[2] Sir John Mordaunt, App. III.

[3] For the king's response, see **182**.

178 *Robert Pichard*[1] *to Sir Robert Plumpton 27 January [1500 × 1503/4] (No. 209, p. 146)*

Right worshipfull Sir, in my best maner I comend me vnto you. And vnderstand þat but layte ye have made clame & pretence vnto a certayne land in Rybstone of long tyme in the tennor [*p. 147*] of one John Ampleforthe,[a] the which, aboue þe tyme wherof is any memory, hath belonged vnto þe person of Spofford for the tyme beying, wher, [...][b] though all vnworthy, at this tyme I occupie þe rowme, & the same land, without any let or interuption hath had at his dissposicion, as is wel known to all ancient & aged persones within the lordship of the same, & nygh in þe country thervnto. Wherfore, Sir, I trust veryly, of your wyssdome, ye will not in þat matter, nor in [...][c] no other, any thing attempt against the right of me & my sayd church more than ye have heretofore done in þe tyme of my predecessorȝ, or of ther deputs and fermors. And if ye redely will, I must defend me & my sayd right as I may, & so will. Neuertheless, if I may have the right of my church with your loue & favor, I wold be right glad, for right loth I wold be, not compelled, to be in troble with you, or any worshipfull of my parishe. Therfor, Sir, I requier you to let me have my right peasiably as my predecessors tofore hath had, & so doing, ye shall have my service, & otherwise not, as this berer, my servant, to whom please yt you to give credence, shall more largly shew you on my behalfe. Wrytten at Pettewoorth[2] the xxvij of January, with the hand of him þat wold, having noo cause to the contrary, owe you his service.

Robart Pichard person of Spofforthe[d]

Endorsed (p. 146): To the right worshipfull Sir Robt Plompton knight

[a] *Marginal note*: Land in Ribston vidz.
[b] of *deleted*.
[c] any *deleted*.
[d] *Appended*: Copied þe 11th of May 1613.

[1] Incumbent of Spofforth (d.1502), presented by the 5th earl of Northumberland, 14 Dec. 1499, shortly after receiving livery of his estates, Kirk, 62; **125**n, **183**.
[2] The Sussex estate of Petworth which belonged to Northumberland.

179 *German de la Pole to Sir Robert Plumpton, [1503]* *(No. 94, p. 53)*

Right worshipfull and my most especiall gud father in law, in my most vmbele manner I recomend me most hartely vnto you, & vnto my lady my mother in law, gladly desiring to haue knowledg of your prousperyte, wellfayre and harts ease, the which I besech almyghty Jhesu long to contynew & increase vnto his pleasure, and vnto your most ioyfull comforth and gladness. Sir, if it please you to vnderstand þat since my last coming into Darbyshire, it was infirmed me þat þer was in Staforthshire a parcell of land, þe which shold be þer at Combryge and Cramarch,[1] þat was not received þe recovery of the size[a] at Nottingham and Derbye. Wherfore, Sir, I toke vpon me in your name to send vnto þe tenants for as much rent as þey were behind, synce þe last payment þat was made vnto Sir John[2] or Preston.[3] And they desired [*p. 54*] my servants to com againe, as þat day sennyt, and they should either haue the rent or be suffered to streyne on such guds as they fond on the ground. And so they did com againe, as they had appoynted them, and in þe meane season, thorow the meanes of one Berdall of Assope, ther had bene iiij of Suttell & Roclife servants, þe which wold haue had þe rent, & your tenants answered þat they knew not wherfore þat they should pay them, & so they went ther way. Howbeit they sayd they wold be ther shortly againe, & for þat cause they wold not pay my servant, as for at þat tyme. Howbeit they promysed them, vpon ther fayth, þat they shall not pay one penny vnto þe tyme þat they haue some word from you.

Furthermore, Sir, if it please you to vnderstand of the great vnkindnes þat my grandam[4] hath shewed vnto me, now latly, as the bringer herof can more planly shew you by much, to whom I besech you to take credence on. For be ye sure, Sir, at I was neuer so vnkindly delt with; &

all is because þat she will know it þat ye are at [...][b] asunder; therfore she thinketh þat she may giue & sell all at hir owne playsure. I will besech you, for the reuerence of Jesu, to be so gud father vnto me & my wyfe, as to mayntayne it þat is my ryght, and to se a remedy for it, as my speciall trust is in you aboue all other creatures livinge.

Furthermore, I wold desire you þat I may haue knowledge how þat you do in your matters, for I here tell þat you dyd well; þat wold be the most ioyfull tydings vnto me þat euer was, or euer shalbe, as knoweth the blessed Rode of Rodeborne,[c] who saue you in his blessed kepinge. Amen. I will besech you, Sir, þat this simple letter may recomend me vnto my brother William,[5] with all your houshold.

By your humble son and beadman G. de la Poole[d]

Endorsed (p. 53): To his right worshipfull & most especiall gud father in law Sir Robart Plompton kt be thes deliuered

[a] *MS* site.
[b] brother *deleted.*
[c] *Marginal note*: Blessed Rood of Rodburn.
[d] *Appended*: Copied þe 26 day of March 1612.

[1] Combridge and Crakemarsh, Staffs, **92**n., **180**.
[2] John Rocliffe.
[3] Sir William Gascoigne's servant, **123**.
[4] Elizabeth de la Pole, **138**, **193**, **159**.
[5] William Plumpton, Sir Robert's eldest son.

180 *German de la Pole to Sir Robert Plumpton, [1503]* *(No. 95, p. 54)*

Right worshipfull and my most singuler good father in law, in my most humblest maner I recommend [me] right hartely vnto you & vnto my lady <my> mother in law, inwardly desiring to haue knowledg of your wellfare and harts ease, the which I besech almighty Jesu of his infinyt mercy and grace shortly to [*p. 55*] send you, vnto your most ioyfull comforth, and to the pleasure of your harte. So it is, Sir, þat I vnderstand by the letter þat I receiued from you, þat ye haue þe kings protection ryall,[1] þe which is the most ioyfullest tydings þat ever I hard, since the tyme þat I was borne of my mother. For now, I doubt not but with dew labor mad vnto þe kings grace, & with þe gud counsell of your lovers & frinds, all the vexation & troble þat ye haue had now laytly for your matters, by the grace of þe blessed Trenity, shall turne vnto your ioyfull comforth & harts ease; considering how falsly & how vnrighteously the size is past against you, contrary to the law, either of God or man.

Furthermore, Sir, I haue bene at Combrige for your rent at your tenaunte William Smith, and I receiued of him for one yeares rent xl*s*, the which I send you by the brynger herof. Howbeit, I lay outside ij dayes or I cold haue it; he was so fearfull to pay it because of Sir Robart Shefell[2] & Emson; and he desireth you to be his gud master & beare him out, þat a be not vexed nor trobled therfore. For be ye sure he is stedfast vnto you. And I wold haue had rent in Crakemarch, but the tenaunts wold pay me none; & I wold haue streaned, but ther could no man shew me which was your ground. Wherfore I supposed þat it should haue hurt your matters to haue streyned, not knowing your ground from his.

Also, Sir, I desired you in my last letter to be so gud father vnto me as to com speake with my grandam for diuerse matters, the which longeth vnto my profit. Howbeit I haue no gud answere of you, but now I will desire you, for the reuerence of Jesu, to doe for me as i will do for you, if my power were vnto my will, & make it in your way to com speake with hir for the welfare & profit of your daughter, my wyfe, & me. Many a gentleman in Darbyshire marvelleth, I being so nere my age, þat ye will not com & speake with hir for my right; & if ye come [...][a] it wil saue me greatly, more [then] ye know, in dyvers matters þat I shall shew you of them, by the grace of Jhesu, who haue you in his gloryous keping.

Your owne son and beadman German de la Pole[b]

Endorsed (p. 54): To his right worshipfull father Sir Robart Plompton knight þes letter be deliuered

[a] *MS* not come.
[b] *Appended*: Copied þe 27 day of March 1612.

[1] **175**n.
[2] Sir Robert Sheffield held land in Crakemarsh in right of his wife, Ellen, **92**n.; App. III; Kirby, in *Church and Chronicle*, 231–2.

181 *Thomas Strey*[1] *to Sir Robert Plumpton [1503]* *(No. 120, p. 72)*

Right worshipfull Sir, I recommend me vnto you. Sir, one John Frobisher,[2] one of the coroners in the county of York, hath bene with me & shewed me your wrytt of atteynt[3] with a panell, whervpon ye were well agreed at Yorke afore him & all his fellowes, as he seeth, and at they should send the writ to me to returne in ther names because they were not expart in making ther returne, because it is somewhat diffuse, & because of this your wrytting. And þat ye [...] the impanell is not [*p. 73*][a] good and indyferent for you, I haue not medled, nor will not, at the disire of the croners, without your assent. And so they haue determyned enough themselves to send the sayd John Frobisher, in all ther names, to put in the same writt. And therfore I will advise you, if ye will labour the kings grace herin, to make all the speed you can, and tery not for any other cause, for this matter towches you nere. I can not intreet the sayd Frobisher to keep the wryt in his hands, but to put it in at the day, as he & all his fellowes wer agred for his & ther honestyes & truth in this matter; for they haue warned the panell iurie and this other partie to kepe ther day at London, according to the wrytt. And therefore without ye be at London afore, & geit some comandement from the kings grace to the said coroners to kepe the sayd wrytt in ther hands, or els to amend the returne; & this must be done & labored with affect. And therfore I will advise you to make you ready to ryde on Munday next at the furdest, for els ye will come behind. And thus far ye well, & God giue you as gud speed in this matter as I wold haue my selfe. From Doncastre, this Sunday.

By yours T. Strey[b]

Endorsed (p. 72): To the right worshipfull Sir Robart Plompton knight be thes deliuered

[a] *Between pp. 72 and 73, a fragment*: Noverint universis per presentes, me, Wilhelmum Ryther, recepisse de domina Johanna Grastock, executrice Willelmi Garcoin, militis – 10 marcas, unde 6 marcas a domino Willelmo Ryther, patre meo, ac 4 marcas a dicta Johanna, 8 April 7 Hen.7.

[b] *Appended*: Copied the 12 Aprill 1623.

[1] Attorney, of Clement's Inn. One of the two regular clerks of assize for the northern circuit, he was known to be favourable to Sir Robert and was displaced temporarily by John Vavasour, senior assize judge for the midlands, Ives, *CL*, 21, 312; Introd., p. 15.

[2] Of Altofts, near Doncaster (d.1543). He may have been the grandfather of Martin Frobisher, Pollard, *Reign of Henry VII*, ii, 142; *Test. Ebor.*, vi, 164; J.W. Walker (ed.), *Yorkshire Pedigrees* (3 vols, Harleian Society, xciv–xcvi, 1942–4), i, 188.

[3] A process for the examination and possible reversal of the verdict of the York assize jury, which was discontinued, but on Sir Robert's obtaining royal protection as a knight of the body precepts were sent to the sheriff of Yorks and others forbidding the serving of writs, precepts or other writings upon Sir Robert as knight of the body, or upon his servants, WYASL, Acc. 1731/9 M-17.

182 *Robert Plumpton to Sir Robert Plumpton, [1503]* *(No. 56, p. 99)*

After most harty & due comendations, I recomend me vnto your mastership & brotherhode; & wheras my brother William, like as I shewed you a byll, hath in his name & myne, put a byll vnto the kings grace agaynst Rocliffe & Suttell, which hath made answere, as appeareth in the byll I sent you by Ball. And the kings Counsell comaunded my brother Wylliam to goe & enter into Okbroke;[1] & so, in his coming home he went thither, & wold have entred, & William Saucheverell[2] wold not suffer him; & he showed þe copie of our deed, & he wold not admyt it; but the tenaunts sayd if he come againe afore Alhallowmes & bryng the deeds under seale, they shold endeuer them to pay us. And I thinke to send Sir Robart North thither with him in the weke next after Alhallowmase. Wherfore I pray you þat ye will lett Sir Robart haue the ijd deed with him in a box, which is of feoffment, thider, to þe intent abousayd, & ye shall haue them deliuered againe vnto you, or my lady, whether ye shall please. And if you wyll my brother Wylliam bring them vp to you vnto London, I shall bynd me þat he shall trewly deliuer you them. [*p. 100*] And of your gud mynd & pleasure in thes premysses, I pray you þat ye will vochsafe to send me knowledge in wryting. And, Sir, I vnderstand your adversaries reporteth your matter shalbe determyned by the kyngs iudges and sergiants, and ther, I dout me, ye gitt but litle favor.[3] Therfore þe sonner ye goe up, I trust yt be þe better for you. And almyghty Jesu perserue you & send you gud speed in all your busines; & þat shalbe my daly prayer, as God knoweth. At York, this Munday.

Your servant Robt Plompton[a]

Endorsed (p. 99): To my right worshipfull <master &> brother Sir [Robart] Plompton knight for þe kings body

[a] *Appended*: Copied þe 24 of Aprill 1613.

[1] **150**n.
[2] **155**n.
[3] This review was Henry VII's response to Sir Robert's appeal against the injustice of the verdicts at Nottingham and York, **166**, **177**, **206**.

183 *The earl of Northumberland to Sir Robert Plumpton, 31 January [1499 × 1503] (No. 52, p. 31)*

Cosin Sir Robart Plompton, I commend me vnto you, & am informed þat ye pretend a tytle & clame vnto a litle land in Rybstone, the which without tyme of mynde hath belonged vnto the parson of Spofford the tyme being, and hath [...][a] always bene at his disposition to now lait that, as I pereciue, ye be aboutward, against all right to imbarr & exclud my [*p. 32*] chapleyn, now parsonn ther,[1] and [...][b] my service is the same; wherof I greatly marvill, considring his predesessors alway hertofore hath quietly & peasibly had it. And furthermore, well assured I am, cousen, that my chaplayn wold not convit to haue it, but for the [...][c] aforesaid, & in the right of his church, the which for that I [am] patron thereof, I must & will, in that I can, helpe to defend as myne owne inheritaunce. Wherefore I desire & pray you noe further to intromete you with the sayd land & right of his church more then ye haue in tyme past, in the dayes of other his predesessours. And in case ye medely will, wherof I wold be right sory, know ye veryly ye cannot haue my good will & favour. And that morover it shalbe greatly against my will that ye or any other shall wrong me in the right of the same, whill I liue. Written in my mannor of Petworth, the last day of January.

Your loving cousin   Hen: Northumberland[d]

Endorsed (p. 31): To my right hartely beloued cousin Sir Robart Plumpton knight

[a] bene *deleted.*

[b] *A gap in the MS.*

[c] *A word, perhaps* reason, *omitted.*

[d] *Appended*: copied the 27 day of February 1612.

[1] Robert Pichard, **178**.

184 *William Stockdale, abbot of Kirkstall,*[1] *to Sir Robert Plumpton 2 December [1501 × 1508]   (No. 68, p. 40)*

Sir, I recomend me vnto you, & pray you take no displeasure þat I cannot content your mynd, informing þat I am not certayne what day or tyme to be called up for certayne matters concerning the weyll of <my> house. Many other causes reasonable to be shewed you which I long to writt. I fere me greatly to be aercharged or I witt, and thus the Lord preserve you. From Kyrkestall the secund day of December. I haue good plegges that will serve me of nothinge at my nede, þe which I am full like to sell, & displese the owners now at my need.

Your beadman   <William> the abbot of Kirkestall[a]

Endorsed: To his right worshipfull and welbeloued frind Sir Robart Plompton knight

[a] *Appended*: Copied the 12 day of March 1612.

[1] Elected abbot of the Cistercian abbey of St Mary of Kirkstall 1501; in office Feb. 1506/7, *VCH Yorks*, iii, 145. His successor, John Ripley was in office in 1508.

185 *Sir Robert Plumpton to Dame Agnes, 13 February 1503/4 (Bodl Lib., MS Dodsworth 148, fols 62v–63r)*

Best beloued, in my most harty wyse I recommend me vnto you. Soe it is I mervaile greatly þat yee send mee not the money þat yee promised mee to send with John Wauker within 8 dayes after you and I departed, for I am put to great lacke for it. Therefore I hartily pray you, as my especiall trust is in you, to send me the said money in all hast possible; and alsoe to send me money, for my cost is very sore and chargeable at this tyme, for I haue spent of the money þat I brought from you more then v *li*. For very certaine, Sir Roger Hastings[1] is at the point of vndoinge because hee hath not money to pay where he ought to pay. Therefore, deare hart, I pray you to remember mee.

And as for my matter, there is no moueinge of it as yet, but the Kings grace is the same man hee was att my last departinge from his Grace and my lord of Winchester[2] and Mr Louell,[3] Mr Gylforth,[4] Mr Weston,[5] with all our good friends are to mee as they were at my last departinge. And as shortly as I can haue any way certaine of my matters I shall send you word. Neuertheless my aduersaries had laboured to haue had a priuy [*fol.63r*] seale against mee, but my lord of Winchester and Mr Deane, of the kings chappell, would let them haue none to tyme were þat they vnderstood whether I was in sicknes or nay.

And for diuerse consideracions and greate hurts might falle to you and mee and our children hereafter, I heartily pray you to remember to haste the money vnto mee, as my especiall trust and loue is in you, as knowes the Holy Trinity, who preserue you euermore to His pleasure. From London, in hast, the Tuesday next afore St Valentines Day.

By your louing husband, Robart Plompton kt

Postscript by Sir Richard Plompton, priest: Madam your bedeman servant, Sir Richard Plompton, hartely prayes you to remember all the matters aboue written, for my masters adversaries and yours purueys them to bee still with the Kings grace, and entends to impouerish my master, and all that will take his part and doe for him.

Endorsed (fol.62v): to my right hartily and mine entyrely beloued wife, Dame Agnes Plompton, bee this deliuered.

[1] Sir Roger Hastings of Roxby, younger brother of Sir Hugh Hastings of Fenwick (d.1489), Gooder, 207–8. This letter is probably one of those missing from the Letter Book, Introd., p. 18.

[2] Richard Fox, bishop of Winchester (d.1528), **112**.

[3] Sir Thomas Lovell (d.1524), chancellor of the Exchequer 1485, and member of Henry VII's and Henry VIII's councils; president of the Council 1502–9, *Anglica Historia*, vi, 149.

[4] Sir Richard Guildford, KG, one of Henry VII's most trusted councillors, Lander, 114–15, 119.

[5] Sir Richard Weston, JCP, Introd., p. 18.

186 *Dame Agnes Plumpton to Sir Robert Plumpton, 19 March [1503/4] (No. 84, p. 47)*

Ryght worshipfull Sir, in my most hartie wyse I recomend me vnto you, euermore <desiring> to here of your prosperitie & wellfaire, & good sped in your matters, shewing you þat I and all your children is in good health, blessed be Jhesu, and prays you for your blessing. Sir, it is so now þat I haue mayd you thewsans of the money þat ye sent to me for, & I haue sent it you with John Walker at this tyme, the which I shall shew you how I haue mayd schift of at your comminge; & I pray you that ye be not miscontent that I sent it no sooner, for I haue made the hast that I could that was possible for me to do; & also, Sir, I will not lett Thomas Croft wife plow nor occupy her fermeald, but saith she <shall> not occupy without yer life;[1] & also I pray you to send me word how you speed in your matters againe, as soone as ye may;[2] & also to send me word where ye will your horses to come to you. No more at this time, but the Trinity keep you. From Plumpton, in hast, the xixth day of March.

By your wife Dame Agnes Plompton[a]

Endorsed: To the [right *deleted*] worshipfull Robart Plompton knight be this byll deliuered in hast

[a] *Appended*: Copied þe 19th of March 1612.

[1] On 20 April 1503 Sir William Conyers, sheriff of Yorks, directed a writ of *capias* to Thomas Spinke, bailiff of Claro, against a number of husbandmen, yeomen and others at the suit of William Plumpton, on a plea of trespass, CB, 820.

[2] On 16 July 1503 the king directed a precept from Collyweston to Sir Christopher Warde and Sir William Calverley to the effect that William, 'son and heir of Sir Robert Plumpton, peaceably inioy the lordships of Plumpton and Idle and the rents &c', WYASL, Acc. 1731/9-m, 18.

187 *William Normanville*[1] *to Lady Plumpton, [9 April 1504]* *(No. 119, p. 72)*

Madam, in my most harty manner I commend me vnto your ladyship, thanking you of your reward deliuered vnto me by Edmund your servant. Madam, here hath bene this day with Master schereffe, Edmunde your awne servant, and also Edmond Ward, your tenant, which was arested at Knaresbrught by dew of a warrant deliuered to the balife. Master Schereffe[2] is good master vnto him, as he can shew you, for this writt shalbe at none harme, nor neuer ether named in the wrytt with him, at this terme.[3] Neuertheless I would advise you wryte to London to some of your counsell, that the wryte may be answered to, or els I thinke veryly ther shall another *capias* come against them the next terme, which if ther doe, I doubt ther wilbe labor made to Master Schereffe for taking of them, which I wold be loth to doe, as knoweth God, who keepe you. Att Ryther, this Tewsday in Ester weeke.

By your poore kinsman William Normanville

Endorsed: To the right worshipfull lady my Lady Plompton <be> this byll deliuered

[1] Under-sheriff of Yorks (d.1521), younger son of Sir John Normanville, of Kilnwick, of an ancient family, Percy retainers, and long associated with the Plumptons, Wedgwood, 637; Gooder, 190; *Test. Ebor.*, ii, 138; *ibid.*, v, 123–4; Stapleton, 185n.

[2] Sir Ralph Ryther, **97**.

[3] His power to delay writs in the interest of one of the parties gave the sheriff considerable influence in local politics, J.G. Bellamy, *Bastard Feudalism and the Law* (1989), 11–13.

188 *Dame Agnes Plumpton to Sir Robert Plumpton, 12 April [1504]* *(No. 89, p. 49)*

[*p. 50*] Right worshipfull Sir, In my most hartiest wyse I recomend me vnto you, desiring to here of your prosperitie & welfayre, & good spede in your matters, the which I marvell greatly þat I haue no word from you. Sir, I marvell greatly þat ye let the matter rest so long, & labors no better for your selfe; for it is sayd with them þat count þat ye myght haue had one hend, and ye wold labor it deligently. But it is sayd þat ye be lease forward and they underworketh falsly; & it is sene and known by them, for they thinke to dryve it þat they may take the Whitsonday ferme; & so it is sayd all the country about.[1] Sir, I besech you to remember your great cost & charges, & myne, and labor the matter þat it myght haue anend, <for they haue taken on> *capias* and deliuered for certayne of your tenants. And so they have taken Edmund Ward at Knaresbrough and arest him, the which is a great nossen in the country,[2] þat they shall get such prosses, and ye dow none them, but let them haue there mynd fullfilled in every case. And the other tenaunts cannot pays there housses, but they shalbe cagid;[3] & also <willing> none of your servants shall not pas the dowers, but they mon be trobled.

And also they haue stopped the contry, that there will no man deale with any of your servants, nether to bye wod, no nor nothing els. Therfore, I pray you þat ye will get some comandment to the scherefe þat the prosses my be stoped. Also, Sir, I send you the copy of the letter þat came from vnder sherefe,[4] & the copy of the cases, & the letter þat came from William Elison, the which I had mynd in for lyssing of Edmund Ward, for I haue gotten him forth by the wayes of William Ellyson. And also, Sir, I am in good health, & all your children, blessed be Jesu, & all your servants is in good health, & prayes delygently for your good speed in your matters. And also it is sayd þat they haue cagments[5] for them þat hath bought the wood, þat they dare not deals therwith, for without ye get some comaundement I wott not how your house shalbe kept, for I know not whereof to levy one pennyworth. No more at this tyme, but the Trenietie keepe you. From Plompton, in hast, the xij day of Aprill.

By your wyfe Dame Agnes Plompton[a]

Endorsed (p. 49): To the [right *deleted*] worshipfull Robart Plompton knight be these deliuered in hast

[a] *Appended*: Copied þe 21 day of March 1612.

[1] Surely unfair. As Sir John Fastolf found in his legal battle with Edward Hull, 'Law went as it was favoured', P.S. Lewis, 'Sir John Fastolf's Lawsuit over Titchwell, 1448–1455', *Historical Journal*, i (1958), 1–2.

[2] The writer may be taken to mean not the 'county', but rather the community of 'them that count' in the neighbourhood, see R. Virgoe, 'Aspects of the County Community in the Fifteenth Century', in M. Hicks (ed.), *Profit, Piety and the Professions in Later Medieval England* (Gloucester, 1990), 4–6; J.R. Maddicott, 'The County Community, and the Making of Public Opinion in Fourteenth-Century England', *TRHS*, 5th ser., xxvii (1978), 38.

[3] Cagid = confined, *NED*.

[4] **187**, **189**. The letter from Elleson has not survived.

[5] Cagments = insults, affronts, *NED*.

189 *Dame Agnes Plumpton to Richard Plumpton, clerk, 13 April [1504]* *(No. 85, p. 47)*

Sir Richard Plompton, I recomend me vnto you, dessiring & praying you þat ye will se some remydy for your prosses, þat they may be stopped; & þat ye will goe to my Lord Dayrsse[1] and make on letter for me in my name, & shew him how they delt with my housband tenaunts & servants, and ye thynke it be to dowe; & I pray you þat ye will se that nether thes nor none other prosses pas, but be stoppyd, as my speciall trust is in you. For I have sent up the copy of the *capias*, with one letter from William Elesson, & one other from vnder sherife, þat ye may, after the scest of them, labor as ye think best by your mynd. Also, Sir Richard, I pray you to remember my [order,][a] for Thomas Stabill hath taken þe west rod & the est rod, and hath mayd the fenses, & so she hath no gresse to hir cattel; & also they sow hir land and will not let hir occupy nothing as yet, & þat discomfortheth <them> much. No more, but the Trenetie kepe you. From Plompton in hast, the xiij day of Aprill.

By me Dame Agnes Plompton[b]

Endorsed: To Sir Richard Plompton be thes byll deliuered in hast

[a] *MS* other.

[b] *Appended*: Copied þe 20 day of March 1612.

[1] Thomas, 1st Lord Darcy of Templehurst (exec.1537), married, secondly, Edith, widow of Ralph, Lord Neville, whose daughter, Isabel, was to become Sir Robert's 2nd wife. Darcy was probably summoned to the parliament which met in Jan. 1503/4, *GEC*; **199**, **200**.

190 *Dame Agnes Plumpton to Sir Robert Plumpton, [26 April 1504]* *(No. 82, p. 45)*

[*p. 46*] Right worshipfull, I in most hartee wyse recomennd me vnto you, desiring to heare of your well faire and good speed in your <matters>, letting you vnderstand that I [...][a] <am in good> helth, with all your children, blessed be Jesu, and pray you of your daly blessinge; and all your servants is [...][b] <in good> helth and is right glad to here of your welfare. Sir, one the eving after the making of this letter your servant Edmund Robynson[c] came home, and so I vnderstand by your letter þat you wold vnderstand if Sir John Roclife servants haue receiued any ferme in Yorkshire, but therof I can get no knowledg as yet, but they haue sould oke wood at Nesfeld, & lettes them stand to the tyme of the yeare, one oke þat is worth xl*d* for xij*d*. And also they haue sold [...][d] <aches> at the saime place; and the okes ar sold to William Clapame & Richard Clapame, and the aches to the towards there about; & also at Idell they haue sold holyn to James Formes & to Thomas Quertin and William Aches; and herof I can geet no more certaintie as yet, nor your seruants nether, at this tyme; but the Trenitie haue you in his blessed keeping. Scrybled in hast, the Fryday next after St Marke Day

By your wyffe Dame Agnes Plompton[e]

Endorsed (p. 45): To the worshipfull Robart Plompton kt be thes byll deliuered in hast

[a] Comend *deleted.*
[b] comend *deleted.*
[c] *Marginal note*: Edm. Robinson.
[d] okes *deleted.*
[e] *Appended*: Copied the 19 day of March 1612.

191 *Maud Rose*[1] *to Sir Robert Plumpton [?1504]* *(No. 127, p. 77)*

Sir, after my dowte of comendations remembering, in my most harty manner I recomend me vnto you. Sir, I desire you to beare in remembrance money the which you caused to be borowed vpon my husband & me, the which money I dyverse tymes sent for, & ye have dyverse tymes appoynted me to send for it, & when I send for it at your poyntment, you brak day ever with me, wherby I canot get my money. Therfore I desire you to send me <word> how I shalbe answered of yt, by this bearer, for if I may have it I were loth to troble you. If you will not send me word how I shall have yt, I wyll take my next remedy, þat you shall well know, yt shalbe to your paine & they that borowed yt. No more at this tyme, but Jesu preserve you to his

pleasure. Written at Killinghall by your loving & frind
Mawd Rose[a]
Endorsed: To Sir Robart Plompton of Plompton kt be these deliuered

[a] *Appended*: Copied the 15 day of Aprill 1613.

[1] Possibly Maud Roos, second wife and residuary legatee of Thomas Roos of Ingmanthorpe (will pr. 1503/4), *Test.Ebor.*, iv, 223. She writes as a social equal.

192 *John Eyre*[1] *to Sir Robert or Lady Plumpton, or to William or Isabel Plumpton, or Richard Plumpton, chaplain* (*No. 174, p. 113*)

Most honorable & worshipfull and my especiall good master, after most hartyest manner I can or may, I recomend me vnto your mastership. Sir, I am a poore beadman of yours, & I am at wayes right glad to here of your welfare, my lady your wyfe, Master William your son & my mystress his wiffe,[2] & all your childer, & all your good frinds & lovers. Sir, the cause of my wrytting to your mastership at this tyme: your mastership remembers þat John Toyllar left me with þe keyes of your schawittey[3] to keepe for your behalfe, in the defalt of a better. Sir, I had the keyes leuered me when John Toyller came to your mastership, & had a fellow lemett to keepe the sayd schawnter with me, & he faylled me in my most neede. In the defalt of him ther come another poore man as my selfe, whose name is called Ingland, & we two keeped yt well & trewly to þe tyme þat your seruant came & discharged vs, whose name called Broweke, your seruant. I leuered him þe keyes, afore John Tayller, in Bondgate, to Sir Thomas Aykryge behalf, by the comandement of Broweke, your seruant. Touching [...] Akryg promysed to content all maner of dues. I beseech you, Sir, þe most enimies þat I have within Rypon is Robert Squire & his wyffe, touching þe right þat John Toyller knowes right well. Desiring your mastership to send me word with this pure boy, how I shalbe demeaned & vnder what forme; & Jhesu preserue you, Sir. I am yours at all tymes.

Your servant & poore beadman of yours John Eyre[a]
Endorsed: To his right reuerent & worshipfull master Sir Robt Plompton knight or my lady his wyfe or ayre William or my mystress or Sir Richard his chaplain or any of you deliuer this byll

[a] *Appended*: Copied þe 27 of Apryll 1613. Words are omytted by cause they are ryuen out.

[1] The spelling of the words 'schawnter' and 'schawittey' is said to indicate that the writer of this letter, whether John Eyre or an amanuensis, was an unlettered man, J.W. Adamson, 'The Extent of Literacy in England in the Fifteenth and Sixteenth Centuries', *The Library*, 10 (1929–30), 165.

[2] William Plumpton and Isabel Babthorpe were married in the autumn of 1496, App. I, 5.

[3] The chantry of the Holy Trinity behind the high altar of the Collegiate church of Ripon, Letters Patent of James I, 2 Aug. 1604, Cathedral chapter House; App. II, 1.

193 *Dame Elizabeth de la Pole to Sir Robert Plumpton, 10 July [1504] (No. 108, p. 64)*

Right worshipfull & my full singuler good master, in the most humble & lowly manner þat I can or may, I humbly recomend me vnto your good mastership & vnto my good lady your wyfe, desiryng hartely to here of your welfare, & also of your good speed in your weighty & great matters, which I haue prayed for, & shall doe dayly. Sir, I receyved a letter from you, which bare dayt the viij day of June, & in þat letter you wrote to me þat it was my sone Germyne mynd & yours, with other his frynds, þat I should occupie still at Rudburne,[1] as I haue done in tymes, as long as we can agre, upon condition þat I wold be as kynd to my sayd son Germyne as he intendeth to be to me. I pray Jesus þat I may find him kynd to me, for it is my full entent & purpose to be kynd and lovyng vnto him & his, whersoever I come. But thus the [*p. 65*] matter is now: þat I haue taken another house within the Freres at Derby, which is but of a smale charge, and ther I intend to dispose myselfe to serue God dilygently & kepe a narrow house & but few of meany; for I haue such discomforth of my son Thomas vnfortunate matters þat it is tyme for me to get me into a litle corner, & so wyll I doe. I will besech you and him to take no displeasure with me for my departing, for it wilbe no otherwyse: my hart is so sett.

Moreover, as touching the costodie of all such evidence as I haue now in my keeping concernyng thenherytance of my sayd son Germayne, a gentleman of your acquantance, Master Henry Arden,[2] hath bene in hand with me for them, & I haue <shewed> him whensoever & to whom it shalbe thought by you most convenyent tyme of the delyverance of them, I wylbe redy to delyver them, for I wilbe glad to be discharged of them; for I will flitt at this next Michelmas, as I am full mynded, or sonner, with Gods grace. I pray you contynew my gud master, & owe me neuer the worse will therfor, for it ryseth on my owne mynd to give ouer gret tuggs of husbandry which I had, & take me to lesse charge; & with Gods grace I shalbe as kynde to him & to my daughter, his wyfe, as euer I was in my life, as well for them, as with them, With the grace of Jesu, who euer preserve you. Wrytten at Rodburne, in hast, the xth day of July

By your poore sister & trew beadwoman Elizabeth Pole[a]

No Endorsement

[a] *Appended*: Copied þe 8th of Aprill 1613.

[1] German de la Pole attained his majority in 1504, **138**; App. III.
[2] Henry Ardern, **196**n.

194 *German de la Pole to Sir Robert Plumpton, [1504]* *(No. 101, p. 60)*

Right worshipfull & my most singular good father in law, in my best maner I hartely recomend me vnto you, right glad to here of [your] whelfare, the <which our> Lord contynew long vnto his pleasure & your most comforth. Father, the cause of this my wryting vnto you of myn owne hand is for a matter þat no man knoweth of but onely my wyfe & I & the partyes. Father, this is þe matter: þer is a gentleman, the which had maryed one of my naunts, whose name is Randolphe Manwring,[1] and he beareth great love & favor vnto my sister Ellynor,[2] & she doth likewyse so vnto him the same;[a] & the gentleman hath desired me to wryte vnto you to know if ye can be contented þat he haue hir in marage to his wyfe, the which, if þat ye so be, he wilbe glad to meet you in any plase þat it please you to apoynt, & to haue a communication in the matter; & I thinke in my mynd þat he wilbe contented to take lesse with her then any man in England wold doe, being of his avyower, because of the great love & favour [. . .][b] þat is betwyxt them. And, father, this I will say by myn vncle Manwheryng: his land is a c marke, & also he is as godly & as wyse a gentleman as any is within a m. myle of his hed. And, Sir, all the whold [*p. 61*] matter lyeth in you, & in noe man als; but if þat she were myne owne born syster I had lever þat she had him, knowing him as I doe, then a man of vj tymes his land. Father, how þat ye are disposed in this matter, I besech you þat I may have answere as shortly as ye can, for my sister Ellynor putteth hirselfe vtterly vnto þat thing, þat is your mynd. And my wyfe & I will doe the same, by the grace of Jhesu, who send you shortly a good end in your matters. Amen.

Your son Germayn Pole

Endorsed (*p. 60*): To my right worshipfull father in law Sir Robart Plompton knight be thes deliuered

[a] *Marginal note*: Randal Manring, Ellen Plompton.
[b] he beareth *deleted.*

[1] Possibly Randall Mainwaring, of Carrington, Cheshire, a cadet branch of the Mainwarings of Over Peover, Clayton, 199–200; M.J. Bennett, 'A County Community: Social Cohesion amongst the Cheshire Gentry, 1400–1425', *NH*, viii (1973), 26, 29, 39.
[2] Sir Robert's daughter, Eleanor Plumpton.

195 *German de la Pole to Sir Robert Plumpton, [10 November 1504] (No. 100, p. 59)*

Right worshipfull & my most singuler good father in law, in the best manner þat I possibly can, I hartely recomend me vnto you, with effectual desire to here of your welfare & gud speed in your great matters. And lykwyse, Sir, doth your poore daughter, my wyfe, & my syster Ellynor, desiring to haue your dayly blessing. Father, I have word brought me, by one Duckmanton of Moginton, from you, þat you had a ioyfull end in all your matters, the which were vnto me the ioyfullest tydings þat cold be thought.

Howbeit, Sir, I haue had great marvell þat I haue not, since þat tyme, had some word from you. Father, pleaseth yt you to vnderstand þat I haue comuned with my vncle Maywheryng, according to the effect of your letter, and veryly, Sir, I can no other wyse perceiue by my sayd vncle, but þat he is reasonable in all causes. For, first, he wilbe contented to make hir xx mark ioynture; & as for such essew as God sendeth them, it is no doubt but he wyll provyd for them þat they shall live like gentlemen or gentlewomen, which soever God suffereth. And veryly, father, I am right sure þat my sister Ellynor had rather [*p. 60*] haue hym, you beyng so content, then a man of far greater lands. And also, father, I know wher þat my sayd vncle myght haue great marrages, as both with great lands and guds. Wheafore, Sir, yf yt [is] your mynd þat the matter goe forward, and the preferment of my syster, your daughter, in this behalfe, I pray you þat I may haue shortly knowledg in writting what your mynd is in this matter, and what you be worthy to give for his large proffers. And you being anything resanable, I am right sure þat ye shall like my sayd vncle as well as euer you liked any man, by the grace of Jhesu, who preserve you. Written at Rodburne, in hast, upon Martinmas even.[1]

By your son in law Germayn Pole[a]

Endorsed (p. 59): To my right worshipfull father in law Sir Robart Plompton kt this letter be deliuered in hast

[a] *Appended*: Copied the 2 day of Aprill 1613.

[1] It appears from this letter and the next that the marriage did not take place, and that Henry Ardern was preferred. It has indeed been suggested that Randall may have been an illegitimate son of a kinswoman, Anne Mainwaring, and John Leeke, a Derbyshire gentleman, Wright, 52–3.

196 *Henry Ardern*[1] *to Sir Robert Plumpton [1504]* *(No. 136, p. 83)*

Right worshipfull father,[a] in my most hartyest manner I recomend me vnto you, desiryng to here of your prosperous welfayre, the which I besech Jesu contynew & increase vnto his pleaser. Father, so yt is þat I lent my lady your wyfe, of whose sole God have mercy,[2] ciij markes & a ryall, of which sume I have receiued all save iiij markes, the which remaynes still in my lady your wyffe handes. For the which matter I sent a letter vnto my lady your wyffe, on whose soule Jesu haue mercy, by Olyver Dickenson, your servant,[3] for the same money, for þe which I besech you for to be gud father vnto me, þat I may haue yt at my need; & if <it>, or I did you any good, I am right glad, & shalbe glad to be at your comandement after the old maner. Also, father, I pray you þat I may be recomended vnto my brother, your sone, with all your servants. Father, I pray you remember the suertyshipe þat belongs vnto, to my brother your sone. No more at this tyme, but I besech you, as dayly wellwiller, þat I may have knowledg by the bringer herof how þat ye do in your great matters, the which I pray Jesu give you good speed, who have you in his gloryous keeping.

Henry Ardarn[b]

Endorsed: Unto the worshipfull knight Sir Robert Plumpton

[a] Right worshipful father *deleted*.
[b] *Appended*: Copied þe 18 day of Aprill 1613.

[1] A man of this name was groom of the chamber to Henry VIII in 1526. He may have been a grandson of Thomas Ardern of Marton, Yorks, who married a daughter of Nicholas Gascoigne of Lasencroft. Stapleton suggests that Henry married Sir Robert's daughter Eleanor, *L & P*, iv, 1939 (8); *Test.Ebor.*, ii, 195; **196**n; Stapleton, 194n.

[2] Sir Robert's first wife, Agnes, died soon after 10 July 1504. In Sept. 1505 he married Isabel Neville, **189**, **199**, **200**; Stapleton, cxiv–xv.

[3] Possibly of a yeoman family living in and around the village of Timble, near Harrogate, he served his master during Sir Robert's imprisonment in the Counter 24 April to 5 Aug. 1510. Six Dickinsons were witnesses on Sir Robert's behalf at the trial at York, Ronald Harker (ed.), *Timble Man: Diaries of a Dalesman* (Nelson, 1988), 10. I am indebted to Mrs Audrey Hammerton for this reference.

197 *Opinion of Counsel [1504 × 1505]* *(No. 212, p. 148)*

Hulme, Lynacre, Algrathorpe. In territorijs de Truberui, Braemenn, Lyvacr & chesterfeld Padenhale.[1]

Sir, wheras it is commoned by your aduersaryes þat if þe kings grace, through þe favor which his Counsell beareth you, grant you any lifflod now, they trust [. . .][a] herafter to recouer it againe by þe law, for they have ther recovers exemplified vnder the kings great seale to the same intent. [. . .] Item. They talke, þat wher ye intitle you by reason of a dede intayled by Sir Robt Plompton & Dame Alice his wyffe, daughter & heire of Sir Godfrays Foliambe, made vnto Sir Thomas [*p. 149*] Rampeston & other;[2] they say if the sayd Sir Robt intaled his owne inherytaunce, the intale of his wiffes inherytaunce made to be voided by *cui in vita*,[3] by many & diverse discontynuances which are exemplified; & they have them redy to be shewed herafter, when they see ther tyme for all such causes. Sir, by the advice of your counsell learned, shalbe vnto the kings grace þat all former recouers & other tytles, which your aduersaryes hath against you & your heires, may be voyded & adnulled & revoked; & þat ye by the aduice of your learned counsell, by authoryty of Parliament, recouer, or otherwyse, as your counsell thinketh most expedient, herafter may be in suerty for all manner recouerse, discontynuances, or any other claime þat your aduersaryes or ther heires myght haue against you & your heires. And this for Gods sake ye se done & perfitly fynyshed; & Jhesu euermore[b] preserve you.[c]

[a] and *deleted*.
[b] *Marginal note*: not and one.
[c] *Appended*: Copied the 12th of May 1613.

[1] The relevance of this legal opinion concerning the ownership of the Derbyshire hamlets of Holme, Linacre, Hackenthorpe, Troway, Bramley and a place near Chesterfield identified by Stapleton as recorded in the Domesday survey is not clear, because the Plumptons do not appear to have had any interest therein. The king's protection to Sir Robert applied only to his Yorks estates, those in the Midlands having been in the occupation of Bubwith and Burgh since the judgement of the Nottinghamshire assize justices in 1501, see the compotus of Edward Brown, bailiff of the Derbyshire estates, for the use of the 2 feoffees 14 Sept. 1504, App. I, 7.
[2] App. II, 6.
[3] The alienation of Alice Plumpton's estates was illegal and could therefore be challenged by the writ of entry, *cui in vita*.

198 *Robert Chaloner*[1] *to Sir Robert Plumpton* *(No. 131, p. 79)*

Right worshipfull Sir, I recomend me vnto you, being glad to here of your welfayre. Sir, according to þe promyse þat ye made with this bearer the last tyme þat he was with you, I pray you þat I may have my money now at this tyme, for I [. . .][a] must occupy much money within [these][b] iiij dayes, as this bearer can show you; & if ye delyver it to this said berer, then he shall deliuer to you your *exigent*, and also an acquitance for the sayd money; & if ye will not delyuer it at this tyme [. . .][c] I will send no more to you for it, but this berer shall goe to the schereff with this *exigent* & have from him a warrant to leve the sayd money, or els to take your body, the which I wold be as sory for as any man in Yorkshire, if I myght other wayes doe, as knowes our Lord, who keep you in worship. At Staynley this St Martyn even.

Yours to his litle power Robert Chaloner

Endorsed: To the right worshipfull Sir Robart Plompton knight be these delivered in hast

[a] have *deleted.*
[b] *MS* thur.
[c] it *deleted.*

[1] Common lawyer of Stanley, Wakefield, App. III.

199 *Dame Isabel Plumpton to Sir Robert Plumpton, [?1506] (No. 90, p. 50)*

[*p. 51*] Sir, in the most hartyest wyse þat I can, I recomend me vnto you; Sir, I haue sent to Wright of Idell for þe money þat he promyst you, & he saith he hath it not to len, & makes choses; & so I can get none nowhere; & as for wood, ther is none þat will bey, for they know ye want money, & without they myght haue it halfe for nought they will bey none. For your son, William Plompton, & Thomas Beckerdyke[1] hath bene euery day at wood sence ye went, & they can get no money for nothing, for tha will bey none without they haue tymmer trees & will giue nothinge for them: & so shall your wood be distroyed & get nought for it. Sir, I told you this or ye went, but ye wold not beleue me. Sir, I haue taken of your tymmer as much as I can get of, or Whitsonday farme, forehand, & þat is but litle to do you any good, for ther is but some þat will len so long afor[a] þe tyme; & your Lenten stoufe is to bey, & I wote not what to do, God wote, for I am ever left of thes fachions.

Sir, ther is land in Rybston feild þat Christofer Chambers wold bey, if ye will sel it, but I am not in a suerty what he will giue for it. But if ye will sel it, send word to your son what ye will doe, for I know nothinge els wherwith to helpe you with. Sir, for God sake take anend, soe we are brought to begger staffe, for ye haue not to defend them withall. Sir, I send you my mare & iij*s* iiij*d* by the bearer herof, & I pray you send me word as sone as ye may. No more at this tyme, but the holy Trenyttie send you good speed in all your matters, & send you sone home. Sir, remember your chillder bookes.

Be your bedfellow Isabell Plompton[b]

Endorsed (p. 50): To Sir Robart Plompton kt be this letter deliuered

[a] *MS* it for.

[b] *Appended*: Copied the 23 day of March 1612.

[1] **171**.

200 *Lady Neville to Dame Isabel Plumpton,*[1] *28 April [?1506] (No. 135, p. 82)*

My nown good Lady Plompton, I recomende me unto yow, & to your gud husband, & right sory I am of his & your troubles. If I could remedy it. But God is where he was, & his grace can & will pooruey euery thing for þe best, & help his seruants at their most needes. And so I trust his Hynes he wildo you. My lord, my husband, recommends <him> unto you both, and sends you yowr obblegasiyn, & has receyued but 4*li* & a [...][a] <marke> of the 20 *li* & 2 *li*. The remnant my lord giues to your good husband & you. And I pray almighty Jesu send you both wel to do, as your own herts can desire. Written in hast [...][b] with the hand of your mother [*p. 83*] the 28 day of April. Give credence to this good bearer, for surely he loues you full well.

Edith Neuill

Endorsed (p. 82): To my Lady Plompton

[a] ryall *deleted.*
[b] by *deleted.*

[1] Dame Isabel Plumpton's mother, although married to Thomas, Lord Darcy, retained her first husband's title (**189**, **201**). She died 22 Aug. 1529. There is an account of her funeral, from a transcript by Dugdale of a manuscript in the College of Arms, cited as MS.I.3, in Stapleton, 268–9.

201 *Dorothy Plumpton*[1] *to Sir Robert Plumpton 18 May [?1506] (No. 93, p. 52)*

[*p. 53*] Ryght worshipfull father, in the most humble manner þat I can, I recommend me vnto you, & to my lady my mother, & to all my brethren & sistren, whom I besech almyghtyie God to maytayne & preserve in prosperus health & encrese of worship, entyerly requiering you of your daly blessing. Letting you wyt þat I sent to you mesuage by Whyghame of Knaresbrough of my mynd, & how þat he should desire you in my name to send for me to come home to you, & as yet I had no answere againe, þe which desire my lady[2] hath gotten knowledg. Wherfor she is to me more better lady than ever she was before, in somuch þat she hath promysed me hir good ladyship as long as ever she shall lyue; & if she or ye can fynd athing meyter for me in this parties, or any other, she will helpe to promoote me to the ultermost of hir puyssuance.

Wherfore I humbly besech you to be so good & kind father vnto me as to let me know your pleasure, how þat ye will haue me ordred, as shortly as it shall like you; & wryt to my lady, thanking hir good ladyship of hir so loving & tender kyndness shewed vnto me, beseching hir ladyship of good contynewance therof. And therfore I besech you to send a servant of yours to my lady & to me, & shew now, by your fatherly kyndnesse, þat I am your child, for I have sent you dyverse messuages & wryttings, & I had never answere againe. Wherfore yt is thought in this parties, by those persones þat list better to say ill than good, þat ye have litle favor vnto me, the which error ye may now quench, if yt will like you to be so good & kynd father unto me. Also, I besech you to send me a fine hatt & some good cloth to make me some keuercheffes. And thus I besech Jesu to haue you in his blessed keeping, to his pleasure & your harts desire & comforth. Wryten at the Hirst, the xviij day of May.

By your loving daughter Dorythie Plompton

Endorsed (p. 52): To the [right *deleted*] worshipfull & my most entyerly beloved good, kind father Sir Robart Plompton knight lying at Plompton in Yorkshire be thes deliuered in hast

[1] Daughter of Sir Robert and Dame Agnes. She subsequently married Henry Arthington.

[2] Dorothy's step-grandmother, **189**n, **200** &n.

202 *Robert Chaloner to Sir Robert Plumpton, 16 December [?1506] (No. 130, p. 78)*

[*p. 79*] Right worshipfull Sir, my duty remembred, I recomend me to your good mastership, praying you to be good master to me as to send me iiij*li*, according to your appoyntement afore my master Gascoygne, at Harwods, the which appoyntment was þat I should send for yt within viij days of Martynmas Day. I thinke, by the grace of God, to goe to London within thes 2 or iij dayes, & therfore I send to you mastership more hastyly, for because I wold have it with me to pay for þe cost of the same suyte, & therfore I besech you to bestowe no more labor in this behalfe; & this my letter, the which this berrer can delyver to your mastership, shalbe a sufficient discharg of all debts & outlares by reason of þe sayd obligacion, as knoweth [...][a] Jesu, who keepe you in worship. At Wakfeald, the xvj day of December.

Your owne to his power Robart Chaloner[b]

Endorsed (p. 78): To the right worshipfull Sir Robt Plompton kt in hast thes [be del *deleted*]

[a] you *deleted*.
[b] *Appended*: Copied þe 16 of Aprill 1613.

203 *Robert Chaloner to Sir Robert Plumpton, 16 April [?1507]* *(No. 132, p. 79)*

[*p. 80*] Right worshipfull Sir, in the best manner þat I can I recommend me to you, praying you to send me þe money which my father lent you at London, þe which is iiij*li*; for your son Edmond[1] promysed me at London if I wold suffer the *exigent* which I had agaynst you not to goe out agaynst you, þat I should have the money now at my comyng into the countre; & therfore, if so be ye will deliuer to this berer the aforesayd money, he shall deliuer to you þe *exigent* & an acquitance sealed with my sygnett for the same; & if not, I will put the *exigend* into the schereffe hands & then ye shalbe outlawd shortly.[2] For if I had not kept it in my hands, ye had bene outlayed or now, as knoweth Jesu, who preserve your mastership in worship. At Standley, the xvj day of April.

Yours to his power Robt Chaloner[a]

Endorsed (p. 79): To the right worshipfull Sir Robart Plumpton kt

[a] *Appended*: Copied the 16 of Aprill 1613.

[1] Edmund Plumpton, to whom this is the only known reference, probably died during his father's lifetime.
[2] Defendants had little to fear from the 'slow and largely ineffectual process of outlawry', Rawcliffe, 169.

204 *Richard Aldburgh[1] to Sir Robert Plumpton [1502 × 1509]* *(No. 144, p. 87)*

Worshipfull vncle, I recomend me to you as hartely as I can thinke; and wher yt is þat my servant, John Tomlynson,[2] hath taken a farmehold of þe abut of Fountayns, after the desseyse of the tenant þat dwelleth theron, which the abott wyll record the taking; & yt is so þat the sone of <him>, the foresayd tenaunt, clameth the farmehold after his father dysseys, & he neuer toylke þe sayd farmehold of þe abott, nor of none other man, but my sayd servant, John Tomlyson. Wher it is so, vncle, at the matter betwyxt my servant & John Forest is put to iiij men and the owmpreght[3] of you. Yt is so, vncle, þat I shold have bene with you þe same day, butt þat I had letting & busynes, but I besech you be gud master to my servant as my specyall trust is in you, & at such a way may be taken to right, & well to my servant; & I besech you giue credence to the berer.

Your cousin & servant Richard Aldburgh[a]

Endorsed: To my vncle Sir Robart Plompton kt deliuer these in hast

[a] *Appended*: Copied þe 19 of Aprill 1613.

[1] Son of Sir Richard Aldburgh (d.1476) and Agnes, daughter of Sir William Plumpton, App. III.
[2] **111, 205**.
[3] Umpire, *OED*.

205 *John Tomlynson*[1] *to Sir Robert Plumpton [before 1509] (No. 82, p. 120)*

Right worshipfull & my especyall good master, I recommend me vnto you etc., shewying you þat at the last end of this terme Sir Richard Aldburgh[2] sold take of me awort, as yt is made me to know, praying your mastership to speake to your atturnay, & poynt yt, if þat so be, & what charge or cost ye be at, I shall content. No more at this tyme, but Jesu preserue you in all causes.

Your bedman & seruant John Tomlinson[a]

Endorsed: To his hartly beloued & <good> master Sir Ro: Plompton kt be these delivered

[a] *Appended*: Copied þe 20 of May 1613.

[1] Of Little Ouseburn, Yorks (d.1507) and a tenant of Fountains Abbey in North Stainley, *Lease Book*, xlv, 105.
[2] Knight of the body to Henry VII by 1509, **204**.

206 *Sir Robert Plumpton to Henry VIII [post April 1509] (Bodl. Lib., MS Dodsworth 50, fols 103r–104r)*

In most lamentable wise complaineth & sheweth to your noble Grace[1] your poore subiect & true liegeman Sir Robert Plompton, knight, þat where the said Sir Robert was seazed in his demeane as of fee of the manors of Plompton & Idell & diuerse other landes & tenements <with> in the county of Yorke, and of þe manors of Mansfeld-wodhouse & Kynalton & diuerse other landes & tenements in the county of Nottingham, & of the manors of Hassop, Darley and Staynton & diuerse other landes & tenements in the county of Darby.

And your said beseecher soe being seazed, one Sir John Rocliffe, kt, & Dame Elizabeth Sotehill, widdowe, by the procuringe & stirrings of Sir Richard Empson, kt, sued diuerse assizes of nouell disseisin in the names of Sir Richard Burgh & Sir Robert Bubwith, clarks, against your said beseecher in the said countyes for the foresaid manors, which Sir Richard by corrupt & vnlawful meanes obteyned the fauour & goodwills of þe sheriffe of the said county of Yorke by giuinge of fees & rewards vnto him, & soe caused þe pannels to bee made after his owne mynd & the mynd of þe said Sir John Rocliffe & Dame Elizabeth Sotehill, & of þe plaintiffes of þe said Sir Richard Empson & Sir John Rocliffe; & other plaintiffes caused the pannels in the counties of Nottingham & Derby to bee made after theire owne mynds, Sir Ralph Longford, then beinge sheriffe, ne [*fol.103v*] his vndersheriffe not being priuy thereto; & for proofe thereof the said Sir Ralph Longford, yet liuinge, if hee bee called thereton, will testify the same.

And the said Sir Richard obteyned diuerse letters missiues from your noble father Kinge Henry þe seauehth, whose soule God pardon, to diuerse greate gentlemen of the said counties to beare theire fauour & goodwill to the said Sir Richard in þe said assizes. And beecause hee wold haue euerythinge ordered after his owne mynd & pleasure, hee rode himselfe in his proper person to þe said assizes, accompanied & attendinge vpon him diuerse knightes, esquires, gentlemen & yeomen of your said noble fathers guard, himselfe rydeing & hauinge his footemen wayteinge on his stirreps, more liker the degree of a duke then a batchelor knight, & for noe other intent but to make vnlawfull maintenance, brasinge & fasinge[2] at þe said assizes, whereby iustice & due order of your lawe should not haue indifferent course, to þe most perillous example that hath beene seene in any country. Wherevpon þe said assizes passed with þe said plaintiffes, & vpon suite made to your said noble father touchinge þe said assizes, & misdemeanours of þe said Sir Richard Empson,[3] his highnes commanded þe title of both partes to bee examined as well before his honourable lordes & counsell as before his councellors & iudges, before whom your said beseecher proued substantially & sufficiently his said title which could not bee auoyded by noe meanes by þe said Sir Richard Empson, Sir John Rocliffe ne Dame Elizabeth Suthell. And yet þe said Sir Richard & [*fol.104r*] Sir John Rocliffe not therewith content, but conspiringe & imagininge the vtter confusion & destruction of your said beseecher and of Mr Plompton his sone & heire foresed, & fayned diuerse false & vntrue offices touchinge þe said manors, whereby they intiteled your said noble father to a greate part of the issues & profits of þe premisses.

And þe said Sir Richard & Sir John, in further executeinge theire cruell malice vpon your poore subiect & his sone, caused an information to bee put into your exchequer, as well against your said beseecher as against his said sone, supposinge by þe same þat they had intruded [on][a] þe kinges possession in þe said manors, & had done greate wast, by reason whereof your said besseecher & his said sone were by þe commandement & meanes of þe said Sir Richard Empson, committed to þe prison of þe Fleete, where they remayned well neare þe space of two yeares,[4] to their importune cost & chardge, & neuer could come out but by your gratious pardon, whereby your said beseecher & also his said sone were set at theire liberty. And þat notwithstandinge, on Sir William Perpont, which hath married the daughter of þe said Sir Richard Empson, which daughter before was married to the sone & heire of þe said Dame Elizabeth Sotehill, which Sir William Perpont, tothe intent to followe such sinister & vnlawfull wa[y]s as his said father in lawe Sir Richard Empson vsed, caused other vntrue informations to bee made vpon your said beseecher in your said exchequer, suposinge by þe same þat your said beseecher had eftsoones intruded vpon your Graces possession of þe moity of þe said manors, by meanes whereof [*fol.104v*] your said beseecher shall bee put to importune costes & chardges, to his vtter vndoinge, vnless your mercifull grace, moued with pitty, be now to him shewed in this behalfe. In tender consideration whereof, & for þat yt was found, now of late, þat þe oyer determiner, by diuerse inquestes, as well in þe county of Yorke as in your counties of Nottinghamshire & Derbyshire, þat sinister & vnlawfull labour, embrasinge of thinquestes & other oppression & maintenance in þe said assizes; and alsoe þe said Sir Richard Empson condempned at your oyer determiner within your citty of London to your said beseecher in 400 *li* for þe said vntrue forginge & other misdemeanour, that it may therefore please your Highnes to dischardge þe said last information, by priuy seale or otherwyse, to the treasurer & barons of your exchequer, soe þat noe further processe bee made from henceforth against your said besecher touchinge þe said information.

And also, in consideration þat þe title of your said beseecher hath beene soe openly & thorouly examined & proued, as well by good guidences as otherwise by greate deliberation, that it may therefore please your Highnes, by the aduise of your lords spirituall & temporall in this present Parliament assembled, þat it may bee ordeyned, enacted & established þat your said beseecher & his heires may stand & bee in as good condition touchinge all such manors, landes & tenements as were recorded by þe said assizes in þe said assizes; & þat þe said recordies may stand & bee as against your said beseecher & his heires, & against all other claiminge to him & to his vse vtterly voide & of none effect, sauinge to þe said plaintiffes, & all other to whose vse [is][b] recorded all such right, title & interest as they had before þe said record.

For þe which your said beseecher shall daily pray to God for þe preseruation of your most noble & roiall estate longe to endure.

Endorsed (fol.103r): to the Kinge our Soueraigne Lord, & to the Lords Spirituall & Temporall, & to the discrett Commons in this present Parliament assembled

[a] *MS* by.
[b] *MS* þe.

[1] This is probably one of the letters missing from the Letter Book, Introd., p. 18.
[2] Brashing = running headlong at; and fashing = wearying by importuning, Wright, *Dialect Dictionary.*
[3] **166**. Empson was executed 17 Aug. 1510.
[4] There appears to be no other reference to this imprisonment, which preceded Sir Robert's confinement in the Counter for debt between May and Aug. 1510, Introd., p. 12.

207 *John Carver*[1] *and John Wythers to Sir Robert Plumpton, 20 October [1509]* *(No. 210, p. 146)*

Right worshipfull, after all due recomendations, pleaseth you to vnderstand þat of late you made great instante labors vnto our singuler good lord, my lord Archbyshop of Yorke,[2] for a chauntory of þe Trenite [*p. 147*] within the church of Rippon,[3] possessed by Sir Anthony Sole; and also ye shewed to our lord Archbishop þat þe foresayd Sir Anthony was intrused. Wervpon your informacion, our sayd lord Archbishop comaunded, by a letter to þe foresayd chapitor of Rippon derected, to admitte Sir Richard Plompton[4] by your presentacion, for because þe foresayd Antony was presented by Richard Emson, & also þat he was his chapelaine, & not after þe true order of law admytted. Master Plompton, according to our sayd lord Archbyshop, at his departing out of England, comaunded to me John Carvar, his vicker general [...][a] & John Wythers, his surveyor & generall reasonner, to wryte vnto you þat foresayd Sir Anthony hath be possessed this iij quartors of a yeare & more peassably; & also presented by the kinge, & nothing belonging to Rich: Emson, and no *quare impedit* of your parte suyd, & as now without remedie by þat wryte. Wherfore, we exhort you & hartyly desire you to patiently suffer this poore preist to occupie peassiabely his poore chavntory, with all <þe> profitts & commoditys to þe said chavntrey belonging, without any desire & commaundement of your parte to þe tenaunts, fermes & occupiers of þe same, without any furder besines or trouble; & it nothinge preiudiciall to your tytle of londis; & thus doing, ye shall please almighty God & to cause our forsayd lord Archbishop to be more synguler good lord in all your causes, busines & trobles; & thus our lord god haue you in his keeping.[5] From yorke, þe xxix day of October, by your faithfull & loving frynds at ther litle powers, as god knowes.[b]

John Carver Vicar General John Wythers[6]
Endorsed (p. 146): To our right worshipfull Sir Robt Plompton kt

[a] Sir J. *deleted.*
[b] *Appended*: Copied þe 12th of May 1613.

[1] Appointed vicar-general 1501, archdeacon of Middlesex and of York (d. by 1515), Emden, *Biographical Register of Oxford*, i, 365–6.
[2] Christopher Bainbridge, provided 22 Sept. 1508, appointed Henry VII's proctor at the Holy See Sept. 1509, died at Rome 1514, *HBC*, 265.
[3] **192**n.
[4] **157**.
[5] On 12 Nov. 1515 it was agreed to settle by arbitration the question whether the Ripon chantry was appurtenant to the manor of Plumpton, CB, 845; App. II, 1, 75.
[6] John Wythers, provost of the church of Hemingborough, brought an action for trespass in Addingham against John Catterall, *Early Chancery Proceedings*, ii (PRO, Lists & Indexes, xvi), 557.

208 *Hamnet Harrington[1] to Sir Robert Plumpton 8 May [1510] (No. 121, p. 73)*

Master Plumpton, I comend me vnto you, letting you vnderstand þat the schereff of the shire of Lancaster sent a balife to my house with a wrytt, and hath seysed into the kings hand al my lands & goods vnto such tyme þat þe merchant of London be content of a c*li* which Sir John Luth knight[2] and I were surty to for you,[3] & the whole sume is layed to my charge. Wherin I marvell greatly þat ye shewed þat ye had gote longer day to pay it in at Whitsontide & Candelmas. Wherfor I pray you to se a way þat I may be discharged, as shortly as ye can, so þat I may occupy my land & goods. If ye will not so doe, I must sue my statute marchant[4] on you & ayre William, your sone, which I wold be loth; & ye had such dayes granted as ye shewed me, ye must [*p. 74*] at the least send to London to the marchant, & get him to send downe to the schereffe, þat I may be discharged; & if ye will not do soe, I will up to London & sue out my statute marchant, as shortly as I can.[5] Take credence to þe bearer therof. At Hyton, the eight day of May.

Hamnet Haryngton esquier[a]
Endorsed (p. 73): To the right worshipfull Sir Robart Plompton kt be this byll delyuered, or to my lady his wyfe

[a] *Appended*: Copied þe 12th day of Aprill 1613.

[1] Died 1528 seised of lands in Farleton, near Kendal, Eskrigg, and Hutton Roof which he held of Thomas, Lord Stanley, to whom they had been granted after the attainder and death of Sir James Harrington, *VCH, Lancs*, viii, 202–3; CB, 833; App. III.

[2] Sir John Bothe of Barton, Lancs, knight of the body 1487, fell at Flodden, Somerville, i, 495; Roskell, *Knights of the Shire for Lancaster*, 119.

[3] The obligation is dated 1 Jan. 1509/10, and the final acquittal 9 May 1516, CB, 833, 847, 848.

[4] The Statute of Merchants (1285) strengthened the creditor's position by authorizing immediate imprisonment of a debtor on proof that he had defaulted on his day, R.B. Pugh, *Imprisonment in Medieval England* (Cambridge, 1965), 45.

[5] Sir Robert was imprisoned in the Counter for debt from 24 April 1510 until the following Aug.; CB, 836 is an account of his expenses during his incarceration (transcribed in Stapleton, cxviii).

209 *Memorandum that the parties have submitted to arbitration, [before 11 May 1514] (No. 128, p. 77)*

Memorandum for the matter of varyance betwyxt Sir John Roclife, Sir William Perepoynt, John Constable, on the one party, & Sir Robart Plompton & William his son on the other party. It is thus ordred by the assent of both the parties: the sayd partys shall abyde the award of my Lord Wynchester,[1] my lord Tresourer, my lord of Surrey, Robt Brudnell,[2] William Fayrfax, iustices,[3] Bryan Palmes, [*p. 78*] John Newdygate,[a] sargaunts at the law,[4] Sir John Norton knight,[5] Richard Sawcheverell,[6] or Sir Andrew Wyndysour,[7] betwixt this & the next assise; & nether of the sayd partyes shall vex other, nor ther partakers, servants, tenants for ther sakes, by entre, dystresse,[b] wrytt, priue seale, indytement, nor otherwyse betwixt this & the sayd assise.

William Farfax[c]

[a] *Marginal note*: Newdigate sergant 10s.

[b] *Marginal note*: Memorandum about the suit on the lands lost by daughters.

[c] *Appended*: Copied the 16 day of Aprill 1613.

[1] William Fox, **211**.

[2] Robert Brudenell, JKB 1507, App. III.

[3] Sir William Fairfax, JKB, App. III.

[4] **38**, **146**, **173**.

[5] Of Norton Conyers, son or grandson of Sir William's feoffee of 1475, Apps II, 35, 36; III.

[6] Richard Sacheverell, possibly a younger brother of Ralph, **147**.

[7] Sir Andrew Windsor of Bradenham, Bucks, royal councillor 1519, *L & P*, iii (i), 196; (ii), 967.

210 *Sir Marmaduke Constable of Flamborough to Sir William Gascoigne, 11 November [1514] (No. 75, p. 42)*

Right worshipfull cousin, I recommennd me vnto you. And where it was appoynted for the matter in traverse betwixt my cousin Plumpton, my cousin Roclife and his cooparsoners,[1] the meetyng to be at Yorke upon Fryday next afore St Wylliam Day, supposing than it had bene the morning next after the twelt day.[2] Cousin, in þat matter we toke the day wronng, for þat same Fryday is veryly the twelt day. Wherfore þat it will like you to apoynt some other day, for þat day cannot keepe, for causes aforsayd. And if it like you to appoynt the Munday or Tewsday next after St William (Day, or) any day in þat weke, I, havyng knowledg from you, I shall not fale to apoynt. [*p. 43*] And the cause why I am desirus to know the day now, is cheifly because I wold common with Sir William Parpoynt,[3] who is now comyng fro beyond the see, and know his mynd thorowly in this matter afore our meting. And thus I besech Jhesu preserve you. Wrytten at Holme, the xj day of November.

Your loving cousin Marmaduke Constable of Flamborgh[a]
Memorandum to appoynt the Tewsday next after Twelt Day.[4]
Endorsed (p. 42): To my right worshipfull cousin Sir William Gascon be these deliuered

[a] *Appended*: Copied the 15 day of March 1612.

[1] Elizabeth Sotehill, widow of Sir John Sotehill, died 21 Sept. 1506, leaving twin granddaughters, Joan and Elizabeth, daughters of her son Henry (d. by 1506) as her heirs. Sir Marmaduke Constable (d.1518) purchased the marriage of Joan Sotehill for his 4th son John (d.1571) and with her the manor of Kinoulton. Elizabeth married Sir William Drury, *CIPM, Henry VII*, iii, 158, 177–8, 256–7; Apps II, 77; III. For the descent of the Sotehill and Rocliffe moieties, see genealogical table, pp. x–xi; App. II, 67.

[2] Friday 6 Jan.

[3] Sir William Pierpoint was married to Joan, widow of Henry Sotehill, and in Jan. 1509 he was granted the wardship and marriage of her twin daughters and custody of their lands, *Test. Ebor.*, iii, 365; *L & P*, i (i), 79, 322; App. III.

[4] The meeting took place on 10 Jan. 1514/15, when the parties agreed to abide by the award of arbitrators headed by Richard Fox, bishop of Winchester, CB, 840, 841; App. II, 74, 75.

211 *Sir Marmaduke Constable to Sir William Gascoigne, 19 November [1514]*[a] *(No. 1, p. 181)*

Right worshipfull coussin, I recomend me vnto you.[b] And this Saterday at thre of the clock at after nowne I receiued your letter, whearby I perceiue that both ye and my coussin Plompton is content to kepe the Tewsday next after the Twelt Day at York, and whether ye think to be theare that Tewsday at viij clock, and haue comunication in that matter vpon Wedsnday by viij or ix of the clock in the morning, or els to be theare the Monday <at> night, and haue our comunication vpon the Tewsday: this I had nede to know before I send to my cossin Parpoint because he comes farre and I wold not disapoint him. And furthermore, coussin, ye rehearse to me in your said letter that you haue spoken with my cossin William Plompton in the matter that ye comond with me of, at that ye trust at our metting to giue me such an<swer>[c] in that matter as I shall be content. Coussin, as towching the matter betwixt Sir Robart Plompton and Sir John Rouclif and his cooparseners, if my sayd coussin be of any towardnes to take end, and to be ordred by frinds in that matter, I shall well content both in that and other things [...] frind apoynted to kepe the day at York, such as ye haue appoynted. And as for any answer or other comunication with my cossin William Plompton in any other matter, but onely this old matter, betwixt my coussin Sir Robart Plompton, his father, and Sir John Rouclif and his cooparseners, I trust verrely that ye think that I, of my honnestey, may neither common nor take answer in that [*p. 182*] matter. And so if that be the princepall cause, or any part of any meting, I wold neither ye, nor I, lost no labor, but rather remit all matters to the common law. And, coussin, for the more perfit and suer knowledg of your mind touching this day of our metting, I shall send a servant of mine, who shall not faill to be with you vpon Thursday at viij clock next coming, and to bring me suer writting from you in þat behalfe. And thus our Lord perserue you. Writtin at Holme the xixth of Nouember.[4]

Your louing coussin Marmaduke Constable of Flaynbrough knight

Endorsed (p. 181): To my right worshipfull coussin Sir Wm Gascoine thes delliuered

[a] *Marginal note*: 1 letter.
[b] *Marginal note*: To Sir Wil: Gascoin by Sir Marm: Constable.
[c] quer *deleted*.
[d] *Marginal note*: Copied the 2 of June 1626.

212 *German de la Pole to Sir Robert Plumpton, [4 June 1515]* *(No. 96, p. 55)*

Right worshipfull father, in the most loving manner that I can, I hartely recomennd me vnto you, and to my lady my mother in law, your wyfe; and likwyse my poor wyfe, your daughter, recomends hir vnto you & my sayd lady, and prayeth you of your daly blessing, & we desire hartely þe knowledge of your prosperous health, worship, & welfare, the which I besech almighty Jesus long to contynue & encrease, to his pleasure & your comforth.

And, father, if you be remembred, I wrote a letter vnto you laytly,[1] [*p. 56*] and sent it vnto you by my servant, in the which letter I instaunced & desired you to shew your fatherly kyndnes vnto my poore wife & me, and to be so gud father vnto us as to make a sure meane þat we myght peaseably enioy and occupie þe land þat I bought of you in Combryge were specified in [...][a] Stafforthshire, for I thought þat unles the sayd land in Combryge were specified in this award, now made betwixt you & Roclife and the heires of Suttell, or els of a liklyhod they wold enter vpon me and disposses me; & you send me word þat you thought they wold not haue it, nor medle with it. But thus it is þat now, within this fortnyth, there were servants of <Sir> William Parpoints and Sir John Roclifes determined to take away the goods þat they could find vpon the ground, and so had they donne, but þat þe tenaunt fortuned to here tell of þer coming, and in all possible hast came to giue me warning. And so, by the helpe of gud masters & frinds, at þe last, by fayre meanes, with very great payne, entreated þem to spare distreyning till such tyme as I had sent vnto you to know what remedy you wold provide herin. Wherfore, at þe reuerence of God, & for the loue þat you owe vnto my poore wyfe & me & our children, remember how we stand vnto you, & be so gud & kind father vnto us to find the meane þat we may peasiably occupie þat litle land which I bought of you and truly payd for; & it shalbe to a discharge of your conscience and, with Gods grace, comforth in lykwyse, for it shall euer succede in your bloud. Father, I besech you thus to doe, to take þe payne vpon you to make such labor vnto Sir John Roclife, þat he will, at your instaunce & by the mediacion of such of your frinds as it shall please you to cause to labor vnto him, make a release of þat land in Combrig.

Father, if it please you to doe your best herin, I doubt not, with Gods grace, but you shall wel bring this matter to passe, considring the familiaritie betwixt you & him now, & þat is like to be. Thus doing, you bynd me and all myne euer to do you þat pleasure þat may be in our smale power. And not doyng thus, all þat know you & me myght well speake vpon it, þat I should, considryng how I stand vnto you, pay such a sume of money to you, & not to be made sure of my bargen; & beside, þat it wold be to me as great discomforth as lightly cold happen me, which wold greve much more then the losse of my money, or of my land. And as you know right well, I haue Slyngsby bonden as your surty in an obligation of x*li* for þe performance of your bargan, which I haue redy in my keping; & the Lord preserve you. From Redburne, in hast, upon Trenetie Munday.[2]

By your faythfull loving son Germayn Pole[b]

Endorsed (*p. 55*): To my right worshipfull father in law Sir Robart Plompton kt be these deliuered

[a] this award *deleted.*

[b] *Appended*: Copied þe 29 of March 1612.

[1] See **180**.

[2] In the final award of 27 March 1515 ownership of the land at Combridge was not established, but a subsequent agreement to refer the matter to arbitration resulted in a decision, dated 12 Nov. 1515 in favour of Pole, CB, 845.

213 *German de la Pole to Sir Robert Plumpton, 3 October [1515]* *(No. 97, p. 57)*

Right worshipfull and my full singuler gud father, in þe most humble and lowly manner þat I can, I hartely recommend me vnto you & to my lady your wyfe, & in lykwyse doth your daughter, my poore wyfe, & hartely prayeth you of your dayly blessing, desiring þe knowledg of your prosperus health & welfaire. Father, so it is þat upon a truth, of Thursday last, oon Richard Bardall of Hassope came in the names of Roclife, Parpoynte, and Connstable to my tennant in Combryg, and also to Crake[marsh], & in their names commannded my tennant þat he should from henceforth pay me no rent, but to make his rent redy for them, shewing eich one of them wold send a servant thither for the rent betwixt this & Martynmas; & told him playnly þat they must haue the sayd land, because it was neither in ther wryting, nor in yours. Father, you sent me word laytly, by my servant, þat you had made it sure to me without any daunger. Yt pleaseth you to let him se your wrytings, and, as I vnderstand, both by you & by him, it is nether expressed in þe wrytings þat towch them, nor you. Yet, not withstanding, vpon myne honestie, they make this sturrying [. . .][a] therin, & so it is to thinke þat if they may finnd any hole or colur therin, they will troble with me for the same; & it were great pytie þat I should haue any troble for þat thing þat I have bought and truly payd for. Wherfore, at the reuerence of God, & for þe love þat you owe to me and my wyfe & our children to make a sure way for me now, at this terme, at London.

And I pray you send me word what tyme you will goe or send to London, and I will send one of my servants to meet you, or your deputie ther; & at his comming, whom, bringing me word þat you haue made it sure to me, without daunger or iopartie, forthwith you shal haue payd you þat, þat myne uncle, Sir Alban,[1] promysed you, and at all tymes the best þat in me may be to you & all yours duryng my natural life, by the sufferance of Jhesu, who haue you in his eternall keeping. From Rodburne, in hast, the iij day of October. Father I besech you at such tyme as recoueres or assurances shalbe made, þat it will please you to let it be expressed by name, þat they may be avoyded & expulsed from ther clame þerin.

Your loving son Germayn Pole[b]

Endorsed: To the right worshipfull & singular gud father Sir Robart Plompton kt be thes deliuered in hast

[a] *Two words deleted.*
[b] *Appended*: Copied þe 29 day of March 1612.

[1] Alban de la Pole, a younger son of Ralph and Elizabeth de la Pole, was probably a cleric, Stapleton, 214n.

214 *William Gascoigne to Sir Robert Plumpton, 18 December [?1515]* *(No. 74, p. 42)*

Uncle Plompton, I commend me vnto you. It is so I am like to haue busines for the lordship of Harwood. The kinge is my good and gratias lord, and hath granted it to me, with all the reuenos and profitts therof duryng þe nowne age of the heire of Heire Ridman.[1] And, as I am enformed, such folkes as be not my louers wold bysie them in the cause; how be it they haue no matter of law, nor right therin. Wherefore I desire you, if there be any cause or matter of danger against me in þat behalfe, þat ye wilbe with me, with such company as you can make, at such tyme as I send to you; [at] which your comyng ye shall se a reasonable suerty to beare me in þe cause.[2] And what ye will doe herin, I pray you send me word in writting be this bearer; & thus our Lord keepe you. At Gaukthorpe, the xviij day of December.

Your nephew William Gascoygne[a]

Endorsed: To my vncle Plompton this letter be deliuered in hast

[a] *Appended*: this letter hath a seale. Copied the 13th day of March 1612.

[1] Joan Redman, only daughter of Henry Redman, of Harewood, and granddaughter of Edward Redman, of Lincoln's Inn (1455–1515), Lander, 96; *Flower's Visitation*, 262; T.D. Whitaker, *Loidis and Elmete* (1816), 166.
[2] The Plumptons and Redmans were related through Sir William's 1st wife, Elizabeth Stapleton, Gooder, 176.

215 *John D.*[1] *to Sir Robert Plumpton 28 June [1516]* *(No. 180, p. 118)*

Right worshipfull Sir, in my most humble maner þat I can I recomend me to your good mastership, & also to my good lady, letting your mastership vnderstand þat Nicholas the messenger hath deliuered a byll into the Stare Chamber of all the prevey seles þat he deliuered in the north country; & as [*p. 119*] many as apereth not, the Councell derecteth proses against them. Howbeyt I made aledgment for your mastership, wherwith they are content, & hath giuen day to All Hallow

Day; & they lay to your charge lxxviij*li* þat your mastership shold be debtable to þe king for þe lordship of Plompton,[a] for ij yeres in King Herre the vijth dayes. This must be answered at the next terme; & Sir, ther is a suyt against your mastership in the excheker for introschon;[2] &, Sir, as for my yong master, þat hath none end as yet.[3]

Sir, the kings grace & the queens lyeth at Wodfeld; & yt is sayd of certayne þat they comes a lyget from Rome to my lord Cartdenall[b] & shall bring to my lord Cardenall the paypis with <full> authoryty & power of all maner of things [in] the reame of England.[4] No more to your mastership, but the Holy Ghost haue you in his keping. From London, in hast, the xxviij of June.

By your seruant Joh. D.[c]

Endorsed (p. 118): To my right worshipfull master Sir Robt Plompton kt deliuer thes in hast

[a] *Marginal note*: Indebted for þe lordship of Plompton to þe king.
[b] *Marginal note*: Newes from Rome.
[c] *Appended*: Copied þe first of May 1613.

[1] John Doddington, **234**. See A.G. Dickens, 'The First Stages of Romanist Recusancy in Yorkshire, 1560–1590', *YAJ*, xxxv (1943), 165.

[2] Having illegally retained possession of Plumpton after its recovery by the feoffees to the use of the heirs general, Sir Robert was now indebted to the king for the issues received during the period up to the date of his legal reinstatement, *CIPM, Henry VII*, iii, 177–8.

[3] The dispute with the Babthorpes, **126**, **216** and *passim*.

[4] Cardinal Wolsey obtained these powers by bull 22 Dec. 1516, Rymer, xiii, 573.

216 *James Emyson to Sir Robert Plumpton, [?1515 × 1516]* *(No. 169, p. 109)*

Right worshipfull Sir, after my loving maner I hartyly recommend me vnto your good mastership, desiryng euermore to heare of your good health & wellfare, the which almighty Jhesu preserve & contynew to his pleasure & to your most singular comforth. [*p. 110*] Sir, þe speciall cause of my wrytting to your mastership at this tyme is this: my lady Ward,[1] your sister, hartely desires your mastership þat ye wold be so good brother vnto hir as for to let hir have Mrs Clare, your daughter, to beare hir ladyship companie this tyme of Christynmas, at Gauthorp; that done, she were much bound to your gud mastership. Letting your mastership vnderstand þat she is a heuy gentlewoman, wherfore, I cannot say.

Letting your mastership to know þat Mr Nevell is come home, and Master Watter Steyckland,[2] in like manner. As for other newes, I here of none. Desiring your mastership to send hir ladyship your mynd by wrytting, or els by word or mouth, be the berer of this letter, what manner she shalbe ordred touching þe primysses of this byll. No more to yor mastership at this tyme, but almighty Jhesu haue you in his keeping & all yors. Amen.

Your owne seruant to his power James Emysonn[a]

Endorsed (p. 109): To his right worshipfull master Sir Robt Plompton kt deliuer these in hast

[a] *Appended*: Copied the 28 of Apryll 1613.

[1] Margaret, wife of Sir Christopher Warde of Givendale (d.1521), sister of Sir Robert's first wife, Agnes Gascoigne, App. III.

[2] Ralph Neville of Thornton Bridge, and Walter Strickland of Sizergh, Sir Christopher's sons-in-law, **138**.

217 *William Elleson to Mrs Isabel Plumpton, [before June 1519] (No. 5, p. 185)*

Sister,[a] I hartilie recommend me to you.[1] Edmond, your servant, shewed me that ye ar aferred that the agrement that my lord of Durram hath made with Beddell[b] shold hurt your title in [...][c] Babthorp. [2] Sister, be ye nothing afeared herof, for ye shall haue as good remede now as ye might haue had before, and as that if your cossin wear at full age; for his nonage shall not hurt you.[3] If any person com from the sherif to take your cattell, obey ye it not,[d] for no cattell shall be taken therby but your husband cattell, and he hat none; and so may ye make the bayly answer. And take good hede of your cattell and of keping your place now whiles your husband is at London. And I pray God send you good spede in your matter. Written this Monday

By your William Elson[e]

Endorsed: To his sister Isabel Plompton be this deliuered

[a] *Marginal note*: Letter 5 by William Eleson to his sister Isabel Plompton.

[b] *Marginal note*: Bedel.

[c] rider *deleted*.

[d] *Marginal note*: Obey no praecept.

[e] *Appended*: Copied the 5 of June.

[1] The writer may have been Isabel Plumpton's half-brother, **129**.

[2] The manor of Babthorpe was held of the bishop of Durham. On 3 April 1506 the Plumptons had been given seisin by the escheator, but by the time this letter was written William Bedell, who had married Christina, widow of William Babthorpe (d.1504) and mother of the present claimant, had occupied Osgodby in right of his wife, who held it in dower, and Babthorpe in right of William Babthorpe, her son, then a minor, Introd., pp. 16–17; App. II, 63, 65, 66.

[3] William Babthorpe, later Sir William (d.1555), App. III, **220**.

218 *William Plumpton to Sir Robert Plumpton, 10 June [?1519]* *(No. 91, p. 51)*

Right worshipfull Sir, after dew recomendations had, I homly recomend me vnto you & to my lady & mother in law, beseching you for your dayly blessing. Sir, I haue bene dyverse tymes before the iudges for my matters, but I can have none <end> as yet, except my cousin Babthorp myght haue all þe lands in Hemyngbroguh [. . .] and I to have Waton, Northcaysse, Medelton, Wyston, and lands in Beverley[1] to the valow of xl*s*, & forest land in Selby to þe valow of xx*s*, and iij*li* land more, or lx*li* in money; & to give answer the first day of þe next tearme. Wherfore, Sir, I besech you of your best counsell herin, by this bearer; & as for your owne matter before Master Dance, Olever hath wrytten to you þe scertayntie therof; and as for Mr Woyd, I had money so much to do as to stope the out lawey this terme. Wherfore, Sir, I besech you to make some search therfore, for yt is a great danger, as the world is at this day; as Jhesu knowes, who preserve you in health. Wrytten at Sacum, the x day of June. Sir, I besech you give credence to this bearer.

By your owne son to his litle power William Plompton[a]

Endorsed: To my right worshipfull and my especiall good [*a word deleted*] <father> Sir Robart Plompton kt be thes deliuered

[a] *Appended*: Coppied the 24 of March 1612.

[1] Waterton, Lincs, North Cave, Middleton and Wistow in Yorks. This may relate to the second attempt at arbitration in June 1519, Introd., p. 17.

219 *Sir William Gascoigne to Sir Robert Plumpton, 3 March [after 1521]* *(No. 70, p. 40)*

Uncle Plompton, I recommend me vnto you, desiring you to call to your remembrance the byrth of my nephew William Farfax,[1] which was borne with you at Plompton, and let me haue the dayt of his byrth. Also I pray you let me haue the dayt <of> the marriage of my cosin Hair[2] & your daughter, which ye haue in wrytting, as I am enformed; & ye thus doyng, bynds me to doe you as great a pleasure, which I shalbe glad to dow, with the grace of God, who preserue you to his pleasure. I thus fare <ye> well. From Gawkthorp, þe third day of March.

Your William Gascoygne kt[a]

Endorsed: To my uncle Plompton be these deliuered

[a] *Appended*: Copied the 13th of March 1612.

[1] Nicholas (d.1571) and William Fairfax were twin sons of Sir Thomas Fairfax, of Walton (d.1521); their mother, Anne Gascoigne, was a daughter of Sir William (d.1487) and sister of the writer, Wedgwood, 364; App. III.

[2] Sir Arthur Eyre, of Padley (b.1481), son and heir of Robert Eyre, married Sir Robert's daughter Margaret c.1500, Wright, 57, 61–62; **139**, **143**, App. III.

220 *Thomas Burgh*[1] *to William Plumpton, 18 July [?1524]* *(No. 35, p. 216; Stapleton, 222)*

[...][a] your frinds of the sid of [...][b] Babthorps,[c] that som of your learned councill did convay, & beside, claime euidence, which neyther yourself, nor any of your frinds wold haue done at any meting. Therfore it is thought that you meting with such learned councill shall take litle efect. But if ye would take one substantiall frind or ij, & he likewise take one or tow, and at my coming home, soe to meate, I shall be glad to meate with you at such time and place as shall be apoynted by you both;[d] & take with me such as is both of good experience and learning, trusting so to set a finall end [...] you and them. I trust we shall commun [...] ther of our matters; and of your mind in the premises, I pray you to acertaine me, and thus hertyly fare ye well. From Aknig, the xviij day of July.

Hertyly yours asured Thomas Burgh

Endorsed: To the right worshipfull Mr William plompton

[a] *The copyist has not transcribed the beginning of the letter.*

[b] *Two illegible words followed by a blank space.*

[c] *Marginal note*: 35 letter by Thomas Burgh.

[d] *The foot of the page is torn and the remainder of the letter missing. The ensuing part of the text is therefore taken from Stapleton, p. 215.*

[1] Possibly Sir Thomas Burgh (d.1549), son of Edward, 2nd Lord Burgh of Gainsborough (d.1528), and grandson of Thomas Burgh, Edward IV's trusted knight of the body and master of the horse. He writes as one accustomed to authority. The family held estates in south Yorkshire, *GEC*; John Warkworth, *A Chronicle of the First Thirteen Years of the Reign of Edward IV*, ed. J.O. Halliwell, (Camden Society, O.S., x, 1839), 8; Morgan, 7, 20; Somerville, 576.

221 *Christopher Hudson*[1] *to William Plumpton, 1 November* *(No. 34, p. 215)*

Right worshipfull Sir,[a] in my hartyest maner I commend me to your mastership and to my mistress your wife, thanking you of the good chear ye maid me at my being with you. Sir, the cause of my wryting vnto you at this time is to beg your mastership to [...][b] to me for God [...][c] else [*p. 216*] ye vtterly vndo me. Wherfore I besich your mastership

I may know your mind in wryting, for I trust, seing I am your tennant, ye will not put me owt, except it wear for som great cause, þat ye would ocupy it yourselfe, as ye promisd me at the beginning. Sir, the gentleman that you said should haue it sayes that the first motion came of you & [not] of him.

Sir, ye spoke with me that you would haue had som good ling fish; wherfore I send your mastership part to se how you like them, & if you do like them, send me word in wryting what substance ye would haue, and I shall helpe to provide you therof, or salt fish in likewise, for I supose ye shall haue as good a penneworth now as ye shal haue afterward. And thus our Lord haue your mastership in his keping. At Beverley, the first day of November.

Your louing frind and tennant at your pleasure Christopher Hudson[d]

Endorsed (p. 215): To the right worshipful Mr Plompton of Plompton this deliuer

[a] *Marginal note*: 34 letter by Christopher Hudson.
[b] *Page torn.*
[c] *Page torn.*
[d] *Marginal note*: Copied the 17 June, Saterday.

[1] A tenant of the Babthorpes in Beverley. On 29 Jan. 1500/1 he and his wife Margaret quitclaimed Sir Robert of all actions, quarrels and demands against them, CB, 808.

222 *Marmaduke Wyvill to William Plumpton, 5 October*[1] *(No. 36; Stapleton, 225)*[a]

[...] in my hartyest wise I recommend me unto you. Sir, whear I was with you upon a time, and did [*blank*] you to be good and loving kinsman to me conserning a litle farmehold lying in Kirk Stainley of vj*s* viij*d* by yeare, and belonging to your chauntre preist in Ripon; even so I hartely require you by this simple letter to be good kinsman to me in the same, as it may do to lie in my lytle power to do you such like pleasure, that I may have it for my farme paying. Cousin, if ye be good to me, I trust your chauntre prist and I shall agre. Sir, I spoke with my cousin, your son, at York, at Lamas sise, and desired him to be meadiater to you for me in that behalfe; and he told me againe, that he put no dought that he would be good and favorrable to me. Sir, ye so being shall bind me, to my litle power, to do you pleasure, as knoweth our Lord who preserve you at his pleasure. From Lytle Burton, the v day of October.

By your loving kinsman Marmaduke Wavell

Endorsed: [...] worshipfull Mr Plompton of Plompton theis

[a] *As this letter is now missing from the Letterbook, the transcript has been taken from Stapleton's edition. See Introduction p. 18.*

[1] The writer and Anne (née Norton), William's daughter-in-law, may have been cousins. The Wyvills, originally of Ripon, had moved to Little Barton, Richmondshire, Pollard, *NE England*, 114; *Flower's Visitation*, 356–7.

223 *Henry Percy*[1] *to William Plumpton, 18 September [before 19 May 1527] (No. 17, p. 196)*

Right trusty and welbeloued,[a] I great you hartly well, and whear there is done & trau<ersed> betwixt you and the tennants of Folefeit Poole,[b] of my lord and father lordship of Spofforth, for our courte in this time within his said township of Folefout, and, as I vnderstand, ye ar contented to bide the order of me and others of the said lord and my fathers cowncell of and vpon the premises, so that an end wear maid before months day next. And so it is now at this time that I haue had, and yet [*p. 197*] hath, such buisenes as I can not attent it this time;[c] wherfore I pray you be contented to giue sparing to the next head cort at Spoforth, at which time ye shall haue an end, with my lord and fathers fauor and mine. And if you doe break and make iij or iiij gaps in Folefout feild, as ye clame to doo, of coustam yearly, thearwith I am content at this time, so that ye doe make noe more buisenes therin to the time when the said matter be ordered or determined. And herof at this time, I pray you faile not, as my trust is in you. Written at the castle of Wresill the xviij day of September.

H: Pearcy[d]

Endorsed (p. 196): To my right trusty and welbeloued William Plompton esquire

[a] *Marginal note*: 17 letter by H. Perce.
[b] *Marginal note*: About riolties in Folifoote vsed by Plompton.
[c] *Marginal note*: 17 letter by H: Perce.
[d] *Marginal note*: Copied 9 of June 1626, Friday.

[1] Henry Percy succeeded his father the 5th earl of Northumberland on the latter's death, 19 May 1527. The two had recently been on bad terms, A.G. Dickens (ed.), *The Clifford Letters of the Sixteenth Century*, (SS, clxxii, 1957), 46; App. III.

224 *Henry Percy, 6th earl of Northumberland to William Plumpton, 17 December 1527 (No. 16, p. 196)*

Right trusty and welbeloued,[a] I commend me unto you, signefiing vnto you I am informed on the behalfe of my right welbeloued in God, the prior of the monestry of St John Euanglist, Helagh Park, of my foundation, of certaine trau[er]sie depending bet[wixt][b] him <and> owne Georg Fulbarne for the right & intrest of one spring liing within the [town]ship[c] of Litle Ribston,[d] within my lordship of Spoforth, which, as I perceiue, you haue bought of the said Georg, and so intendeth to fell it to your loss. I desire, and also chargeth[e] you that ye sufer the sauing of it vnto the time the better we may know to whome the right of the same belongith. Written at Siningfeild the xvij day of December in the xix yeare of the reign of our souraign lord King Henry viij.

H: Northumberland[f]

Endorsed: To my right welbeloued William Plompton esquire

[a] *Marginal note*: 16 letter by H: earle of Northumberland.
[b] *MS* betelbe.
[c] *MS* celbinship.
[d] *Marginal note*: A spring liing in Litle Ribston.
[e] *prefex* dis *deleted*.
[f] *Marginal note*: Copied the 9 of June 1612, Friday.

225 *Sir Robert Constable*[1] *to Ann, Lady Rokeby,*[2] *22 April [before February 1531]* *(No. 2, p. 182)*

Madam,[a] in my best and hartest manner I recomend me vnto you, and I dout not but ye haue hard of the vniust & crafty dealing of Geruis Chawood against me. Your late husbend, whose sowle God pardon, was clearely expulsed and put forth of his ofic, which he had vnder þe chapter seale for tearme of his life,[b] by the said Cawood, and the said Cawood receiued your husbands fee; and what accounts and reckinings he maid vnto your late husband hereof I know not. And þat if I may know from you how many yeares the said Cawood reseiued your hosbonds fee, if ye doe acertin me herof, and make me a letter of atturney vnto some of your frinds, aboute to clame your arrearages. I will help him forward for your helpe, the best I can. And I pray you to accertaine me the truth by your writting by this bearer. And thus our Lord send you good life and long, to his pleasure. Written at Holme in Spald[ing] this 22th day of Aprill.

By your louing frind Robart Constable knight[c]

Endorsed: To my very good Lady Rokeesby deliuer this

[a] *Marginal note*: A letter to Lady Rooksby. This Lady Rokesby liued and dyed at Plompton.
[b] *Marginal note*: By Sir Rob: Constable for abuses of Cawood. W. Cocks br.
[c] *Marginal note*: Copied the 2 of June 1626.

[1] Son and heir of Sir Marmaduke Constable of Everingham, he was executed 1537.

His sister, Elizabeth, married Lady Rokeby's nephew, Ralph Ellerker, *Flower's Visitation*, 66, 109; **211**; App. III.

[2] Daughter of Sir Ralph Ellerker of Rusby, Lincs, and widow of Sir Ralph Rokeby of Mortham, North Yorks, App. III.

226 *Sir Marmaduke Constable*[1] *to Ann, Lady Rokeby, 17 December [before February 1531]* *(No. 3, p. 183)*

Madam, in my harty wyse I recommend me to you,[a] and right so doth my wife, and we ar very glad that ye be in good health & that I hear you like so well with Mr Plompton; & I send you your indenture by this berrer, which hath stayd your son[2] Newport;[b] then I trust ye shall hear more of him but good toward you, and when your prest at Boyton had song out all your ten pound, he kepes him still at his cost, and will kepe a prest sining at Boynton[c] as long as he liues, which example ye began. My coussin Portington,[3] as I doth sopose, hath brought your through[4] to [...][d] Resby church,[5] to be laid of your husband Rokesby by this time. And our Lord preserue you long in good health. At Everingham, this xvij of December.

Your owne asured Marmaduke Counstable knt[e]

Endorsed: To my good Lady Rokesby at Plompton

[a] *Marginal note*: 3 letter. To the Lady Rooksby by Sir Mar: Constable fro. Eueringham.

[b] *Marginal note*: Son Newport.

[c] *Marginal note*: A priest singing at Boynton for his life.

[d] to *repeated*.

[e] *Marginal note*: Copied the 3 of June 1626.

[1] Of Everingham, App. III.

[2] Presumably Thomas Newport, Lady Rokeby's son by a previous marriage, who sold the manor to William Strickland in 1549, *VCH, Yorks, East Riding*, ii, 314.

[3] A member of the Howdenshire family who held the manor of Speeton, near Flamborough, *VCH, Yorks, East Riding*, ii, 102.

[4] Thruff-stone = tombstone, Wright, *Dialect Dictionary*.

[5] Rusby in Lincs was Lady Rokeby's childhood home.

227 *Ann Abbott to Ann, Lady Rokeby, [before February 1531]* *(No. 4, p. 183)*

Maddam,[a] after my most louely I recomend me to your ladyship, evermore desiring to wit of your good well fare, which is my dayly prayer to Jesus, to inquete to your harts most comfort. Maddam, I doe wryte to you, praying not your ladyship to be wroth with my husband for the money that he receiued of my mistress your daughter,[b] that he send not to you by this bearrer. It was my consent, for in good faith,

Madam, in a maner we weare either to haue lost our farme, for Mr Trey is so trobled in the law that he may not for beare his rent no whyle.

Madam, I had my husband take [*p. 184*] your money, and I said I trust your ladyship wold not be discontent for your money for a season, the which shall be befor Lamas, by the grace of God. For in good fayth, Madam, we must haue else sold iij of our key, the which had beine a great hindrance to us. For in good faith we buy that we spend in our howse, and I am faine to eate browne bread and drinke small [...][c] alle my selfe, and liues as hardly, as God knowes, and must do for this yeare. I trust to God it shall be ammended the next yeare; for I thanke God we had not a better cropp toward this good whyle.

And God reward your ladyship; we had liued most hardly if þat your ladyship had not bene. And I pray you, Madam, let not my mistress your daughter wit of it, for then she will nether trust my husband nor me. God reward hir, which I am much bownd vnto. I can doe nothing for your ladyship and hir, but for to pray for your prosperity. I pray you Madam, let not my husband know of this letter, and send me word trewly with this bearrer in a little bill of your owne hand ij or iij words, that he know not of your mind. No more, but Jesus kepe your ladyship in good health.

By your power beadwoman Ann Abott[d]

[a] *Marginal note*: 4 letter. To the Lady Rooksby by Ann Abbot.
[b] *Marginal note*: Money lent by L[ady] Rokesbys daughter to Abbot.
[c] ale *deleted.*
[d] *Marginal note*: Copied the 3 of June 1626.

228 *Sir Robert Neville*[1] *to William Plumpton, [16 November 1532]* *(No. 33, p. 215)*

Right worthy and welbeloued coussin,[a] in my full hertily maner I recommend me to you. The cause of my writing to you at this time is that I wad be very glad to speake with you as touching my cousin Robart Sheifeld,[2] whose soule Jesus haue mercy, for my frinds in Lincolnshire hath letten me haue vnderstand<ing> that ye haue some knowledgeging in the thing touching that matter, the which I would desire you that I may know. For surely if ye can let me haue knowledge of any thing [...][b] <concerning the same,> ye do vs a great pleasure, and a great deade of charrety to bring to knowledg, for I assure you I would to take great paine to come to perfit knowledge. Wherfor, coussin, if it would please you that I might know your mind perfetly in wryting by this my servant, or that it like you that I might speake with you my selfe, I will be at Harrwood of Monday next, with grace of God, and that ye will take a litle paines to come thider, that I might speak with you. I shall take paines to labor twice as far, if ye call of me, with grace of Jesus, who kepe you. From Liversay, this Saterday after Martinmas Day.

By your louer asured Robart Nevill knight[c]

Endorsed: To the right worshipfull & his welbeloued cousin Will: Plompton esquire

[a] *Marginal note*: 33 [Letter by] Robart N[evill] knight.
[b] touching the same *deleted*.
[c] *Marginal note*: Copied [17] June, Saterday.

[1] Sir Robert Neville of Liversedge (d.1542), son of Thomas Neville (d.1499), whose 2nd wife was Isabel, daughter of the lawyer Robert Sheffield, **92**; App. III.
[2] Sir Robert Sheffield died 14 Nov. 1532, App. III.

229 *Robert Plumpton*[1] *to Mrs Isabel Plumpton, 12 January [c.1535/6] (No. 12, p. 191)*

Right worshipful mother,[a] I humbly recommend mee unto you, desiring you of your dayly blessing, praing Jesu long to continew your helth to his pleasur. Mother, I thank you for the [*blank*] at[b] you send mee, for yf you were not, I were not able to liue, for this same Christmasse hath cost mee as much as you send mee. Wherfor I am afraid I shal not haue money to serue mee to Easter. Also I wold desire you to send mee word of the letter that I wrote to my father and you, for to mooue my Lady Gascoin[2] to write to my lord her brother[3] not to bee only his seruant, but of his houshold and attending unto him, for els he wold do as other lords do, knowes not half their seruants. Wherfor I desire you that you wil mooue my Lady Gascoin to writ so to my lord that I may bee his houshold seruant.

Also, mother, I wold desire you to mark wel my letter that I sent you by Mr Oughtred.[4] And here I send you a godly New Testament by this bearer, and yf the prologue[5] bee so small that ye cannot wel reade them, ther is my fathers book, and they are bothe one, and my fathers book hath the prologue printed in bigger letters. Yf it wil please you to read the Introducement ye shal see maruelous things hyd in it. And as for the understanding of it, dout not, for God wil giue knowledge to whom he will giue knowledg of the Scriptures, as soon to a shepperd as to a priest, yf he ask knowledg of God faithfully.[6] Wherfore pray to God, and desire Jesus Christ to pray for you and with you. No more to you at this tyme, but God fill you with al spiritual knowledge, to the glory of God, helth of your soule, and the profit of

your poor nieghbor. Written at the Temple, the 12 day of January.[c]
By your sonn Robart Plompton[d]
Endorsed: To his mother at Plompton be this letter deliuered

[a] *Marginal note*: 12 letter by Rob: Plompton who died 38 Henry 8.
[b] *The surface of the page is rubbed.*
[c] *Marginal note*: Copied the 7 of June 1626, Wednesday.
[d] *Appended*: Wherfor pray. Written at the [...].

[1] William and Isabel's eldest son, who died 1546. James Ryther of Harewood accounts for the Plumptons' predilection for the name 'Robert' by their proximity to the shrine of St Robert of Knaresborough, W.J. Craig, 'James Ryther of Harewood and his Letters to William Cecil, Lord Burghley', *YAJ*, lvi (1984), 103 &n.

[2] Margaret, daughter of Richard, Lord Latimer (d.1530) was the 2nd wife of Sir William Gascoigne (d.1551).

[3] John Neville, Lord Latimer (d.1542), joined the Pilgrimage of Grace but claimed that it was against his will. His third wife, Katherine, daughter of Sir Thomas Parr, later married Henry VIII, *GEC*; *Test. Ebor.*, vi, 159–63; Reid, 58–9.

[4] Robert Ughtred of Kexby, son of Sir Henry (d.1510), **161**.

[5] Attached by Tyndale to this and subsequent editions of his *New Testament*, A.G. Dickens, *Lollards and Protestants in the Diocese of York* (Oxford, 1959), 132–3.

[6] For Prof Richmond's view of Robert as one of the gentry 'moles' who helped to 'destroy a healthy flock', see Harper-Bill, 149.

230 *Robert Plumpton to Mrs Isabel Plumpton [?1535–36]* *(No. 13, p. 191)*

Right worshipfull mother,[a] I humbly recommend me vnto you, desiringe Jesus long to continewe your healthe to the pleasure of God. Worshipfull mother, I am bounde to write to you, yea & you were not my mother, because it hathe pleased God, of his inestimable goodnes, to send me some vnderstandinge in the Scriptures; for everie man or woman that it shall please God to sende knowledge [*p. 192*][b] in the Scriptures is bounde to instructe theire brethren in the lovinge of the Gospell. Wherefore it is my dutie to instructe you, moste principalle of all other, which hathe shewed to me so muche kindnes, besides all motherly kindenes. Wherefore I desire you, moste deare mother, that ye will take heede to the teachinge of the Gospell, for it is the thinge that [...][c] all we muste live by;[1] for Christ lefte it that we shoulde altogether rule our livinge thereby, or els we cannot be in favoure with God. Wherefore I would desire you, for the love of God, that you woulde reade the New Testament, which is the trewe Gospell of God, spoken by the Holy Ghoste. Wherefore doubte not of it, dearely beloved mother in the Lorde, I write not this to bringe you into anie heresies,[2] but to teache you the cleare lighte of Goddes doctrine. Wherefore I will never write nothinge to you, nor saye nothinge to you concerninge the Scriptures but will dye in the quarrell.

Mother, you have muche to thanke God that it woulde please him to geve you licence to live vntill this time, for the Gospell of Christe was never so trewly preached as it is nowe. Wherefore I praye to God that he will geve you grace to have knowledge of his Scriptures. Ye shall heare perceive what the profession of our baptisme is, which profession we muste have written in our hartes. Which profession standeth in two thinges, the one is the knowledge of the lawe of God, vnderstandinge it spiritually as Christe expoundeth it, Math: v, vj, & vij chapters, so that the roote & life of all lawes is this: love thy lorde God with all thy harte, all thy soule, all thy mighte, & all thy power, & thy neighboure as thy selfe, for Christes sake; & love onely is the fullfillinge of the lawe, as saithe S. Paule; & that whatsoever we doe & not of that love, that same fullfillethe note the lawe in the sighte of God; & what the lawe dothe meane, ye shall finde in the prologue to the Rom: in my fathers booke called the New Testament. I wryte vnto you because that I knowe you have a fervent [*blank*][d] & his lawes[3] [*blank, unfinished*][e]
Endorsed (p. 191): To his right worshipful mother bee this deliuered with speed

[a] *Marginal note*: 13 letter by Robert Plompton who dyed at Waterton 38 of Henry 8 about Christmas.

[b] *At the foot of the page* RN.

[c] we *deleted.*

[d] *Marginal note*: Copied 7 of June 1626.

[e] *At the foot of the page*: Mistress Ann Scrope, daughter to Sir Edw: Plompton of Plompton, ded die in December the 16 1650. Lord Jesus rest hir sowle in heven. Edward Cholmlay. *The handwriting suggests one of the copyists.*

[1] Robert predeceased his mother but she expressed her love for him in her will, *Test. Ebor.*, vi, 260–2.

[2] The Plumptons remained loyal to the old faith and suffered the penalties for recusancy. Robert's son William (d.1602) was presented as a recusant in 1582, and the last heir in the direct line, Robert Plumpton, died unmarried 8 Aug. 1749 at Cambrai, where his aunt was a Benedictine nun, H. Aveling 'The Catholic Recusants of the West Riding of Yorkshire 1598–1790', *Proceedings of the Leeds Philosophical and Literary Society*, X, vi (1963), 196, 306; J.J. Cartwright, *Chapters in the History of Yorkshire* (1872), 239; Stapleton, cxxxviii.

[3] The writer's concluding passages derive almost entirely from Tyndale, Dickens, 134–5.

231 *John Doddington*[1] *to William Plumpton, 22 February [1538/9] (No. 25, p. 203)*

Right worshipfull,[a] my deuty to you premised, in my most hertyest maner I recomend me vnto you, and likewise to my good mistress, your wife, trusting in Jesus that you with all your children be in good health, the continuence wherof I pray Jesus increase. It may please you to be advertised I haue receiued your gentle letters datted at Plompton the ix of January, by the which you required me to helpe Tho: Compton,[2] your nephe, to some honiest ocopation at London, with him to be bownd prentis, which I wad gladly to the vttermost of my power and the helpe of my frinds haue don, as I am bownd, in case he had come vnto me, as he did not. The bringer of your said letters informed me that your said nephew was determend to kepe in his owne countrie & not to cum to London.

And where your pleasure in your said letter is that I shold giue you notise if theare wear any thing in varience [*p. 204*] within your maner or lordship of Sacomp, to the intent you might send your pleasure therin by your baly at his next coming to Sacomp. Sir, thear is one thing in varience for title of copehold land ther, which one Edward Glidall, your late farmer, hath, which land was somtimes one Flegs, vnto the which one Flege now maketh title, and hath don longtimes past. And abowt Chrismas last past, the same Flegge deliuered a *supenea* [...][b] to Glidall for the same, as I am informed, but what is don therin I know not. Of this matter Settil, your servant, can informe you better than I.

Allso ther is one Slepe, dweling abowt St Albones, who at your last court thear maid clame to a percill of grownd of your said copehold in the tenner of Marston, of the which the same Marston hath a cope. Soeuer the less, said Slepe aledgeth that his brother, of whome the said Marston bought the same ground, never maid sirrender <therof>, according to the [...][c] custome of your maner. Albeit, it apereth plainely in a bill remaining with the said Merston, that the brother of the said Slepe sold vnto Merston all his intreast in the <said> coppehold. The same Slepe at your last court required your baly [...][d] <ther, with the asent> of the said Merston, [...][e] <to make search in your court rowl that if any such surrender war maid, acording as> it is mentioned in the said copie remaining with the said Marston, which cope, as I remember, was made in the[f] [*p. 205*] fowerth or fifth yeare[g] of the reign of our souaraigne lord the king that now is, whear the said rowle would not be found. Howbeit, theare was all the rowles of this king reigne, but onely that of that yeare. Sir, as me thinks your rowls theare be not kept as they ought to be, the cofer wherin your said court rowles lieth is nought and the lock therof not worth a pene, and it standeth in the church at Sacomp, wheare every man may com at his pleasure. Wherfore, in my simple mind, it should be nesary for you to provide som other meane for the safe custody of your said rowles.

Also, Sir, sith the time I haue bene your farmer ther I haue paid, and must pay within tow yeares next to come vj fiftens for the farme of yur maner of Sacomp: the first payment xxiiij*s*, the second xxx*s* viij*d*, and either of the other fowr years xxiiij*s*, which amounteth in the hole vij*li* x*s* viij*d*. I marvill greatly that your said manor shold be so highley charged, considering the hole fiftene of your towne of Sacomp is but lix*s*. I could never se no writing of the sesment therof, but only by the report maid of your tennants ther by word of mouth. Sir, I wright this vnto you because in case you haue any sertinty therof in wryting, I might know it. I wold be sory to charge your said maner with any more then ought of right to be; and yet I haue paid the same bycause I am loth to stand in contentions with my neighbors [*?until*][h] the truth therin be known.[*p. 206*]

Further[i] I haue receiued the letter sent to you by Sir Philip Butler,[3] knight, wherin he wrighteth that you haue bene insensed against him by the report of lewd and evill disposed persons – by whome he meaneth the same, I may not iudge, howbeit I think rather by me then any other. His sones ar discontented with me because I kepe greyhounds and hownds at your said maner, saieng that it becometh not me to kepe grey howns and howns so near theyr fathers nose, with many other things which I remite for lake of time.

And whear your pleasure is in your said letter, that I shold shew Mr Butler that in case he wold giue you such fine for your milne of Sacomp as your baly did demaund for the same, you wear contented that he shold be amited tennant therof. Sir, with the receit of your said letter I haue not spoken with the said Mr Butler, because I haue bene, and yet am at London, as this bearrer can informe you. Albeit, at this Hillary tearme I spoke woth one Mr Hide,[4] who maried the said Mr Butlers daughters and lieth and continueth within the said Mr Butlers and is the greatest doer about him, to whom I shewed your pleasure therin, requiring him to informe Mr Butler therof, and of your said pleasure. Whervpon the said Mr Hide said that you demaunded an vnreasonable fine for the same, and that his father did ofer you double the fine that ever was paid by any man for the same. And further, he said that in case ye wold not take such fine as shold stand with reason and good conscience, he trusted that my lord Chaunceler of England,[5] vpon the matter hard before him, wod se such fine for the same as shold stand with right and good [*p. 207*] consience.[j] And whear also the said Mr Butler, amongst other things, wryteth in his said letter that your tennants thear be daly in his danger, and that he might pot them daily to trobles, if he wold.

Sir, I trust you haue no tennant thear but that is the kings trew subiect and obedient to Gods law and his Graces. And as long as the be so I dought not but that we, having so noble and gratious a king as we haue, power men shal liue in rest, doing their deuty to his Grace as they and all other men ar most bownd to do. Sir, Mr Butler, of himself, is a good and gentle knight, in case he wear not otherwise counciled, as knoweth Jesu, who ever preserue you and all yours in good and prosperus health, with long continuance of the same, to his pleasure. From London, the xxij day of Febuary.

Your fermar and servant John Dodington[k]

Endorsed (p. 203): To the right worshipfull and his singuler good master Mr William Plompton esquire at Plompton Hall in the countie of York giue theis

[a] *Marginal note*: 25 letter by John Dodington.
[b] of *deleted.*
[c] said *deleted.*
[d] *therwith the asent* deleted.
[e] that the brother of the said Slepe sold vnto the said Marston *deleted.*
[f] *Marginal note*: Thomas Cholmley desiers Mister William Faerfax to sufer all he can posible for the good of the comanwelth, and long lokt for will cum at last.
[g] *Marginal note*: 25 letter by John Dodington.
[h] *Illegible word.*
[i] *Marginal note*: 25 letter by John Dodington.
[j] *Marginal note*: *As above.*
[k] *Marginal note*: Copied the 13 of June, Tewsday.

[1] John Doddington (d.1544), farmer of the manor of Sacombe, Lincs, part of Isabel Plumpton's inheritance, **126**.
[2] Stapleton suggests that Thomas Compton came of a Lincs family and was 'nephew in half-blood' to Isabel Plumpton, 238n.
[3] Sir Philip Boteler, of Woodhall, Herts, four times sheriff of the county, Somerville, 405.
[4] Leonard Hide married Anne Boteler, Stapleton, 240n.
[5] Probably Lord Audley (d.1544).

232 *William Plumpton to Robert Plumpton, 14 November [?after 1538] (No. 14, p. 194)*

Son Robart Plompton,[a] I hertely recommend me to you, and sending you and your brother[1] God blesing and mine. The cause of my writing to you now, that I wold you should helpe this bearer, yong Letham, in such buisenes as he hath in the court of augmentation, for certaine power for yong children of one Berkine, deceased, as conserning one farme hold late belonging to the hold of St Robarts, which you know I did speake to the ansurer[2] for the vse of the said children, and he permised not to suit them. That not withstanding, John Benson would haue entred, and now made many great riots vpon the said children, and therfore he is indited with diuers persons with him. And now forther, he hath brought a preue seale against old Leatham & yong Leatham, and also the eldest child; and for that diuers and many of their frinds hath moued me [*p. 195*] to wryte to you[b] to help them in the said matter. And if it be that you can make any frinds to shew Mr Chauncelor[3] the planer, and through in every thing, [...][c] <and> this bearrer can instruct you, and then, I pray you do the best for them.

And also I would haue you to speak with Mr Latham the goldsmith,[4] lanlord to Robart Oliuer, and shew him how that he will not make his diches and fences belonging to his farme, but that my corne and gras is spoyled at Watterton[5] by that meaner. And if he will not seake remedy therof, let Mr Fox enter a action of trespas against [...][d] the said Robart Oliuer for dispoyling my gras at Watterton to the valew of fiue mark. And as far as I fele, Mr Norton[6] comith not up. I shall make your rents to be gathered, and send it to you as shortly as I can. And thus hartely far you well. From Plompton, this 14th day of November.

By your loving father William Plompton[e]

Endorsed (p. 194): To my welbeloued son Robart Plompton at the Inner Temple in London be this

[a] *Marginal note*: 15 letter by Mr William Plompton.
[b] *Marginal note*: 15 letter by his father.
[c] thou *deleted.*
[d] him *deleted.*
[e] *Marginal note*: Copied this 8 of June 1626, Thursday.

[1] William Plumpton's second son Denis was one of his mother's executors, *Test. Ebor.*, vi, 260–2.

[2] The local receiver responsible to the Court of Augmentations for rents and profits, Walter C. Richardson, *History of the Court of Augmentations 1536–1554* (Baton Rouge, 1961), 140n.

[3] Sir Thomas Audley, chancellor 1533–44, created Lord Audley 1538, *HBC*, 86.

[4] Ralph Leatham, of Upminster, Essex. Christopher Twistleton was his grandson, Stapleton, 235n; **238**.

[5] Robert Plumpton and his wife lived at Waterton, near Gainsborough, a manor acquired as part of the Babthorpe inheritance, App. I, 5.

[6] Sir John Norton, of Norton Conyers. Stapleton suggests that this letter was written after his daughter's marriage to Robert Plumpton, 20 Sept. 1538, 235n; **209**.

233 *Edward Lee, archbishop of York*[1] *to William Plumpton, 9 August 1539 (No. 18, p. 197)*

Mr Plompton, after my herty comendations,[a] wheras some contreverse hath bene betwen Sir William Mydleton[2] and Sir Oswold Wilesthorpe[3] for a tith which the said Sir William Mydleton hath certaine yeares had in his own hands; for as much as afore me they be condescended and agred that the said tith shall be gathred and inned by some man indefferent, and in place semblable, and of all other hath thought you most convenient and indefrent frind to chouse such men as shall se the ining and ordering therof as to the place. This is, first on my behalfe, and eftsones theirs, to desire you hertely to take the paines betwene them, to apoynt alwayes such men as place infefrent, [*p. 198*][b] so that it may remaine in the said place and custode to such a day as they haue apoynted that further order shold be taken for the same. And thus far you hartyly [...][c] well. From Cawood, the ix day of August 1539.

Your loving frind Edw: Eborum[d]

Endorsed (p. 197): To my louing frind William Plompton of Plompton esquire

[a] *Marginal note*: 18 letter by Edward Eborum.
[b] *Marginal note*: 18 by Edward Eborum.
[c] far *deleted*.
[d] *Marginal note*: Copied the 9 June 1626, Friday.

[1] Sir Oswald Wilstrop, son of Guy Wilstrop (d.1530) and his wife Agnes, daughter of Sir Ralph Pigott of Clotherholme (d.1467), grandson of Miles Wilstrop, *Flower's Visitation*, 355; **18**, **40**, **89**.

234 *George Johnson to Robert Plumpton, jnr*[1] *(No. 14, p. 193)*

Right worshipfull Sir,[a] my deuty donne vnto your mastership, and as letting you know that I haue receiued your indenture and deliuered it to Robart Poclington, and he is content with that, sauffing that he wold desire your mastership to set in the indenture whear that he should pay his money at his rent dayes. For the indenture specefies his money unpaid xxj dayes, you or your heires to recouer of him all the hole, which wear a undowing to him, to take that he should make his living on for the place unknowne whear þat he shold pay his rents, [...][b] or what place. And I also letting you know that Mr Leades flate with him verry fast afar his neighbors, [...][c] since he cam from you. As I say, he shall not occupy it but has the lase, for he hath no right to it, nor you neither, and he said he had no lawfull warning that he will take a discharge for, but that he will occopy alsoe. I had Poclington plow and put him of over the lands, that he haue no intrest; and send me word what his deade is and his words, and I shall send you word. For in your absence, I had him send me word and I shold come ouer to him and se what he sayes and take his answer.

And also if it please you to send me money I will [*p. 194*] do the best for you I can at all times.[d] As for barley, is now much redy and in chambers; for wheat, that such that now [...][e] <ready>, the substance is gon. Yowr men also kiln dry. Beanes is at Gainsbrough[2] vj*li* score, and barly at 4*li* and xiij nobles a skore, and wheat is at Hull at ij*li* a skore. I pray you send me word in a bill what ye will haue done as conserning this writing in all condittions. And thus Jesus preserue you.

By yours to his litle power Georg Johnson clerk[f]

Endorsed (p. 193): To Mr Robart Plompton the yonger be this deliuered

[a] *Marginal note*: 14 letter by Georg Johnson, clerk.
[b] to *deleted.*
[c] *A word deleted.*
[d] *Marginal note*: 14 letter by Georg Johnson, clerk.
[e] had *deleted.*
[f] *Marginal note*: Copied the 8 of June 1626, Thursday.

[1] So styled during the lifetime of his uncle, Robert Plumpton, of Knaresborough.
[2] Near Robert Plumpton's estate at Waterton.

235 *John Doddington to Mrs Isabel Plumpton, 22 February [?1539–40] (No. 6, p. 185)*

Right worshipfull and my singler good mistress,[a] my duty to you premised, in my most hertyest maner I recomend me vnto you. Pleaseth you to vnderstand I haue receiued your letter, by the which I vnderstand that your pleasure is that I shuld lett Edward Glydal haue such parcels of ground of your maner of Sacomburs as which he[b] think to be nessary for him, and which parcils I think be minded to be let. Mistress, as yet I haue let no percill of the same, your maner, to no person. So ever the les, I haue oferd Glidall that if I let any persill of the sam, that he shold haue the perfirment therof before any other person, and as farr as I can prevaile, he hath in mind to haue ney percill of the same land. He hath taken a [*p. 186*] farme[c] of my lord of Essex,[1] and that he intendeth to inhabit and dwell; and his eldest son, which lately dweld in a coppie hold of his father in Sacomb, hath taken and dwelleth in a farme of [...][d] <Mr Holts> in Lankeshire, about Wouden.[2] And the same copie hold the said Edward Glidal wold haue me to take of him and put in account therin my self, and that then I shold & might tach land of the sam, your said maner, to the said coppiehold I shuld think expedient, and I as yet am not minded to take any copehold. Soeuertheless, if Gladall himselfe or his son be minded to occupie any of the said land that I shall be minded to let, he shall hau the preferment therof, and your [...][e] <comaundment> in that behalfe, or in any other thing that in me lieth to be obse[ru]yd and kept to the [...][f] best of my power by the same, as Jesus [knoweth,] who preseue you in good and prosprus health, with long continuance of the same. In hast, from London, the xxijth of Febuary.

Your servant & to camaund John Doddington[g]

Endorsed (p. 185): To the right worshipfull Mrs Isabell Plompton this with speede

[a] *Marginal note*: 5 letter by John Dodington.
[b] *MS* he which.
[c] *Marginal note*: Letter 5 by John Doddington.
[d] his father *deleted*.
[e] contenment *deleted*.
[f] lease *deleted*.
[g] *Marginal note*: Copied the 5 of June 1626.

[1] Henry Bourchier, earl of Essex (d. March 1540), or Thomas Cromwell, raised to the earldom 18 April 1540 and executed the same year. Mackie, 404, 414n.
[2] The manor of Wodden, near Eccles, formerly an estate of Whalley Abbey, was granted to Thomas Holcroft (kntd 1544), who later transferred it to the senior branch of the family, headed by his brother, Sir John Holcroft of Holcroft, *VCH, Lancs*, iv, 372.

236 *John Doddington to William Plumpton, 6 June* *(No. 22, p. 200)*

Right worshipfull,[a] in my most hartyest maner I commend me to you, and likewise to my good mistress your wife, trusting to Jesus that you and all your children and family be in good health. And wheare I perceiue by Robart Setell, your servant, that the perty who oweth the lease you sent vnto me to be exemplefied, thinketh long for the same, and suposes the same lease to be [*?lost*],[b] Sir, truth it is the same lease is and remaineth in the custody of Mr Henley[1] of the court of augmentation of the kings maiesties crown, and is assigned with the hands of Mr [*p. 201*] Chauncler[2] and councell[c] of the court aforsaid, & vpon the iiij day of this present month of June was deliuered to Duke, clarke of the said councell, to ingrosse in parchment, and then to be sealed with the seale of the same court, which shall be done and finished within fower or 6 dayes next coming. And shortly also, I shall send you the same with a bill of such somes of money as I haue & shall disburse for the same, so that I trust the said party haue no cause to mistrust the having therof. He may not haue that leases in revertion be sold on Alowed Sent Leasur. And frindship, as knoweth our lord God, who ever preserue you. Scribled in hast at London, the 6th day of June.

Yours to comaund John Dodington[d]

Endorsed (p. 200): To the right worshipfull and his singuler good master Mr Wm Plompton esquire this

[a] *Marginal note*: the 22 letter by John Dodington.
[b] *MS* best.
[c] *Marginal note*: 22 letter by John Dodington.
[d] *Marginal note*: Copied the 10 of June, Satterday.

[1] Walter Henley, formally appointed solicitor of augmentations 16 Dec. 1537. He held the office until the autumn of 1547 when it was reported that he was seriously ill and almost blind, Richardson, *Augmentations* 43n, 140n., 492; *L & P*, xiii (1), 67, 109, 253, 1093.
[2] Lord Audley was succeeded as chancellor in 1544 by Thomas, Lord Wriothesley, *HBC*, 86.

237 *John Doddington to William Plumpton, 7 October [?1542] (No. 24, p. 202)*

Right worshipfull Sir,[a] my deuty to you premised, in my hartyest maner I commend me vnto you and to my mistress, your wife. Pleaseth yt you to vnderstand my master[1] hath wryten his letter to Mr Goldsbrough[2] for a do for your mastership in Bilton park, or the peark of Heay,[3] at your pleasur. I trust it will be signed, and if it be not, [*p. 203*] my master[b] desires your mastership to send him word therof. The same letter is herin closed. And I pray your mastership if ther be any service that I doe your mastership, it will please you to commaund me as your servant. And thus pray almighty God to preserve you. Scribled in hast the vij day of October.

Your servant to comaund John Dodington[c]

Endorsed (p. 202): To the right worshipfull Mr William Plompton esquire

[a] *Marginal note*: 24 letter by John Dodington.
[b] *Marginal note*, as above.
[c] *Marginal note*: Copied the 12 June, Mondey.

[1] Robert Plumpton.
[2] Possibly Edward Goldsborough, king's sergeant at arms (d. by Oct. 1543), who received a regrant for life of the office of feodary of Knaresborough with the forestership of wards in Knaresborough forest, 6 July 1523, Somerville, i, 526; *L & P*, xv, 473; xvi, 432, 708; xviii (i), 184.
[3] Hayah Park, Knaresborough.

238 *John Doddington to William Plumpton, [26 March 1543] (No. 23, p. 201)*

Right worshipfull,[a] in my most hertyest maner I commend me vnto you, and likewise to my good mistress your wife, and very glad wold be to heare of your good health and all your children. Theas be to certifie you that it hat pleased God Almightie to take into his mercy the late person of Sacomp, Mr John Petty.[1] He departed this tronsetory life vpon Easter Day last at vij of the clock before nowne, whose sowle I pray Jesus perdon. And let vs pray that he shall succede him be of no worse sorte than he hath bene.

I and all my neighbors hartyly desire your mastership in also he that shall [*p. 203*] haue the same[b] be minded to be resident and abid vpon the same personage, than that you will moue him that cumes: Sir Christopher Bird, person, who honestly did kepe the cure vnder the forsaid late person and the maintenment of God service, and may be his depete, as he was to the other late person; wherof I and all your other tennants wold be very glad.

Sir, I haue sent you the kings writ of *dedimus potestatum* by Mr Birnand[2] with a letter sealed in a box, which I trust is come to your hands; and what your pleasure shal be to commaund me in the premises, I pray you let me know and I shall be glad to accomplish the same. And I pray you haue me hartyle commended to Mr Robart Plompton, your son, and to my mistress [...][c] <his> wife, and to Mr Dinis, your son, and Mr Birnand. And I pray you informe Mr Birnand his son is [...][d] <mery> and in good health, thanks be to Jesus, who euer perserve you and all yours. Scribled in hast at your maner of Sacomp, the Monday next after Easter Day.

By your <to> commaund John Dodington[e]

Endorsed (p. 201): To the right worshipfull Mr Wm Plompton of Plompton in the county of York esquire deliuer with speed

[a] *Marginal note*: 23 letter by John Dodington.
[b] *Marginal note, as above.*
[c] your *deleted.*
[d] well *deleted.*
[e] *Marginal note*: Copied the 12 of June, Monday.

[1] John Petty's successor at Sacombe was Richard Sharp, admitted 3 May 1543, on presentation of William Plumpton in right of his wife.
[2] Probably John Birnand of Knaresborough (d. by 1545), son of Robert Birnand (d.1502). John was receiver of Knaresborough and Pontefract, 1526 for life, an appointment which 'may well have been due to some connection with the steward, Lord Darcy', and to his professional skill rather than prominence in West Riding society, Smith, 68; Somerville, 517, 526; **24**, **40**.

239 *Christopher Twistleton*[1] *to William Plumpton, 28 December [?1543] (No. 26, p. 207)*

Also, in my most hartiest manner,[a] as vnaquainted, I haue me hartile commended vnto you. And whearas I am informed by Oliuer, my [...][b] <tennant>, that the kings maiesties oficers requireth of you and of me and diuers other [...][c] <tennants> of Watterton to be contribetors to the charges and staving of the watters of Ancotes, and that you haue suficent writing for your discharg and mine in that behalfe; therfore this shall be to desire you, in voidin farther trobles and charges that might insue against vs both, that you will deliuer [*p. 208*] vnto my said tennant[d] a trew coppe of the said writing, if you haue any such, whearby I and my frinds and counsill, with your frinds [and] councill, at this next tearme may might to geather and may take som order and derection in that behalfe, as may be for the safte of vs and our heires, if your deed will maintaine the same.

And further, whear I am informed by my said tennant that you haue partly denied him his wey to his mor,[e] which my tennants haue alwayes hertofore had, desiring you therfore that he may gentle haue the same, as one gentleman and gentlewoman may vse one another with fauor, and in so doing you shall [receiue][f] at my hands such pleasur as I and my frinds can do for you, as knoweth our lord God, who euer haue you in his keping. From Dertford, the xxviij day of December.

By your loving frind Christopher Twistleton[g]

Endorsed (p. 207): To the right worshipfull Mr Plompton of Plompton in Yorkshire this be deliuered

[a] *Marginal note*: 26 letter by Christopher Twistleton.
[b] servant *deleted.*
[c] gentlemen *deleted.*
[d] *Marginal note*: 26 letter by Christopher Twistleton.
[e] *Marginal note*: Watreton ne.
[f] *MS* atuie.
[g] *Marginal note*: Copied the 13 of June, Teusday.

[1] Of Barlby, near Selby, son of Alderman John Twistleton, citizen and goldsmith of London, and his wife Alice, daughter of Ralph Leatham, Stapleton, 235n., 245n.; **224**.

240 *Sir Henry Savile*[1] *to William Plumpton, [?1544]* *(No. 28, p. 209)*

Cossin Plompton,[a] in as harty manner as I can think I recomend [me] to you. First, all your frinds ar in good health heare. I have bene very sick since ye went, but I am well now, I thank God. I haue vewed Christall: þe rent of it, as it is now letted, x*s* iiij*d* score, xv*li* viij*s*; and Arthington[2] is about xx*li* at þe end of xvj yeares; the will be iij score pownd aboue þe rent. And the woods, my man sayes he dar giue a thowsand marke for them, but he thinks without dowt he will make a thowsand *li*. I haue written to my cossin, Henry Savill of Lapset,[3] to go thorowgh with my lord of Canterbury for it.[4] Acording to the comunication, and ye and my cossen John Gascoyne[5] shall haue a part if ye will wryte to me that ye will strike to it, and I will haue a part, and Robart Savill[6] and Henry Savill of Lapsit will stand to tow parts. I think the woods will giue vs our money and more, and the lease cleare to be gotten [*p. 210*] for laying out of the money[b] till we can make it againe of the woods. I haue sent you a rental of it, what it is euery cloase. I pray you let my cossen John Gascoyne se this letter & þe rentall. Kepe it secret from all other. I pray God send vs merry meting. All written in my ship at Timmoth. Cussin Gascoyne, your children ar mery.

Your asured kinsman Henry Savill[c]

Endorsed (p. 209): To my cosen Plompton of Plompton this deliuer with spede

[a] *Marginal note*: 28 letter by Henry Savill knight.
[b] *Marginal note, as above.*
[c] *Marginal note*: Copied the 14 of June, Wedsday.

[1] Of Thornhill, Yorks, App. III. I am grateful to Mr Michael Collinson for his suggestion that this letter could date from late April 1544 before Sir Henry, who held a captaincy in the army mustered for war against the Scots, sailed on 1 May from Tynemouth after waiting a week there for a fair wind.
[2] Formerly a house of Cluniac nuns, [Sir William Dugdale], *Monasticon Anglicanum* (6 vols, 1817–30), iv, 518.
[3] The Saviles of Lupset, a collateral branch of the Thornhill family, were descended from Thomas Savile (d.1501/6).
[4] Thomas Cranmer, archbishop of Canterbury 1533–55. On 7 June 1542 he acquired lands and woods belonging to the former Cistercian monastery of Kirkstall and the nunnery at Arthington, *L & P*, xvii, 256.
[5] Probably John Gascoigne of Lazencroft (d.1557), of a collateral branch of the Gascoignes of Gawthorpe, Smith, 290; *Flower's Visitation*, 45.
[6] Robert Savile of Howley (d.1583), Sir Henry's illegitimate son, who ultimately acquired the whole property in fee. It later descended to the Brudenells, hence the prevalence of 'Brudenell' and 'Cardigan' in the street names in this part of Leeds, Stapleton, 247n., App. III.

241 *Sir Henry Savile to William Plumpton, 8 November [1544] (No. 32, p. 213)*

Cossin Plompton,[a] I recomend me to you, and as I perceue by my son Robart servant, ye say ye will com over and hunt with me. And it please you so to do, ye shall be as hertyly welcome as any man that cam heare of a good space. Ye shall se your arrow fly and your grayhound run, and all thos that comes with you, winter and somer, when it please you to come, as long as I liue.

As for the other matter, I pas not a litle of it. I haue yet waide it with my councill, and as ye shall know at our meting, as I am informed, and as I take it, thear ar many dowts by yt. When I speak with you I will hide nothing from you in this then in no other cause. When ye intend to come, let me know what time, [*p. 214*] or els ye may hape[b] neither to haue me then nor my son at home; but my wife ye shal be sur to find, & she will send som with you that shall let you se both rid and fallow, if ye will take the paine. I haue killed a hind or tow of late, & they ar very fatt this yeare, both in the woods at Tankersley[1] and in my gardin at Thornehill. I think ye weare never yet in no grownd of mine, and I never say no man naye. Therfore the faut is in you and not in me: ye may amend the faut when it pleas you.

The cause of my sending of my servant at this time is this: he informes me that in your countrie thear is a man that can kill otters very well; wherfor I haue sent him to git him to me for a weke. I asure you they do me exceding much harme at diuers places, and especiall at Woodkirk & Thornhill, & lyes in small becks. My folks se them dayly and I can not kill them: my hownds be not vsed to them. From Sothill the 8 of November.

By your asured kinsman Henry Savill knt

After the making herof, or it was sealed, cam my son home from London. Of Wedsday came my lord of Norfock[2] to the court. The Spanish duke is gon; the earle of Hertfort,[3] the bishop of Winchester,[4] with the French ambasador[5] is gon to the emporer;[6] the duke of Sufolk,[7] with other remaines at Calisse. The Frenchmen that wear of sea [...][c] <ar> gon to Depe haven, and the Inglish men ar of the sea, but the cold weather [...][d] <will> sufer no man long to continew of the water. As conserning news of Scotland, giue credence to this bearrer.[8] This is my owne hand.[e]

Endorsed (p. 213): To my cossin Plompton of Plompton this be deliuered

[a] *Marginal note*: 32 letter by Henry S.
[b] *Marginal note, as above, but the page is torn.*
[c] by *deleted.*
[d] *An illegible word deleted.*
[e] *Marginal note*: Copied 16 June, Friday.

[1] South of Dewsbury in the West Riding.
[2] Thomas Howard, 3rd duke of Norfolk (d.1554).
[3] Edward Seymour, earl of Hertford, created duke of Somerset 1547, exec. Jan. 1551/2, *GEC*.
[4] Stephen Gardiner held the see, 1531–55, *HBC*, 259.
[5] Claude d'Annebault.
[6] Charles V.
[7] Charles Brandon, duke of Suffolk (d.1545). On 4 Sept. 1544 an army under Norfolk as captain-general had captured Boulogne, *GEC*.
[8] On 4 May 1544 Hertford, as lieutenant-general in the North, landed at Newhaven; he burnt Edinburgh, and laid waste the surrounding countryside before retiring to Berwick, *GEC*.

242 *Sir Henry Savile to William Plumpton, 28 November 1544* (*No. 31, p. 212)*

Cossin Plompton,[a] I hartely recommend me vnto you, thanking you for all your goodnes at all times. I haue receiued your letter by Roger Brindell, and wheare that ye wryte thear is noe dowghts if the matter had come to comunication. Ye ar the man that I trust, & by you I wold haue bene ordered, and if ye had so thought, I would haue confeined my selfe to you. But I perceiue the parte is not minded to commone with him; his wife thinks him to light. And I think, consider his qualeties, his living, his posabilete, and confer al together, I think, as good chepe as this I shall git a living for him, both as good and as fare;[1] <&> I am sur ther haith bene <comredis won with other far wars> then he, <excep> one faute. And as for that, ther is and haithe bene many good men with that faut: it is the thing that he cannot amend. It lets him not to eat, drink, slepe; he can liue as well of it I haue giuen him, as though it had desendit to him. And if his brother dy without isew, in all by gift he shall haue v hundreth mark land, [...][b] <& if> he were but inheretable by the law, [*p. 213*] he shold be heir to him;[c] but for defaut of heirship, I thinke he will not change his estate in this case; and for defaute of heires of my body lawfuly begotten he shall inherit all that I haue. But in the meane onely his fault so shall not hirt him in no profets. Let this matter pas. I hertyle thank you as much as if it had come to pase. He is much bownd to you; and, if euer he be able to do you pleasure. I trust ye shull se him git a living ere þe yeare is past. At York, if ye will come and kill a hind, ye shal be hertyly welcom. Wryten at Sothill[2] the xxviij of November, anno 1544, 36 H.8.

Your asured frind Henry Savill knt[d]

Endorsed (p. 212): To my right worshipfull coussin Mr Wm Plompton of Plompton esquire this deliuer

[a] *Marginal note*: 31 letter by Henry Savill.
[b] *A word deleted.*
[c] *Marginal note, as above.*
[d] *Marginal note*: Copied 16 June, Friday.

[1] The writer's determination to endow his illegitimate son adequately was fully realised, App. III.

[2] The estate near Thornhill, acquired by Sir Henry in right of his wife, Elizabeth Soothill, who inherited a large part of the Yorks possessions of her father, Thomas Soothill (d.1535), Smith, 217.

243 *Sir Henry Savile to William Plumpton, 28 May 1545* *(No. 29, p. 210)*

Cossin Plompton,[a] after my hartie recommendations. Your seruant sheweth me ye were & haue bene very sick, wher<of> I am very sory; & if your sicknes continue wheare the commaundment comes forth, send forth your servants & tennants, and send forth your excuse to my lord lieutennant, with a letter of the trough of your sicknes, & of the time of the continuance therof; and being advertised of the truth he will excep of your lawfull and reasonable excuse. And thus hertely far you well. From York, the xxviij of May, anno 1545, 37 H.8.

Your asurred kinsman Henry Savill[b]

Endorsed: To his right worshipfull coussin Will: Plompton esquire this deliuer

[a] *Marginal note*: 29 letter by Henry Sauill knight.
[b] *Marginal note*: Copied the 15 of June, Thursday.

244 *Sir Henry Savile to William Plumpton, 5 May 1546* *(No. 30, p. 210)*

Cossin Plompton,[a] I hartely recommend me vnto you. The caus of my wryting to you is for that Roger Ramy said to me he thought ye would abowte Low Sonday be at Thornhill. Ye shall come to a old howse cleane downe and as yet litle amended, but ye shall be very welcome, as I can think. I wold be sory that ye shold take paine and I not at home when ye come. To morrow begging Thursday I must of force ride to Tankersley viij [*p. 211*] myles hence[b] and mete my lord of Shrewsbury,[1] who will be thear to morrow by ij of the clock, and se a showt at [. . .][c] <a> stage, as my keper hath sent me wourd.

And of Monday, Tewsday & Wedsday thear is apoynted a great number of gentlemen to mette at cocxs at Sheifeild, whear I entend, God willing, to be, and every night will ly at Tankerslay. Soe it will be Friday or I come to Thornhill, which is the xviij of May. Wherfore, I desire you either put of your comming to that day, or take so much paine to come the viij myles to Tankerxlay, whear I haue no lodging, but you shall haue the best bed the keper hath, and ye shall se a polard or tow, both rid and falow, and se all our good coxs fight, if it plese you, and se the maner of our cocking. Ther wilbe Lanckeshre of one parte, and Derbeshire of another parte, & Hallomshire of the third parte.[2] I perceiue your cocking varieth from ours, for ye lay but the battell; and if our battell be but x*li* to v*li*, theare wilbe x*li* to one laye or the battell be ended. And whensoeuer ye come, I require you to take time to hunt with me for one weke. Bring bowes and grayhounds, and at the time of the year, hownds. A polard is swet now, and I loue it best now, at this season. And by Whytsonday this year I shall haue fatt bucks, & or any red deare be fatt it will be July, as far as my experience serves. Com when ye will, and such as I haue, ye shall se. And bring good strife, for I warne you they ar wild abowt Tankerxlay and ill to cach. And if all fale, I haue that ar tame enough.

I make all these brages to cause you to come, for I neuer yet did se you in thease parts; and ye shall come no time wrong, fence time then other. I haue tame plenty lyeth out; [*p. 212*] I can make you game[d] at rid and falow, and stir noe rascall. I besich Jesus send vs merry meting. Thus hertyly far ye well, this Wendsday, at Thornhill, the vth of May, anno 1546, 38 H.8.

Your asured frind Henry Savill knt[e]

Endorsed (p. 210): To my cossin Plompton this be deliurerd

[a] *Marginal note*: 30 letter by Henry Savill knt.
[b] *Marginal note, as above.*
[c] the *deleted.*
[d] *Marginal note*: 30 letter by Henry Savill knt.
[e] *Marginal note*: Copied 16 June, Friday.

[1] Francis Talbot, 5th earl of Shrewsbury (d.1560), son of George Talbot, **108**.
[2] Suggesting that the 'county might have become a focus for loyalty and affection', Roger Virgoe comments on the intercounty rivalry displayed here, in Hicks (ed.), *Profit, Piety and the Professions*, 6.

245 *Robert Savile to William Plumpton, 14 September [1546]* *(No. 27, p. 208)*

Right worshipfull,[a] after my most hartiest manner I recommend me to you. I receiued your letter of Friday. I was buisie a hunting, but as for your suerty, ye shall never be bownd to me, for I will not sew you: I had rather louse it. I went immeaddetly to Mr Gargraues[1] howse, & he was with my father, and so I mist of him. I haue drawn an obligation to be sealed afore you and your servant, Settill, for a knowledge, and my servant shall deliuer a hundred marke; & for because I am in no seurty wheare I shall be when ye or any frind of yours shall call,[*p. 207*] I shall let[b] another hundred marke [with][c] [...][d] the bearer herof, of an owre warning to be redy, vpon reasonable seurty to be repaid within one yeare. And to this bearrer I haue declaired my mind to shew you in all things. And thus I bid you hartely farwell. From Sotthill, þe xiiij of September.

Your asured to his power Robart Sauill[e]

No endorsedment

[a] *Marginal note*: 27 letter by Robart Savill.
[b] *Marginal note, as above.*
[c] *MS* whe.
[d] his *deleted.*
[e] *Marginal note*: Copied the 14 of June, Wedsday.

[1] Sir Henry Savile's mother, Elizabeth Paston, daughter of William Paston (d.1490), a younger son of Judge Paston (d.1444), married Robert Gargrave of Gargrave and Nostell as her fourth husband, N. Davis, *The Paston Letters and Papers of the Fifteenth Century* (2 vols, Oxford, 1971–6), i, pp. lii, lvii.

246 *Renold Besey to William Plumpton, 7 August [1546]*[a] *(Probably no.37; Stapleton 252–3)*

After harty commendations premised, this shall be to advertise you, that my lord Presedent[1] and other of the kings honnerable comishiners hath delivered to me a precept to cause to com befor them at the castle of York, the xvith day of this month of August, a certane number of worshipfull men of Yorkshire, wherof ye be one. Wherfore, I require you to accept this my letter for a sufichent warning, for ye to be at the castle the same xvith day, at x of the clock before nowne, to inquire upon certaine articles and matters which shall be then and thear by the said comishioners declared upon our sovarayne lord the kings behalfe. Wherfore, I pray you, faile not, as ye will answer to the said comishioners. Thus hartely far ye well. From York this viith day of august

By yours to comaund Renold Besey clerk of the castle of York
Endorsed: To the right worshipfull Mr Plompton esquire deliver theis

[a] *As there is now no trace of this letter the transcript is taken from Stapleton's edition, pp. 252–3.*

[1] Cuthbert Tunstall, bishop of Durham (d.1559), was appointed president of the Council in the North in 1537. In *c.*1550 he was succeeded by Francis Talbot, 5th earl of Shrewsbury, Reid, 151–2, 169; *DNB.*

247 *William Hungate*[1] *to William Plumpton, [July 1547]*[a] *(Probably no.38; Stapleton, iiin)*

Right worshipful Sir,[2] in my most lowly manner I recommend me unto you for all kindness shewed to me and all myne, and for the good chear that you, my mistress your wife, maid me at my last being with you. And the cause of my wryting to you at this time [*blank*] yt will please you to call to your remembrance [...]

[a] *As there is now no trace of this letter in the Letterbook the transcript is taken from Stapleton's edition, p. iv. n.*

[1] Of Saxton, Yorks, whose will was proved in 1548, Thoresby, 247; G.D. Lumb (ed.), *Testamenta Leodiensia, 1539–53* (Publications of the Thoresby Society, xxvii, 1930), 200–1; Kirby, *Documents*, 270.

[2] William Plumpton died 11 July 1547, his will was proved 12 Aug. following, *Test. Ebor.*, vi 258–60. When his grandson received seisin of the Yorks estate 23 Nov. 1564 it was valued at £68 8s 9½d p. a., WYASL, Acc.1731/4, fol. 27.

248 *William Woodruffe*[1] *to Mrs Isabel Plumpton, 25 March [1548]* *(No. 10, p. 189)*

With most harty commendations in Christ Jesus,[a] good Mrs Plompton, this is to advertis you of the dispatch of such matters as you did commit vnto me at my last being with you, wheare that I haue traueled as I might of, partly by the ade and help of Mr Bill,[2] your very frind, I think, who hath him most hartily recommended <both> [...][b] to you and Mr Dynes, and hath sent your lozengs[3] for a token. Ye shall allso receiue with this bearrer a letter to Mr Haymond,[4] feodarry, for your lease, procurred by Mr Bill, who shewed me that your charges in the cheker is dispacht, and your cossin Girlington[5] hath brought your acquitance.

And order is taken for you at the court of the wards, and all is well stayd but yet not paid. Your request was moued to [...][c] <Sir> Arthur Darcy[6] first, who taketh the matter frindly, as ye shall know. The other gentleman was then by chaunc from the court, which was the cause of the first talke with Sir Arthur, but in such wise as we may, and shall with honesty take the way which shalbe thought the best to you and your frinds.

Because ye may se the effect of my lord Treasurrers letters[7] for your lease, I haue sent it to you patent and open; and that knowing the efect therof, then ye may send it to the feodary your [*p. 190*] selfe,[d] which wear good that ye did with spede conuenient. Thus I comit you to the permishion, to Him that canne, to will iustice, [who] all your lawfull <deedes> of honesty desires no dought, who I pray long to preserve in health. From my lodge at Howell, the Palme Sunday.[e]

Yours to my litle power William Wodrif[f]

The cause þat I came not now to you is a broken shin, which hath much vexed me.

Endorsed (p. 189): To the right worshipfull Mrs Plompton at Plompton Hall

[a] *Marginal note*: 10 letter by Will. Wodrif.

[b] vn *deleted.*

[c] and *deleted.*
[d] *Marginal note*: 10 letter by Will. Wodrif.
[e] *Marginal note*: Copied the 7 of June 1626.
[f] *Appended:* From my lord at Howell.

[1] Younger son of Thomas Woodruffe, of Woolley, near Wakefield, William was a tenant of James, Lord Mountjoy in Howell Grange, a property of the former Nostell Priory. He may have sought his lord's favour to promote Isabel Plumpton's interests. In her will she refers to him as her 'lovinge frende and kynsman', *Test.Ebor.*, vi, 260–2; *Flower's Visitation*, 350–1.

[2] Thomas Bill, physician to Edward VI, having purchased the wardship and custody of Isabel's young grandson William, 16 Nov. 1547, granted it to Isabel, 12 Nov. 1549, App. II, 83, 84.

[3] Lozenges. Possibly lozenge-shaped shields on which the arms of a widow were emblazened, *OED*.

[4] William Hammond, an officer of the court of wards, *CSPD, 1566–69*, 278; Kirby, *Documents*, 269.

[5] **250**.

[6] Second son of Thomas, Lord Darcy (exec. 1538).

[7] Edw. Seymour, 1st duke of Somerset, deprived 10 Oct. 1549. Succeeded 3 Feb. 1550 by William Paulet, earl of Wiltshire.

249 *William Woodruffe to Mrs Isabel Plumpton, [1549 × 1550]* *(No. 11, p. 190)*

Right worshipfull Mistress,[a] in my harty wise I commend me to you, with thanks giuen to you for all your genntlenes. Certyfying you that as yet my wife hath not laid her belly, but remaineth at hir wits end. And since me being with you I haue not had iij dayes of health: I thank God albeit. I am better now, which aple, that I was thinking, by Gods helpe, to se you after the holadayes. In the mean time I haue sent this knowen bearrer to you for to se you, because I am not all well. Praying your aduertis me of your health and wellfarre, which I will be glad to hear of as I wold be any frind I haue, as God knowes, who haue you in his keping. And so, fare you well. From Howell Grang, this Palme Sunday.

Yours to my litle power withowt gile Wiliam Wodrife[b]

I am sory [...][c] of the heuines of the death of Mr Dinis wife.[1]

Endorsed: To the right worshipfull Mrs Plomton at Plompton Hall widow

[a] *Marginal note*: 1 letter by Will. Wodrife.
[b] for your *deleted.*
[c] *Marginal note*: Copied the 7 of June, Wednesday.

[1] Ursula, daughter of Richard Aldburgh of Aldburgh, great-great granddaughter of Sir William Plumpton (d.1480), and niece of Ralph Aldburgh, writer of **250**. She and Denis (d.1596) were married 4 July 1547, and she left a son, Richard, WYASL, Acc. 1731/9-M3.

250 *Robert Girlington*[1] *to Mrs Isabel Plumpton, 10 February [1549/50] (No. 8, p. 187)*

Right worshipfull and my singuler good Aunt,[a] my deuty to you premised, I haue me recommended vnto you. This shall be to certyfy you that according to your commaundment haith kept your cort at Sacompte, and there Setle, your servant, reseiued of [...][b] <tow> men that was admited tennements at this your cort iiij*li* saue 40*d*; and of one power woman xiij*s* 4*d*; [...][c] <which> was admitted tennements in reverscion he did receiue xj*s*, which I haue written to you, ouer and aboue your rents and your estreats. And I desire you, good Aunt, to let me know how you will haue your corts ordered, whether you will haue them kept one or tow times in the yeare, by your next letter; and I, acording to your commaundement gevin I shold doe, with the grace of almighty Jesus, who haue you, yours and all your houshold in his blessed keping. Written the xth of Febuarij

By yours to comaund Robart Girlington[d]

Endorsed: To his right worshipfull aunt Mrs Isabell Plompton at Plompton Hall deliuer this

[a] *Marginal note*: 8 letter by Rob: Girlington.
[b] Tolle *deleted.*
[c] whitch *deleted.*
[d] *Marginal note*: Copied the 6 of June 1626, Tewsday.

[1] Possibly Robert, a younger son of Nicholas Girlington, of Hackforth, Richmondshire. His father, or grandfather, supported Sir Robert at the York assizes 1502. Stapleton suggests that Robert may have been related to Isabel Plumpton through his father's marriage with William Elleson's sister Joan, *Flower's Visitation*, 141; Stapleton, 256n.; CB, 824; **129**, **162**; App. II, 68.

251 *Ralph Aldburgh to Mrs Isabel Plumpton, 2 February [?1551/2] (No. 9, p. 187)*

Aunt,[a] this is to certife you that my father in law[1] sent one to me ij letters þat came from London from Robart Girdlington, one to you which is in hast, as far as my father sent me word to send them [*p. 188*] as shortly as I could[b] send þem to you. Furthermore, I wold haue you them sent with Langton; them I giue, and he wold not carry them, and so I haue spoken vnto Mr Egeme<ton> for barneckles, and so I shold haue gon ouer to Lodington to haue bought them, and so I let them aloane. And so I desire you haue me remembred to my mistres,[2] and to let her know that my lady servants Hilyeard[3] demaunds halfe a quarter of beanes for their fat swine, and if it weare in condition or no; and if it be not, to alowe the same in the xx quarters that she shold haue, and barly [...][c] <in> like case. And so to let you know that barly rises of pease, as they say, and I haue sold none as yet; and that they ar threshing in the one lath beanes and barley both, for swine makes il work, and so I make them labor as hard as <they> can for the same; & soe by this bearrer I send ij letters, and I giue him for his labour xij*d* for coming. No more ouer to you, but Jesus haue you in his kepping. Written this Lady Day at night in hast. And to let you know whearas ye told me of 6 horses, the which they say the sorrell nag is not of yours, and sayes that ye haue but 5; and so I wold answer it. For your hofer, it likes not, I shud a sold it, I trust, for 4*s* or better, if ye will.

By me Rafh Audbrough[d]

Endorsed (p. 187): To the right worshipfull Mrs Plompton of Plompton Hall be this deliuered

[a] *Marginal note*: 9 letter by Rafh Audbrough.
[b] *Marginal note, as above.*
[c] of *deleted.*
[d] *Marginal note*: Copied the 6 of June, Tewsday 1626.

[1] Stapleton implies that the writer, 3rd son of Sir Richard Aldburgh (d.1514), was married to Robert Girlington's sister, and that Isabel Plumpton was aunt to both, 218–19n., 237.

[2] Anne, widow of Robert Plumpton (d.1546). The manor of Waterton, where Robert died, was part of her dower, **232**; App. III.

[3] Joan, widow of Sir Ralph Hillyard of Winestead in Holderness, son or grandson of Sir Robert Hillyard (d.1501) and descendant of Robert Hillyard of Winestead, identified erroneously in a number of sources as Robin of Holderness, leader of an abortive Percy-inspired rebellion of 1469, Ross, *Edward IV*, 127; *Test. Ebor.*, iv, 11–12.

252 *Mrs Ann Pole[1] to Mrs Isabel Plumpton,[2] 6 March [1551/2] (No. 7, p. 186)*

Right worshipfull sister,[a] after most harty and louing commendations, with like desire of your good health and the long continuance of the same, this shal bee to giue you most harty thanks for al your gentlenes unto mee shewid, and in especially for your goodness shewid unto John Pool my son: he hath you most hartily commended, as your poor kinsman and bedesman, and he desires you and I both to take no displeasure with him for his long tarrijng here, for as yet he is at no point for his childs part of my husbands goods. Therfore I desire you, as my trust is, that you wil bee so good aunt unto him. Also, I desir to haue me commended to my sister Clare and to my son Dennis [*p. 187*] sending him Gods blessing and mine,[b] and to al other my kin and frends. Also my son Richard and John commends them unto [...][c]

<you> and their Aunt Clare, and to Master Dennis, and to al other their good frends. And so Jhesu preserue you. From Rodburne, the 6 of March,

By your sister to her power Ann Poole[d]

Endorsed (p. 186): To her worshipful sister Mistress Plompton at Plompton Hall deliuer these

[a] *Marginal note*: 7 letter by Mrs Ann Poole.
[b] *Marginal note*: 7 letter.
[c] you *deleted*.
[d] *Marginal note*: Copied the 5 day of June 1626, Munday.

[1] Daughter of Sir Robert Plumpton and widow of German de la Pole (d. Jan. 1551/2), **138**n.
[2] Isabel Plumpton died 30 July 1552, *Test. Ebor.*, vi, 260–2; Introd., p. 17, App. II, 86, 88.

APPENDIX I

Transcripts of Selected Documents from the Plumpton Coucher Book and Other Sources

1 *Letter to Sir Robert de Plumpton, 24 May 1416* *(CB, 378)*

Unto the worshipfull & reuerent Sir, Monsire Robert de Plompton, steward of the forest of Knaresburgh, or to his deputies, William Bedale, mercer, Richard Bellingham, mercer, John Vnthanke, spicer, William Garnet, bower, Thomas Constable, fletcher, & Thomas Lincolne, citizens of Yorke, send honor & reuerence. For als mekill als an John of Lawe, chapman, sold unto Richard Clerk of Burebrig a pak with diuers mercery therein & a horse for xxie nobles of the kings coyn, on Thursday next after St Elen Day last past, in the towne of Burebrig, als wee are fully by true men enformed; and for als mekill als it is needfull & necessary thing to all Christen men to record & beare witness to the soth, we do ye to witt that the gude quilke the foresaid John sold att Burebrig was his awen proper gude, and leley and truly bought & sold; and a gude man of name and fame euer that was & is halden among us, and for non other neuer that was halden ne reccond. And this witnesse we by this our present letter, written & seald att Yorke, the xxiiij day of May in the yeare of King Henry fift after the Conquest of England, fourth.[a]

[a] *Appended:* This letter hath six seales. Copied 3 February. 1615.

2 *Testimony of Witnesses, 26 October 1503* *(WYASYAS, MS 650, p. 243[r])*

Be itt knowne to all men yatt forasmuch as itt is meritorie and medefull for euery true Crysten man to testify and bere true wytnes is euery true matter or cause; therefore we, William Ratcliffe, berying the age of v^{xx} yeres, Nicolas Whitfeld, of $iiij^{xx}$ and viij yeres, and John Thornton of $iiij^{xx}$ yeres, will record, and testify, for verrey trouthe, that the Lord Sir Thomas Clifford marryed Elizabeth his daughter vnto Roberte Plompton, the eldest son and heyr of Sir William Plompton, when she was bot of six yeres of age, and they were wedded att the chappell within the castell att Skypton, and the same day one John Garthe bare her in hys armes to the said chappell. And also itt was agreed att the same tyme yt if the foresaid Roberte dyed within age, that then the said Lord Clifford should haue the second son of the said Sir William Plompton vnto his said daughter. And they were bot iij yerre marryed when the said Roberte dyed. And when she came to the age of xij yeres she was marryed to William Plompton, second son to the foresaid Sir William. And the said Sir William promised the said Lord Clyfford that they should not lygg togedder till she came to the age of xvj yeres. And when shee came to xviij yeres she had Margarete, now Lady Roucliffe.

And how as euydenes hath ben imbeseld, or what as hath been doon syns, we canott tell, bott all that ys aforerehersed in this bill wee wyll make itt gode and, if nede be, depely depose afore the kynge, or his cownsell yt itt is matter of trawth, in any place where we shalbe commanded, as farr as ys possible for any such olde creatures to be carryed to. It witnes hereof to this true byll of record we, the seyd William, Nicolas and John hath sett our sealls the xxvjth day of October in the xixth yere of the reane of Kyng Henry the vijth.

[1] Copy of Bodl.Lib., Dodsworth MS vol. LXXXIII, fol. (transcripts of evidences from Skipton Castle).

3 *Indenture between Sir William Plumpton and Henry Sotehill, 11 February 1464* *(CB, 562)*

This indenture, made the xj day of February the third yeare of the reigne of King Edward the iiijth betwene Sir William Plompton, knight, on the one party, and Henry Sotehill, squier, on the other party, witnesseth that the said Sir William hath granted, & by thes presents granteth to the said Henry the keping & mariage of Elizabeth, cossin & one of the heirs apparants of the said Sir William, that is to say daughter of William Plompton, squier, son to the said Sir William.[a] Also it is agreed betweene the said Sir William & Henry that John, theldest son & heire apparent of the said Henry shall, with the grace of God, take to wife the said Elizabeth, & the said Elizabeth shall, with the grace of God, take to husband the said John; and in case that the said John decesse, that then any son of the said Henry that shalbe heire apparant to the said Henry shall take the said Elizabeth to wife, and she him into husband, if the law of the Church will suffer it.

Which Elizabeth the said Sir William hath deliuered to the said Henry. For the house keeping & marriage of the said Elizabeth in the manner & forme aforesaid, to be had, the same Henry hath paid to the said Sir William c *li*, and shall, afore the feast of St Michaell tharchangell next coming, find surety to the said Sir William, Brian Rouclif & Sir Richard Hammerton, knight, by his seuerall obligacion, to pay to them ccxxxiij *li* vj*s* viij*d* in the forme following, that is to say xx *li* att the feast of the Natiuity of St John Baptist next coming, and xx *li* at the feast of St Michaell tharchangell then next following, & xx *li* att the feast of Pasche that shalbe in the yeare of Our Lord 1465; and xx *li* att the feast of St Michaell that shalbe in the same yeare, and xx *li* att the feast of Pasche that shalbe in the yeare of Our Lord 1466; and xx *li* att the feast of St Michaell that shalbe in the same yeare, and xx *li* att the feast of Pasche that shalbe in the yeare of Our Lord 1467; and xx *li* att the feast of St Michael that shalbe in the same yeare, and xx *li* att the feast of Pasche that shalbe in the yeare of Our Lord 1468; and xx *li* at the feast of St Michael that shalbe in the same yeare, and xx *li* att the feast of Pasche that shalbe in the yeare of Our Lord 1469; & xx marcs att the feast of St Michaell that shalbe in the same yeare, vpon such condicion in euery of the said obligacions to be made, that if the said Elizabeth dy afore the day of payment in any of the said obligacions comprised, that then the same obligacion be voyd & of none effecte. All which obligacions shalbe deliuered to the keeping of Guy Fairfax by deliuery to them, the said Sir William, Brian & Richard when the said Sir William shall haue made a feoffement of manors, landes & tenements to the yearly value of xlvj marcs, after thintent, use & effect hereafter following.

And the said Sir William granteth to the said Henry by thes presents that the said Sir William shall, afore the feast of St Michael tharchangell next coming, make a do to be made by deed indented, whereof the said Henry shall haue the one part a sufficient & sure estate to Bran Rouclif, third baron the king's exchequer, Richard Hammerton, knight, George Darrell, knight, Richard Aldburgh, knight, John Gresley, knight, Walter Wortesley, knight, Richard Fitzwilliam, knight, John Sotehill, of Sotehill, squier, & Guy Fairfax to them & to their heires for euer, of manors, landes & tenements to the yearly value of xl marcs ouer all charges & reprises, they to haue the said manors, landes & tenements in trust, & to thintent, vse & effect that if the said Elizabeth dy within the age of xij years, that then the said Henry or his executors shall haue & perceiue yearly the issues, rents, fermes and profitts of the said manors, landes and tenements to the yearly vallue of xx marcs immediately after the decesse of the said Elizabeth, during the life of the said Sir William; & immediately after the decesse of the said Sir William the said Henry or his executors shall haue & perceiue yearly thissues, rents, fermes & profitts of the said manors, landes & tenements to the yearly vallue of xl marcs vnto the tyme that the said Henry or his executors shall haue taken & perceiued all such sumes of money as it shall hap him to haue paid to the said Sir William for the said marriage, for the said death, a parcell of the c *li* paid afore the date of this indenture, as the residew in the forme aforesaid to be paid. And that the said feoffez stand in the said feoffment, or other feoffez by them to be made, to thuse of the said Sir William & his heirs after the said money be content & paid.

And the said Henry granteth to the said Sir William by thes presents that if Margrett, sister to the said Elizabeth, dy without issue, the said Elizabeth than being alife & within thage of xiiij years, and if the said Sir William take a wife in time to come, & haue not issue masle by her, than being in life, which ought to be his heire masle apparent, that then the said Henry shall pay to the said Sir William ccc marcs, that is to say within a yeare after the decesse of the said Margrett, c marcs, if the said Elizabeth than liue & be within thage of xiiij yeares, noon such heir masle had by the said Sir William in the forme aforesaid, and within a yeare next sewing c marcs, if the said Elizabeth than liue & be within thage of xiiij yeares, noon such issue masle had by the said Sir William in the forme aforesaid; & within a yeare then next sewing c marcs if the said Elizabeth then liue & be within thage of xiiij yeares, none such issue masle had by the said Sir William in the forme aforesaid.

And if the said Elizabeth dy within thage of xiiij yeares, than such payments as shall hap to be behind of the same ccc marcs not paid cease, and pat for that some or payments of the said ccc marcs that shall hap to be paid at the tyme of the death of the said Elizabeth, the said Henry or his executors shall haue & perceiue yearly during the life of the said Sir William xx marcs of the foresaid manors, landes and tenements. And after his death xl marcs yearly of the foresaid manors, landes and tenements vnto the time that the said Henry or his executors be satisfied of as much money as it shall hap him to haue paid of the foresaid ccc marcs, and that the same feoffees stand in the same feoffment, or other feoffees by them to be made, to the same intent & effect, and as parcell for repayment of the same ccc marcs, as for repayment of the xc marcs abouesaid.

And the said Sir William granteth to the said Henry by thes presents that the said Henry or his executors shall take & perceiue yearly thissues, rents, fermes & profitts of thes the said manors, landes & tenements in forme aforesaid, parcell the payment afore rehersed, without interupcion of the said Sir William, his heirs or assignes. Moreouer, Sir William granteth to the said Henry by thes presents that if hereafter the said Sir William take a wife and haue issues masle by her which ought to be his heire masle apparant, that the said Henry shall haue the keping & marriage of the same issue masle, to be married to one of his daughters, for which marriage to be had the said Henry to pay to the said Sir William cc marcs, that is to say the day of the deliuery of the said issue masle to the said Henry c marcs, taking then of the said Sir William sufficient surety that in case the said issue masle dy afore the age of xiiij, that then the said Henry to be repaid of the c marcs. And that day xij moneths after the said deliuery of the said issue masle c marcs, taking then, in likewise, surety of the said Sir William that in case the said issue masle dy after the said age, that then the said Henry to be repaid of the said cc marcs.

And the same Henry granteth by thes presents to the said Sir William that he shall vnto John his son, or vnto him that shall hap to be heir apparant vnto the said Henry, who shall hap to haue, or take into wife the said Elizabeth, after the decesse of the said Henry & of Anne his wife, of John Boyvile & Alinor his wife, landes & tenements to the yearly value of c *li* in fe simple or fe taile, whereof the said Henry shalbe seized, or other to thuse of the same Henry, or of him that shall hap to be his heire apparent, wedded or to be wedded to the said Elizabeth after the decesse of the said Henry, Anne, John Boyvile & Alinor, his wife.

And the said Sir William granteth by thes presents to the said Henry, & faithfully promiseth that the same Sir William, nor any feoffe to his vse shall not alien nor charge any landes or tenements whereof he or any to his vse is seized but vnto him that by his said wif shalbe vnto the said Sir William heire masle apparent, except the alienation afore rehersed, and that it shalbe lawfull to the said Sir William to giue & grant, or to make to be given & granted for terme of lyfe to his wife that he shall wed in tyme to come, & to other certeine persons landes & tenements to the yearly value of c marcs, whereof vnto certeine persons to be named at the pleasure of the said Sir William, landes & tenements to the yearly value of c marcs. And also vnto Elizabeth, late the wife of the said William Plompton, squier, landes & tenements to the yearly value of xl *li* for terme of life.

And also the said Sir William granteth by thes presents to the said Henry that he, nor none of his stirring nor comaundment for him, shall perceiue nor stirre the said Elizabeth, nor Elizabeth hir mother to disagre to the said marriage, but faithfully he hath promised to be wele willed that they shall both agre to the said marriage.

And to all these covenantes aboue rehersed to be performed of the party of the said Sir William, the said Sir William byndeth himself & his heirs to the said Henry by thes presents in vjc *li* of sterling. And all these covenantes aboue rehersed to be performed of the party of the said Henry, the said Henry bindeth him & his heirs to the said Sir William by thes presents in vjc *li* of sterling. In witnesses whereof to the one party of this indenture remaining toward the said Henry, the said Sir William hath sett his seale. And to thother party of this indenture remaining toward the said Sir William, the said Henry hath sett his seale, the day & yeare aboue said.[b]

[a] *Marginal notes:* The marriage of Elizabeth Plumpton with John Suthill being the coheir of William Plumpton. *Anno* 1464 3 Edw.4 11 February.

[b] *Appended:* This indenture hath a seale att the coppying the 19th day of June 1616.

4 *Valors of the Principal Estates of Sir William Plumpton, 1479* (*BL, Add.MS 6698, fols 3v–4*)

Veri valores dominorum, maneriorum, terrarum, tenementorum nuper Willelmi Plompton, militis, in comitatibus Eborum, Nottinghamiae, Derbiae et Staffordiae in ano 19° Edwardi quarti in Annoque Domini 1479

Plumpton[a] in comitatu Eborum
Valet per annum per estimacionem —— £60
Valet in redditibus et firmis, tam libere tenencium quam ad voluntatem domini per annum – £32 4*s* 0½*d*.
Perquisita curie ibidem hoc anno – £4 3*s* 7*d* [?£4 3*s* 8*d*][b]
inde in redditibus resolutis – 13*s* 4*d*; feodum custodis bosci hoc anno – 30*s* 4*d*. Et valet de claro —— £34 4*s* 0½*d*

Dominium de Steeton in comitatu Eborum
Valet in redditibus et firmis, tam libere tenencium quam tenencium ad voluntatem domini ibidem – £29 17*s* 6*d*. Perquisita curie ibidem hoc anno – 50*s* inde in redditibus resolutis – 13*s* 4*d* per annum; feodum ballivi – 10*s* (hoc anno – £1 3*s* 4*d*).
Et valet de claro —— £31 4*s* 2*d*

Dominium de Idle in comitatu Eborum
Valet in redditibus et firmis per annum – £20.
Perquisita curiarum hoc anno – £4 6*s* 5*d* inde in fine pro respectu homagii et fine pro secta curie relaxanda hoc anno – 10*s*; feodis ballivorum – 20*s* (hoc anno – 30*s*).
Et valet de claro — £22 16*s* 5*d*

Summa valorum dominicorum predictorum — £153 19*s* 0½*d* [£153 1*s* 7½*d*]
Inde in redditibus resolutis ut supra – 36*s* 4*d*; feodis ballivorum ut supra – £3 0*s* 4*d* – £4 16*s* 8*d*
Et remanent —— £148 4*s* 11½*d*

Dominium de Kinoulton in comitatu Nottinghamiae
Firma manerii Kinoulton per annum – £32. Redditibus firme, tam libere tenencium quam tenencium ad volun-

tatem domini ibidem per annum – £5 10*s*. Perquisita curie ibidem hoc anno – 38*s* 10*d* [£1]; inde in redditibus [fol. 4] resolutis – 3*s*.
Et valet de claro — £38 7*s* 0*d*

Ockbrook in comitatu Derbiae
Valet in redditibus et firmis, tam libere tenencium quam tenencium ad voluntatem domini ibidem per annum – £17 6*s* 8*d*. Perquisitis curie – 20*s* ibidem hoc anno (£18 6*s* 8*d*); unde in redditibus resolutis – 5*s*; feodi custodis bosci – 13*s* 4*d* (hoc anno – 18*s* 4*d*).
Et valet de claro — £17 18*s* 4*d* [£17 8*s* 4*d*]

Spondon in comitatu Derbiae
Valet in redditibus et firmis tenencium ad voluntatem domini per annum — £2 1*s* 4*d*

Chaddesden in comitatu Derbiae
Valet in redditibus et firmis, tam libere tenencium quam tenencium ad voluntatem domini ibidem hoc anno – £11 9*s* 3½*d*. [Perquisita curie – nichil hoc anno] inde in redditibus resolutis ac fine pro secta curie hoc anno – 40*s* 4*d*. Et valet de claro — £9 8*s* 11½*d*

Dominium de Stanton in comitatu Derbiae
Valet in redditibus et firmis, tam libere tenencium quam ad voluntatem domini ibidem per annum – £3 9*s* 8*d*. Perquisita curie ibidem, nil, hoc anno, inde in redditibus resolutis manerio de Elton per annum – 20*s*
Et valet de claro — £2 9*s* 8*d*

Dominium de Darley in comitatu Derbiae
Valet in redditibus et firmis tenencium, tam libere quam ad voluntatem domini ibidem per annum – £11 6*s* 11*d*. Perquisita curie ibidem – 16*s* 8*d* hoc anno (£12 3*s* 7*d*), inde in redditibus resolutis hoc anno – 23*s* 10*d*.
Et valet de claro — £10 19*s* 9*d*

Edensor in comitatu Derbiae
Valet in redditibus et firmis, tam libere tenencium quam ad voluntatem domini per annum – £16 15*s* 4*d*. Perquisita curie ibidem – 20*s* 4*d* hoc anno (£17 15*s* 8*d*) inde in feodo ballivi hoc anno – 30*s* 4*d*.
Et valet de claro — £16 5*s* 4*d*

Pilsley in comitatu Derbiae
Valet in redditibus et firmis, tam libere tenencium quam ad voluntatem domini hoc anno – 7*s* 9*d*. Perquisita curie – 12*s* hoc anno (£8 1*s* 0*d*).
—£8 1*s* 0*d*

Hassop
Valet in redditibus et firmis, tam libere tenencium quam ad voluntatem domini hoc anno – £13 4*s* 9*d*. Perquisita curie ibidem – 6*s* 8*d* hoc anno (£13 11*s* 5*d*) inde in redditibus resolutis per annum – 2*s*.
Et valet de claro — £13 9*s* 5*d*

Ballivatus de Wormhill
Valet in redditibus et firmis per annum – £22 13*s* 8*d*. Perquisita curie ibidem hoc anno – nichil (£22 13*s* 8*d*) inde in redditibus resolutis cum fine pro secta curie relaxanda hoc anno – £4 10*s* 9½*d*; quam feodum ballivi — 20*s* hoc anno (£5 10*s* 9½*d*). Et valet de claro — £17 2*s* 10*d*
[£17 2*s* 10½*d*]

Newbold – valet ad firmam per annum de claro — £2 13*s* 4*d*
Broughton – valet ad firmam per annum — £1 13*s* 4*d*
Combridge in comitatu Staffordiae per annum — £2
Crakemarsh in eodem comitatu – valet per annum de claro — £1 10*s*

Summa totalis valorum dominicorum predictorum — £307 19*s* 7*d*
[£309 0*s* 7*d*]

Inde in redditibus resolutis et feodis ballivorum — £17 5*s* 3½*d*
Et valet de claro — £290 14*s* 3½*d*
[£291 15*s* 3½*d*]

[a] *The place-names in this document have been modernised, and, since the figures in the MS are Arabic, the modern symbol for the pound is used.*
[b] *Figures within square brackets are the editor's corrections.*

5 *Indenture between Sir Robert Plumpton and William Babthorpe, 11 May 1496* *(CB, 781)*

This indenture, maid the xj day of May the xj yeare of our souereigne lord King Henry the vij betwene Sir Robart Plompton, knight,[a] of the one partie, & William Babthorp, gentleman, of the other partie, witnesseth that it is couenanted, granted and agread betwene the said parties in forme folowing, that is to say that William Plompton, son & heire apparant to the said Sir Robart, shall, with the grace of God, marry & take to wife Isabell Babpthorp, cossin & heire to Dame Isabell Hastings, late deceased, late wife to Sir John Hastings, knight, & neace to the said William Babpthorpe before the feast of St Michell tharchangell next coming, & that the said Isabell shall, by the said grace, marry & take to husband William Plompton before the said feast; & also it is agreed that if the said William Plompton decease, as

God defend, before carnall knowledg betwene him & the [said] Isabell, that then the son of the said Sir Robart that then shall be his heire apparant shall, within xx weekes next after that, marry & take to wife þe said Isabell, if the said son & the said Isabell will <thereto> agre; & that the said Sir Robert shall obtaine & git licence suficent in the law for the said mariage or mariages to be had & solemnised, according to the law of Holy Church, at his proper costes & charges.

And the said Sir Robart granteth, by thes presents, that the said William, his son, after the marriage solemnised betwene him & the said Isabell, shall continue the same without disagrement or dissputing to the same, vpon his partie. Also it is agread that the said Sir Robart shall beare the costs of the array of the said William, his son, and his son to be married to the said Isabell in forme afforesaid, the day & days of the said mariages, & the costes of the meat & drink to be expended at the mariage & mariages, & that the said William shall beare the costes & charges of tharay of the said Isabell the day of hir first mariage.

And also it is couenanted & agread betwene the said parties that the said Isabell shall haue to hir heire the manor of Saccompt in the countie of Hertford, & Watterton in the countie of Lincolne & all other lands, tenements & herrediments with their appurtinences in the said countie of Hertford, & in Hotoft, Amcotes & Watterton in the countie of Hertford, & in Hotoft, Amcotes & Watterton in the countie of Lincolne, & in Estoft,[1] Selby & Kirkby vpon Wharfe in the county of York, except certaine closes in Selby called the Flates, wherof Sir Robart Babpthorp, knight, or Dame Elizabeth, his wife, grauntseer & grauntmoder to the said Elizabeth, or Sir Raufe Babpthorp, knight, vnkell to the said Isabell, or any of them, weare seased of anie estaite of enhirritaunce, without let of the said William Babpthorp or his heires for ever.

And the said William Babpthorp granteth for him and his heires by these presents pat he & his heir shall doo as much as shall be in their power to make the said Isabell assure of the said maner, lands, tenements & herediments, with their appurtinances, except before excepted, by fine, feoffment, release, with warrant, sufferance of recoueres, or otherwise as shall be avised by the said Sir Robart & William, his son, & other son of the said Sir Robart being husband to the said Isabel, & his or their councill, at his or their charges & costs, whensoever the said William Babpthorpe or his heir shall therto be reasonable required by the said Sir Robert, William, his heir, or other his sones, husband to the said Isabell.

And over this, it is agreed that the said William Babthorp shall haue him & his heire all the lands, tenements & herediments with their apurtinances in the parish of Hemyngburgh, Midleton vpon the Wold,

North Cave, Hundsley, Loftsowe,[b] & Wistow in the county of York, & in Colby in the county of Lincolne, with their appurtinances, wherof the said Sir Robart Babpthorpe, Sir Raufe Babpthorpe, knights or Master Thomas Babpthorp, clerk, or any of them, weare seased of any estaite of any enheritance; & also the said closes in Selby, before except, in satisfaction of all theas lands, tenements & herediments with their appurtinances that wear or be in tailed to any of the name of Babpthorpe, his anchestors, or to the heire male of any of their bodies, without let or interruption of the said William Plompton & Isabell, or any other son of the said Sir Robart, husband to the said Isabell, & heire of the said Isabell for ever.

And the said Sir Robart granteth by thease presents that he shall doo & cause the said William Plompton, or other his son that shall hapen to be husband to the said Isabell, and also the said Isabell to doo as much as shall be in his or anie of their power to doo to make the said William Babpthorp & his heir asurance of the said lands, tenements & herediments with their appurtinances in the parishes of Hemyngburgh, Midleton, North Cave, Hundsley, Loftsowe & Wistow abouesaid; & also of the closes befor except, and of the lands, tenements & herediments in Colby before said, with their appurtenances, by fine, feoffment, release, warrant, suferance of recoueries & otherwise as shall be advised by the said William Babpthorp & his heire, & his or their counsill at his or their cost & charges whensoever the said Sir Robart, William, his son, or any other his son, husband to the said Isabell, & the said Isabell shall therto be reasonable required by the said William Babpthorpe or his heires.

And it is agread betwene the said parties that the said William Babpthorpe & his heire shall haue all the euidence & munniments touching the said lands, tenements & herediments with their appurtinances in Hemyngburh [etc.] beforesaid, & the aforesaid closes in Selby called the Flates, & tofice of the steward & master forester of the forest [of] Galeres,[c] or any of them, in or to whose hands the said evidence, escript or munnements, or any of them be, or shall, come; & that the said Sir Robart Plompton, knight, shall haue all the evidence, escripts or muniments towching or conserning the residew of the mannors, lands, tenements, herediments with their appurt-enances that any time weare the said Sir Robart Babpthorpe, Rauffe Babpthorpe, or anie ancestors of the said Isabell, or any parcell of them to the vse & behalfe of the said Isabell & hir heires in, or to whose handes the said evidence, escript & munniments be, or shall, com.

Also the said Sir Robart [...][d] granteth by theas presents that he shall make, or cause a sure, suffice & lawfull estate in fee simple <to> be maid before the said feast of St Michele to Niccolas Mydleton, Richard Grene, Robert Haldynby, esquires, and Richard Plompton, clerk, of lands & tenements to the clear yearly valew of xx mark over all charges, to the vse & intent that the said feofees shall make estate of the said lands & tenements with their apertinances to the said William Plompton & Isabell,[2] or other son of the said Sir Robart, as is abouesaid, within six weakes next after the said Isabell cometh to the age of xvij yeare; & over this the said Sir Robart [...][e] granteth by thease presents that he, before the said feast of St Michell, shall make all manner such suerti to the said William Babpthorpe as shall be advised by him & his counsill, & thought reasonable by Niccolas Mydleton & Richard Grene, at the costs & charges of the said William Babpthorpe, that al things rehearsed in this indenture [...][f] done by the said Sir Robart and William his son, or any other his sone, as is aboue said, & the said Isabell [...][g] or anie of them to the said William Babpthorpe [...][h] or his heire shall be trewly executed & performed of their partie, according to the trew intent of the same.

And the said William Babpthorp will, & granteth by thease presents, that he before the said feast of St Michell shall make all maner such suretie to the said Sir Robart as shall be advised by him & his counsill, & thought reasonable by the said Niccolus Mydleton & Richard Grene, at the cost & charges of the said Sir Robart, that all things rehearsed in this endenture hereafter to be done by the said William Babpthorpe & his heire to the said Isabell & her heires shalbe trewly executed & performed of his partie, according to the trew intent of the same. In witnes of all the promisses the parties abouesaid to thes indentures haue in[ter] changeable set their seales, the day and yeare abouesaid.[i]

[a] *Marginal note:* Cope the will of this Sir Robart being date 10 of April 1523.
[b] *Lofthouse.*
[c] *Galtres.*
[d] *MS* William *included in error.*
[e] *MS as above.*
[f] *MS several words obliterated.*
[g] *as above.*
[h] *MS* granteth by these presents that he before the said feast of St Michael *crossed out.*
[i] *Appended:* Copied the 17 August 1627 then hauing a seale by Mr Edward Arthington to which agrement will be deposed.

[1] Not to be confused with Eastoft, Lincs.
[2] The feoffment comprising the Derbyshire manor of Hassop with appurtenances in Hassop and Rowland is dated 14 Sept. 1496, App. II, 55.

6 *Memorandum: the Case for the Plaintiffs* *(BL, Add.MS 6698, fols lv–2v)*

Sir William Plompton, chivalier, seisitz de divers maners in les contes de Everwick, Nottingham, Derby et Stafford, avoit issue per un feme Robert & William; et puis le dit Sir William fyt covenaunt ove Thomas,

Signeur de Clifford, que le dit Robert espouse Elizabeth, file de dit Signieur de Clifford et le dit Sir William graunta quil ferra feoffment a les dits Robert et Elizabeth des maners, terres, ove tenements a le valure de xl livres, a aver a eux et a les heires le dit Robert et le dit Elizabeth engenderount, le remainder al droit heires de le dit Sir William. Et que toutz autres maners et hereditaments que le dit Sir William ou autre a son use adonqz avoit, deveoit apres le mort le dit Sir William remainer descender et reverter a le dit Robert et a ses heires sauns disinheritance ou incumbrance de ceo ent a fair per le dit Sir William ou ses feoffees.[1] Et puis le dit Sir William de touts ses maners, terres et tenements in les contes de Everwike, Nottingham, Derby et Stafford enfeffet Johan Tempest, chivalier, et autres in fee, sur condition que les dites feoffes, quant ils serrount per le dit Sir William requises, enfeofferount le dit Sir William et un tiel en fee quil epousa, de certen de dits maners a le valure C marcs, a aver a eux pur terme de lour vies, le remainder al dit Robert et a ses heires, et quil ferroit autre estate des tenements a le valure xx marcs a un fitz le dit Sir William qui le nomera pur terme de [vie], le remaynder a le dit Robert et ses heires in fee. et de touts les resideu des tenements avant dits, que les dits feoffes apres le mort le dit Sir William enffe le dit Robert et ses heires en fee, pourveu touts foits, que si le dit Robert morust, vivant le dit Sir William, que ben lirra a le dit Sir William [fol. 2] in touts les tenements avant dits, ultre les tenements a le dit Sir William, ses femes et ses fitz en le furme avant dit, etc.,[2] dones et lesses a rentrer. Puis le dit Robert deine xiiij annz &c.[3]

Et puis le dit Sir William relezeroit lez premers covenaunts de marriage covenauntes ove Seigneur de Clifford, que le dit William, adonque son fitz et heire apparaunt epouseroit le dit Elizabeth,[4] et le dit Sir William graunta quil ferra feoffment a les dits William et Elizabeth des certens maners et tenements a le valure de xl *li*, a aver a eux et a les heyres de le dit William del corps le dit Elizabeth engendres, le remaynder pur default tiel issue al heyres de le dit Sir William. Et outre graunta quil ferra anuel estate de auters terres et tenements a les ditz William et Elizabeth a le valure x*li* a aver a eux et apprender les profitz apres le mort Margaret de [Rempston], aylesse a le dit Sir William.[5] Et auxi le dit Sir William graunta quil ferra escripts indentis de les premisses in due et loiall manner, accordant a les dits escript indentis faits sur le dit premer [. . .] marriage; per force de quell le dit William espousera le dit Elizabeth, et avoit issue inter eux ij files, silz Margaret et Elizabeth. Et le dit William devia.[6]

Puis le dit Sir William fit covenant ove Briane Roecliffe pur certen sumes dergent a lui paies, que le dit Margaret, un des heyres apparaunts, espousera Johan, fitz et heyre apparaunt a le dit Brian, et outre graunta quil ne autre de ses feffes ferroit alyenacion ne discontinuance dacun de ses manors et hereditaments, mes quil entierment apres son mort descenderont et returner a les heyres le dit William,[7] per force de quel le dit John espousa le dit Margaret, heyre le dit William. Et apres le dit Sir William graunta a un Henry Sothill, pur certen sumes dergent a lui payes, que Elizabeth, son consin et auter de les heyres, epousera un John, fitz et heyre apparaunt a le dit Henry. Et outre graunta quil nul de ses feffes ferrount acun feoffment ne discontinuance sil ne soit a seluy qui ferra son fitz et heyre male apparaunt, excepts terres et tenements a le valure de c*li* quil poit doner a terme de vie ou des vies.[8] Come appeart en un indenture fait lan le tierce le roy Edward le iiijte, le dit Sir William infeffa un Richard Fawbergh et autres persons de touts ses terres et tenements in les countes de Nottingham, Derby et Stafford,[9] per force de quel ils fueront ent seisis tanque par le dit Sir William disseises. Et le dit Sir William issint eut seise, et enfeffa le dean de Evewike et auters en fee, qui prist estates a luy pur terme de vie, le remaynder a un Robert Plumpton, chivalier, et a ses heyres de son corps engendres.[10] Et apres le dit Sir William murroit.[11] Apres [fol. 2v.] que mort le dit Sir Robert entra, sur que le dit Richard Fawbergh et les feffees entraient, devant le statute de Richard le tierce.[12] Et un Richard Fawbergh, un des enfeffes qui surveyquist son confeffes reentra et enfeffe ceux qui porte le . . .[13]

Item: le dit Syr William Plumpton enfeffa un Richard Redman et autres de tous ses terres et tenements en le counte de Everwyke en fee,[14] per force de quel ils fueront seises tanque per le dit William disseisez. et puis le dit Syr William recyaunt seisin, enfeoffa auters persons en fee; sur que bien le dit Richard, qui fuit en le graunte, entra et enfeffa auters persons al use Margaret et Elizabeth . . .[15]

[1] 10 Aug. 1446, App. II, 11.

[2] 31 Aug. 1449, App. II, 13.

[3] Robert died 20 July 1450. By 1453 Sir William was married to Joan Wintringham, App. II, 30.

[4] There is no record of this marriage in CB.

[5] App. I, 3; II, 8.

[6] William died in 1461 and his daughters were subsequently admitted as copyhold tenants to lands in and near Knaresborough, 24 Feb. 1462, App. II, 20, 21.

[7] 26 Nov. 1463, App. II, 23.

[8] Note 3 above.

[9] The deed is dated 1 June 1464, App. II, 28,29.

[10] Between 12 Oct. and 7 Nov. 1475. Sir William's marriage had been declared valid 13 July 1472, and their son was therefore recognized as legitimate, App. II, 33.

[11] 15 Oct. 1480, App. II, 33.

[12] 16 Sept. 1483, App. II, 48.

[13] The account breaks off at this point.

[14] There is no record of this deed in the cartulary, but see App. II, 8.

[15] It was John Ingilby who conveyed the Yorkshire manors to Robert Bubwith and Richard Burgh, 7 May 1502, App. II, 62.

7 *Compotus of Edward Brown, 14 September 1503 to 14 September 1504* (*BL, Add.MS 6698, fols 2v–3*)

Compotus Edwardi Browne ballivi et collectatoris redditorum ibidem ad usum Ricardi Burgh et Roberti Bubwith, clericorum, a festo Exaltatione Crucis, anno regni Regis Henrici 7 19° usque idem festum proximum sequentem per unum annum integre.

Idem reddit compotum de v*s* ix*d* de redditibus tenentium liberorum per annum in Darley, ut patet per rentale unde in vigilia Sancti Michaelis archangeli dicti domini Regis xvij particulariter factum.
Et de viij *li* xj*s* iiij*d* de redditibus tenentium ibidem ad voluntatem domini, ut patet per &c.
Et de [fol.3] iij *li* x*s* j*d* de diversorum tenentium in Stanton ad voluntatem domini, ut patet &c.
Et de xij *li* xij*s* vij*d* de redditibus diversorum tenentium in Hassop ad voluntatem domini, ut patet &c.
Et de xx*s* x*d* de quodam redditu annuatim per villatam de Rowland ad predictos terminos, ut per idem rentale ibidem.
Totalis oneris ———xxvi *li* xix*d* [?xxvi *li* ix*s* ix*d*]

De quibus petit allocari de redditu domino Regi resoluto castello suo de Alto Pecco xv*s* iiij*d* per annum pro terris in Darley.
Et de vd solvendis eidem Regi annuatim pro pallefrido ibidem.
Et de vij*s* ij*d* annuatim solvendis domino de Bakewell ibidem.
Et de vs annuatim solvendis Henrico Columbell, armigero, pro terris ad voluntatem infra clausuram ibidem, manerio pertinent.
Et de ix*d* de redditu annuatim solvendo Christophero Allen pro terris suis infra clausuras manerij ibidem, manerio pertinent.
Et de xiij*s* iiij*d* in decasu redditus unius clausure super moram ibidem, nuper in tenura Henrici Columbell, pro defectu inclusionis, quod reddere solebat xvij*s* viij*d* modo dimittitur pro iij*s* iiij*d*, et sic in decasu, xiij*s* iiij*d*.
Et de xx*s* de redditu annuatim resolvendo Henrico Foljambe, armigero, pro terris in Stanton.
Et de ij*d* *ob* solvendis domino Regi pro pallefrido in Stanton.
Et de ij*d* *ob* solvendis domino Regi annuatim pro quodam auxillio vicecomitatis ibidem.
Et de xij*s* resolutis Henrico Vernon, militi, pro parcella terre vocata le Milnehill annuatim et pertinencijs in Hassop.
Et de ij*s* vj*d* solvendis annuatim domino Regi pro pallefrido in Hassop.
Et de ij*s* solvendis domino de Ashford quolibet anno pro [...][a]
Et de liij*s* iiij*d* solvendis Henrico Vernon, militi, pro feodo suo hoc anno.
Et de liij*s* iiij*d* Thomo Babington, armigero, pro feodo suo hoc anno.
Et de xxvj*s* viij*d* solvendis Rogero Vernon hoc anno [...][a] (caetera dec.t).

[Total of allowances as shown above —— £10 12s 2d]

[a] *MS left blank.*

8 *The Earl of Cumberland's Memorandum, 18 December 1582* (*BL, Add.MS 6698, fols 7v–8)*

Lands sould in fee farm and in the countess of Shrewsbury's lease, that they be offered to her at forty years purchase. Moredale: It being 10*s*, rent valued at most worth £5 per annum. Priced to the countess of Shrewsbury at £50.
Whetson [Wheston]: For a tenement there, rent, 9*s* 10*d*. to my lady at 100 years purchase for £60.
Tideswell: For two acres and half there, worth at most 16*s*. To be sold for £16.
Hassop: The moiety of the demesnes containing 260 acres, and is worth by the year £34 6*s* 8*d*. Valued at £1,000. Also one tenement and one oxgang containing by estimation 15 acres in the occupacion of Henry Watts, valued at £120.
Edensor: The moiety of the demesnes containing 142 acres, and valued at 5*s* an acre by the year, worth per annum £35 10*s*, & the purchase whereof at 25 years amounteth to £881. [fol. 8] The moiety of the oxgang of land in the occupation of the countess of Shrewsbury contaning 210 acres, after the rate of 15 acres to an oxgang, at 5*s* an acre, is worth £26 5*s* by the year.
The purchase price, £656 5*s*.
The free rents there with the services thereto belonging rated at thirty years purchase.
Item: The moiety of 5 oxgangs in the hands of several tenants, which after the rate of 15 acres to an oxgang amounteth to 75 acres, & valued at 5*s* an acre, amounteth to £9 7*s* 6*d*, and after 25 years purchase cometh to £134 1*s* 6*d*.
The common pasture land is not here valued, as it may be included with the rest.
The heirs and assigns of Henry Ticksall hold freely of the said manor 2 messuages, 19 acres of land, 2 acres of meadow, with appurtenances, at yearly rent of 9*s*, a moiety whereof is 4*s* 6*d* due to Clifford. Rated at 30 years purchase, which is £6 15*s*.
Item: the yearly rent of 13*s* 4*d* paid to Clifford in right of the said manor after 30 years is £20.
Heriott Land: The lands and tenements in fee farm in Edensor, Pillesley and Stanton Hall being heriottable are to be valued at 50 years of purchase.

Lands that pay a relief: Lands and tenements in Wormhill, Bakewell, Whetston, Chelmorton, Hurdlow, Wardlow, Flagge, Martinside, and Betfield, which are held in fee farme and pay relief to be valud at 40 years purchase or thereabouts. Lands leased by Sir Ingram Clifford to Henry Cavendish, esq.,: The parcells contained in the lease granted by Sir Ingram Clifford to Henry Cavendish, esq., dated 10 May 16 Eliz., namely his lands, rents & tenements in Edensor, Hassop, Darley, Carlton, Pillesley, Rowland, Bakewell, Moredale, Mugginton and Duffield in Derbyshire. These be charged with chief rents: Wormhill, Whetston, Martinside, Betfield, and Combes.

9 *Valuation of certain lands in Derbyshire by Commissioners acting for George, earl of Cumberland and Francis Clifford, esq., his brother, 1584* (*BL, Add.MS 6698, fols 7–7v.*)

Darley: The moiety of the demesnes, 33 acres at 6*s* 8*d* per acre, after £11 per annum – £240. The moiety of 2 oxgangs of land containing by estimation 15 acres at 5*s* per acre, price, £80. The fourth part of the mill, valued at 20*s* per annum, price, £15. The particular farms in Darley to be valued by the ordinary rent after 120 years purchase – £180. [fol. 7v.] Darley farm valued another time at £347 8*s* 1½*d* and the common and 4 enclosures to go in with the values aforesaid. Kenalton: A manor house and demenes in the tenure of William Rayner, the moiety whereof being 91 acres at 6*s* 8*d* per acre per annum is £63 13*s* 4*d*, which after the rate of 25 years purchase amounts to £1,591 13*s* 4*d*.
Broughton: The moiety of a tenement containing 36 acres valued by the year at £9, and of old rent, 12*s*, price, £133 6*s* 8*d*. Sold for £180.
Herberger Meadow: The fourth part of 2 closes there containing 7½ acres, rent, 8*s*; value per annum, 50*s*; price, £40.
Twyford: The moiety of a croft and 6 acres of land and meadow, rent, 20*d*; value per annum, 17*s* 6*d*, price, £21.
Chaddesden: The moiety of the demesnes there valued at £18 15*s* per annum, price, £400.
Burghwash: A tenement there, 16 acres, 4 cottages, 6 acres of land.
Spondon: Three tenements and 1 croft.
Lockhawe: 5 acres [*These three*] valued in the book of survey at 120 years purchase at the old rent.
The lands in Herbeger Meadow, Twyford, Chaddesden, Burghwash, Spondon and Lockhowe being about 140 acres, rent, £5 9*s* 9*d*. Sold for £600.

APPENDIX II
Calendar of Selected Documents from the Plumpton Coucher Book and Other Sources

1 *25 January 1346, Ripon*

Tripartite indenture of William Plompton, kt,[1] granting, by licence of the king and of William Whittlesey, archbishop of York, to God, to the Holy and Undivided Trinity, to the Blessed Virgin and all the Saints, to the altar of the Holy Trinity behind the high altar in the collegiate church of Ripon and to Sir Henry de Plompton, chaplain, a messuage with buildings and appurtenances near Bedern in Ripon; 24s rent from his water-mill at Plumpton; a messuage with a bovate of land and appurtenances in the vill of 'Kirkstainley'; 3 tofts and a mark of annual rent with appurtenances in Kirkby Malzeard, and 28s 0¼d rent with appurtenances in Grewelthorpe. To be held of him and his heirs so that divine service may be celebrated in perpetuity under conditions below stated: viz. that the said Henry shall have for life all the aforesaid premises, with authority to appoint and remove at will a suitable chaplain to serve in his place. After the death of the said Henry it shall be for the donor or his heirs to present to the Chapter of Ripon, within 40 days next ensuing, a suitable chaplain to be instituted and inducted to the chantry and its appurtenances, and thus at each vacancy following. In case of such appointment not being made within 40 days the Chapter of Ripon shall appoint a chaplain, who, after swearing an oath faithfully to perform divine service and to preserve, and never to sell, let to farm, mortgage, pledge or otherwise dispose of the books, chalices and ornaments, lands, rents and tenements pertaining to the chantry, shall be instituted and inducted.

The chaplain shall celebrate daily, without interruption, for the beneficial estate of the donor during his lifetime and for other benefactors of the chantry, saying Placebo and Dirige, with appropriate prayers and commendations for the souls of the donor's progenitors and ancestors, for his soul and those of his heirs and successors, for Sir Henry Plompton and those to whom he is beholden; also for Sir John Schupton, chaplain, and his progenitors and for all the faithful departed.

Any sale, mortgage or alienation of any property pertaining to the chantry shall be held to be invalidated by force of this tripartite charter.

The donor's seal, together with the seal of the Chapter of Ripon, of the second part, is appended and is to remain with the donor; the seals of the Chapter and of Sir Henry, of the third part, have been appended and shall remain with the Chapter; the seals of the donor and of Sir Henry are appended.

Witnesses: Lord Thomas de Bourne, lord of Studley, Andrew de Merkingfeild, Richard de Goldsburgh, kts, Simon Ward, John de Cloutherow, Roger de Hewyk and others. Ripon, Wednesday, the feast of the Conversion of St Paul (25 Jan.), 1346.

[Latin]

[copyist's note.] This deed hath att the copying the 28 of July 1615 two faire seales, the first being a ram, & the other the five fusils vpon a triangle with the corner uppermost, & hath written in the circumference Sir William Plompton.

[CB, 215]

[1] CB,215 is an almost verbatim copy of this one; it bore the same 2 seals.

2 *28 May 1396*

Charter of William Sparrow, chaplain, granting to Thomas Pynchebeck, chaplain, his messuage and its appurtenances in Nether Ousegate, York, which he had of the gift and feoffment of John Lindlay, citizen of York, which lies around William de Selby's land and alongside the highway called Nether Ousegate as far as the cemetery of the church of St Michael near the bridge over the river Ouse, and near 'Cayllomhall' on either side of the river, to have and hold in perpetuity to the aforesaid Thomas and his successors as chaplains to celebrate for the repose of the soul of John de Gisburn, formerly citizen and merchant of York, and for the good estate of Ellen de Gisburn, his widow,[1] for the souls of John's mother and father, his ancestors and for all the faithful departed at the altar of St Nicholas in the church of St Martin in Micklegate, York, where Thomas and his successors shall say mass daily with due formality and without any interruption.

If it should happen that Ellen has failed to bestow the said premises, then the heirs of the said John are to have the right of appointing another suitable priest. Isabel, one of the heirs of John de Gisburn and her heirs is to have the first presentation to the chantry, and Alice, the other heir, is to have the second, and so on alternately, in perpetuity.

Witnesses: William Frost, then mayor of York, John More and John de Hamden, then sheriffs of the city, Thomas Era, John de Braithwaite, William Salley, William de Cestr' of York, and many others.

[Latin]

[Copyist's note.] This deed hath 3 faire seales of red wax att the copying the 20th of Sept: 1615.
[CB, 300]

[1] Sir Robert Plumpton's maternal grandparents.

3 *3 February 1412, Westminster*

Final concord made at Westminster the day after the Purification 1412 before William Thyrning, William Hankford, John Cokayne, John Colpeper and Robert Hill, justices, and others,[1] between Robert Babthorpe and Margaret, his wife, plaintiffs, and William Babthorpe and William Bekby, chaplains, defendants, whereby the manor of Babthorpe with appurtenances, and 3 messuages, 11 bovates and 141 acres of land and 7 acres of woodland with appurtenances in Brackenholme, Woodhead, Hemingborough, Wistow and Selby, and a moiety of the manor of Lofthouse with appurtenances were acknowledged to be the right of the defendants, since they held them by gift of the aforesaid Robert. By agreement, fine and consent the same William Babthorpe and William Bekby granted to Robert and Margaret the aforesaid manor and lands by surrender in court, to have and hold to them and the legitimate heirs of Robert[2] of the chief lords of that fee by due service, in perpetuity. In case of lack of heirs the premises are to remain, after the deaths of Robert and Margaret to the right heirs of Robert.
[Latin]
[BL, Add.MS 32, 113, fols 215v–216]

[1] See no. **86** below.
[2] Until this date the estates of the Babthorpes had been transmitted by hereditary descent in the male line, Thomas Burton, *The History and Antiquities of the Parish of Hemingborough in the County of York* (York, 1888), 182.

4 *6 November 1416, Plumpton*

Feoffment by Robert de Plompton, esq., to Henry, Lord FitzHugh of Ravensworth, Dame Margaret Rempston, Dame Alice de Plompton, his mother, John Grene of Newby, William Forman, parson of the church of Kirkby Overblow, and John Brennand of Knaresborough of the manor of Plumpton with appurtenances and the advowson of the chantry in the collegiate church of Ripon; also the manors of Idle, Nessfield and Steeton with appurtenances, together with the reversion of lands, tenements, reversions and services in Grassington and Studley, which Dame Alice de Plompton, his mother, holds for life,[1] and which,

after her death, descend by inheritance to the heirs of Robert. *Witnesses*: Nicholas de Middleton, kt, William de Beckwith, Richard de Stathington and John Poleyn.
[Latin]
[Copyist's note.] This deed hath a very faire seale att the copying the 15 of February 1615.
[CB, 384]

[1] Dame Alice de Plompton, formerly Alice Gisburn, died in 1423, CB, 293, 325, 341, 381; Stapleton, xxix–xxxii.

5 *1 April 1418, Plumpton*

Memorandum that Robert de Plompton, kt, enfeoffed Henry FitzHugh, lord of Ravensworth and treasurer of England, Dame Margaret de Rempston, Dame Alice de Plompton, his mother, John de Grene of Newby, William Ferman, parson of Kirkby Overblow and John Brennand of Knaresborough in the manors of Plumpton Nessfield, Idle and Steeton with appurtenances, together with the reversions of all his lands and tenements, rents, reversions and services in Grassington and Studley held for life by the aforesaid Alice, with reversion to Robert by inheritance after her death, as is plainly set out in his charter of feoffment.

Condition: that the aforesaid feoffees shall secure to Godfrey, son of Sir Robert, a life annuity of a clear 20m from land or rents out of the aforesaid premises. If it should happen that Sir Robert, about to go on foreign service, should not return, the feoffees are to secure to his son Robert a life annuity of a clear 20m out of the same properties. If either Godfrey or Robert should die, his portion is to remain to the other, with remainder after the deaths of both to the feoffees in perpetuity.

Above this the feoffees are to enfeoff Sir Robert's valet John Wode for life in a tenement in Plumpton now in the tenure of John Lightfoot; likewise Sir Robert's servant Robert Norton in a tenement with appurtenances in Plumpton, which he sometime held, with reversion after the deaths of these two beneficiaries to the feoffees in perpetuity.

Also the feoffees are to pay Sir Robert's debts and carry out his wishes as expressed in his testament.

Also Joan[1] and Alice Sir Robert's daugthers, and his sisters Isabel and Katherine are each to receive marriage portions of 40m out of the issues of the manor of Nessfield, and Richard Plompton his brother is to have a life annuity of 40s out of the same issues.
[Latin]

[Copyist's note.] This indenture hath no seale left att the copying the 28 of Feb. 1615.
[CB, 399]

[1] Joan later married John Greene, App. III.

6 *24 September 1420, Plumpton*

Feoffment by Robert de Plompton, kt, to Alice de Plompton his mother, Richard de Norton, chief justice of the court of common pleas, Thomas de Rempston, kt, John Buttler, esq., and John Grene of his manors of Plumpton, Idle, Steeton in Airedale, and Nessfield with appurtenances, rents and services, with the advowson and presentation of his chantry of the Holy Trinity in the church of Ripon, with the reversion of 50m issuing from the manor of Plumpton which Dame Isabel, formerly the wife of Robert de Plompton, kt, his grandfather, has for life by his grant in lieu of a feoffment and dower after the death of the aforesaid Robert, her husband; also the manors of Grassington in Craven, and Little Studley, near Ripon, after the death of Alice, his mother.
Witnesses: Thomas de Markenfield, Roger Ward, Richard de Goldesbrough, Halnath Malleverer, kts, William de Bekewtih, William Pensax, William de Hopton, Henry de Chambre, John Pulane and others.
[Latin]
[Copyist's note.] This deed hath a seale att the copying the 7 of March 1615.
[CB, 405]

7 *13 September 1423, Topcliffe*

Notification by Henry Percy, earl of Northumberland, that he has authorized William Whitehall, his sister Elizabeth, Lady Clifford's steward, to distrain and receive the farms of the tenants of Steeton in Airedale, to which the earl is entitled during the minority of Sir Robert Plompton's heir. The issues to be remitted to Richard Fairfax, squire. Sir John Langton, steward, John Aske and the officials of Spofforth are to assist, if necessary by distraint.
[Latin]
[Copyist's note.] This deed hath a seale att the copying the xth of Aprill 1616.
[CB, 419]

8 *10 April 1439*

Feoffment by William de Plompton, kt, to Thomas de Rempston, kt, Dame Agnes Stapilton, Brian Stapilton, kt, Ranulph Pygot, esq., William Rempston, rector of the church of Bingham, Robert Rempston, Richard Redman, snr, Richard Askham and William Wood, chaplain, of the manors of Kinoulton, Hassop, Wormhill, Pilsley, Stantonhall, Chelmorton and Combridge with lands [etc.] in Bakewell, Tideswell, Wheston, Flagfield, Martinside, Combes, Wardlow, Hurdlow, Spondon, Lockhaw, Twyford, Turndike, Broughton, Crakemarsh, Monyash, Chesterfield and Chaddesden, with the advowsons of the chantries in the churches of Bakewell and Mansfield Woodhouse, together with the reversion of the lands and tenements held for life by Dame Margaret Rempston of Sir William's inheritance.
Witnesses: Richard Vernon, Henry Pierrepont, Hugh Willoughby, Robert Eyre, John de Middleton, Robert Rikhill, Robert Pageham, and others.
[Latin]
[Copyist's note.] this deed hath att the copying the 27 of Aprill 1616 a very faire seale being the Plompton arms quartered with the Foliambes arms & the roebuck, & being supported by a woman, & hath William Plompton de Plompton written in the circumference. It is the first deed that is to be sealled with the same seale.
[CB, 443]

9 *10 April 1439, Kinoulton*

Letter patent of Sir William Plumpton appointing Robert Maderyche, John Rylay and William Jackson of Hassop, attorneys, to deliver to Thomas Rempston, kt, Dame Agnes Stapilton, Brian Stapilton, kt, Ralph Pigott, esq., William Rempston, rector of the church of Bingham, Robert Rempston, Richard Redman, senior, esq., Richard Askham, William Wood, chaplain [the properties named in no. 8] with all other lands, tenements and rents, and with villeins and their progeny, in Notts, Derbyshire and Staffs, with the advowson and presentation appurtenant to the chantries in the churches of Bakewell and Mansfield Woodhouse, together with the lands and tenements held for life by Dame Margaret Rempston of the inheritance of the feoffor.
[Latin]
[Copyist's note.] this deed hath the same seale that the former hath [no. **8**], and was copyed the 27 of Aprill 1616.
[CB, 444]

10 *19 February 1442, London*

Grant by Henry Percy, earl of Northumberland and lord of the honor of Cockermouth, to William Plompton, kt, of the office of steward of all his manors, lordships, vills and tenements in Yorks for life, for which, and for his service well and faithfully hitherto performed, and for good and faithful future service he is to receive an annual fee of £10, payable by the earl's Yorkshire receiver at Pentecost and the feast of St Martin in Winter in equal portions. He is to enjoy the perquisites pertaining to the office, and is entitled to be shown aid, favour and obedience by all and singular officers, tenants and ministers within the county.
[Latin]
[Copyist's note.] This deed hath a seale att the copying the 29 of May 1616.
[CB, 524]

11 *10 August 1446, Derby*

Feoffment by William Plompton, kt, to John Harrington, kt, William Gargrave, Thomas Garth, John Garth and John Elys, clerk, of the manors of Darley, Stanton, Pilsley, Wormhill, Chaddesden and Spondon, with appurtenances in Derbyshire, together with lands and hereditaments there and in Edensor, Wardlow, Bakewell, Martinside, Wheston, Tideswell, Hurdlow, Chelmorton, Flagfield and Castleton, with the exception of a chantry in the church of Bakewell and two closes named 'Bussenhay' or Combes and Betfield. Condition: that within five years they shall enfeoff Robert Plompton, son and heir of Sir William, and Elizabeth daughter of Thomas, Lord de Clifford and Westmorland, kt, in the same, to hold to them and to the heirs of their bodies, with remainder, in case of lack of issue, to the right heirs of Sir William.
Witnesses: Richard Vernon, Henry Parpoint, kts, John Curson, Thomas Foljamb, Robert Ayre and others.
[Latin]
[Copyist's note.] This deed hath no seale att the copying the 30 of May 1616.
[CB, 531]

12 *1 November 1447*

Letter patent of Henry Percy, earl of Northumberland and lord of the honor of Cockermoth, reciting that whereas he has granted to Sir William Plompton, kt, an annual fee of £10 from the rents and farms of his Yorks lordship of Leathley, payable [as in no. **10**]. Now for good and faithful service performed and to be performed in future the fee is increased to £20 payable at the same terms. In case of the payment being in arrears, Sir William, his assigns, farmers or tenants may enter the vill to take distress, and distrain until the payment is made.
[Latin]
[Copyist's note.] This deed hath a seale att the copying, 31 May 1616.
[CB, 533]

13 *31 August 1449*

Feoffment by William Plompton, kt, to John Harrington, John Tempest, Brian Stapilton and John Conyers, kts, Thomas Thwaites, Richard Banks of Newton, Thomas Garth, William Gargrave, Geoffrey Pygot, John Vavasour of Newton, Guy Fairfax and John Fawkes of all his manors in Yorks, Derbyshire, Notts and Staffs. Condition: that they enfeoff within 5 years, Robert Plompton, son and heir of Sir William, and Elizabeth, daughter of Thomas, Lord de Clifford and Westmorland, kt, to hold to them and to the heirs of their bodies, with right of re-entry reserved to Sir William in case of lack of issue.
Witnesses: Robert Roos, Roger Ward, Richard Vernon, Henry Parpont, Thomas Chaworth, Gervase Clifton, kts, Richard Hamerton, John Curson, William Babyngton, and others.
[Latin]
[Copyist's note.] This deed hath a seale att the copying the 31 May 1616.
[CB, 535]

14 *23 August 1453*[1]

Grant by Thomas Rempston, kt, to William Plompton, kt, of his manors of Plumpton, Idle, Steeton in Airedale, Nessfield, Grassington in Craven and Little Studley, near Ripon, with their appurtenances, rents and services, together with the advowson and presentation of the chantry of the Holy Trinity in the church of Ripon, Yorks, which all and singular premises were held by Alice de Plompton, Richard de Norton, chief justice of the court of common pleas, John Butelere, esq., and John Grene, all now deceased, by the gift and feoffment of Robert Plompton, father of William Plompton, kt, and Godfrey his brother. To have and hold the aforesaid premises to William and his lawfully begotten heirs male of the chief lords of that fee and by services thence owed and accustomed by right. Remainder in case of the death of William without male heirs is to Godfrey and his heirs male, to be held [etc.], and in case of Godfrey's death without heirs male to the right heirs of William in perpetuity, to hold [etc]. Warranty.

[Latin]

[Copyist's note.] This deed hath a very faire seale att the copying the xth day of June 1616.

[CB, 537]

[1] On 25 Aug. following, Sir Thomas appointed Richard Lowder and Robert Smith of Plumpton his attorneys to deliver seisin of the premises to Sir William, CB,539.

15 *23 August 1453*[1]

Grant by Thomas Rempston, kt, to William Plompton, kt, of his manors of Kinoulton, Hassop, Wormhill, Pilsley, Stanton, Chelmorton and Combridge with their appurtenances, and of all his lands and tenements in Bakewell, Tideswell, Wheston, Flagfield, Martinside, Combes, Wardlow, Hurdlow, Spondon, Twyford, Lockhaw, Broughton, Crakemarsh, Monyash, Chesterfield and Chaddesden, with all other lands, tenements, rents and services, whether free or of villeins with their progeny, and with all other appurtenances belonging to the above premises in Notts, Derbyshire and Staffs, with the advowsons and presentations of the chantries in Bakewell and Mansfield Woodhouse, together with the reversion of what was held by Dame Margaret Rempston for life upon the said Thomas and his heirs, all by reason of the feoffment made by the said William Plompton, kt, to Dame Agnes Stapleton, Brian Stapleton, kt, Ralph Pigott, esq., William Rempston, rector of the church of Bingham, Robert Rempston, Richard Redmayn, sen., esqrs, Richard Askham and William Wood, chaplains, all now deceased. To have and hold to the aforesaid William Plompton, kt, and his legitimate heirs male of the chief lords of that fee, and by due services, with remainder in case of lack of heirs male to Godfrey Plompton, his brother, and his heirs male, and in case of the death of Godfrey without heirs male, to the right heirs of Sir William in perpetuity. Warranty.

[Latin]

[Copyist's note.] This deed hath a faire seale att the copying the xith day of June 1616.

[CB, 538]

[1] On 25 Aug. following Sir Thomas appointed John ... and Roger Jackson his attorneys to deliver seisin of these premises to Sir William, CB, 540. At the foot of this deed: 'These 4 last deeds have all one seale being very faire and undefaced at the copying the xith of June 1616, and haue written on the circumference *Sigilla Thomae Remyston militis.*'

16 *10 July [1454 or earlier], 'Hert.'*

Attestation by Thomas, Lord Clifford,[1] that a rent which, as he is informed, Sir William Plompton proposed to grant by *nisi prius* to Thomas and Alice Kempe out of lands in Chaddesden and Spondon would constitute an alienation from the estate already settled upon William Plompton and Elizabeth Clifford.
[English]
[Copyist's note.] This deed hath a seale att the copying the 29 day of May 1616.
[CB, 526, transcribed Stapleton, lxv.]

[1] Lord Clifford died in 1454.

17 *12 October 1455*

Indenture between Sir William Plompton, kt, and Thomas Beckwith, esq., witnessing an agreement between the parties for a marriage between Thomas's eldest son, William, and Elizabeth Plompton, daughter of Sir William. Within 8 days of such marriage Thomas is to make to William and Elizabeth a legal estate in lands and tenements yielding a clear annual income of £10 13s 4d entailed upon them and their lawful heirs male. Also lands, tenements, rents recoveries and services held by Thomas in sole seisin within the town of Clint between the river Nidd and Thornton Beck, and within the towns of Muston, Filey, Halnaby,[1] Little ... and 'South Ethington' in Yorks shall revert to William after Thomas's death, free of all rent charges, statute merchant or causes of execution made or to be made by Thomas. Also lands held in jointure by Thomas's wife Elizabeth shall remain to William and his heirs after her death, similarly discharged [etc.]. furthermore any feofee or feoffees holding lands to the use of Thomas, except those held by feoffment to the use of William and Elizabeth, as above stated, are to make lawful release to William and his heirs male within six months of his request for such release, or to his next heir or heirs male at his or their request, free of rent charges, statutes merchant or causes of execution. Provided always that Thomas or his feoffees may have use of such lands to the yearly value of £4 to hold to them or one of them for life.

For his part Sir William is to pay to Thomas £23 6s 8d on the wedding day, and with other sufficient persons jointly and severally to give bond for the payment to Thomas of £10 at the feast of St Wilfrid thereafter [12 Oct.], £20 at the feast of St Peter *ad Vincula*, known as Lammas [1 Aug.] and three further annual payments of £20 at the latter feast.

Should Elizabeth die without a surviving male heir by William[2] the sums due on dates following her decease shall not be leviable.

[English]

[Copyist's note.] This deed hath a seale att the copying the xijth day of June 1616.

[CB, 541]

[1] (?) Hunmanby, near Filey.

[2] See no. **54**.

18 *2 January 1461, Epworth*

Grant by Katherine, duchess of Norfolk, to William Plompton, kt, of the office of chief warden and master of her chace and warren within her honor and lordship of Kirkby Malzeard and Nidderdale in Yorks, to have and hold the office exercising it himself or through a sufficient deputy during her lifetime and his own. For holding and exercising the office well and faithfully he is to receive from her aforesaid lordship 100s yearly, payable at Pentecost and Martinmas in Winter in equal portions by the receiver, bailiff or prepositus in office for the time being. All farmers, tenants and inhabitants there are to give Sir William their obedience and aid.

[Latin]

[copyist's note.] This deed hath a very faire seale att the copying the xiijth of June 1616.

[CB, 546]

19 *5 February 1462*

Pardon by Edward IV, of his abundant special grace, certain knowledge and mere motion, to William Plompton, kt, *alias* William Plompton formerly of Kinoulton, Notts, *alias* the same, formerly of Knaresborough, Yorks, *alias* the same, formerly sheriff of Yorks, *alias* the same, formerly sheriff or Notts and Derbyshire, kt, or under whatsoever other

name he is assessed, of all transgressions, offences &c.[1]
[Latin]
[Copyist's note.] This pardon hath a faire large seale of yellow wax att the copying, the vj of June 1616.
[CB, 551]

[1] This general pardon followed a term of imprisonment, beginning 12 June 1461, for failure to redeem a bond of £2,000 entered into on 13 May 1461. On 10 Sept. 1462 Sir William obtained a release from all claims resulting from the bond, CB, 549,550, 552; Stapleton, lxviii–ix.

20 *24 February 1462*

A court held at Knaresburgh. William Plompton, esq., son of William Plompton, kt, held of the king according to the custom of the forest 1 acre of land in the hamlet of 'Fellescliff' within the vill of Clint called 'Kirkacre', formerly in the tenure of John Malham; a messuage, 16 acres and a '*denarium*' per annum in the hamlet of 'Rowdon' within the lordship of Clint, formerly held by William Hebden and Margaret his wife; a half-acre of land in the hamlet of Birstwith, formerly held by William Webster; 2 acres of meadow called 'Moracres' in Clint, formerly held by Thomas Malham; a messuage with 7 acres and a '*denarium*' per annum in 'Rowdon', formerly held by William, son of Robert Tilleson; 1 *obulat*' of newly assarted land in Birstwith, formerly held by John Curtas and Joan, his wife; a messuage with 2 acres of land in the vill of Killinghall, and half a messuage with 2 acres of land in the hamlet of Hampsthwaite within the vill of Clint, formerly held by Ralph Beckwith; a messuage with 16 acres of land called 'Crookesnab' and a pasture called 'Stockbrignure' Close, formerly held by Richard Brennand and Elizabeth his wife. After *diem clausit extremum* following the death of William Plompton, esq., his daughters and heirs Margaret and Elizabeth came and took of the king the aforesaid premises to them and their heirs and assigns to hold according to the custom of the forest, saving the life interest of Elizabeth, formerly the wife of the said William Plompton.
[Latin]
[CB, 500]

21 *24 February 1462*

Court held at Knaresburgh. William Plompton, esq., son of William Plompton, kt, held according to the custom of the manor 2 acres of waste in Knaresborough, formerly held by John Thorner, chaplain; 3 acres of land in Ferrensby upon 'Panchorn', formerly held by Ellen, wife of Mathew Daker; a parcel of land in Knaresborough marked by boundary stones called 'Castleings'; a messuage with 18 acres of land in Arkendale Loftus; 26 acres and a rood of land and meadow, a ½ acre and a messuage, a cottage with an acre of land, and 14 acres of waste in Knaresborough, Scriven and Ferrensby, formerly held by Richard Brennand and Elizabeth his wife. After *diem clausit extremum* following the death of William Plompton, esq., Margaret and Elizabeth, his daughters and heirs came and were admitted, to hold to them and their heirs, with reserved right [as above, CB, 500].
[Latin]
[CB, 501]

22 *28 May 1462, Westminster*

Letter patent of Richard Bingham, JKB, reciting that writs of appeal having been served in the king's bench by Thomasin, widow of Henry Perpoint of Holme, esq., against Robert Grene late of Plumpton, near Knaresborough, gent., and others named therein of the death of her husband, and by Richard Grene, nephew and heir of the late John Grene, against John Perpoint late of Rodmanthwaite and others named therein, Sir William Plompton, kt, and Henry Perpoint now stand bound in mutual obligations of £100, dated 24 May 1462, payable at Pentecost next coming, each to be nullified on condition that Thomasin and Richard abide by the award and judgement of Richard Bingham, chosen by both parties, otherwise the obligations are to remain in force. The award is to be given in writing and sealed before Pentecost next coming.

Having called the parties before him and heard the reasoned answers to their quarrels he delivers his sealed judgement on the morning after Ascension Day – within the time specified – as follows: that neither Thomasin nor Richard shall pursue their appeals in the king's bench, but shall be recorded as non-suited before Pentecost next coming.
[English]
[Copyist's note.] This deed hath some wax remaining att the copying the 17 of June 1616.
[CB, 552]

23 *26 November 1463*

Indenture between Sir William Plompton, kt, and Brian Roucliffe, 3rd baron of the Exchequer, witnessing that Sir William granted the keeping and marriage of his granddaughter and co-heir Margaret Plompton, daughter of his son William Plompton, deceased, to be married to John Roucliffe, Brian's son and heir apparent, at a convenient and speedy time, and at Brian's expense. Also that Sir William will endow the couple and their lawful heirs before Easter next coming after the date of this indenture with the manor of Nessfield with appurtenances, with reversion, in case of lack of such heirs, to Sir William and his heirs. Moreover that Sir William is to retain the issues of the manor for the next 5 years, and for 5 years thereafter a yearly sum of 10m therefrom. That if Sir William should die within this period his executors are to have no claim upon the premises.

For which marriage and feoffment Brian Roucliffe is to pay to Sir William, in addition to the sum already paid by him 400m, that is 100m 'in hand', and 20m a year payable at Pentecost and St Martin in Winter by equal portions until the whole sum is paid. It is agreed that if John Roucliffe should die within 10 years Brian and his executors are to receive £50 as reimbursement out of the issues and profits of Sir William's lands. The parties undertake that all these covenants are to be performed without fraud or bad faith.

[English]

[Copyist's note.] This deed hath a seale att the copying the 19th day of June 1616.

[CB, 558]

24 *Undated*

Bond in 100m by Brian Rocliffe of Cowthorpe, gent., to William Plompton, kt, payable to William, his heirs or executors at Christmas next, for which payment Brian, his heirs and executors are bound under seal, Given 30 Nov. 1463. Condition: that if the aforesaid Brian pays to the aforesaid William the sum of £46 13s 4d, that is 10m at Pentecost next and 10m at the following Martinmas, and thus 10m yearly at the aforesaid feasts until the whole sum of £46 13s 4d is paid, that then the obligation shall be void, otherwise it is to endure in force and effect.

[Latin]

[Copyist's note.] This bond hath a seale att the copying the 19th day of June 1616.

[CB, 559]

25 *13 December 1463*

Indenture between Elizabeth Plompton and Brian Roucliffe, witnessing that as Sir William Plompton, kt, and the said Brian have concluded an agreement for the marriage of Brian's son, John, and Margaret, daughter of Elizabeth and her deceased husband William Plompton, esq., son of Sir William, and also for other causes, Elizabeth grants the keeping and marriage of her daughter to Brian to the intent that the marriage shall take place at a convenient time.
[English]
[WYASYAS, MS 650, p. 188[r]]

26 *20 January 1464, Westminster*

Letter patent from Edward IV to all mayors, sheriffs escheators, bailiffs, constables and other ministers,[1] informing them that William Plompton, kt, having been acquitted of all accusations against him, is now fully exonerated, and hereby declared to be a true and faithful liegeman. Therefore neither he nor his are henceforth to suffer illegal molestation or vexation to their persons or property, or be subjected to rudeness or discourtesy. He is to be at liberty to go where he will, as other the king's true lieges are free to do. Disobedience to this order will incur the king's displeasure and punishment at law.
Westminster, under signet.
[English]
[CB, 561, transcript, Stapleton, lxx.]

[1] This followed Sir William's acquittal on a charge of uttering treasonous words, Stapleton, lxix; Introd. p. 7

27 *12 May 1464*

Power of attorney by Brian Rocliffe, 3rd baron of the Exchequer, Richard Hamerton, George Darell, Richard Aldburgh, John Gresley, Walter Wrottesley and Richard FitzWilliam, kts, John Sothill of 'Sothill', esq., and Guy Fairfax, sergeant-at-law, appointing John Byrd, gent., and John Inskypp their attorneys to enter and take seisin of the manors of Ockbrook, Hassop, Chaddesden, Spondon and their appurtenances, together with all lands, tenements, rents, reversions and services there, in accordance with the form and effect of the charter by which William Plompton, kt, granted the same to them, their heirs and assigns.[1]
[Latin]

[WYASYAS,MS 650, p. 258]

[1] No. **28**.

28 *1 June 1464*

Charter of William Plompton, kt, granting to Brian Rocliffe, 3rd baron of the Exchequer, Richard Hamerton, George Durell, kts, Guy Fairfax, sergeant-at-law, Richard Pygot, sergeant-at-law, Henry Sotehill, Thomas Beckwith, Stephen Hammerton, esqrs, Lawrence Kighley and Godfrey Grene his manors of Plumpton, Grassington, Steeton, Idle and Studley Roger and all other manors, lands, tenements, rents, reversions and services, together with military fees, advowsons and presentations to churches, chantries and other benefices, with all and singular their appurtenances, profits and commodities in Yorks and the city of York. To hold in perpetuity of the chief lords of those fees, by the service thence owed and accustomed by right. Warranty. Appointing Roger Jaceson and Thomas Billop, Stephen Croft, Richard Fou ... ch, Roger Faukene and Thomas Croft his attorneys jointly and severally in his name to deliver full and peaceful seisin of and in the premises to the above-named feoffees, in accordance with the form and effect of this charter.
Witnesses: Peter Ardern, JCP, Brian Stapleton, Richard Goldsburghe, kts, Robert Roos of Ingmanthorpe, Ranulph Pigott, esqrs, and others.
[Latin]
[Copyist's note.] This deed hath a seale att the copying 21st June 1616.
[CB, 565]

29 *1 June 1464*

Charter of William Plompton, kt, granting to Walter Blount, kt, Brian Roucliffe, 3rd baron of the Exchequer, Richard Hamerton, George Darell, kts, Guy Fairfax, Richard Pygott, sergeants-at-law, Henry Sotehill, Thomas Beckwtih, Stephen Hamerton esqrs, Lawrence Kyghley and Godfrey Grene, also Edward Goldsburgh, John Byrd, John Askham, Richard Fawbergh and Thomas Allestre his manors of Kinoulton in Notts, Edensor, Darley, Stanton, Wormhill and Pilsley in Derbyshire and Crakemarsh in Staffs, and all other his manors, lands, tenements, rents reversions and services, with all and singular their appurtenances and profits, together with military fees, advowsons of churches and chantries and other benefices in the same counties. Excepted are lands and tenements held of the king in chief. To hold the aforesaid premises in perpetuity of the chief lords of those fees by due service and right customs. Warranty.

Appointing Roger Jackson, William Jackson and Thomas Wylde jointly and severally his attorneys to deliver full and peaceful seisin of and in all the above premises to the feoffees.

Witnesses: John Markham, kt, CJKB, Richard Bingham, kt, JKB, William Vernon, kt, Thomas Foljambe, Richard Bingham and many others.

[Latin]

[BL, Add.MS 6698, fols 1–1v.]

30 *13 February 1468*

Evidence given by Robert Littester, aged 40,[1] chaplain to Sir William Plompton, kt, before the official of the civil court at York to the effect that about 11 years previously he had accompanied Sir William as far as Skipton-on-Swale when the latter was riding to a muster called to meet a threat from the Scots. Before they parted Sir William revealed to him the secret of his marriage to Joan Wintringham, asserting that she was indeed his true, married wife, and charging him with the duty of testifying to the legality of the marriage when called upon to do so, should Sir William chance to die in battle.

[English]

[Copyist's note.] This deed hath a seale att the copying the xxvth day of July 1616.

[CB, 631, transcript Stapleton, lxxiv.]

[1] The testimonies of Richard Clerk, parish clerk of Knaresborough, and John Croft who were present at the wedding in St John's church, Knaresborough, were given 6 July 1472, CB, 682, (transcribed Stapleton, lxxvi–vii).

31 *25 May 1471*

Award of Robert Roos of Ingmanthorpe, Robert Gascoigne, Thomas Clapham and Lawrence Kighley, reciting that whereas William Plompton, kt, and the minister of the house of St Robert are bound in mutual obligations of £100 to observe this award,[1] the arbitrators ordain that each party shall be friendly and loving towards the other, that William shall be good master to the bretheren and tenants of the convent, and the minister a good father and neighbour.

Also that Sir William shall repair his mill and dam on the river Nidd, cleanse and free the goit, and not allow the workmen ...[2] so that the goit shall be in use before St Margaret's Day [8/20 July]; that Sir William and his heirs shall retain possession of these premises without interruption from the minister and his successors, and that the minister shall certify this by sealed deed before the feast of St Peter called Lammas Day. The minister shall also grant to Sir William the farm of the fishing of the convent's water mill from Grimbald Bridge as far as the mill. Sir William is to grant to the minister and his successors licence in pure and perpetual alms, before the feast of St Peter to ... his mill from the convent's mill that stands at the east end of the goit, as long as it shall not [?impede] the water supply to his mill. He is to relinquish all claim to the convent's mill.

Also Sir William shall not suffer William Husworth, William Rute, Christopher Craven, Richard Dryver, Richard Warter and John Ripley, friars and bretheren of the convent ... as John Cock, William Parker, Thomas Choldeyn, William Haworth and John Nonnes,[3] indicted and ... over their ... after the form of the law. Also the minister is to deliver to Sir William a cross ... belonging to him before Easter.

Sir William is to release the minister and bretheren before St Peter's Day from all personal actions moved before St Ellen's Day next before this award [3 May], and likewise the minister shall release Sir William, provided always that if either party wishes to vary the wording of this award, it shall be modified according to our true intent by two, three or by the four of us, whereof two must be trustees representing each of the parties.

[English]

[Copyist's note.] This award hath fawer seales att the copying the 25th day of June 1616.

[CB, 573]

[1] CB, 571.

[2] A 17th cent. copyist described this deed as 'so dimmed Þat it cannot be read', Acc. 1731/6, fol. 230v., hence the illegible words/phrases indicated here.

[3] Friars who had been indicted and outlawed by Sir William during his dispute with the convent, **9**, **18** above pp. 31–2, 42–3.

32 *20 June 1471*

Charter of the minister, Robert Bolton, and convent of the house of St Robert of Knaresborough granting to William Plompton, kt, and his heirs licence to farm the fishery of the mill-pond and water of their water mill from a certain place called Grimbald Bridge as far as the mill, upon ground belonging to the said minister and house. The grant is ratified and confirmed to William and his heirs of and in the water belonging to the mill.

[Latin]
[Copyist's note.] This deed hath a seale att the copying the 25 day of June 1616.
[CB, 574]

33 *13 July 1472, York*

Certification by Dr William Poteman, official of the civil court of York, that whereas Sir William Plompton of Plumpton in the parish of Spofforth, said to have harboured a certain Joan Wintringham in his house, to the great peril of his soul and the grievous scandal of the faithful, having come before the court in the cathedral church of York on the 26 July 1468[1] to answer the charge against him, declared that the said Joan was not his concubine but had been for many years his true wife; that a child had been conceived after their clandestine marriage in Knaresborough parish church about 20 years past, and that he was now prepared to submit to the Church's censure and make amends. Having heard the evidence of witnesses to the truth of Sir William's claim it is hereby declared, acknowledged and published to all the faithful that they are and have been truly married.
[Latin]
[Copyist's note.] This deed hath a seale att the copying the second day of July 1616.
[CB, 583]

[1] This was Sir William's first appearance before the court, Stapleton, lxxiii.

34 *28 September 1472*

Lease by Richard, duke of Gloucester, chief seneschal of the Duchy of Lancaster to Sir William Plompton, kt, of the farm of the corn mills of Knaresborough and of the new mill at Bilton, together with the office of bailiff of the borough of Knaresborough for 12 years, at an annual rent of 20m for the first, and 46s 8d for the second and third.
[Latin]
[Copyist's note.] This deed hath a seale att the copying the 2 of July 1616.
[CB, 584]

35 *12 October 1475*

Charter of William Plompton, kt, granting to Master Richard Andrewes, dean of the cathedral church of York, William Eure, clerk, John Norton, kt, Ralph Pigot, John Arthington of Arthington, Godfrey Grene and Richard Knaresborough his manor of Plumpton, Yorks, with its appurtenances, together with the advowson or nomination of a chantry of the Holy Trinity in the collegiate church of Ripon, also all other his lands, rents, reversions and services appertaining in the vill of Plumpton. To have and hold the same to those grantees their heirs and assigns in perpetuity of the chief lords of that fee and by services thence owed and accustomed by right. Warranty.[1]

Appointing John Justyppe as his attorney to enter the premises in his name and with his authority to deliver full and peaceable seisin to the grantees of and in the premises.
[Latin]
[Copyist's note.] This dede hath Sir William Plompton's seale at armes att the copying the 4th day of July 1616.
[CB, 586]

[1] Sir William conveyed all his properties between 12 Oct. and 6 Nov. 1475, CB, 589, 591, 593, 596, 598.

36 *23 October 1475*

Re-settlement by the grantees [named in no. **35**] to William Plompton, kt, of their manor of Plumpton in Yorks with its appurtenances, together with the advowson or nomination of a chantry of the Holy Trinity within the collegiate church of Ripon, also all other their lands and tenements, rents, reversions and services with all and singular their appurtenances in Plumpton (except a pasture with a house built thereon called Rudfarlington)[1] for the term of his life, so that after William's death the premises (except those excepted) may pass to Robert Plompton, junior, his son, and Joan wife of the aforesaid William and to the legitimate heirs of Robert. Remainder, in case of lack of such heirs, to the right heirs of William in perpetuity, holding of the chief lords of that fee [etc.].

Appointment by the grantors of Robert Plompton, senior, as their attorney with full powers to enter the premises (except those excepted) and in their name to deliver [etc.].[2]
[Latin]
[Copyist's note.] This deed hath 7 seales att the copying, 4 July 1616.
[CB, 587]

[1] See nos. **79**, **80**.
[2] The remaining properties were in like manner resettled between 23 Oct. and 7 Nov. 1475, CB, 588, 590, 592, 594, 597, 600, 603.

37 *13 July 1477*

Indenture between Sir William Plompton, kt, and William Gascoigne, esq., witnessing an agreement for the marriage of Robert son and heir of Sir William and Agnes sister of William Gascoigne, the marriage to take place between this day and the forthcoming feast of St Andrew [30 Nov.]. Sir William will provide within a month of the marriage a sufficient estate in jointure to them and their lawful heirs, worth a clear £20 a year, out lands and tenements within the lordship of Kinoulton, Notts. Remainder, in case of lack of heirs, to the right heirs of Sir William.

Sir William guarantees that neither he nor any other feoffee to his use shall make any lease or feoffment of any lands or tenements belonging to him for the agreements already entered into with Henry Sothill and Brian Roclif without the knowledge of William Gascoigne. Should it be held by the advice of Gascoigne's council that insufficient provision had been made for Robert and his heirs, the insufficiency will be made good by Sir William; fines and recoveries only excepted.

For the marriage, William Gascoigne shall pay £100 by installments, viz.: £20 on the day of the wedding, or within a month thereafter, and 40m a year thenceforward, for which payment he and two others shall be bound to Sir William by their several obligations. The wedding dinner and the bride's clothing are to be provided by William Gascoigne. Sir William Plumpton is to be bound in the sum of 400m for the performance of his obligations.
[English]
[Copyist's note.] his deed hath a seale att the copying the 12th of July 1616.
[CB, 604]

38 *1 May 1478*

Charter of Sir William Plompton, of Plumpton, Yorks, kt, granting in perpetuity to his son Robert Plompton and to Robert's heirs and assigns all his goods, of whatsoever kind, moveable or immoveable, alive or dead, together with whatsoever debts are due to him, of whatsoever kind or form within any part of the kingdom.
[Latin]

[Copyist's note.] This deed was copied on Saturday the 27 of January 1626, and then it had a seale.
[CB, 685]

39 *1 May 1478*

Charter with warranty of Sir William Plompton of Plumpton, kt, granting to Robert his son, his heirs and assigns all right, status and possession of and in his lands, tenements, rents and services with all their appurtenances in Yorks, also of all other lands and tenements, rents and services with their appurtenances in Notts, Derbyshire and Staffs. To be held to Robert his heirs and assigns of the chief lords of those fees [etc.].
Witnesses: Master William Eure, clerk, Brother Robert Benson, minister of the house of St Robert, Ralph Pygott, Thomas Medelton, John Ardington, esqrs, and others.
[Latin]
[Copyist's note.] This deed was copied the day and yeare last above written Saturday, 27 Jan. 1626, and then it had a seale.
[CB, 687]

40 *8 April 1479*

Charter of Dame Cecilia Fuljambe, widow of Edward Fuljambe, kt, granting to William Plompton, kt, her manor of Elton in Derbyshire with appurtenances and also all other lands and tenements, rents, reversions and services with all and singular their appurtenances in Elton; also the fifth part of the manor of Newton near Blithfield, Staffs, with all and singular its appurtenances; also demising and releasing to Sir William all her right, status, title, claim, possession and interest in Elton and its appurtenances there and in Stanton and in the fifth part of the manor of Newton. To have and hold [etc.]. Warranty.[1]
[Latin]
[Copyist's note.] This deed was copied on Wednesday, the 31 of January 1626 and then it had a seale.
[CB, 693]

[1] See no. **48**.

41 *29 May 1480*

Bond by Brian Roucliff, 3rd baron of the exchequer, John, his son, Thomas Roucliff and Peter Ardern, esqrs, to stand firmly in an obligation to William Plompton of Plumpton, kt, and Robert Plompton, junior, esq., in the sum of 1,000m, payable to them or their lawful attorneys at Michaelmas next after the date of these presents, 29 May 1480. Condition: that Brian, John, his son, and Margaret, his wife, abide by the award of Thomas Burgh, William Gascoigne, Robert Constable, Hugh Hastings, kts, Robert Sheffeld, William Eland, Thomas FitzWilliam, Thomas Middleton, Edward Saltmarsh, Miles Metcalf, John Everingham and John Dawney, arbitrators chosen by both the above parties, 10 or 8 of them, of whom the aforesaid Thomas Burgh, William Gascoigne, Robert Sheffield, Thomas Middleton, John Everingham and John Dawney are to be 6, either William Eland or Thomas FitzWilliam to be a seventh, and Edward Saltmarsh or Miles Metcalf to be the eighth. To adjudicate on the right, title, possession, claim and interest in all and singular lordships, manors, lands and tenements with their appurtenances which are of the aforesaid Sir William or of any to his use or that of his heirs. Also upon all causes of dispute between the parties, provided the award is given in writing before 2 Feb. next, otherwise the obligation will be null and void.[1]
[Latin]
[Copyist's note.] This deed hath fower seales att the copying the 15th day of July 1616.
[CB, 610]

[1] Sir William died in Oct., see no. **46**.

42 *10 November 1480*

Inquisition at Wetherby before William Nettilton escheator of Yorks by authority of a writ of *diem clausit extremum* directed to him and to the inquisition. Percival Lyndley, John Arthington, Thomas Hawkesworth, esqrs, William Exilby, Henry Arthington, John Rawden, John Chambre, William Lyndley, gents, Richard Saxton, John Baildon, William Angram, William Stead, George Swale and John Herryson say on oath that at his death William Plompton, kt, held lands of the king in chief in Yorks in demesne and not by villein service; that on the day before his death he was seised in his demesne as in fee of the manor of Plumpton with appurtenances in Yorks, together with the chantry of the Holy Trinity in the collegiate church of Ripon; that by his charter submitted in evidence to the jurors he granted these premises to Master

Richard Andrewes, dean of York, William Eure, clerk, John Norton, kt, Ralph Pygot, John Arthington, Godfrey Grene and Richard Knaresburgh, their heirs and assigns in perpetuity, to be held of the chief lords [etc.]. In virtue of this grant the feoffees were seised of the same, and, by their charter exhibited in evidence to the jurors, demised and granted to William Plompton for life the aforesaid manor and advowson, except for a messuage, 20 acres of land and 40 acres of woodland with appurtenances called Rudfarlington, within the vill, and parcel of the manor of Plumpton, with remainder of all save the lands above excepted to his son, Robert Plompton, jnr, and the legitimate heirs of his body, and to Joan, wife of Sir William, remainder, in case of lack of heirs, to the right heirs of Sir William in perpetuity.

Also that the feoffees were seised of the aforesaid Rudfarlington, and by another charter submitted in evidence they demised these premises to William and Joan Plompton without imputation of waste, so that after the deaths of William and Joan the same to remain to Robert and his legitimate heirs, remainder in case of Robert's death without such heirs to the right heirs of William. And Joan has sole seisin of Rudfarlington in survivorship in her demesne as by free tenure, remainder to Robert and his legitimate heirs.

Also that being similarly seised in his demesne of the manor Steeton and its appurtenances William demised and granted these to the same feoffees [etc.], as appears in a charter exhibited in evidence. The feoffees, then being seised, conveyed the premises to William and Joan to hold for their lives without imputation of waste, remainders [etc]. As survivor, Joan has sole seisin of the premises which after her death pass to Robert [etc].

Also that the manor of Idle, together with the advowson of the chantry or altar of St Nicholas in the church of St Martin in Micklegate, York, held by William as of his demesne and in fee were similarly demised by him to the same feoffees, who, having seisin, thereafter demised them in the same terms to William for life, remainder to Robert [etc., as above].

Also that the manor of Grassington was conveyed by Sir William in like terms to the same feoffees, who demised them to William and Joan for life. The latter as survivor has sole seisin. Remainders [etc., as above].

Also that the manors of Plumpton, Steeton, Grassington, the advowson and appurtenances and Rudfarlington are held of Henry, earl of Northumberland by military service as of his manor of Spofforth, not of the king. And that the manor of Idle with appurtenances is held of the king as of the honor of Pontefract, parcel of the Duchy of Lancaster, by fealty and a rent of 3s yearly for all services.

Also that the clear value of the manor of Plumpton, together with the aforesaid advowson is 40m yearly, that of the manor of Steeton is 20m yearly, of the manor of Grassington is £20 yearly, and of the manor of Idle with the advowson of the chantry in York, £10 yearly. The clear value of Rudfarlington is 5m yearly.

Also that William Plompton, kt, died 15 Oct. 1480, and that Margaret, wife of John Rocliffe and Elizabeth, wife of John Sotehill are '*consanguines*' and heirs of Sir William, viz.: daughters of William Plompton, son and heir of Sir William, and that Margaret is aged 20 years and more and Elizabeth 19 years and more.
[Latin]
[CB, 624]

43 *18 December 1480*

Inquisition at Derby before Edmund Perpoint escheator of Derbyshire by authority of a writ of *diem clausit extremum* directed to him and to this inquisition. Henry Columbell of Derby, Henry Tykhull of Chaddesden, Godfrey Pilkington of Stanton, John Ashby of Chellaston, John Smalley of Alvaston, William Frounches of Little Chester, Robert Tibnull of Dale, gents, John Stapulford of Alvaston, Nicholas Cuger of Chaddesden, Nicholas Brashaw of Windley, William Condrom of 'Lutchworth', Robert Cokke of Spondon, Nicholas Cokke of the same, George Lister of Little Chester, William Merry of Chellaston and Thomas Tykling of Kirk Langley[1] say on oath that on the day before he died William Plompton, kt, was seised of the manors of Ockbrook, Chaddesden, Darley, Stanton, Edensor, Pilsley, Hassop, Wormhill, Chelmorton, Castleton, Rowland, Carlton, Lees, Flagfield, Wardlow, Bakewell, Bely, Twyford and Lockhaw with appurtenances in Derbyshire, and of two messuage with appurtenances in Spondon, a messuage with appurtenances in Broughton, 2 messuages within 2 gardens and appurtenances in Tideswell, and a messuage with appurtenances in Newbold, and of the advowsons or nominations to the chantries of the Holy Cross in the church of Bakewell and the Blessed Mary in the church of Elton, and also of other lands and tenements in Wheston, Martinside, Combes, Betfield and Hurdlow. Thus seised, he, by charter now submitted in evidence, conveyed the premises to feoffees [names as in no. **42**], who in virtue of this grant were seised of the same and, by their charter submitted in evidence, demised them to William for life without imputation of waste, remainder to Robert Plompton, jnr, his son, and the legitimate heirs of his body, remainder, in case of lack of heirs, to the right heirs of William in perpetuity.

Also that the manor of Ockbrook is held of the king in chief, by fealty only, and its clear value is £13 6s 8d yearly. The manor of

Chaddesden and 2 messuages in Spondon with appurtenances are held of the king as of his honor of Tutbury, parcel of the Duchy of Lancaster, by fealty and a rent of 32s yearly for all services. Clear value, £6 13s 4d. The manor of Darley with appurtenances is held of the king as of the honor of Tutbury by fealty and a rent of 3s yearly. Clear value, £5 6s 8d yearly. The manor of Stanton with appurtenances is not held of the king, but of whom, they are ignorant. The manor of Edensor with appurtenances is held of the king as of the aforesaid honor, by fealty and a rent of 8s yearly. Clear value, £10 yearly. The manor of Pilsley with appurtenances is held of the king as of the aforesaid honor, by fealty and a rent of 5s yearly. Clear value, £5 6s 8d yearly. The manor of Hassop with appurtenances is held of the king as of the aforesaid honor, by fealty and a rent of 3s yearly. Clear value, £7 yearly. The manor of Wormhill with appurtenances in Wheston, Martinside, Combes and Betfield is held of the king as of his castle of the High Peak, by fealty and a rent of £3 13s 10d yearly. Clear value, £8. The manor of Chelmorton with appurtenances in Hurdlow is held of the king as of the honor of Tutbury, by fealty and a rent of 6d yearly. Clear value, 16s 8d. The manor of Broughton with appurtenances is held of the prior of Tutbury, by fealty and a rent of 7s yearly. Clear value, 13s 4d yearly. 2 messuages and a garden with appurtenances in Tideswell are held of Joan Meverell by fealty only. Clear value, 6s 8d yearly. A messuage in Newbold with appurtenances is held of the abbot of Welbeck, by what services they are ignorant. Clear value, 23s 4d.

Also that on the day of his death William Plompton, kt, held no other lands in Derbyshire. Also that he died 15 Oct. 1480, and that Margaret, wife of John Rocliffe, and Elizabeth, wife of John Suthill are '*consanguines*' and next heirs of William namely, daughters of William Plompton, esq., son of the aforesaid Sir William. Also that Margaret is aged 21 and more and that Elizabeth is aged 20 and more.
[Latin]
[CB, 626]

[1] MS, Erkingley.

44 *20 December 1480*

Inquisition held at Lenton, Notts, before Edmund Perpointe, escheator, by authority of a writ of *diem clausit extremum* directed to him and to the inquisition. William Bingham of Car Colston, William Bowes of 'Cortingswark',[1] Henry Plompton of Arnold, William Smithe of Ratcliffe upon Soar, gents, Richard Tayler of Bunny, William Smallwood of Wysall, Nicholas Botiller of Ratcliffe upon Soar, Richard Ebb of

Rempston, John Bealle of the same, John Savour of West Leake, John Milner of Sutton Bonnington, Thomas Lawrence of the same, Henry Wheatly of Bunny, William Milnes of East Leake and William Clement of Kingston, say on oath that William Plompton, kt, on the day of his death held certain lands of the king in chief in demesne, namely the manor of Kinoulton held in his demesne as in fee, a messuage with appurtenances in Mansfield Woodhouse, and the advowson of a chantry of the Blessed Mary in the church of Mansfield Woodhouse, all of which premises he, by his charter now exhibited in evidence, conveyed to Richard Andrewes [and others named in no. **42**] to have to them their heirs and assigns in perpetuity. Thus these grantees, being legally seised of the premises granted them by their charter here exhibited to William Plompton and Joan his wife for their lives without imputation of waste, with remainder after their deaths to their son Robert Plompton, jnr, and the legitimate heirs of his body in perpetuity. In case of lack of such heirs remainder in perpetuity to William's right heirs. Joan is thus seised in survivorship of the premises in her demesne as of free tenure.

Also that Kinoulton is held of the king as of the honor of Tickhill, parcel of the Duchy of Lancaster, by fealty and a rent of 3s 4d. The farm is worth ...[2] yearly, and the clear value of the manor is £26 13s 4d yearly. Also the messuage and advowson are held of the king as of the manor of Mansfield by fealty only, and that their clear annual value is 6s 4d.[3]

Also that the said William died 15 Oct. 1480, and that [the heirs are the same as in nos **42–3**]. Margaret is aged 21 and more, and Elizabeth is aged 19 and more.

[Latin]

[Copyist's note.] Copied 24 Feb. 1626, hauing many seales.

[CB, 710]

[1] (?) Keyworth.

[2] Figures illeg.

[3] This figure is almost illegible and may therefore be incorrect.

45 *26 April 1481*[1]

Letter patent of Brian Redeman, son and heir of Richard Redeman, snr, esq[1]., deceased, granting power of attorney to John Sotehill, Richard Middilton of Skipton, esqrs, Christopher Radeliffe, gent., John Barnby and John Markingfeld to enter the manors of Plumpton, Grassington-in-Craven, Idle, Steeton and Little Studley, near Ripon, with their appurtenances and take full and peaceful seisin for him and in his

name, having whomsoever is thereupon removed and expelled, and thus resume his possession.
[Latin]
[WYASYAS,MS 650, p. 260.]

[1] On 10 July 1481 Brian Redman enfeoffed Thomas Burgh, William Parr, Thomas Fitzwilliam, kts, and William Hopton of Swillington in these premises. Witnesses: Guy Fairfax, kt, JKB, Thomas Worteley, James Danby, kts, Miles Wilstrop and William Calverlay, jnr, esqrs, WYASYAS, MS 650, p. 260.

46 *21 March 1482*

Obligation by John Roclife and John Sothill, esqrs, in £2,000 to Joan Plompton, widow, and Robert Plompton, jnr, esq., their executors or legally appointed attorneys, payable at Pentecost next after the date of thses presents, to which obligation they, for themselves, their heirs and executors affixed their seals, 21 March 1482. Condition,[1] that they and all those having right or title through Margaret, wife of John Roclife and Elizabeth, wife of John Sothill, daughters and heirs of William Plompton, esq., of and in all and singular the lordships, manors, lands, tenements and hereditaments with appurtenances, of which William Plompton, kt, was seised, are to stand and obey the arbitration and judgement of the Lord Richard, duke of Gloucester, Henry, earl of Northumberland, William Parr, James Harrington and Hugh Hastings, kts, John Vavasour, sergeant-at-law, Robert Sheffeld, William Eland, Miles Metcalf and John Dawney, arbitrators, chosen indifferently by the parties.

They John Rocliffe, John Sothill and others having right or title are to hold and adhere to the ordinances of the arbitrators, provided they be given in writing and sealed with their seals before the feast of Pentecost next after the above date, otherwise the obligation is to be void and of no effect.
[Latin]
[Copyist's note.] This bond hath 2 seales att the copying the 23 day of July 1616.
[CB, 629]

[1] On 14 Feb. 1483 the condition was altered to hold to the award to be given in writing by Edw. IV before 7 July next, but his death, 9 April 1483, supervened and the bond was renewed 12 Sept. 1483, and judgement was given 16 Sept. 1483, CB, 720, 721.

47 *13 July 1482*

Will of Robert Plompton of Plompton, esq. Whereas he has enfeoffed his mother Dame Joan Plompton and others of his manors, lands, tenements, rents, reversions, advowsons and commodities in Yorks, Notts, Derbyshire and Staffs, his will is that in the event of his death Dame Joan and Dame Agnes, his wife, are to receive jointly and without disturbance the revenues, offices farms and profits therefrom and raise a sum of 400m as a portion for his daughter Jane, should she be granted 'the grace of life'; that they should lose no time in paying his dues and debts, and in rewarding his servants according to their deserts. After the deaths of his wife and mother the feoffees are to make a lawful estate of all the premises to Jane Plompton his daughter and her heirs in perpetuity.
Witnesses: Brother Robert Bolton, minister of St Robert's Thomas Middleton, esq., Robert Gylyngham.
[English]
[Copyist's note.] This deed hath a seale att the copying the xxvth day of July 1616.
[Marginal note.] his will was made he being in minority and not knighted, and Sir William Plompton lately deceased.
[CB, 630]

48 *16 September 1483*

Arbitration award of Richard III[1] on matters in dispute between Joan Plompton, widow, and Robert Plompton, kt, of one party, and John Roucliff, esq., and Margaret his wife and John Sotehill and Elizabeth his wife of the other, namely the right, title, claim and interest in all the premises of which the late Sir William Plompton, kt, or any to his use were seised, and other matters, actions and demands at issue between them.

Reciting that the parties were bound by mutual obligations dated 12 Sept. 1483,[2] the king having examined the matters and taken the advice of the lords of his council and of his judges has made his award as follows: [1] Margaret and Elizabeth the heirs general are to have a sufficient and lawful estate in the manors of Grassington and Steeton with appurtenances, lands, tenements, rents, services and reversions therein. Also other lands, tenements, rents, services reversions and hereditaments with appurtenances within the manors and towns of Chaddesden, Spondon, Ockbrook, Broughton, Wormhill, Wheston, Tideswell, Martinside, Combes, Betfield, Hurdlow, Chelmorton, Wardlow, Castleton, Burgh, Newbold, Pilsley, Edensor, Carlton and

Lees in Derbyshire, together extended at a clear 224m. Sir Robert and Dame Joan and any feoffees to the use of Sir William, and all others having use or title in the same are to make over to the heirs general a sufficient and lawful estate therein before the 29 Aug. next. Remainder in case of lack of heirs of Margaret and Elizabeth to the right heirs of Sir William. The legal instruments for the implementation of the above are to be approved by Sir William Hussey, CJKB, and Sir Guy Fairfax, JKB, and made at the expense of the grantees. [ii] Sir Robert and Dame Joan are to have a sufficient and lawful estate in the residue of all lordships [etc.] which were of Sir William Plompton, kt, or any other to his use. The heirs general are to make over a sufficient and lawful estate in the premises [as above] at Sir Robert's expense, and to the satisfaction of the same two justices.

[iii] John and Margaret Rocliffe are to retain the manor of Nessfield which was settled upon them by Sir William. Any lands there or in Langbar shown to the satisfaction of the two judges not to have been parcel of the manor of Nessfield are to be to Sir Robert and his heirs. Remainder in case of lack of heirs to the right heirs of Sir William. A sufficient and lawful estate in the above exceptions shall be made by John and Margaret at Sir Robert's expense.

[iv] The heirs general shall pay an annual rent charge of £40 with distress clause to Sir Robert, payable at Martinmas and Whit Sunday in equal portions, for the life annuity due to Elizabeth, widow of William, son of Sir William Plompton. Sir Robert shall execute the grant to her before the 11 Nov. next at his expense.

[v] The manor of Elton with Stanton, Derbyshire, and a fifth part of the manor of Newton-by-Blithfield, Staffs, are to be enjoyed by whichever party shall recover them[3] until the party shall have recovered half the cost of recovery, the other party then being recompensed to the extent of half the cost. The parties are to receive sufficient and lawful estates in the moieties.

[vi] Rents, services and issues levied and paid to Sir Robert and/or Dame Joan since Pentecost 1481 in respect of properties awarded to the heirs general shall be handed over to them before next Easter, as directed by the advice of the two justices.

[vii] Each party shall surrender and hand over to the other before next Easter all evidences relevant to the premises awarded to them.

By privy seal, 16 Sept. 1483.

[English]

[Copyist's note.] Copied the 29th March 1627 hauing a seale, and signed with the king's hands.

[CB, 722]

[1] The document is transcribed in full in *Harleian MS 433*, 133–6, and Stapleton, xc–xcv.

[2] No. **46**n.
[3] See no. **40**.

49 *Undated*

Charter of Robert Plompton, kt, appointing his beloved Edward Plompton his true and lawful attorney with power to act for him and in his stead in all confidential causes, negotiations, motions and matters before whatsoever persons, spiritual or temporal; to proceed with legal process and litigation in his absence, negotiating costs, drawing up and evaluating documents, and by appearing, proving, defending, excepting, making replication in legal contest, viewing and, if necessary, increasing valors, do whatever is necessary for concluding legal actions, and generally by special authority, take all and singular actions and expediants that may be necessary for the forwarding of matters. He is appointed attorney to act for and in the name of Sir Robert in all matters as if he were present in person.
[Latin]
[CB, 729]

50 *22 November 1486, Plumpton*

Indenture between Robert Plompton, kt, and John Willymott witnessing that Sir Robert let to farm to John Willymott the manor of Kinoulton with the demesne and a close on the south side of the barn between the manor and a tenement held by Brian Smith, for nine years from the 3 May next coming, at a yearly rent of £22 for the manor, and 20s for the close, payable at the feasts of Martinmas in Winter and Pentecost in equal portions.

The tenant is to provide free stabling, fodder, hay and grass twice yearly for four days for Sir Robert's horses and those of his retinue to the number of 20. In case of a longer stay the tenant shall receive ¾d a day (viz. 24 hours) per horse, and 1½d per horse for a week's pasturage. For the period of their visit Sir Robert, his menie and servants shall occupy the hall, chamber, bakehoue, brewhouse, kitchen and stables whilst the tenant and his household confine themselves temporarily to the hall and chambers at the other end thereof, and to all other offices belonging to the manor.

The tenant shall maintain the walls of the building with stone and earth and the roofs with thatching, and carry out hedging and ditching. At the end of his tenure he shall bear the cost of removal and leave the premises in good order, making good any deficiency which may be

found at the time of his departure. He shall provide meat and drink for Sir Robert's steward and reeve and their servants when they come on Sir Robert's business, and hay, litter and provender for their horses. He shall not fell timber. Re-entry clause.
[English]
[Copyist's note.] Copied 22 June 1627, then hauing a seale.
[CB, 744]

51 *1 June 1490, Padley*

Indenture between Sir Robert Plompton, kt, and Ralph Haigh, witnessing that after disagreements and controversies between the parties regarding the right, title and possession of the manor of Darley with appurtenances, valued at 10m yearly, the parties agreed to obey the award of Robert Eyre, esq., who, having knowledge of the titles, replications, records and allegations of both parties, agreed to their request and makes his award as follows: [i] Ralph Haigh is to deliver into his custody within 6 days after the date of this award all his evidences concerning Sir Robert Plompton for safe-keeping until Sir Robert shall have granted him an annuity of 5m payable at Pentecost and St Martin in Winter by equal portions, from the issues of manors and tenements held by Sir Robert in Hassop. The annuity is to be made before the 10 Nov. next and must include a clause allowing for distraint. [ii] On the day of the making of the annuity the parties are to make mutual acquittances of all manner of actions, causes and demands between them.
Witnesses: Thomas Meverell, the younger, esq., Robert Plompton, gent., John Waston, chaplain, Henry Fox, yeoman and others.
[English]
[Copyist's note.] Copied 6 July 1627, then hauing a seale.
[CB, 756]

52 *26 August 1490*

Indenture between David ap Griffith and Sir Robert Plompton, kt, witnessing that the former has leased to Sir Robert the keeping of Haverah Park with the herbage and pannage and all other profits, offices, commodities and farms belonging to the same, as is more plainly expressed in the patent. Sir Robert or his deputy is to hold the office for 6 years from 25 March next coming, paying £8 yearly at the feasts of St John the Baptist and the Assumption of Our Lady by equal portions. Provided always that Sir Robert or his deputy shall discharge

yearly the said David to the king and his officers of all manner of charges belonging to the said David for the park during the term of the lease, if the said David continue as patenter there. To perform all covenants aforesaid upon the part of Sir Robert, Sir Richard Langton and Sir John Langton, clerks, are bound in £20, as appears by their obligation.
[English]
[Copyist's note.] Copied 9 July 1627, then hauing a seale.
[CB, 758]

53 *22 November 1490, Plumpton*

Award by Robert Plompton, kt, relating that whereas William Plompton, late of Kirkby Overblow, bastard, had by his obligation dated 1 Oct. 1490 bound himself in the sum of £100 to abide by the award of Sir Robert Plompton, assisted by Thomas Midleton, John Vavasor and William Hill, on all manner of variances, quarrels, trespasses, debates, askings, suits, actions, and claims, real and personal between Sir Robert and William arising before the above date. The award is to be given in writing before the 30 Nov. next.

Therefore Sir Robert with the advice of his council ordains that William shall reimburse him 30s for the herbage of Haverah Park and 20s for dues to the pallessers; he is also to pay the fees and dues owed by him to Thomas Ward since the 8 Sept. last. At the request of Thomas Midleton, John Nelson, William Hill and other friends Sir Robert agrees to grant William a life annuity of 3m payable at Martinmas and Whitsuntide in equal portions, or within 40 days after each feast, provided that he remain loyal and honest in his dealings and performs his due service, his allegiance only excepted, to Sir Robert and his heirs. Also Sir Robert remits 26s 8d of the total sum of £5 owed to him by William, who is to pay the residue of 23s 4d before next Whitsuntide.
[English]
[Copyist's note.] Copied 13 June 1627, then hauing a seale.
[CB, 761]

54 *19 August 1496, Plumpton*

Release with warranty by Elizabeth Beckwith, widow of Sir William Beckwith, kt,[1] on behalf of herself and her heirs, to Sir Robert Plompton, kt, and his heirs of her whole right, title, claim and interest to and in the manors of Plumpton, Grassington, Steeton, Idle, Nessfield, Studley

Roger and Ripon, with the advowson of the chantry of Holy Trinity in the collegiate church of Ripon, with all their appurtenances in Yorks, and in the manors of Kinoulton, Owthorpe, Hickling, Colston and Mansfield Woodhouse, with the advowson of the chantry of St Mary in the church there, with their appurtenances in Notts, and in the manors of Ockbrook, Chaddesden, Stanton, Edensor, Pilsley, Hassop, Wormhill, Chelmorton, Darley, Hurdlow, Flagg, Wheston, Combes, Martinside, Betfield, Tideswell, Castleton, Wardlow, Rowlond, Bakewell, Carlton, Lees, Bely, Broughton Twyford, Spondon, Newbold and Lockhaw, together with the advowsons of the chantry in the chapel of St Margaret at Elton and of the chantry at the altar of the Holy Cross in the church of Bakewell with their appurtenances in Derbyshire, and in the manors of Crakemarsh and Combridge with appurtenances in Staffs, and in all other premises whatsoever which were sometime held by her father, Sir William Plompton.
Witnesses: William Gascoigne, Ralph Pigot, Christopher Warde, Peter Midleton, kts, John Wanseford, John Arthington, Nicholas Midleton, esqrs, and others.
[Latin]
[Copyist's note.] Copied August 1627, then hauing a seale.
[CB, 782]

[1] See no. **17**.

55 *14 September 1496, Plumpton*

Feoffment with warranty[1] by Robert Plompton, kt, to Nicholas Middilton, Richard Greave and Robert Halderby, esqrs, and Richard Plompton, clerk, of the manor of Hassop with its appurtenances in Derbyshire, also lands and tenements in the vill of Hassop and Rowland. To have to them, their heirs and assigns, holding of the chief lords of that fee by due services and right customs.

Also power of attorney to Thurston Lawe and Richard Wall, severally and together, to enter the premises, take full seisin in the name of the grantor and then to deliver full and peaceful possession to the aforesaid grantees according to the from and effect of the above charter.
Witnesses: William Gascoigne, Ralph Pygot and Christopher Warde, kts, Tristram Bolling, Walter Baildon and many others.
[Latin]
[Copyist's note.] Copied 22 August 1626, hauing a seale.
[CB, 783]

[1] Feoffment in pursuance of the terms of the contract for the marriage of William Plumpton and Isabel Babthorpe, App. I, 5.

56 *26 September 1497*

Indenture between Robert Plompton, kt, and William Babthorpe, esq., witnessing that William delivered to Robert a deed in tail of the manor of Sacombe and other lands in Herts sealed in red wax with a seal of arms comprising, in the escutcheon of the name, between a Chevron 3 Squerells seriant, and the king's letter patent of licence for the same to keep to the use of Isabel, wife of William Plompton and the heirs of her body. The tenor of which deed of entail with warranty being that on 11 Sept 1420 Richard Gott, clerk, brother and heir of Hugh Holte, esq., demised to Ralph Babthorpe, kt, the manor of Sacombe with appurtenances, a messuage, 2 ..., 3 ..., 8 acres of woodland and 40s rent, with appurtenances in Staunton and Sacombe, to be held by Robert for life with remainder to Ralph Babthorpe his son and heir and Katherine his wife and the heirs of their bodies. Remainder in default of such heirs to the right heirs of Robert. Witnessed by Robert Onwhit, John Leventhorp, John Hotoft, John Fray.
[Latin and English]
[Copyist's note.] Copied 20 September 1627, hauing a peace of a seale.
[CB, 791]

57 *5 March 1500*

Quitclaim by John Vavasour of Newton, esq., to Robert Plompton, kt, of all right and claim which he has of the grant and feoffment of William Plompton, kt, father of the said Sir Robert and in all manors, lands and tenements in Plumpton, Follifoot, Idle, Grassington, Braham, Stockheld and Steeton. These to be held by Sir Robert and his assigns in perpetuity of the chief lords of those fees and by services [etc.].
[Latin]
[Copyist's note.] Copied 28 September 1627, hauing a seale.
[CB, 796]

58 *2 July 1500*

Power of attorney by Robert Bubwith, clerk, and Richard Burrow, chaplain, to William Saucheverell and William Sanderson, their attornies and deputies, to take and receive full and peaceful possession and seisin of their manors of Edensor, Darley, Stanton and Pilesley and their appurtenances in Derbyshire, and of their manors of Combridge and Crakemarsh in Staffs with their appurtenances, also of all other manors, lands, tenements, rents, services and reversions with all and singular their appurtenances and profits whatsoever, together with military fees and advowsons of churches, chantries and other benefices in the same counties, according to the form and effect of the charter indented to them and their heirs made by Richard Fawberg.[1]
[Latin]
[BL, Add.MS 6698, fol. 2v.]

[1] See no. **29**.

59 *6 October 1500*

Charter of Robert Plompton kt, granting to Thomas Lindley, John Swayle, snr, Richard Kigheley, esqrs, John Allan, clerk, and William Lindley of Pottergate, his manor of Steeton in Yorks with appurtenances, and also all other lands and tenements, rents, reversions and services there, also his manor of Grassington in Craven, Yorks, with appurtenances and all other lands and tenements, rents reversions and services therein. To have and hold to them, their heirs and assigns, of the chief lords [etc.]

Appointing Ralph Knowley and William Crooke his attorneys jointly and severally to enter for him and in his name all the aforesaid premises, and deliver full and peaceable possession and seisin to the feoffees.
[Latin]
[Copyist's note.] Copied 22 of October 1627, hauing a seale.
[CB, 805]

60 *16 July 1501*

Indenture between John Yaxley, sergeant-at-law and John Pulan, gent., witnessing that John Yaxley is to be present at the next assizes to be held at York, Nottingham and Derby as counsel representing Sir Robert Plompton, kt, in such actions as shall be required. For his services,

including his expenses and labour, John Pulan is to pay him 40m on the 8 Sept. next, or within 8 days thereafter, of which £5 is to be paid on account. If he is given due notice that his services are required only at Nottingham and Derby Yaxley is to receive £15 in addition to the sum paid on account, and if he is given due warning that his services will not be required at all, then he will retain only the £5 paid on account for his good will and labour. Sir Robert shall pay Yaxley's expenses at York, Nottingham and Derby.
[English]
[copyist's note.] Copied the 5 of October 1627, hauing no seale.
[CB, 802, transcribed Stapleton, 152–53n.]

61 *4 August 1501, Westminster*

Letter Patent from Henry VII appointing his justices John Vavasor and John Fissher together with those associated with them to hold an assize of *novel disseisin*, to which Thomas Lindeley, John Swayle, snr, Richard Kyghley, John Allen, clerk and William Lindley[1] are to be summoned by the king's writ versus John Roucliffe, kt, and Margaret his wife and Elizabeth Sotehill, widow, in respect of tenements in Edensor and Pilsley. They are to hold the assize by royal mandate on a certain day and place, and do justice in accordance with the law and custom of England, saving the king's amercements thence issuing. The sheriff of Yorks is to issue a writ of *scire facias* stating the date and venue to bring the contestants into court. Signed, William Warham.[2]
[Latin]
[Copyist's note.] Copied the 6 of October 1627, hauing a seale.
[CB, 803]

[1] See no. **59**.
[2] An identical warrant of the same date was issued to Humphrey Coningsby and James Hobart regarding the manors of Steeton and Grassington. This was copied 22 Oct. 1627 and had a seal, CB, 804.

62 *7 May 1502*

Charter of John Ingilby, esq., granting to Robert Bubwith and Richard Burgh, chaplains, his manors of Plumpton, Idle, Steeton, Grassington in Craven and Little Studley, near Ripon, Yorks with their appurtenances, to have and hold in perpetuity to them, their heirs and assigns of the chief lords of that fee [etc.]; constituting and ordaining John Johnson and Gilbert Walleron his attorneys and deputies jointly and

severally to enter, move and expel those in unlawful possession and deliver full and peaceable possession and seisin thereof to the grantees of their assigns.
Witnesses: Thomas Foss, Richard Goldsburgh, John Acclome and James Rober, esqrs, and others.
[Latin]
[Copyist's note.] Copied the 6 of November 1627, hauing a seale.
[CB, 818]

63 *Undated*

Memorandum that James Hobart, kt, king's attorney, came before the barons of the exchequer [date left blank] and on behalf of the king informed the court concerning Babthorpe, a manor with appurtenances in Brackenholme and Hemingborough, at present in the king's hands following the death of John Hastings, kt, who held the premises of the king in chief on the day he died as by courtesy of England, because they are of the inheritance of Isabel Hastings, deceased, formerly his wife. On 15 July 1504 Thomas Babthorpe, clerk, formerly of Heminghorough, John Stamper, yeo. and Thomas Andrew, both of Hemingborough, entered Babthorpe arrayed in manner of war, namely with staves and cudgels, to the great injury of the king's property, as appears from the record of the exchequer. From the aforesaid date they have appropriated all the profits and issues therefrom and have hitherto made no response to the king, to the utter contempt and injury of the king himself. Hence James Hobart sought the advice of the court.
[Latin]
[BL, Add.MS 32,113, fol. 219]

64 *15 January 1505*

Testimony given at the request of Sir Robert Plompton, kt, by William Gascoygne and Christopher Warde, kts, Henry Vavasor, Thomas Pigot, Henry Ughtred, Thomas Fairfax, Richard Maulevery, Richard Kyghley, Nicholas Gascoigne, Robert Chylton, Thomas Ratcliffe, Walter Bayldon, Thomas Nawdon and Walter Woode, esqrs, 14 gentlemen and 47 yeomen [names supplied] with others as to the conduct of the trial at York which Sir Richard Empson, accompanied by Edward Stanhopp, Gervase Clifton, Robert Dimmoke and William Perpoynt, kts, with more than 200 gentlemen and yeomen, and with certain liveried members of the king's guard attended for the purpose of maintaining the suit of the plaintiffs Robert Bubwith and Richard Burgh against Sir Robert for the recovery of the manors of Plumpton and Idle to the use of Sir John and Lady Rouclife.

John Vavasor, then associated with Justice Humphrey Conyngsby, produced a fine exemplified under the great seal as proof that the disputed properties had been entailed to the heirs general, and on the court's refusal to allow Sir Robert's counsel to examine the deed his friends, fearing it might be genuine, urged a settlement. A meeting of 4 arbitrators, Sir Marmaduke Constable, kt, and Brian Palmes for the plaintiffs and Sir William Gascoigne, kt, and William Eleson for Sir Robert then took place in the chapel on York bridge. Claiming the fine was spurious Sir Robert refused an offer by the opposing side and produced a box containing deeds which proved that the lands in question were entailed to the heirs male of Sir William Plompton, kt. Negotiations were then broken off.

[English]

[Copyist's note.] Copied the 12 of November 1627 hauing 69 seales besides them that is broken off.

[CB, 824, transcribed Stapleton, cvii–ix]

65 *12 July 1505*

Indenture between Henry VII and William and Isabel Plompton, witnessing that the king agreed to grant special livery of all the lordships, manors, lands, tenements and other hereditaments to which they were entitled by virtue of Isabel's inheritance from Dame Isabel Hastings, deceased. Nevertheless to the end that the king may be apprised of the true value of all the premises, a parchment roll containing a valor, dated as above, and certified as accurate by William by oath upon the Holy Evangelist before the king's council, is attached to this indenture.

For his part William grants that the king's auditor shall be given full facility, at his expense, to inspect the estates, to adjust any which may have been undervalued or concealed and to charge William with any surcharge. In case of concealment William shall pay double the yearly value of the property or properties concerned.[1] Signed Dudley.

[Latin]

[CB, 445]

[1] The following extent may have been appended, giving the annual value of the estates in question: manor of Babthorpe, 10m; vill of Brackenholme, 8m; manor of Sacombe, £20; vill of Hemingborough, 33s 4d; vill of Selby, 20s; vill of Estoft, 33s 4d. Total, £36 6s 8d. Included also may have been 2 properties in which Thomas, younger brother of Sir Ralph Babthorpe, had a life interest: vill of Wistow, 40s; vills of Hundesby and Middleton-on-the-Wolds, £5, WYASYAS,MS 599 (unpaginated). See the licence for

entry into these lands without proof of age, 12 Nov. 1505, *CPR*, *1494–1509*, 481.

66 *3 April 1506*

Livery by William Crouch, escheator of Yorks, to William Plompton, esq., and Isabel his wife, heir to Isabel Hastings, formerly wife of John Hastings, kt, of the manor called Babthorpe with appurtenances in Yorks, and of the manors or vills of Brackenholme, Estoft, Selby and Hemingborough in Yorks, as directed by the king's letter of 13 Feb. last past.[1]
[Latin]
[Copyist's note.] Copied 15 November 1627, hauing a seale.
[CB, 828]

[1] This deed has not survived.

67 *12 February 1507*

Inquisition *post mortem* delivered into court, by Richard Empson, kt.

Inquisition held at Newark, Notts, on 16 Jan. 1507 before Robert Arderne, escheator, by authority of a writ of *diem clausit extremum* directed to him and to the inquisition after the death of Elizabeth Sotehill, widow. William Naylor &c. say on their oath that at the time of her death Richard Burgh was seised of a bovate of land in Mansfield Woodhouse, together with a pasture and an assart there lying near Wadgate in his demesne as of fee, to the use of Margaret, wife of John Rawcliffe, kt, and the aforesaid Elizabeth and their heirs in perpetuity.

Also that after Elizabeth's death her moiety descended to Joan and Elizabeth Sotehill, her granddaughters, namely daughters and heirs of Henry Sotehill, deceased, her son and heir.

Also that before her death Robert Bubwith and Richard Burgh, clerks, recovered, by *novel disseisin* versus Robert Plompton, kt, before John Vavasour and John Fysher, justices of assize, the manor of Kinoulton, Notts, to the use of Margaret and Elizabeth and their heirs in perpetuity. Afterwards Margaret and John Rawcliffe and Elizabeth Sotehill, by their charter now produced in evidence, demised the said manor to Richard Empson, kt, for life, to hold in his demesne as of free tenure, with reversion to Bubwith and Burgh to the use of the aforesaid Margaret and Elizabeth and their heirs in perpetuity.

Also that Burgh outlived Bubwith, and after the death of Elizabeth the use of her moiety descended to the aforesaid Jane and Elizabeth, her heirs.

Also that Kinoulton is held of the king as of the honor ot Tickhill, parcel of the Duchy of Lancaster, by fealty and a rent of 3s 4d for all services, and its clear yearly value is £20. The aforesaid bovate and pasture in Mansfield Woodhouse are held of the king in chief by the service of hunting the wolf in Sherwood Forest, and their clear value is 8s.

Also that neither Elizabeth nor any other to her use holds any other lands of the king, neither of any other in demesne, in fee, reversion, or by service on the day she died.

Also that Elizabeth died 1 Sept. 1507 and that Joan and Elizabeth Sotehill are '*consanguines*' and her nearest heirs, and that Joan was aged 1 year on Ascension Day last past, and Elizabeth the same age on the same feast day.

[Latin]

[WYASL, Acc. 1731/9-P]

68 *3 March 1507*

Indenture between William Plompton, esq., and Isabel, his wife, and William Girlington, gent., witnessing the bargain and sale to William Girlington of all the lands, tenements and hereditaments of which William Plompton is seised in Estoft in Yorks in right of Dame Isabel, his wife, or of any other to their use or the use of either. The vendors are to make a sufficient and lawful estate in fee simple to the purchaser in terms devised by him or by his council. Furthermore William Plompton shall seek to persuade Sir Robert Plompton, his father, to release to the purchaser all his right, title and interest in the premises in terms devised by the purchaser and with warranty. For which estate, recovery and release William Girlington has paid to William and Isabel £33 13s, whereby they are fully paid and William Girlington is discharged. William Plompton shall therefore hand over to the purchaser all deeds, evidences and muniments relating to the property by Easter next ensuing.

[English]

[CB, 830]

69 *Undated*

Bill of William Bedell, esq., servant to His Highness's dear mother, complaining to the king that having been in peaceable possession of the lordship of Babthorpe for at least 2 years, on 3 April last William Plompton, esq., and 10 riotous persons, namely Robert Wright, Edmund

Roland, Edmund Johnson, Thomas Bikerdike, William Brocke, John Toller, Ralph Knotts, Richard Waddington, Robert Gibson and James Jackson, yeomen, entered by force upon land belonging to the complainant, armed with bows and arrows, spears, swords and bucklers and removed 5 of his horses, which he had been unable to retrieve. The complainant requests that a privy seal be sent to each miscreant requiring attendance in court to answer the charges.
[English]
[BL, Add.MS 32,113, fols 219v–220]

70 *[1507–08]*

Replication of William Plompton, claiming for himself and the others named in William Beddell's bill that there was no case to answer, and desiring to reserve their position until the dispute should be heard at common law.

The land entered is parcel of the inheritance of Isabel, wife of William Plumpton, as daughter of Robert Babthorpe, deceased, brother and heir of Ralph Babthorpe, kt, who died 5 March 1490, at which time the king claimed primer seisin of the manor of Babthorpe on the ground that other premises were held of him in chief, as found by the *IPM* after Sir Ralph's death, in which Isabel Plompton was named as cousin and next heir. William and Isabel sued livery of Babthorpe and of the other lands held of the king in chief, and a writ of livery directed to the escheator authorized him to put William and Isabel in possession of the premises.

The escheator with the assistance of the said Robert, Edmund, Thomas, William and John put William and Isabel in possession of the premises, by force of which they had seisin thereof, and there found the five horses on their land, which they removed to a lawful pound.

They deny the charge of forcible entry and of unlawfully removing the horses, as well as all other charges contained in the bill. They also deny that William Beddell had been in possession of the premises by any good title. They are ready to prove their case and ask that costs be awarded against their adversaries.[1]
[1507–8]
[English]
[BL, Add.MS. 32,113, fols 220–220v.]

[1] The justices of the king's bench awarded a writ of restitution to Thomas Bedell, fol. 223.

71 *6 May [?1508], Greenwich*

Mandate by Henry VII to Sir William Gascoigne, knight of the body, Sir John Everingham, kt, Sir William Skargill, kt, and William Eleson, learned man, justices of the peace for Yorks, informing them that Sir Thomas Babthorpe, provost of Hemingborough, Sir Thomas Andrew, priest, Henry Pullen, chaplain, Robert Templer and John Stanhope, with 35 other persons [names included] were reported to have assembled in arms and forcibly entered the manor of Babthorpe and there committed riot. The king, urgently requiring to have a report on the truth of the allegations, commands the justices to investigate the matter diligently, impartially and with the utmost speed. Greenwich, under signet, 6 May [?1508].[1]
[Latin]
[BL, Add.MS 32,113, fol. 221]

[1] The commissioners found that on 29 April 1508 Thomas Babthorpe and 39 named persons had entered Babthorpe in arms, committed riot and threatened Isabel Plumpton with arrows so that her life was in danger. To the chagrin of the Plumptons only 3 of the named persons were indicted, and they the least important, ibid., fol. 222v.

72 *Undated [?1508]*

Rejoinder of Thomas Babthorpe, provost, Sir John Andrews, priest, Sir Henry Pullen, chaplain, Robert Templer and John Stanhope to the replication of William Plumpton.

They claim that the manor of Babthorpe belongs of right to William Babthorpe by inheritance from his deceased father; that William, late bishop of Durham was possessed of his wardship and the custody of the said manor, both of which he sold to William Beddell, who was therefore lawfully in possession when William Plumpton and his following entered unlawfully. The trespassers were indicted and Beddell was restored by award of the justices of the bench. Beddell then sold the wardship and custody to Thomas Babthorpe, who thence retained lawful possession until Plumpton and his riotous following entered and were prevented from expelling the farmer, who was in his bed at the time, by the arrival of Thomas Babthorpe and the above-named persons who re-established lawful possession.

They deny [i] that the manor descended to Isabel Plompton as cousin and heir of Dame Isabel Hastings by reason of an old entail made by one of her ancestors; [ii] that Isabel Plompton was ever lawfully seised of the manor; [iii] that the ancestors from whom she claims to have inherited enjoyed peaceable possession for 200 years, as

claimed by William Plumpton in his replication; [iv] that William Beddell never entered the possessions of William and Isabel by force; or that he retained the manor by force until the said 29 April last; or that it is recorded that he and other persons were indicted for the entry before Sir William Gascoigne, and other the king's commissioners; [v] that Thomas Babthorpe and the others confessed that they entered with a force of 30 persons as described by William Plompton; [vi] that Thomas had confessed to having entered the property unlawfully. They claim that the manor of Babthorpe belongs to William Babthorpe by right of inheritance, and they pray that they may be awarded their reasonable costs and charges.
[English]
[BL, Add.MS 32,113, fols 223–4]

73 *29 April 1511*

Bond by Thomas Babthorpe, provost of the church of Hemingborough, to stand in an obligation to William Plompton, esq., of £100, payable on 24 June 1511. Condition: that Thomas Babthorpe and William Beddell, during the minority of William Babthorpe, shall keep and perform the judgement of Thomas, Lord Darcy and Marmaduke Constable, kt, arbitrators chosen by the parties to determine the right, title and possession of the manor of Babthorpe and the lands and tenements in Brackenholme and Hemingborough, which William Plompton claims in right of Isabel, his wife, and of the lands in Lincs claimed by Thomas in right of the aforesaid William Babthorpe, now under age, and of all other disagreements and debates between the parties before the date of this obligation, provided the award, sealed by the arbitrators, is delivered in writing to the parties before the feast of Michaelmas next coming, otherwise this obligation shall be void.
[Latin and English]
[Copist's note.] Copied 23 November 1627, hauing a seale.
[CB, 835]

74 *Undated*

Bond by Marmaduke Constable, kt, of Yorks, John Constable, esq., of the same, John Rocliffe, kt, formerly of Cowthorpe, Yorks, and William Perpoynte, kt, formerly of Holme, Notts, to stand in an obligation of 1,000m to Robert Plompton, kt, formerly of Plumpton, Yorks, and William Plompton, esq., formerly of Waterton, Lincs, his son, payable at Easter next coming after the date of these presents, 20 March 1515.

Condition: that they abide by the award of Richard Fox, bishop of Winchester, Sir Thomas Lovell, kt, treasurer of the king's household, Robert Brudenell, justice, and John Earnley, king's attorney, arbitrators chosen by the parties, *viz.* Sir John Rocliffe and Dame Margaret, his wife, as cousin and heir to Sir William Plompton, kt, deceased, Sir Marmaduke Constable and John, his son, and Sir William Perpoynte as guardians of Elizabeth and Jane Sotehill, also cousins and heirs of Sir William, of one party, and Sir Robert Plompton, kt, and William, his son, of the other, to decide upon the right, title and possession of and in all the manors, lands, tenements and hereditaments in Grassington, Steeton, Studley Roger, Idle, Plumpton and within the parish of Spofforth, the Derbyshire manors of Edensor, Hassop, Darley, and the Notts manor of Kinoulton, together with the advowsons of the churches, chapels and chantries, all formerly of the inheritance of Sir William Plompton or to persons to his use. Also upon all other matters at issue between the parties before the above date.

They, Sir Marmaduke Constable and others having claim to the disputed premises shall hold and adhere to the award of the arbitrators, provided it is given in writing before Easter, otherwise the obligation will be void.

[Latin and English]

[Copyist's note.] Copied 27 of November hauing 4 seales.

[CB, 840]

75 *Undated [27 March 1515]*

Arbitration award by Richard Fox, bishop of Winchester, Sir Thomas Lovell, kt, treasurer of the household, Judge Robert Brudenell and John Earnley, king's attorney, dated 27 March 1515, reciting that whereas there had been discord between Sir John Rouclife, kt, and Dame Margaret, his wife, one of the cousins and heirs of the late Sir William Plompton, kt, Sir William Perpoynte, kt, guardian of Elizabeth Sotehill, cousin and heir of Sir William, Sir Marmaduke Constable, snr, kt, and John Constable, esq., guardians of Jane Sotehill, another of the cousins and heirs of Sir William Plompton, of the one party, and Sir Robert Plompton, kt, and William his son and heir apparant of the other, of and upon the right and title to certain lands, the arbitrators after hearing the depositions of the parties, and with their consent, make their award as follows: [i] Sir Robert and William shall have and enjoy the manor of Plumpton with its appurtenant lands in Plumpton or within the parish of Spofforth, to have and hold to their heirs male. In default of such heirs, remainder shall be to Dame Margaret Rouclife, Elizabeth and Jane Sotehill. [ii] The heirs general and other interested

parties named above, including Dame Joan Perpoynte, mother of Elizabeth and Jane, and Elizabeth and Jane themselves when of full age shall quitclaim Sir Robert in such terms as he shall devise. [iii] The heirs general are to have and enjoy the residue of all the manors &c. according to their inheritance from the late Sir William Plompton. [iv] Sir Anthony Seale, clerk, shall have and enjoy the chantry in Ripon, hereafter to be in the gift of the lords of the manor of Plumpton, if it may be proved of right so to belong.[1] All other benefices are to remain to the heirs general. [v] In case of Sir Robert being able to prove to the arbitrators within a year of this date the purchase or recovery by legal action at his expense, or proof of title to any premises awarded to the heirs general of the same yearly clear value as the lands in Studley Roger, then the heirs general shall cede Studley Roger to Sir Robert in exchange for the lands purchased or recovered by him. Any excess shall be adjusted by a sum of money calculated at the rate of 16 years' purchase. Signed Richard Winchester, Thomas Lovell, Robert Brudenell, John Earnley.
[English]
[Copyist's note.] Copied 10 December 1627, hauing 4 seales.
[CB, 841]

[1] See pp. 245–6. On this chantry becoming vacant Sir John Rocliffe appointed William Cooke of Ripon and Henry Bell to present Stephen Clarkson as chaplain, who was duly admitted. The result was an action by William Plumpton against Christopher Cragley, clerk, and the above-named persons; a jury was summoned 30 May 1530 to determine whether Sir Robert Plumpton was legitimate or a bastard, and hence on William's right to present to the chantry, CB, 857.

76 *Undated*

Recovery, before Robert Reade, kt, and his fellows, justices, in the Hillary Term 1515/16, by John Norton, Richard Mawlevery, Thomas Fairfax and William Mawlevery, kts, through George Rolle, attorney, against Robert Plompton, kt, and William, his son and heir apparent, of the manor of Plumpton with 4,000 acres of land, 100 acres of meadow, 50 acres of pasture, 200 acres of woodland, 40 acres of moorland, 40 acres of commons and 10s rent with appurtenances and all rights and hereditaments in the parish of Spofforth, for which they called John Roucliffe, kt, and Margaret his wife, through their attorney, Thomas Hatche, to give warranty.[1] Hence John, Richard, Thomas and William hold the premises in due form by warranty of Sir John and Lady Roucliffe.
Enrolled at Westminster, Hillary Term 1515/16.
[Latin]

[CB, 864]

[1] On 10 July 1516 Richard Burgh, clerk, released these premises to the 4 knights named in the recovery, CB, 865.

77 *27 March 1515*

Indenture between Sir William Pierpoint, kt, guardian of Elizabeth Sotehill, and Sir Marmaduke Constable, kt, and John his son, as guardians of Jane Sotehill, Sir John Rocliffe, kt, and Dame Margaret, his wife of the one party and Sir Robert Plompton, kt, and William his son of the other, witnessing that after divers variances over the right, title and possession of the manor of Plumpton and other lands, formerly the estate of the late Sir William Plompton, the parties have agreed to stand and perform the award of the arbitrators [no. **75**] who having awarded the manor of Plumpton [etc.] to Sir Robert and William and the lawful heirs male of Sir Robert, Sir John Rocliffe and others of the aforesaid first party agree to meet Sir Robert's reasonable requirements for the making of a legal settlement of the premises thus awarded to him.

Also Sir William Pierpont and Sir Marmaduke Constable and his son agree to enfeoff 8 persons in an estate to the clear yearly value of £40 out of certain lands in Yorks or Notts that are of the inheritance of each to secure the agreement of Jane and Elizabeth Sotehill and their husbands when of full age. In case of their refusal the feoffees shall be seised of the premises to the sole use of Sir Robert and William and the heirs male of Sir Robert, but if they agree to the legal arrangements entered into as above, then the feoffment shall remain to the sole use of the feoffors. The costs of the feoffment in either case are to be borne by Sir Robert and his son, or they to pay 53s 4d to the other party.
[English]
[Copyist's note.] Copied 11 December 1627, hauing 3 seales.
[CB, 842/A]

78 *2 May 1515*

Indenture between Robert Plompton, kt, and William, his son and heir, witnessing that William is to have charge of the household and goods at Plumpton, whilst his father and stepmother are to live in retirement under his roof, and at his expense. To meet the expenses of the household, William is granted the revenues and profits issuing from the lordship of Plumpton, from which he is also to meet all necessary expenses incurred by his brothers and sisters, except those of his sister Clare which will be met by his step-mother. All goods, alive or dead, due to the household shall be delivered there and accounted for. William shall keep as many servants as he deems necessary for the proper conduct of the household, including 3 to be chosen by Sir Robert. He shall pay Sir Robert an annual income of £10 payable on Whit Sunday and Martinmas, or within 12 days following each feast, in equal portions. Also he shall pay Sir Robert's debts to the extent of £20, and the cost of making the present indenture. He is to render an annual account to his father in order that the latter may be satisfied that the debts are being met.

William shall have the letting of vacant farms, taking the advice and counsel of his father, similarly sales of wood shall be made only with his father's approval, until the aforesaid debts are discharged. In case of disagreement both parties agree to have recourse to the minister of St Robert's and Sir John Alan, parson of Burghwallis, as arbitrators. [English]

[Copyist's note.] Copied the 12 December 1627, hauing 4 seales.

[CB, 843, transcript Stapleton, cxxiii–iv.]

79 *6 March 1519*

Indenture between Sir Robert Plompton, kt, and Dame Isabel, his wife, and William Plompton, his son and heir apparent, witnessing an agreement between the parties that both shall make to William Ingleby and Guy Willesthorpe, esqrs, Robert Plompton, the younger, gent., and Sir Thomas Angrom, clerk, their heirs and assigns, a sufficient estate in law of and in a messuage or tenement called Rudfarlington and all the lands, meadows, pastures and woods thereto pertaining, now in the tenure of Richard Paver, also in all other lands [etc.] within the lordsip of Plumpton, Yorks, except 2 closes held for life by Richard Plompton, chaplain, also in these 2 closes after Richard's death, and in all the lands and tenements [etc.] with their appurtenances called Moorehouse within the said lordship, now in the tenure of John Wright, also in 3 burgages, and all the lands [etc.] with their appurtenances in Knaresborough, now in the several tenures of Edward Gibson, William Smith and William Parke, all of which premises shall be to the use of Sir Robert Plompton, kt, and Dame Isabel, and to the survivor of them, to secure therefrom in jointure a clear 20m per annum without impeachment of waste, with remainder to William and his heirs male. In default of such heirs, remainder in tail male to the heirs of Sir Robert, and in default of such heirs, to the next heirs of Sir Robert.

The above feoffees shall make a sufficient estate of a clear £10 per annum out of other lands and hereditaments in Yorks to the use of Sir Robert for life, with remainder to the use of Robert Plompton the younger, Marmaduke and Neil, the 3 younger sons of Sir Robert, for life, to be divided equally between them, and with remainder to William Plompton and his heirs mele, remainder in default [as above].

Sir Robert shall make to the aforesaid feoffees and their assigns a sufficient legal estate in the manor of Plumpton, and in all other lands [etc.] which he or any other to his use has within the county to the use of the said Sir Robert for life, with remainder to William and his heirs male, remainder in default [as above].

[English]

[Copyist's note.] Copied the 21 January 1627, seale.

[CB, 867]

80 *6 March 1519*

Conveyance by John Norton, Richard Mawlevery, Thomas Fairfax and William Mawlevery, kts, at the special request of Robert Plompton, kt, and William Plompton, esq., his son and heir apparent (in accordance with articles of agreement dated 6 March 1519)[1] to William Ingleby and Guy Wilstrop, esqrs, Robert Plompton, jnr, gent., son of the aforesaid Sir Robert, and Thomas Angram, clerk [of the properties in Rudfarlington (including the reversion of the 2 closes there after Richard Plumpton's death), Moorehouse and Knaresborough, as set out in no. **79**]. To have and hold the aforesaid messuage, burgages, lands, meadows, pastures and woods with their appurtenances in Rudfarlington, Moorehouse, and Knaresborough to the aforesaid feoffees and their assigns in perpetuity, to the use of Sir Robert and Dame Isabel Plompton for life, without impeachment of waste, remainder, after the decease of both, to William Plompton and his heirs. The grantors appoint William, Guy, Robert and Thomas to be their attorneys to deliver the premises.

[Latin]

[CB, 869]

[1] Nos **78**, **79**.

81 *9 March 1519*

Conveyance By John Norton, Richard Mawlevery, Thomas Fairfax and William Mawlevery, kts, at the special request of Robert Plompton kt, and William Plompton, esq., his son and heir apparent (in accordance with an agreement between the two dated 6 March 1519) to Thomas Linley, Robert Lampton and John Birnand, esqrs, of their manor of Plumpton, Yorks, and all other lands, tenements, messuages, burgages, pastures, meadows and woods, with all and singular their appurtenances in Yorks which were recovered before Robert Reade, kt, and his fellows in the Hillary Term 1515/16 against the aforesaid Sir Robert and William, except the properties in Rudfarlington, Mooreshouse and Knaresborough [specified in no. **79**], and those worth £10 yearly designated to the use of Sir Robert with reversion to his 3 younger sons [no. **79**]. To be held of the chief lords of those fees and by services thence owed and accustomed by right. The grantors appoint the aforesaid Thomas, Robert and John to be their attorneys to deliver the above premises, reversions and all and singular appurtenances.
[Latin]
[Copyist's note.] Copied 1 Feb. 1627, hauing 4 seales.
[CB, 870]

82 *27 June 1519*

Bond by William Babthorpe, esq., to stand in an obligation of 1,000m to William Plompton, esq., payable at Michaelmas next. Condition: that if William Babthorpe and Agnes his wife and others their feoffees and heirs shall keep the award of the king's justices Robert Brudenell, kt, and Humphrey Coningsby, kt, arbitrators indifferently chosen by the parties, *viz*. William and Agnes Babthorpe and William and Isabel Plompton, to determine the right title and possession of all the manors, lands &c. which formerly belonged to Ralph Babthorpe, kt, or any of his successors, and all other quarrels and disagreements between the parties, and all costs and charges sustained by William Babthorpe. The award is to be given in writing and delivered to the parties under the seals of the arbitrators by the 18 Oct. next. If the arbitrators should make no award before St Luke's Day, then William and Agnes shall fulfill and obey the judgement of the Lord Cardinal, Thomas, legate of the Holy See, archbishop of York and chancellor of England, provided it is given in writing under his seal, and delivered before the 1 Nov. next, otherwise the obligation shall be null and void.
[English]
[copyist's note.] Copied the 19 December 1627, hauing a seale.
[CB, 850]

83 *16 November 1547*

Indenture between Edward VI and Thomas Bill, one of the royal physicians, witnessing the king's grant of the farm of all that part and portion of the lordship and manor of Plumpton with appurtenances in Ripon lately held by William Plompton, esq., deceased, and in the king's hands owing to the minority of his cousin and heir, William Plompton, the king's ward. Exempted and reserved from the grant are the advowsons, woods, wards, marriages, lands and hereditaments granted to Anne Plompton, mother of the ward, for life, and to Denis Plompton and Ursula his wife.

Thomas shall hold the premises to himself and his assigns from Pentecost last past for the duration of William's minority paying £8 15s 8½d at Martinmas in winter and Pentecost by equal portions. In addition, he is to pay the following annuities: to Neil and Robert Plompton, the ward's uncles, £6 13s 4d; to Isabel Plompton, widow of the late William Plompton, for her dower, £13 14s; to John Poly, 40s, Marmaduke Bellingham, 26s 8d, Thomas Gardiner, 24s, Richard Davy, 20s, and in addition £13 6s 8d granted by the king's letters patent for the ward's education. On the death of any of these annuitants the court[1] is to be informed and the appropriate sum paid to the feodary.

Thomas and his assigns shall maintain the premises at their expense, being supplied with lead at the king's expense, on the advice of the officers of the court of wards. They may also take, from time to time, timber for repairs, and 'palebot', 'halebot', 'hedgebot', and 'firebot' as necessary. They are to hold the courts as heretofore, and have the court rolls engrossed so that these and all other relevant documents may be handed over to the heir at the appropriate time without concealment.

The grantees are neither to perpetrate nor allow any waste of wood, neglect of ditches, palings or hedges, illegal entry, reduction of rent or services, nor expel any tenant without the knowledge and agreement of the master and council. Within 6 months of the date hereof Thomas is to submit his part of this indenture for enrollment by the auditor of the court, and the master and council reserve the right of re-entry after 2 months in case of arrears of rent, and on the expiry of 1 month, after due warning given, in case of non-observance of the covenants.[2]

[English]

[Copyist's note.] Sealed with the seale of the said court of wards and liveries, the daie and yeare aboue said.

[WYASL, Acc 1731/4, pp. 23–24]

[1] The court of wards whose master was Sir William Paulet, Joel Hurtsfield, 'Corruption and Reform under Edward VI and Mary: the Example of Wardship', in Idem, *Freedom, Corruption and Government in Elizabethan England* (1973), 163–64.

[2] Thomas Bill was also granted the custody and marriage of William Plumpton, 3 Feb. 1548 for 20m a year, WYASL, Acc 1731/4, pp. 25–26.

84 *9 February 1548*

Indenture between Thomas Bill, esq., and Isabel Plompton, widow, late wife to William Plompton, esq., deceased, witnessing that by the king's letters patent of 3 Feb. 1548 Thomas was granted a yearly rent of 20m out of the manor of Plumpton and its appurtenances in Yorks, late in possession of William Plompton, esq., deceased, who held of the king by knight service, and in the king's hands by reason of the minority of the heir, by assignment by the master and council of the court of wards and liveries. Also the custody and marriage of the heir, William Plompton, without disparagement, to have and hold to him, his assigns and executors until William's attainment of full age or until Thomas should have received the benefit of William's marriage. In the event of William's death before full age and/or marriage, Thomas was to continue to receive the rent-charge and to have the custody and marriage of the next heir or heirs, without disparagement, as long as he or they remained under age.

Now, in consideration of a sum of money paid to him, whereof, by these presents he acknowledges himself fully satisfied and hereby acquits Isabel Plompton and all other persons, he has bargained, sold and granted to Isabel the custody and marriage of the aforesaid William Plompton, together with the annuity of 20m, thus transferring to Isabel a parcel of the said letters patent granting to Thomas the aforesaid annuity, custody and marriage.

[English]

[WYASL, Acc 1731/4, pp. 25–26]

[1] MS gives the date 12 Nov. 1 Edw. VI. Surely an error.

85 *28 February 1565*

Indenture between the Rt Hon. Sir William Cecill, kt, master of the court of wards and liveries and Robert Keilwaie, esq., surveyor of the same, on behalf of the queen, and William Plompton, gent., cousin and heir of William Plompton, esq., deceased, witnessing the court's grant to William, the cousin, of a writ of *oustrer le mayne* of and in certain lands held of the queen as of her manor of Spofforth by knight service, to which he is heir by right of inheritance.

So that the queen shall be informed of the true value of the premises William has to-day submitted to the master and surveyor a schedule indented in Parliament of all the lands pertaining to the writ which will be removed from Her Grace's hands.[1] He agrees also that auditors chosen by the queen or by the court shall, at his expense, and at such times as it may be thought necessary, survey and view the premises and the tenurial arrangements of the same. In case of undervaluation, omission or concealment William, his assigns or executors shall reimburse the queen to the extent of double the yearly value of the affected premises; or they may be required to surrender them until sufficient sureties can be produced, to the satisfaction of the court, for the payment of all monies outstanding.
[WYASL, Acc. 1731/4, p. 26]

[1] A valor of 1564, which may have been submitted to the court, estimates the value of estates in Yorks held by William Plumpton at his death in 1547 at £68 8s 9½d (editor's total – £87 12s 9½d), WYASL, Acc 1731/4, p. 27.

86 *Undated*

Memorandum that Nicholas Bacon, kt, lord keeper of the Great Seal of England,[1] came before the queen at Westminster on Friday next after the Trinity Term [1565] and delivered a certain record of proceedings heard in chancery in the Michaelmas Term 1563 in which it was recounted that according to a certain inquisition held at Tadcaster on 8 Nov. 1564 before Christopher Nelson, then escheator of Yorks, by authority of a writ of *de quo plura* directed to him[2] following the death of Isabel Plompton, Oswald Wylstroppe, kt, Richard Malyverer, Mathew Redman, Henry Johnson, James Ryther, Lawrence Kyghley, esqrs, William Barnaby, Richard Bankes, Richard Barley, Henry Tonge, Henry Copley and William Halteley, gents, Robert Tomson, George Bettyson, Michael Thomson, John Robynson, John Whartesale and Richard Steede, yeoman, said on oath that on the day before Isabel's death a certain Robert Babthorpe, her ancestor, was seised in his demesne as of fee of the manor of Babthorpe with appurtenances, and in 3 messuages, 11 bovates and 141 acres of land and 7 acres of woodland with appurtenances in Brackenholme, Woodhead and Hemingborough, by virtue of a final concord levied in court on 3 Feb. 1412[2] before William Thurnynge, William Hankeford, John Cokayne, John Colpeper and Robert Hill, justices, between Robert Babthorpe and Margaret his wife, plaintiffs, and William Babthorpe and William Brokeby, chaplains, defendants [no. **3**], by which the defendants granted to Robert and

Margaret the said premises in the same court, to be held to them and to the heirs of Robert, of the chief lords of that fee.
[Latin]
[WYASYAS, MS 599]

[1] Attorney of the court of wards 1547–61, Hurstfield, 177.
[2] *CPR, 1563–66*, 1000.

87 *20 October 1565*

Award by Richard Weston and John Walshe, justices of the court of common pleas, reciting that the opposing parties, Sir William Babthorpe, kt, and William Plompton of Plumpton, Yorks, esq., both claimed lands and tenements lately held by Sir Ralph Babthorpe, kt, deceased, the former as heir male, the latter as heir general. Sir William Babthorpe is awarded the manors of Babthorpe and Osgodby and William Plompton the manor and lordship of Waterton with appurtenances in Hotoft, Coleby and Amcotts in Lincs and 'Estoft' and Hunsley, Yorks, without let or hindrance.
[English]
[WYASL, Acc 1731/6, fol. 317 (Red Booke, fol. 139)]

88 *Michaelmas Term 1567*

Decree of the court of wards and liveries, reciting that according to an inquisition at Tadcaster, 8 Nov. 1564, held by authority of a writ of *de que plura* directed to Christopher Nelson, escheator of Yorks, into lands held at her death, 30 July 1551, by Isabel Plompton, she was said to have died seised of the manor of Babthorpe and 3 messuages, 11 oxgangs, 141 acres of land and 7 acres of woodland with appurtenances in Brackenholme, Hemingborough, Wistow, Selby, and Woodhead, in demesne as of fee tail, namely to her and her heirs, held of the queen by knight service. Her heir, William Plompton, her grandson, was then stated to be aged 20 years, 9 months and 20 days.

Upon her death William Babthorpe, kt, entered the premises, which were forthwith taken into the queen's hand. Sir William then obtained a licence from this court to come into chancery on 21 Nov. 1563, where he took the premises to farm and traversed the inquisition *post mortem* of Isabel Plompton and all the matters therein contained, claiming title to the said manor and lands. His suit was opposed by the queen's attorney. Having recited the descent of the premises through the heirs male before the fine of 3 Feb. 1412 in which the entail was to the heirs of Robert Babthorpe,[1] the pleading was delivered to the justices of the bench by Sir Nicholas Bacon, and on the 15th day of the Trinity Term 1565 the queen's attorney withdrew his plea. The lands were then ordered to be removed from the queen's hand and Sir William was put in possession, as appears in a transcript of the record ordered to be sent into this court by a writ of *mittimus*.

Therefore the court of wards decrees that Sir William's reinstatement be carried into effect. Also that the clerk of the court cancel all obligations, bonds and recognizances taken of William, or of any on his behalf, provided that if at any time it may be shown that this decree should not stand, then the same to be void and of no effect.

[English]

[WYASYAS, MS 599]

[1] See p. 247.

APPENDIX III
Biographical Notes

Aldburgh, Sir Richard (d.1475)

Of Aldburgh, near Boroughbridge.[1] An impetuous Percy feedman, it was as a supporter of Lord Egremont that he and his father, also Sir Richard, appeared at York sessions in 1453/4 accused of disseising one of the Nevilles in Swaledale.[2] During a period of Lancastrian ascendancy in June 1460 he was put on the North Riding commission of the peace,[3] and in the aftermath of the battle of Wakefield he and his future father-in-law Sir William Plumpton, with Sir George Darrell, Sir Richard Tunstall, and a gang of Percy desperados captured and butchered the Yorkist chieftain Richard, earl of Salisbury, though he had been granted his life.[4]

After the death of his first wife, a daughter of Sir Roger Warde of Givendale, he married Agnes Plumpton, whose father, Sir William, as steward of the Percy lordship of Spofforth, was directed by the 4th earl of Northumberland to compel Aldburgh to restore distrained or stolen cattle to Dame Isabel Ilderton, widow of one of his most trusted retainers.[5]

His son Richard (d.1514) knighted *c.*1503, held the offices of constable and porter of Pontefract, and married Jane, daughter of Sir Thomas Fairfax of Walton.[6]

[1] *CIPM sive Escaetarum*, p. 381.

[2] R.A. Griffiths, 'Local Rivalries and National Politics, the Percies, the Nevilles and the Duke of Exeter, 1452–55', in Idem, *King and Country: England and Wales in the Fifteenth Century* (1991), 324.

[3] Ibid., 362.

[4] Davies (ed.), *An English Chronicle*, 107.

[5] CB, 555; **23**; Lawson-Tancred, 136; Robert H. Scaife (ed.), *Register of the Guild of Corpus Christi in the City of York* (SS, lvii, 1872), 185.

[6] Somerville, 56.

Babthorpe, William (d.1500/1)

By 1496 the eldest surviving son of Sir Robert Babthorpe of Babthorpe, East Yorkshire (d.1466), William negotiated the marriage of his niece Isabel Babthorpe, daughter of his deceased elder brother, with Sir

Robert Plumpton's eldest son William, securing to himself and his heirs the entail of Babthorpe and other lands in Yorkshire and Lincolnshire,[1] but was soon faced with the task of countering the Plumpton's spurious claim to the exempted estates.[2]

Probably a lawyer, he was active in local administration as commissioner of array and *de wallis et fossatis*, and as a JP for the East Riding from 1492 until his death.[3] With legal colleagues such as Thomas Middleton, William Fairfax and Brian Palmes, Robert Constable and Richard Danby he was entrusted with enquiries into concealed crown lands and unpaid dues, and with adjudication in a case concerning the ownership of the North Yorkshire manor of Gilling;[4] after the death of Northumberland in 1489 he was commissioned by Archbishop Thomas Rotherham, with others of the earl's trusted servants, to convey their master's valuables to St Mary's Abbey, York, for safe-keeping.[5]

His marriage with Christian, daughter of Henry Sotehill of Stockerston, allied him with another victim of the predatory Plumptons. After his death his widow married William Beddell, who purchased from the bishop of Durham the wardship and marriage of her young son, and with the boy's uncle Thomas Babthorpe took upon himself the obligation of protecting the Babthorpe family's interests.[6]

[1] CB, 781; Introd., p. 13.
[2] Introd., p. 16, **126, 129, 130, 142**.
[3] *CPR, 1494–1509*, 52, 150, 239, 506, 667.
[4] *CPR, 1485–94*, 478, 397, 437.
[5] *Test. Ebor.*, iii, 310.
[6] Introd., p. 16.

Babthorpe, Sir William (d.1555)

Said to have been aged over eleven at the time of his father's death, William came of age soon after 1511, and was granted knighthood, 20 February 1547. A bencher of the Inner Temple, his marriage (*c*.1529) with a daughter of the sergeant-at-law Brian Palmes of Naburn (d.1519/20), whilst doubtless furthering his own career, made available to him the resources of this legal family in his numerous lawsuits with the Plumptons.[1]

In the 1530s he was a member of the 5th earl of Northumberland's council, and as legal counsellor to Thomas, Lord Darcy was employed in attempts to settle the disturbances arising from the objections raised by the tenantry to his employer's enclosures at Rothwell, near Leeds. Appointed to the Council in the North in 1525, his friendship with Wolsey secured for him the stewardship of the archbishop of York's lordship of Beverley.[2]

It was another country gentleman and London lawyer, Robert Aske, with whom he appears to have been on terms of close friendship, who drew him into the northern uprising of 1536, known as the Pilgrimage of Grace.[3] Like his fellow councillors Robert Chaloner and Sir Marmaduke Constable he took the Pilgrims' oath, joined the insurgents at Pontefract, and after entertaining Aske to dinner on 22 October, was almost certainly present at the Pilgrims' muster at Doncaster two days later.[4] On 6 December he and nine other selected gentlemen received from Norfolk a verbal assurance of the kings full and free pardon, on receipt of which Aske and many of the leaders dispersed.[5] He subsequently exerted a moderating influence, but appears to have been deceived by Norfolk at their meeting, 1 February 1537, as to the duke's real intentions regarding Aske, for he assured his friend that he had nothing to fear. Like Chaloner he probably suffered the shame of having to impose the king's vengeance upon his former allies.[6]

In 1537 he joined the re-organized Council at an annual fee of £50,[7] and in the following decade significantly increased his East Riding estates through the purchase of former monastic land.[8] Between 1546 and his death he was at work surveying chantries, colleges, hospitals and church goods in various parts of Yorkshire, including the city of York;[9] in December 1546 he sat at York as a justice of oyer and terminer, and at sessions convened for trying those who had offended against the Six Articles.[10] He also served as MP for Yorkshire, 1547 and April 1554; JP for the East and West Ridings from 1525 until his death; commissioner of sewers, and collector of the relief granted by Parliament in 1548–9.[11] By bill of the court of wards, issued 16 June 1555, his heir and namesake was authorized to enter his deceased father's estate.[12]

In view of his activities in promoting aspects of the Protestant Reformation, it may be noted that by 1620 the Babthorpe household, in which Mary Warde was brought up, was firmly recusant.[13]

[1] *CIPM*, *Henry VII*, ii, 595–6; WYASYAS, MS 599; *Tonge's Visitation*, 66; Bindoff, i, 357, *Register of Admissions to the Inner Temple, i*, 12.

[2] *L&P*, i (1), Addenda, 782, 841; *ibid.*, v, 822; Reid, 104, 491.

[3] *L&P*, xii (1), 46, 64.

[4] *L&P*, xi, 622; *ibid.*, xii (1), 392 (p. 191).

[5] *L&P*, xi, 841, 1243.

[6] *L&P*, xii (1), 156–7, 171, 315; Reid, 133–4, 137–8.

[7] *L&P*, i (1), Addenda, 1270; *ibid.*, xviii (1), 272.

[8] *L&P*, xviii (1), 623 (34); *ibid.*, (2), 107 (67); *ibid.*, xix 35; Cliffe, 15.

[9] *L&P*, xxi (1), 69, 302 (30); *CPR, 1548–49*, 135, 394, 417.

[10] *L&P*, xxi (2), 596.

[11] *L&P*, iv (1), 1610 (11); *ibid.*, (2), 5083 (10); *ibid.*, (3), 5243 91, 92; *ibid.*, *1553–54*, 26, 35, 353, 354; Bindoff, i, 357.

[12] *CPR*, *1554–55*, 80.

[13] John Bossy, *The English Catholic Community, 1570–1850* (1973), 128, 160. See below, p. 342.

Babthorpe, Sir William (d.1581)

By bill of the court of wards dated 16 June 1555 William obtained licence to enter into his inheritance,[1] and six years later paid £113 for a 21-year-lease of lands formerly belonging to Drax Priory, thus significantly enlarging his estates.[2] By the following year (1562) he was a member of the East Riding bench and had received knighthood by 1575.[3]

His first wife, Barbara, daughter of Sir Robert Constable of Everingham died before 1565 when he and his second wife, Frances, daughter of Sir Thomas Dawnay of Sessay, appeared before the royal commissioners at York to answer for their failure to attend their parish church. Ordered to hear a sermon in York minster and receive holy communion in Hemingborough parish church they submitted and were dismissed with a caution, but remained under suspicion in 1581 as suspected supporters of Edmund Campion, who almost certainly visited Osgodby early in the year.[4] Nevertheless, like other popish gentlemen he continued to hold a position of responsibility in local government.[5]

His son Sir Ralph, who succeeded to the estates in July 1582, paid dearly for his devotion to the old Faith, although the financial disaster that befell the family after his death seems to have been the result of a combination of heavy fines, extravagance and bad management.[6]

[1] *CPR, 1554–55*, 80.
[2] *CPR, 1560–63*, 215; *ibid., 1575–78*, no. 573.
[3] *CPR, 1560–63*, 436; *ibid., 1563–66*, 117; *ibid., 1572–75*, no. 2692.
[4] T. Burton, *The History and Antiquities of Hemingborough*, ed. J. Raine (YAS, extra ser., i, 1888), 314–15; Cliffe, 168, 173; A.G. Dickens, 'The First Stages of Romanist Recusancy in Yorkshire 1560–1590', *YAJ*, xxxv (1943), 165 &n.
[5] Cliffe, 240; *CPR, 1575–78*, nos 1886, 1962.
[6] Cliffe, 229–30.

Bingham, Sir Richard (d. 1476)

A descendant of a knightly family of Car Colston in the hundred of Bingham, Nottinghamshire,[1] that died out in the main line towards the end of the 14th century, Richard's prospects at birth were poor. His father, a younger brother of Ralph Bingham, the head of a cadet branch, appears to have had legal qualifications, and represented the county in the Parliaments of March 1416 and December 1420. He was employed as county coroner in which office Richard joined him in the 1420s.[2] In August 1430 he was appointed to the quorum of the Nottinghamshire bench; in March 1431/2 he arbitrated in a dispute between Sir William Plumpton and Ralph Neville, earl of Westmorland.[3]

On 14 February 1443 he was called sergeant, and subsequently recorded in the Year Books. Soon afterwards raised to the bench as a JKB, he was retained by Edward IV and continued through the Readeption, by then described as 'knight'. The king did not include him in the patent after his return, however, possibly at Sir Richard's own request, because of advancing years.[4]

After the death of his first wife Elena, widow of William Wastner (d.1420), he married Margaret Freville, widow of Sir Hugh Willoughby (d.1448), and co-heiress of Sir Baldwin Freville of Tamworth, Staffordshire (d.1402), whose fortune was increased by Sir Hugh's generous settlement which was to the detriment of his children by his first marriage. Her longevity deprived her son by Sir Hugh of his inheritance and her grandson was aged forty by the time she died in 1493. Fortunately Sir Richard proved a conscientious administrator of her estates, which were therefore spared the disasters which befell other less fortunate heirs.[5]

His son, also named Richard, married Margaret, daughter and coheiress of Sir Thomas Rempston of Rempston, Notts, a kinsman of the Plumptons.[6]

[1] Payling, *Political Society*, 179–80.
[2] Ibid., 9, 35, 57, 58, 73.
[3] Stapleton, li.
[4] E. Foss, *Judges of England … 1066–1862* (9 vols, 1848–64), iv, 419–20.
[5] C. Carpenter 'The Fifteenth-Century English Gentry and their Estates', in M. Jones (ed.), *The Gentry and Lesser Nobility in Late Medieval Europe* (Gloucester, 1986), 41–3.
[6] Stapleton, 4; *Test. Ebor.*, ii, 225.

Blount, Sir James (d.1492)

Younger son of Sir Walter Blount, later 1st Lord Mountjoy, of Barton Blount, Derbyshire.[1] He married Jane, one of the daughters and coheiresses of Sir James Delves who, with his father, Sir John, lost his life at Tewkesbury[2] – her sister Ellen married the sergeant-at-law, Robert Sheffield.[3] By 1472 he had indented with William, Lord Hastings and in the same year was elected MP for Derbyshire.[4] Appointed captain of Hammes, he defected to Henry of Richmond, escaping with others of the garrison, including his prisoner, John de Vere, earl of Oxford, to join Henry's invading force which landed at Milford Haven, where he received knighthood.[5] He allegedly slew his wife's cousin Sir John Babington at Bosworth, 'more motivated by the prospect of an inheritance than zeal for the Tudor cause'.[6]

The grant to him of the Staffordshire manor of Apedale, near Uttoxeter, was excluded from the Act of 1485 reversing the Delves attainder, but he needed all his influence at court to avoid ejection, and it was eventually recovered by the Delves family.[7] Marks of the high esteem in which he was held by Henry VII were the grant of the stewardship for life of the important Duchy honor of Tutbury, and reinstatement on the Derbyshire bench.[8] He was also effective head of the family during the minority of his nephew.[9]

In 1490 he and Robert Sheffield, casting covetous eyes on the Delves manor of Crakemarsh, part of the jointure of Ellen, Lady Delves, widow of Sir John Delves, were baulked by her unwillingness to succumb to what was probably considerable pressure.[10]

[1] *Collectanea*, viii, 325.
[2] Warkworth, *A Chronicle of King Edward the Fourth*, 18, 19.
[3] *Collectanea*, viii, 324.
[4] Wright, 116; *Return of Members of Parliament*, i (House of Commons, 1878).
[5] Bennett, *Bosworth*, 64, 86, 112.
[6] *Collectanea*, viii, 325.
[7] M.A. Hicks, 'Attainder, Resumption and Coercion', in Idem, *Richard III and his Rivals*, 68; *RP*, vi, 218–19; *Crowland*, 181.
[8] Somerville, 540.
[9] Wright, 85, 107.
[10] J.T. Rosenthal, 'Other Victims: Peeresses as War Widows 1450–1500', *History*, lxxii (1987), 213–230; **92**.

Chaloner, Robert (d.1555)

A common lawyer, of Stanley, Wakefield,[1] he married Margery, daughter of Sir William Scargill, of Thorpe Stapleton[2] (**68**, **70**). In 1528 and 1530 he received annuities of 13s 4d and 6s 8d, respectively, from Thomas Ryther and William Bradford, attorney. The latter, who appointed him executor, included Thomas Strey (**181**) and Sir Robert Plumpton's attorney John Pullein among his beneficiaries. Sir John Rocliffe described him as a 'wellbeloved and faythfull friend' on appointing him an executor in 1534.[3]

Appointed to the Council in the North in 1530, he was retained as counsellor by Henry Clifford, 1st earl of Cumberland, and as feedman by the dean and chapter of York. One of three JPs active in the repression of the rising in Craven in the summer of 1535,[4] he was nevertheless one of five members of the Council in the North who joined the pilgrims' council at York in 1536, put themselves at the head of the conspiracy, and later advised on the articles of the treaty with the king, drawn up at Pontefract. The government retaliated by reappointing the five to the reorganized council and isolating them from the Commons by forcing them to preside over the trials and executions of their kinsmen and erstwhile allies. Thereafter, since 'there was none to whom they might look for help if they offended the king', they remained 'fit agents' for the royal will.[5]

[1] **198, 202**.
[2] *Test. Ebor.*, iii, 369.
[3] *Ibid.*, v, 226, 285, 287, 323; vi, 369.
[4] R.W. Hoyle, 'Letters of the Cliffords, Lords Clifford and Earls of Cumberland, *c.*1500–*c.*1565', *Camden Society, Miscellany* xxxi (1992), 130–1; Idem, 'The First Earl of Cumberland: A Reputation Reassessed', *NH*, xxii, 77.
[5] Reid, 113, 137–8, 140, 152; *L&P*, xi, 820; xii (1), 1022; xii (2), 393.

Colt, Thomas (d.1467)

A lawyer, originally from Carlisle, he acquired an estate in Roydon, Essex, and married Jane, daughter of Lawrence Trusbut, who survived him and subsequently married Edward IV's comptroller, Sir William Parr.[1]

Described as 'the great commoner of the Yorkist revolution', Colt became a close adherent of Richard, duke of York, whom he accompanied to Ireland in the late 1450s, and for whom in 1454 he acted as mainpernor in the duke's purchase of a ten-year lease of the farms of the Devon and Cornish mines.[2] In 1459 he and two others of York's council were accused by Sir William Skipwith of ousting him from valuable offices for refusing to follow the duke to the first battle of St Albans. After fighting under York at Ludford, Colt was proscribed in the Coventry Parliament, and badly wounded at Wakefield, allegedly by a rival at the Exchequer.[3] Edward IV's accession brought his restoration and subsequent appointment as administrator of York's former estates, also membership of the royal Council. In February 1462 he was granted lands in Essex and Suffolk for good and faithful service.[4]

In the 1460s he moved close to Warwick, to whom he became personal advisor. As Chamberlain of the Exchequer he was one of three custodians to whom the temporalities of Durham were committed after their seizure by Edward in December 1462; the following year he and four household officers were granted the custody, wardship and marriage, for three years, of all minors holding land in fee, and of the temporalities of archbishoprics and bishoprics during voidance.[5]

Retained by the Duchy as apprentice in 1462, he served as MP for Cumberland 1455–6, 1460–2, and Carlisle 1449–50, 1463–5; JP for Cumberland 1453–4 and 1459, and Essex from 1461 until his death. He was also employed on several important diplomatic missions.[6]

In February 1462 licence was granted to him for the alienation of land in Kent to provide a chantry with two chaplains and two secular clerks to pray for the good estate of the king and others, including

Colt, himself, during their lifetimes, and for their souls after death; also for the souls of Richard, duke of York, the earls of Rutland and Salisbury, and Kentish men killed during the battles of Northampton, St Albans and Towton. His grandson Thomas was brought up in the household of Sir Thomas More.[7]

[1] **6**; J.W. Clay, *The Extinct and Dormant Peerages of the Northern Counties of England* (1913), 157; Pollard, *NE England*, 294, 297.

[2] P.A. Johnson, *Duke Richard of York 1411–1460* (Oxford, 1988 repr. 1991), 144, 199; Roskell, *Commons*, 253; *CPR, 1452–61*, 158.

[3] *CPR, 1452–61*, 552–53; Jalland, 497; *Foedera*, xi, 455; *RP*, v, 348.

[4] *CPR, 1461–67*, 107, 116.

[5] Jalland, 497; Pollard, 294; *CPR, 1461–67*, 217.

[6] Somerville, 455; Wedgwood, 208n.; *CPR, 1452–61*, 572, 583, 663; *ibid., 1461–67*, 563, 613.

[7] Wedgwood, 208n.; *CPR, 1461–67*, 215, 192.

Constable, Sir Robert (1423–88)

Of Somerby, Lincolnshire, and Flamborough, son and heir of Sir Robert of Flamborough and his wife Agnes Gascoigne. One of the biggest landowners in the East Riding, he married Agnes, daughter of Sir Philip Wentworth – in 1473 both were admitted to the Guild of Corpus Christi, York.[1]

A political trimmer, he remained on the East Riding bench throughout every political revolution from 1453 until his death, in spite of his obligations as a Percy feedman. He was present with the Percies at Heworth Moor on the 24 August 1453.[2] MP for Lincolnshire in the Coventry Parliament of 1459 when the Lancastrians were in the ascendant, he was included in the revised commission of the peace in 1461, empowered to round up remaining Lancastrians.[3] At the same time he was granted the stewardships of certain lordships, including Spofforth, formerly the property of the attainted Henry Percy.[4] On the 4th earl's restoration he succeeded in resuming an amicable relationship: thus in his will the earl directed that Sir Robert be paid his fee for life, provided he continued to serve the heir.[5] Said to have kept a low profile during the Readeption, he emerged with Edward's return and was granted lands in the East Riding belonging to the attainted Sir Thomas Roos. He was part owner of a ship whose master attacked a Scottish merchantman, in contravention of a safe-conduct.[6]

Prominent in local government as JP for Lindsey and the East Riding, sheriff of Yorkshire and Lincolnshire, and MP for a second time in 1477, he was frequently a commissioner, whether of array, *de wallis et fossatis*, survey and inquisition.[7] In accordance with well-tried practice, he accepted the outcome of the dynastic unheavals of 1483 and 1485. Through the marriages of his daughters he allied himself with important Yorkshire gentry families – Metham, Eure, Bigod and Ryther.[8]

[1] Horrox, in *Richard III and the North*, 90.
[2] Lander, 96; K. Dockray, 'Sir Marmaduke Constable of Flamborough', in *Richard III, Crown and People*, ed. J. Petrie (1985), 218.
[3] *CPR, 1452–61*, 560, 609; *ibid. 1461–67*, 31, 39, 567, 576.
[4] *CPR, 1461–67*, 39.
[5] *Test. Ebor.*, iii, 304–10; Hicks, *NH*, xiv, 87n.
[6] *CPR, 1467–77*, 409, 418.
[7] *CPR, 1467–77*, 381, 636, passim; *List of Sheriffs*; Gooder, 208; **14**.
[8] C.H. Hunter Blair (ed.), *A Visitation of the North of England c.1480–1500* (SS, cxliv, 1930).

Constable, Robert (d.1501)

Of North Cliffe, which he purchased together with other lands in the East Riding, lawyer. Second son of Sir Robert (d.1488), he married Beatrice Hatcliffe, widow of Ralph, Lord Greystoke; she took the veil in 1502.[1]

He was admitted to Lincoln's Inn in 1477 and gave his first reading in 1489. Soon after his celebrated third reading on the royal prerogative in the autumn of 1495 he was called to the coif, together with Thomas Frowyk, of the Inner Temple, and John Yaxley, of Gray's Inn,[2] both of whom were to be retained by Sir Robert Plumpton, but his promotion as justice of assize for the south-western circuit precluded him from appearing for Sir Robert's opponents: John Pullein's report suggests that he would have been a formidable opponent.[3]

In her will his widow left provision for their son Marmaduke's education at Cambridge and subsequent training in the law.[4] Marmaduke entered the Middle Temple, 8 April 1520, but died five years later.[5] His eldest son was to have training in the law, prior to entry into the household of Sir Robert Constable (exec. 1537), the testator's cousin.

[1] Ives, *CL*, 458.
[2] Idem, *TRHS*, 5th ser. xviii (1968), 145; S.E. Thorne, *Prerogativa Regis, Tertia Lectura Roberti Constable de Lyncolnes Inne anno 11 H.7* (New Haven Conn., 1949); S.E. Thorne (ed.), *Readings and Moots at the Inns of Court in the Fifteenth Century* (Selden Society, lxxi, 1954), pp. xlix, 171–237.
[3] **126, 153**; CB, 802.
[4] *Test. Ebor.*, iv, 237.
[5] *Register of Admissions to the Honourable Society of the Middle Temple from the Fifteenth Century to the Year 1944* (3 vols, 1949), i, 11.

Constable, Sir Marmaduke (*c.*1455–1518)

Son and heir of Sir Robert Constable of Somerby and Flamborough. Known as 'Little Sir Marmaduke', he married Joyce, daughter of Sir Humphrey Stafford.[1] Knighted by Northumberland during the Scottish campaign of 1480–3, he was an East Riding JP, 1479–80, and in the latter year sheriff of Yorkshire.[3] Like his father a consummate trimmer, he transferred his allegiance to Richard III, who made him a knight of the body and employed him as one of the main vehicles of royal authority in Kent and the Midlands – the more effective because during the lifetime of his father he had few family responsibilities.[4] He moved south in January 1484, whilst serving as JP and commissioner in Kent, on his appointment as ruler of the Stafford estates including Penshurst and Tonbridge.[5] By March 1484 he had replaced Buckingham as steward of Tutbury, Donington and the High Peak, with instructions to secure by oath the exclusive loyalty of the tenants to the crown. Thus between May and December his sphere of activity was transferred to the Midlands, where he served as JP and commissioner of array for Derbyshire and was given charge of the lands of an attainted midlands rebel, including the manor of Bosworth. His acquisitions of lands and offices in this period are said to have brought him, by conservative estimate, an annual income of £300.[6]

He survived Bosworth, where as steward of Tutbury he may have headed the Duchy contingent, and, after a temporary set-back, received a pardon, 18 November 1485. By the following May he was again a knight of the body and thereafter gave loyal service to the Tudors as sheriff of Staffordshire, 1486, and Yorkshire, 1488, 1491 and 1509. JP for the East Riding, 1491–4 and 1507 until his death; MP for Lincolnshire, Staffordshire or Yorkshire in most of the Parliaments from 1486 onwards. Among his rewards was the custody of some of the Percy lands during the minority of the 5th earl.[8]

He accompanied Henry VII to France in 1492, and served the new régime as a member of several important diplomatic missions.[9] Three years before his death he captained the left wing of Flodden, riding on to the field with his son-in-law, William Percy, his brother William, his sons Sir Robert, Marmaduke and William, with kinsmen and allies from Yorkshire and Northumberland, some of whom were knighted after the battle.[10]

Buried in Flamborough church, his epitaph records his career, although without mention of the name of Richard III.[11]

[1] DNB; *Test. Ebor.*, i, 337.
[2] Hicks, *NH*, xiv, 106.
[3] *CPR, 1476–85*, 578; *List of Sheriffs.*

[4] Horrox, in *Richard III and the North*, 98–9, 191–2; Dockray, in *Richard III, Crown and People*, 219–23.
[5] *CPR, 1476–85*, 398, 563; Wolfe, 132.
[6] *Harleian MS, 433*, ii, 187–8, 197; Wedgwood, 212; Somerville, 540 and passim; *CPR, 1476–85*, 400, 471, 490, 557.
[7] Gooder, 216, 231.
[8] *List of Sheriffs; Return of Members of Parliament*; *DNB*.
[9] Wedgwood, 212.
[10] *Anglica Historia*, 217.
[11] Gooder, 231.

Constable of Everingham, Sir Marmaduke (d.1548)

Second son of Sir Marmaduke Constable of Flamborough (d.1518), he married Barbara, daughter and co-heiress of Sir John Sotehill of Everingham, near York, through whom he acquired the estate.[1] After fighting under his father's command at Flodden he was knighted on the field, 9 September 1513.[2]

Like Robert Chaloner he was appointed to the Council in the North in *c*.1530; and in 1536 as a crown commissioner he was responsible for making a new survey of Conishead and Drax priories.[3] Nevertheless he and his elder brother Sir Robert were among those who joined Lord Darcy at Pontefract, yielded the castle to Aske and took the Pilgrims' oath. After the collapse of the rebellion he and other quondam leaders were re-appointed to the Council, and thus forced to preside over the indictments, trials and executions of their former comrades. Sir Robert Constable, who had initially received a pardon was committed to the Tower after the rising of Sir Francis Bigod, and executed at York in June 1537.[4]

Sir Marmaduke's son married Elizabeth, daughter of Ralph Ellerker of Rusby, Lincolnshire, a niece of Anne, Lady Rokeby.[5]

[1] *DNB*; *Flower's Visitation*, 66, 109.
[2] *Anglica Historia*, 216–20. His effects included a pair of standing pots engraved with the arms of the king of Scots, *Test. Ebor.*, vi, 201.
[3] Reid, 113; Somerville, 291.
[4] Reid, 133–4, 137–8, 143–4, 150; Hoyle, *Camden Miscellany* xxxi, 130; *DNB*.
[5] **226**.

Darrell, [Darell], Sir George (d.1466)

Of an ancient family first recorded about the same time as the Plumptons – towards the end of the twelfth century – Sir George's father Sir Edmund Darrell, of Sessay (d.1437) sat as MP for Yorkshire in 1433, and the following year was appointed a commissioner of array.[1]

George married Margaret, daughter of his neighbour and fellow Percy feedman Sir William Plumpton (d.1480), who survived him and afterwards married John Neville of Womersley.[2] Having taken part with his father-in-law in the attack on the earl of Salisbury at Wakefield in December 1460, the two entered into bonds of £1,000, 31 May 1462, on condition that they complied with the award of adjudicators.[3] Although not attainted after Towton, Darrell was held under bond of £2,000 as recognizance for good behaviour, and, like his father-in-law, was eventually granted a release.[4]

In February and June 1464 he was appointed a feoffee for the indenture and settlement made by Sir William Plumpton pursuant to the marriage of Elizabeth Plumpton and John Sotehill.[5]

His wife's jointure included seven manors and other lands in the West Riding. As his three sons, including Marmaduke, the heir, a minor in 1466, died without issue, the estate devolved upon their sister, Joan, the wife of Sir John Dawnay of Cowick (d.1493).[6]

[1] *Test. Ebor.*, ii, 27–8; Gooder, 190.
[2] *Collectanea*, i, 707.
[3] *CCR, 1461–68*, 135. The judgement has not survived.
[4] *CPR, 1461–67*, 39, 77; *VCH, Yorks, North Riding*, i, 447.
[5] CB, 562, 565.
[6] *Test. Ebor.*, iv, 172; **83**.

Eyre of Padley, Robert II (d.1498), Robert III (d.1502)

A knightly family, distrained between 1430 and 1509, with lands in the northern uplands of Derbyshire, the Eyres made themselves useful to landowners like the Plumptons with estates in the county by their expertise in estate management.

Robert II probably succeeded his father, Robert I (d.1460), who witnessed a Plumpton feoffment of 1446, as a member of Lord Hastings's retinue, and as steward of the Derbyshire lands of the earl of Shrewsbury and Francis, Lord Lovell. Both also held office under the Duchy in the High Peak.[1]

From Edward IV Robert II received a grant of 100s a year from the issues of Hallamshire during the minority of George, earl of Shrewsbury, and was appointed a commissioner to enquire into unpaid farms and other dues owing to the crown.[2] Sheriff of Nottinghamshire and Derbyshire in 1480, he served the county as JP, 1472–75 and from February 1481 through the Tudor usurpation until 1493, though he had been an usher of the household under Richard III, and busy as a Derbyshire commissioner of array during the crisis of 1484–5.[3]

He married Elizabeth, daughter of Thomas Fitzwilliam of Mablethorpe. His son, or perhaps younger brother, Robert III, who seems to have been steward of the Plumptons' Derbyshire lands, acted in the Plumpton interest during the latter's dispute with Empson. His son, later Sir Arthur, married Sir Robert Plumpton's daughter Margaret.[4]

[1] CB, 531; Wright, 22, 61–2, 79, 115, 203, 207, 213, 256; Somerville, 524.
[2] *CPR, 1467–77*, 408, 419.
[3] *List of Sheriffs*; *CPR, 1467–77*, 611; *ibid., 1476–85*, 400, 490, 557; *ibid., 1485–94*, 484, 485; Horrox, *Richard III*, 247.
[4] Meredith, 2, 13; *CIPM, Henry VII*, iii, 431; **143**n.

Eyre of Hassop, Stephen (d.1487)

A younger son of Robert I of Padley, he married Catherine, daughter of Nicholas Dymock of Kyme in Lincolnshire, and became the progenitor of a branch of the family established at Hassop, a manor he leased from the Plumptons.[1] Both he and Sir William Plumpton received pardons in December 1471, possibly for implication in the landing of Queen Margaret in the North; specifically, for a long list of riots, robberies and murders committed before 30 September 1471.

Bailiff of the earl of Westmorland's manor of Ashford, near Bakewell, of which his brother Philip held the rectory,[2] he may have served the Plumptons in a similar capacity. He died leaving a son, Rowland, and a daughter, Elizabeth, who was married as a child to John Curzon of Kedleston. His widow was granted a renewal of the lease of Hassop by Sir Robert Plumpton and his mother.[3]

The family, who made a fortune out of Derbyshire lead, became, like the Plumptons, recusants in the seventeenth century.[4]

[1] CB, 695. Most of the material for this note has been taken from Meredith.
[2] Wright, 62.
[3] CB, 751.
[4] Bossy, 87, 237–8.

Fairfax, Sir Guy (d.1495)

Of a family which produced several distinguished lawyers, Guy was a younger son of Richard Fairfax of Walton, from whom he inherited the manor of Steeton in Craven, where he built a castle. He married Isabel, sister of Sir Richard Ryther of Ryther, near Harewood.[1]

Retained by the Duchy as apprentice, 1460–5; called sergeant, 1466, king's sergeant, 1468; chief justice at Lancaster, 1480, he was a justice of the king's bench by Trinity 1477, and as a justice of assize for the midland circuit was re-appointed by Henry VII in 1485. JP for the West Riding, 1456–93, and for Warwickshire, Leicestershire and Lincolnshire, his career continued unabated through each demise of the crown.[2]

A Percy annuitant, legal councillor and feoffee, the 4th earl directed that his fee be continued for life in return for service to the heir.[3] Other patrons included Richard of Gloucester, the duke of Buckingham, who in 1475 retained him as counsellor at law and attorney at Westminster, the dowager duchess of Norfolk, John Lord Scrope and the city of York, where he was appointed recorder in 1476.[4]

His numerous commissions included array, enquiry into persons uttering treasonable speeches (1459), and into the lands of the attainted duke of York (1460), when Sir William Plumpton was a fellow commissioner. With Henry Sotehill, Robert Sheffield and others he was appointed custodian, during his absence abroad, of the lands of George, duke of Clarence (1475). During the troublous early years of Henry VII's reign his activities included investigations into conspiracies in various parts of the country, notably in the city of York, after the northern rebellion of 1489, in which Northumberland lost his life, and in London and Middlesex following Warbeck's invasion of 1495.[5]

A legal colleague John Dautre bequeathed him a Great Register formerly the property of William Gascoigne CJKB.[6]

[1] *DNB*; Ives, *CL*, 452, 460–1.
[2] Somerville, 452, 469; *CPR*, passim.
[3] *Test. Ebor.*, iii, 304–10; Hicks, *NH*, xiv, 87n.
[4] Horrox, *Richard III*, 66; Reid, 44–5; Ross, *Richard III*, 51n.; Rawcliffe, 226; R.B. Dobson (ed.), *The York City Chamberlains' Account Rolls 1396–1500* (SS, cxcii, 1980), 151.
[5] *CPR, 1429–36*, 522; *ibid., 1452–61*, 518; *ibid., 1485–94*, 106, 179, 283; *ibid., 1494–1509*, 29, 30, 31, 285.
[6] *Test. Ebor.*, ii, 233.

Fairfax, Sir William (d.1515)

Of Steeton and Bolton Percy, eldest son of Sir Guy. He and his younger brother Thomas followed their father into the legal profession. Both were benchers of Gray's Inn, and both were called to the coif, William in 1504.[1] Recorder of York, 1490–6; JP for the West Riding from 1496, he was appointed under-steward of Knaresborough in November 1499 to assist the deputy stewards Sir Reginald Bray and William Senhouse, bishop of Carlisle, whose public duties precluded them from exercising the office. By 1509 he was second justice at Lancaster, and soon afterwards a JCP.[2] Shortly before his death he was appointed one of the arbitrators who, under Richard Fox, bishop of Durham, pronounced the final judgement on the case of Plumpton v. Sotehill and Rocliffe.[3]

He and Thomas married, respectively Elizabeth and Cecily, daughters of Sir Robert Manners. For her marriage with Henry Ughtred of Kexby William provided his daughter Elizabeth with a portion of 400m.[4]

[1] Ives, *CL*, 452, 461; Foss, iv, 162–3.
[2] Somerville, 473, 524.
[3] **209**.
[4] **161**.

Frowyk, Thomas (1460/1–1506)

Son of Sir Thomas Frowyk, mercer, alderman and mayor of London, and grandson of Henry Frowyk of South Mimms, mercer, Thomas may have been educated at Cambridge, whence he is thought to have entered a chancery inn before being admitted to the Inner Temple, aged about fifteen.[1] Called to the bar in 1483/4, and in July 1486 appointed common pleader of London – 'A strangely inexperienced "utter barrister" for so important a city', he was by Easter 1489 thoroughly launched on the brilliant career that earned him the reputation of being an 'oracle of the law'.[2]

JP for Middlesex in 1493, he was called to the coif two years later, after performing learning exercises before Thomas Kebell in the early 1480s. In the protracted *cause célèbre* of Pilkington v. Ainsworth – a struggle over an estate in the Derbyshire village of Mellor – he appeared for the defendants, with John Kingsmill and Robert Constable, whilst Thomas Kebell and Robert Brudenell acted for the plaintiffs.[3] In 1497 he was in arms against the Cornish rebels.[4]

By Michaelmas 1501 he had been appointed king's sergeant and a JP for the western circuit. Two years later he owed his promotion to CJCP to the generosity of the mayor of London, Sir John Shea, who paid Henry VII 500m to obtain the office for the city's 'favourite son'.[5]

He married Elizabeth, daughter and heiress of Thomas Jakes, a fellow bencher of his Inn, and purchased land extensively in London and the home counties. He died prematurely, leaving a wealthy daughter, Friedeswide, who married Sir Thomas Cheyney. His widow desired to be buried beside him in the church of St Giles, South Mimms.[6]

[1] Ives, *CL*, 463–4; H.L. Gray, 'Incomes from Land in England in 1436', *EHR*, xlix (1934), 637–8; Bertha Putnam, *Early Treatises on the Practice of Justices of the Peace in the Fifteenth and Sixteenth Centuries* (Oxford, 1924), 127; Wedgwood, 358–9.
[2] Hastings, 65; Putnam, 127–9; Ives, 54; Emden, *Cambridge*, I (ii), 182.
[3] *CPR, 1485–94*, 493; Ives, 123–4.
[4] *Anglica Historia*, 94.

[5] **153**; Ives, 500.

[6] E.W. Ives, 'The Common Lawyers in Pre-Reformation England', *TRHS*, 5th ser., xviii (1968), 159; *Collectanea*, iii, 104.

Gascoigne, Sir William (1450–87)

Of the senior branch of a landed family descended from Henry V's chief justice Sir William Gascoigne, of Gawthorpe (d.1419).[1] Sir William's father and namesake (d. by 1477) married Joan, daughter and co-heiress of John Neville of Womersley, whose second wife was Margaret, daughter of Sir William Plumpton and widow of Sir George Darrell.[2]

His son's marriage with Margaret Percy, daughter of the 3rd earl of Northumberland promoted his advance under his brother-in-law the 4th earl, to whom he owed his appointment as deputy steward of Knaresborough.[3] Both had been attainted after Towton, but whereas William was pardoned in July 1461,[4] Henry Percy had remained nearly ten years in the wilderness. His close relationship with Percy notwithstanding, Gascoigne succeeded in maintaining a foot in both camps, for he was knighted by Gloucester on campaign near Berwick in 1481, and appointed a knight of the body with an annuity of £20 after Richard III's accession.[5]

Several times a commissioner of array, he was also a West Riding JP from February 1472 to November 1473, and from August 1481 to February 1485.[6] In July 1480 he obtained a licence to crenellate his house at Gawthorpe and impark over 2,000 acres of his demesne in and around the manor.[7]

If, as reported, he was present at Bosworth, it is likely he fought at the king's side rather than with the immobile Percy contingent. He died in March 1487 leaving his eldest son a minor, aged eighteen or nineteen.[8]

[1] *Flower's Visitation*, 44; Gooder, 180, 186.

[2] App. II, 37; Gooder, 216; *DNB*; *Test. Ebor.*, i, 390–5, 402.

[3] Somerville, 524; **28**.

[4] Pollard, *NE England*, 293. Strictly, the attainder related to the deceased 3rd earl.

[5] Horrox, *Richard III*, 20; Hicks, *NH*, xiv, 91. But he is described as 'knight' in July 1480 (in error), note 7, below.

[6] *CPR, 1466–77*, 199, 349; *ibid., 1476–85*, 399, 492, 580, 638. The number of JPs was reduced in November 1475: Sir William Plumpton lost his place also, **28**.

[7] *CPR, 1476–85*, 205.

[8] *CPR, 1485–94*, 179.

Gascoigne, Sir William (d.1551)

On 25 November 1487, although still a minor, aged about nineteen, William received knighthood at the coronation of Elizabeth of York, and thereafter was appointed a knight of the body. In the following month he was given livery, without proof of age, of his deceased father's estates in the West Riding lordships of Gawthorpe, Thorpe Arch and Burghwallis, and lands in the East Riding and in Staffordshire.[1] He seems later to have acquired the manor of Harewood through the marriage of his third son Marmaduke with the heiress of the Redmans.[2] By 1545/6, with subsidy assessments, respectively, of £533 and £400 from land in the West Riding, he and Sir Henry Savile of Thornhill were by far the most substantial of the local gentry, and recognized as such by Thomas Cromwell.[3] The size of his household at Gawthorpe is suggested by his ability to provide thirty men for the muster of 1539, and fifty towards the troops required for garrisoning the Borders in March 1545.[4]

He married, first, Alice, daughter of Sir Richard Frognall, secondly Margaret, daughter of Richard, Lord Latimer, thirdly Maud Lindley, a widow, and lastly Bridget, daughter of Robert Stokes of Bickerton, near York.[5]

Under Henry VII he was active locally as commissioner of array, sheriff and MP (1495), as JP for the West Riding from 1493 until the end of the reign, and for the town of Ripon from 1500 to 1507. On 11 May 1509 he attended the king's funeral.[6] He continued to serve on the West Riding bench under Henry VIII, and as one of the collectors of the subsidy of 1524–5.[7]

Between 1525 and 1533, together with Robert Chaloner and William Babthorpe he was engaged in pacifying Lord Darcy's embattled tenants in Rothwell; in the latter year, as her chief almoner, he attended Anne Boleyn's coronation.[8] A commissioner of array in June and July 1511 and August 1512, he probably provided a contingent the following year for the Scottish campaign, and was perhaps present at Flodden, where his eldest son William was knighted by the earl of Surrey.[9]

Although he had shown some support for the Reformation (in June 1534 he reported to Cromwell that he had committed one 'light fellow' to prison for maintaining papal authority),[10] when ordered to fulfill his undertaking to provide 100 men to serve under Lord Darcy in October 1536, both men threw in their lot with the Pilgrims, and at a conference at York in November Gascoigne was appointed to be one of the party deputed to meet Norfolk at Doncaster on 6 December.[11] Like Chaloner, Babthorpe and Sir Marmaduke Constable, he avoided condign punishment, but was appointed a juror for the trials of the rebels at York.[12] On 25 June 1537, following the execution of Sir Robert Constable,

Gascoigne wrote to Cromwell asking his help in obtaining exemption from forfeiture of his daughter's jointure. On 2 November he wrote again, explaining that Dorothy's marriage with Sir Robert's grandson Marmaduke Constable had cost him 1,000m., and pleading that 'for an old man's comfort' the matter might be dealt with expeditiously[13] (indeed, a letter dated 27 April 1526 and apparently signed by him is said to reveal the hand of an already elderly and infirm man).[14]

In 1534, suffering from 'a great defect of the emmerodes', and unable to ride more than sixteen miles a day, he had been arrested by Thomas Legh and brought to London, possibly to answer in Star Chamber one of the numerous suits that were brought against him between 1499 and *c.*1535, most of them for acts of violence or the use of his superior power for selfish ends.[15]

His financial irresponsibility caused Alderman William Nelson of York considerable exasperation, and another merchant, Thomas Tong sued in the city of London for his outlawry.[16] In *c.* 1525 he was dissuaded by Wolsey from laying claim to the earldom of Westmorland.[17]

By the early seventeenth century the family were catholic, though possibly conformist, and at times in the 1630s, they, like the Constables and Fairfaxes, maintained a domestic priest, 'though these arrangements usually broke down in periods of economic difficulty and retrenchment ...'.[18] The house at Gawthorpe survived until 1770–3, when it was demolished during the landscaping of Harewood Park.[19]

[1] Gooder, 216; *CPR, 1485–94*, 169, 197; *Materials*, ii, 214; Smith, 145–56.
[2] *L&P*, i (1), Addenda, 146; Whitaker, *Loidis and Elmete*, 166.
[3] Smith, 60, 290, 292; *L&P*, vii, 1669.
[4] *L&P*, xiv (1), 316; *ibid.*, xx (1), 339 (2).
[5] *Star Chamber Proceedings*, i, 74; Wedgwood.
[6] *CPR, 1494–1509*, 2, 122, 668, 669; Gooder; *L&P*, i, (1), 16.
[7] e.g. *L&P*, iv (2), 5083 (10); *ibid.*, xx (1), 622, 318; *ibid.*, iv (1), 378.
[8] *L&P*, iv (1), 1285, *ibid.*, i (1), Addenda, 538; *ibid.*, vi, 355, p. 247.
[9] *L&P*, ii (2), 2246 (4, ii).
[10] *L&P*, vii, 638.
[11] *L&P*, xi, 212, 464, 522, 688 (3), 1155 (2). *ibid.*, xii (1), 137, 306.
[12] *L&P*, xii (1), 1199 (4), 1227.
[13] Reid, 143–44; Gooder; *L&P*, xii (2), 137, 1018, 1019.
[14] Hoyle, *Camden Miscellany* xxxi, 155.
[15] *L&P*, vi, 1326; Smith, 145; H.B. McColl (ed.), *Yorkshire Star Chamber Proceedings*, ii (YASRS, xlv, 1911), 50–56; Wm Brown (ed.), *Yorkshire Star Chamber Proceedings*, iii (YASRS, li, 1914), 4, 7.
[16] Kirby, *NH*, xxv, 108; *L&P*, i, (1), Addenda, 660.
[17] J.J. Cartwright (ed.), 'Subsidy Roll for the Wapentake of Skyrack of the 15th Hen. VIII', *YAJ*, ii (1873), 292.
[18] Bossy, 84, 260.
[19] Hoyle, *Camden Miscellany* xxxi, 185.

Greene of Newby, John, Robert, Richard

A landed family settled at Newby, near Boroughbridge, at least since early in the 14th century, Richard Greene, who died in 1421, appears to have been the father of John and Robert – the former a son-in-law of Sir Robert Plumpton (d.1421) – who were implicated in the affair on Papplewick Moor. On 20 Oct. 1423 their widowed mother Margaret granted her manor of Dalton, near Topcliffe, to John and his wife Joan Plumpton.[2] Appointed a feoffee by his future father-in-law in 1416 and again in 1418, John was later employed by Sir William as steward of his estates, at a fee of 4m from the issues of Grassington and 'livery according to his degree'; he also held the deputy-stewardship of Knaresborough prior to 1437, when he was promoted to the stewardship for a brief period.[3] His younger brother Robert, groom of the pantry to Edward IV, obtained the bailiwick of Boroughbridge on 8 Sept. 1462 – an office that was exempted from the schedule of resumptions ordered by Parliament in 1467.[4] His son Richard, apparently a lawyer, also served the Plumptons.[5]

Nothing is known of Godfrey Greene, although he was almost certainly a member of the same family.

[1] *VCH*, *Yorks*, *North Riding*, ii, 76; **5**; App. II, 22.
[2] M.J. Hebditch (ed.), *Yorkshire Deeds*, ix (YASRS, cxi, 1948), 57.
[3] App. II, 4, 5, 6; CB, 418; Somerville, 524.
[4] *RP*, V, 593.
[5] **154**.

Harrington, Sir James (1430–87)

Of Brierley, Yorkshire, second but eldest surviving son of Sir Thomas Harrington of Hornby, Lancashire, an ardent Yorkist who, with his eldest son Sir John, perished with Richard, duke of York at Wakefield in 1460.[1] James's marriage with Joan Neville, widow of Sir William Gascoigne (d.1460), whose step-mother was Margaret Plumpton, widow of Sir George Darrell, gave him a foothold in both camps.[2]

His services to the Yorkists included the capture near Clitheroe of the fugitive Henry VI, whom he conveyed to London, receiving a reward of 100m.[3] For his support of Edward IV, whom he joined at Nottingham soon after the king's return from exile in 1471, he was granted Sir Richard Tunstall's castle of Thurland.[4]

He and his brother Robert, who was knighted at Tewkesbury,[5] fell foul of Edward over their attempt to deprive Sir John's two young daughters of their inheritance. In 1468 the king's attorney having sued for them to appear in chancery to answer charges against them, they were briefly confined to the Fleet, whilst the wardship and marriages of the heiresses were granted to Thomas Stanley, who promptly married them to Stanley husbands. The brothers re-occupied Hornby during the Readeption and held it stubbornly until the king lost patience and they were forced to capitulate.[6] No penal action was taken against them and they continued to prosper in royal service as members of Gloucester's affinity and knights of the body after his assumption of the crown. Also a ducal councillor, Sir James was permitted to crenellate at Brierley in 1475.

A busy public office-holder, he was pricked for the shrievalty of Yorkshire in 1466 and 1475;[7] elected MP for Lancaster, 1467 and 1468; appointed deputy steward of Pontefract under John Neville, and steward of Bradford, 1471; deputy forester of Bowland under Gloucester, 1471, chief forester, 1485; served as JP for the West Riding, 1472–3, 1477–85; commissioner of oyer and terminer, 1482, and of array, May and December 1484.[8]

Although attainted after Bosworth he was admitted to allegiance in 1486, but in the following year joined Lambert Simnel, and after the defeat of the rebels at Stoke his sequestrated estates were given to Sir Edward Stanley, husband of his niece Anne Harrington. He is believed to have died in poverty, leaving an only, but illegitimate son, John, as his heir.[9]

[1] Wedgwood; Jalland, 490.

[2] Somerville, 514.

[3] A. Goodman, *The Wars of the Roses: Military Activity and English Society 1450–97* (1981), 98–9; Jones, 39; I. Grimble, *The Harrington Family* (1957), 53–4.

[4] *Arrivall*, 7; Wedgwood; Horrox, *Richard III*, 41.

[5] Wedgwood, 425–6.

[6] Ross, *Edward IV*, 408–9; Goodman, 99.

[7] Grimble, 56; Reid, 44–5; Jones, 40.

[8] Somerville, 508, 514–15; *List of Sheriffs*, 162; Jones, 41.

[9] Goodman, 99; Jones, 42; Grimble, 59–60; Wedgwood; Gooder, 202–4; *CPR*, *1476–85*, 399, 492; *ibid.*, *1485–94*, 133; *RP*, vi, 397.

Ingoldesthorpe, Joan, Lady (d.1494)

Sister of John Tiptoft, earl of Worcester (exec. 1470), and widow of Sir Edmund Ingoldesthorpe of Borough Green, near Newmarket, and Rainham, Norfolk, who died in 1456 seised of twenty-four manors in eight counties, at least a third of which were held in dower by his widow. He also had an annuity of 500m from the Exchequer as kinsman and next heir of Sir Thomas de Braddeston (d.1361), to whom it had been awarded in perpetuity by Edward III in consideration of his services. An important landowner, Sir Edmund served as JP for

Cambridgeshire, 1448–55 and MP, 1445, 1449 and 1453–4.[1]

Custody of their only daughter and heiress, Isabel, having been secured by Queen Margaret, she was married to Warwick's brother Sir John Neville, afterwards earl of Northumberland, subsequently Marquis Montague (d.1471). Their only son, George, duke of Bedford (1465–83) was deprived of his dukedom and peerage by Act of Parliament in 1478, and died unmarried.[2]

Lady Ingoldesthorpe continued to enjoy the royal annuity, part of which was paid out of the proceeds of the subsidy and ulnage of cloth in East Anglia and Essex.[3] With Geoffrey Downes, her employee (possibly steward) and friend, she founded a chapel and lending library at Pott Shrigley in Cheshire. In April 1589 a visitor to the chapel saw in the east window the figure of a woman kneeling between coats of arms, and beneath it the inscription: *Orate pro bono statu dominae Johannae Inlesthorpe. . . .*[4]

Her ultimate heirs were her great grandson, John Stonor, and her three granddaughters.[5]

[1] Wedgwood; Hicks, in *Richard III and his Rivals*, 293; *CFR, 1452–61*, 51, 84, 167.

[2] Wedgwood; *GEC*; Hicks, 291–6.

[3] *CPR, 1446–52*, 258–59; *ibid., 1461–67*, 525.

[4] Kirby, in *Church and Chronicle*, 230; Richmond, in *Religious Belief*, 121–2, 125–6; J.P. Earwaker, *East Cheshire Past and Present* (2 vols, 1880), ii, 325, 327; **9**, **10**, **18**.

[5] *CIPM, Henry VII*, i, 1985–8.

Mauleverer, Halnath (Alnathus)

Son of John Mauleverer of Allerton Mauleverer, near Knaresborough, and his wife Isabella, daughter of Sir Thomas Markenfield of Markenfield, near Ripon.[1] His elder brother Sir John became a committed Neville supporter, and in May 1461 was commissioned to arrest Sir William Plumpton's younger brother Godfrey for his implication in an affray in Knaresborough market place.[2] His role as arbitrator in the dispute between Sir William and the House of St Robert of Knaresborough appears to have caused him some irritation, although Halnath's letters suggest that he had appointed Plumpton as one of his feoffees.[3]

Halnath Mauleverer, apparently a brother of the House of St John of Jerusalem at Clerkenwell, may possibly be confused with his nephew and namesake.[4] An usher in Edward IV's household, he moved south and settled at Ashdown in Devon following his marriage with the west country heiress Joan Carminew,[5] and was endowed by Richard III with land and offices in the southern counties after Buckingham's rebellion, in accordance with the king's policy of extending royal influence through trusted lieutenants.[6]

Sheriff of Cornwall in 1470 and of Devon in 1483, when he was commissioned to arrest and imprison the rebels,[7] he was a JP for Devon 1470–71 and of Devon and Cornwall 1483–84;[8] commissioner of array for Cornwall, and of oyer and terminer concerning treasons committed in Devon.[9] In September 1484 he was granted the constabulary of Launceston for life, and in December, as an esquire of the body, received Edward Courtenay's manors of Bosconnock, Glyn and Braddock in tail male, in recognition of his service in quelling the rebellion in the South-West.[10]

The pardon issued to him on the 19 Nov. 1485 as 'late of Allerton Mauleverer, alias late of Clerkenwell, alias late of Ashwater, alias late of Boconnok', does not mention his presence on the field of Bosworth, but his nephew Sir Thomas Mauleverer, who also received a pardon, as a knight of the body probably rode with the king on his last charge.[11] Neither was included among those former Ricardians who were employed by Henry VII.

[1] *Tonge's Visitation*, 54.
[2] *CPR, 1461–67*, 29.
[3] **18**, **40**, **41**.
[4] **40**.
[5] *CPR, 1476–85*, 122; Pollard, *NE England*, 351.
[6] Horrox, *Richard III*, 191.
[7] *CPR, 1476–85*, 201, 490, 371; *List of Sheriffs*.
[8] *CPR, 1476–85*, 556, 558.
[9] *CPR, 1476–85*, 398, 490, 493.
[10] *CPR, 1476–85*, 502, 503.
[11] *CPR, 1485–94*, 21, 39; Bennett, *Bosworth*, 114; Hicks, *NH*, xiv, 97.

Middleton, Thomas

Younger son of Sir William Middleton, of Stockeld, near Plumpton, and his wife Margaret, daughter of Sir Stephen Hammerton.[1] Having qualified at Gray's Inn as an attorney, he probably practised as a Westminster man of law – an advantage in securing retainers from influential local clients.[2] In spite of the family's strong Percy links Thomas and his brother Richard were retained also by Gloucester, the latter as a member of the ducal household.[3] In 1468 Thomas married Joan, daughter of Sir William Plumpton in the chapel of the Holy Trinity at Plumpton Hall.[4]

A feoffee of the 4th earl of Northumberland in the 1470s, he was also retained as counsel by the city of York, Durham Priory (from 1478), and by the bishopric of Durham, first as counsel, afterwards as steward (1467–84).[5] JP for the West Riding, he was of the quorum from 1473,[6] and a frequent executor and feoffee.

In June 1471 and February 1483 he served under Gloucester on important commissions, the former to enquire into reports of arson perpetrated by Scottish men and women alleged to be roaming at large in the Yorkshire countryside; the latter to investigate disturbances within the forest of Knaresborough. In June 1485 he was engaged in assessing and appointing the collection of a West Riding subsidy.[7]

He and his wife were buried in Spofforth church, where Stapleton saw and recorded the funerary inscription on their tomb.[8]

[1] **78**
[2] Ives, *CL*, 141; **11**, **14**, **132**.
[3] Horrox, *Richard III*, 63–4; 92.
[4] CB, 570.
[5] Hicks, *NH*, xiv, 87; Pollard, *NE England*, 134–5.
[6] Arnold, 126; *CPR*, *1476–85*, 580.
[7] *CPR*, *1467–77*, 385; *ibid.*, *1476–85*, 50; *ibid.*, *1485–94*, 242.
[8] Stapleton, 75n.

Mordaunt, Sir John (d.1455–1504)

One of a group of lawyers, including Empson, Dudley, Hobart and Lovell, who ran the country under the personal direction of Henry VII,[1] his father was the obscure William Mordaunt of Turvey, Bedfordshire (d.1481). A brilliant career at the Middle Temple culminated in his call to the coif and appointment as king's sergeant in 1495.[2]

He married an heiress, Edith, daughter and co-heiress of Sir Nicholas Latimer of Duntish, Dorset, became CJ of Chester before the turn of the century and chancellor of the Duchy of Lancaster for life in 1504. A frequent commissioner and a JP for Bedfordshire from June 1483 until his death, by 1494 he had become a member of seven other county commissions.[3] Elected as speaker of the Commons in the Parliament of 1487,[4] he fought at Stoke and was knighted in 1503 on the occasion of the creation of Prince Henry as Prince of Wales.[5]

His son John was summoned to Parliament as Baron Mordaunt of Turvey.[6]

[1] **177**.
[2] *Register of the Middle Temple*, 2; Ives, *TRHS*, 5th ser. xviii (1968), 145, 156–7.
[3] Wedgwood; *CPR*, *1485–94*, 481–83 and passim; *ibid.*, *1494–1509*, passim.
[4] Roskell, *Commons*, 114, 299–300.
[5] Wedgwood.
[6] *Register of the Middle Temple*, 5.

Percy, Henry, 4th earl of Northumberland (*c.*1449–89)

Only son of the 3rd earl who was slain at Towton 29 March 1461, Henry was committed to the Fleet and afterwards to the Tower, and his sequestrated lands, together with the earldom, were granted to Sir John Neville, Lord Montague (**19**). But Percy had inherited his family's potent influence in the North-East, where an insurrection in the spring of 1469 led by one calling himself Robin of Holderness, aimed at his restoration.[1] After Warwick's escape overseas Edward IV released him, 27 Oct. 1469, restored the earldom to him, 25 March 1470, and in 1472 granted him custody of his estates pending the reversal of his father's attainder.[2] In June 1470 he was appointed to the family's traditional office as warden of the East and Middle Marches, and in the following year was granted the stewardship of Knaresborough for life, 28 June 1471.[3]

He married Maud, daughter William Herbert, earl of Pembroke, whose wife was the queen's sister, and in whose household he had spent the latter part of his confinement.[4]

The dominant figure in Northumberland and the East Riding, he had estates also in the North and West Ridings, Cumberland, the Midlands, Suffolk and London. He soon set about recruiting to the Percy affinity, decimated in 1461.[5] The Readeption having brought him no advantage – indeed the wardenship was transferred to Marquis Montague – Northumberland did nothing to impede Edward IV's progress after his return from exile, 14 March 1471, but 'sat still' – possibly he would have been unable to persuade his followers actively to support the Yorkist king.[6] He was not trusted, however, and Clarence ordered that spies be set to watch him.[7]

In his efforts to rebuilt his authority in the North, Percy came into conflict with the rapidly-growing power of Gloucester, but the indentures of 28 July 1474, formulated by the king and Council, whilst establishing the duke's superior authority put limits on his power, and enabled Northumberland to avoid ruinous competition and thus ensure the perpetuation of traditional Percy influence.[8] The strength of the tie is seen in Northumberland's part in Gloucester's usurpation, of which he must have had prior knowledge, for he presided over the trial of Earl Rivers, Sir Richard Grey and Thomas Vaughan, an act which committed him to Richard's cause.[9] Presumably, he then led the northern army which overawed London whilst Richard accomplished his plan, 6 July 1483.[10] Soon afterwards Percy retained a number of former ducal supporters, including Sir Thomas Mauleverer, Sir Richard Conyers and Sir James Strangeways, but Richard III was determined to maintain his hold over the North, and the royal household proved a potent rival attraction.[11]

As king, Richard bid high for Northumberland's loyalty but failed to grant him the prizes he most coveted – the chief stewardship of the Duchy, wardenship of the West March, presidency of the Council in the North. Furthermore the generous accretion of estates awarded to him did not include significant holdings in the North.[12] These may indeed be reasons why his conduct at Bosworth could be interpreted as treason. 'He was', says a Ricardian historian, 'the shame of the North, and four years later the North would avenge its shame by killing him'.[13]

Far from showing gratitude, Henry VII imprisoned the earl but released him under surety, 6 December 1485, and subsequently restored him to many of his offices, though the warden-generalship was granted only on an annual basis.[14] He had little influence with the new king and lacked political allies. He spent most of the remainder of his life in the North where he did sterling service during the troubles which beset the early years of the reign as sheriff of Northumberland and as a member of thirteen commissions of the peace.[15]

His murder at South Kilvington (Cocklodge), near Thirsk by a riotous mob led by Robert Chaloner of Ayton, 28 April 1489, has been linked by some with memories of Bosworth. The only casualty, he would not have died if his retinue had done their duty (**74**).[16] His will is said to have been written in his own hand.[17]

[1] Goodman, 67.

[2] *GEC*; *RP*, vi, 16.

[3] J. Bain (ed.), *Calendar of Documents Relating to Scotland*, iv, *1357–1509* (1888), no. 1387; Somerville, 524.

[4] Hicks, *NH*, xiv, 83–4.

[5] J.C. Hodgson (ed.), *Percy Bailiffs' Rolls of the Fifteenth Century* (SS, cxxxiv, 1921), passim; Hicks, 81.

[6] Hicks, 97; Goodman, 208; Storey, *House of Lancaster*, 195; *Arrivall*, 6–7; A. MacKay, 'A Castilian Report on English Affairs 1485', *EHR*, lxxxviii (1973), 92–9.

[7] C.L. Kingsford, *English Historical Literature of the Fifteenth Century* (Oxford, 1913), 392.

[8] Hicks, 84, 87; Ross, *Edward IV*, 199.

[9] Hicks, 88–9.

[10] Gillingham, 221, 224–5.

[11] Hicks, 104–5.

[12] *DNB*; Bennett, *Bosworth*, 74; Horrox, *Richard III*, 204–5, 216–18; Gillingham, 241.

[13] *Crowland*, 179; P.M. Kendall, *Richard III* (1955), 368.

[14] *Rotuli Scotiae*, ii, 470, 484–5.

[15] *Crowland*, 58; Goodman, 103.

[16] **74**; Hicks, *NH*, xxii, 40; Raphael Holinshed, *Chronicles of England, Scotland and Ireland*, ed. Henry Ellis (6 vols, 1807–8), iii, 769; *Test. Ebor.*, iii, 304.

[17] McFarlane, 240.

Percy, Henry, 5th earl of Northumberland (1478–1527)

After his father's death the new earl took the field, aged eleven, on Henry VII's behalf.[1] Eight years later he commanded the northern horse for the suppression of Lord Audley's rebellion.[2] Although brought up at Henry VII's court he was never trusted by the king, who imposed large recognizances and obligations upon him.[3] The year before achieving his majority he was given livery of his estates without proof of age, and in the same year (1498) was sworn of the king's Council, though not until later was he appointed to the Council in the North.[4] He married, before 1502, Catherine, daughter and co-heiress of Sir Robert Spencer of Spencercombe, Devon.[5]

Although granted the stewardship of Knaresborough for life the wardenship of the Marches eluded him, perhaps because he was 'too incapable and froward to be trusted', or indeed because he refused the office.[6] Apparently overbearing and headstrong, his quarrel with the archbishop of York, Thomas Rotherham, provoked an order from the Council, 19 Nov. 1504 enjoining both parties to order their servants to lay down their arms and to refrain from bringing large contingents of followers to Westminster. Twelve years later after examination in Star Chamber on unspecified charges, and confinement for 12 days in the Fleet, it was feared by his friends that through tactlessness and petulance he might further exacerbate his predicament.[7] Made a KG before April 1499, he was appointed to the Westmorland commission of the peace, but not until 1500 to that of Sussex, and later still to those of the West and East Ridings.[8]

Most notable for the magnificence of his entourages when escorting the Princess Margaret from York to Berwick for her marriage in 1503 to the king of Scots, and at the Field of the Cloth of Gold in June 1520, in October 1523 he assembled a force of 850 men at Alnwick to repel a threatened invasion.[9] He and his wife were buried beneath a magnificent tomb in Beverley minster.

[1] M.J. Bennett, 'Henry VII and the Northern Rising of 1489', *EHR*, cv (1990), 51.

[2] G.T. Clark, 'Annals of the House of Percy by E.B. de Fonblanque', *YAJ*, xi (1891), 8; **125**.

[3] Bernard, 11.

[4] *CPR, 1494–1509*, 138.

[5] *GEC*.

[6] Stapleton, 88n.; Bush, 42; Condon, 118.

[7] C.G. Bayne (ed.), *Select Cases in the Council of Henry VII* (Selden Society, lxxv, 1958), 41–2; Bernard, 14–15.

[8] Lander, 30.

[9] *GEC*; *Collectanea*, vi, 280.

Percy, Sir Robert (?d. c.1485)

Eldest son of Robert Percy of Scotton, near Knaresborough (*fl.*1474/5), he may have been educated in the household of Richard Neville, 'the Kingmaker' at Middleham, together with Richard, duke of Gloucester. A committed Yorkist, he brought an action in chancery against Sir William Plumpton for injurious treatment after the battles of Ludlow and Wakefield. He remained close to Gloucester, receiving knighthood on 5 July 1483, prior to Richard's coronation, and with Frances, Viscount Lovell served the king and queen at their coronation banquet. In the same year he was made comptroller of the royal household, a privy councillor, and, for his support against the rebels, was granted land in Essex, Cambridgeshire and Norfolk, and, in reversion, on the death of Thomas, Lord Stanley, the manors of Scotton and Brearton, with other properties in the neighbourhood. As rumours of invasion spread during 1484 he was appointed to a crucial commission of array in December of that year.[2]

He married, first, Eleanor, daughter of Sir Ralph Bewley, secondly, Joyce, daughter of Norman Washbourne of Wichenford, Worcestershire, for whose jointure he purchased from Robert Walkingham the lease of lands in the lordship of Arkendale.[3]

According to the Crowland Continuator he fell at Bosworth, though some sources aver that he escaped after the battle. He was not attainted and may have died soon afterwards. His son and namesake, attained for complicity in Lovell's rebellion of 1487–8, was granted a pardon and restitution of goods two years later.[4]

[1] Joseph Hunter, *Familiae Minorum Gentium*, ed. J.W. Clay (4 vols, Harleian Society, xxxviii–xl, 1894–6), ii, 873.

[2] W.E. Hampton, 'Sir Robert Percy and Joyce, his Wife', in *Richard III, Crown and People*, 184–5, 188; A.R. Myers (ed.), *The Household of Edward IV: The Black Book and the Ordinance of 1478* (Manchester, 1989), 289; Horrox, *Richard III*, 219–20; *CPR, 1476–85*, 434–5, 492.

[3] Hampton, 188; **104–106**.

[4] Myers, 289; Hampton, 185; Ross, *Richard III*, 225; RP, vi, 397; *Crowland*, 183, 574; *CPR, 1485–94*, 222.

Pierpoint, Henry (d.1457)

Originally of Pierrepont, near Grandcourt in Picardy, the family settled at Hurstpierpoint soon after the Conquest and moved to Holme Pierpoint, Nottinghamshire in the mid-thirteenth century.[1] Henry's father, Sir Henry (d.1452), who had witnessed Sir William Plumpton's settlements of 1449,[2] held office under the Duchy.[3] Maimed, allegedly, by Thomas Foljambe of Walton in January 1433 in the course of a murderous feud between the two families, both parties were indicted – Sir Henry by a jury, which included Plumpton (whose mother was a Foljambe) that placed responsibility on the Pierpoints and their allies.[4]

His son and namesake headed the family for only five years before meeting his death at the hands of a Plumpton kinsman during the affray on Papplewick Moor.[5] After the death in 1499 without issue of his son Sir Henry,[6] the estates passed to the latter's nephew Sir William, who played a part in the later affairs of the Plumptons.[7]

[1] Payling, 21; Thoroton, 77, 87–91.
[2] CB, 531, 535, 544, 552.
[3] Somerville, 556.
[4] Blatcher, 79; Wright, 129–30; Payling, 199.
[5] **5**; *Flower's Visitation*, 203; Payling, 113, 200–1.
[6] Wedgwood, 683–4; *CPR*, 1467–77, 624–5; Morgan, 11.
[7] **210, 211.**

Pigott, Richard (d.1483)

Of an ancient and comparatively affluent gentry family whose main branch lived at Clotherham, near York, Richard, a younger son of the lawyer John Pigott of Ripon (d.1427), entered the Middle Temple and was called to the coif in 1463, having already embarked upon his outstandingly successful legal career. JP for the North Riding from 1460, later for Bedfordshire, Buckinghamshire, Cambridgeshire and other counties, he was appointed deputy steward of Knaresborough under Warwick in 1461 – a position he held until Sir William Plumpton regained it in 1463; King's sergeant, 1467, retained by the Duchy as sergeant, 1467, and in the same year appointed a justice of assize for the East Anglian circuit; second justice at Lancaster, 1480.[1]

He married Joan, daughter and co-heiress of William Romanby, inherited an annuity of 40m, and eventually, on the death of his elder brother, the parental lands.[2]

A member of several powerful royal commissions, including oyer and terminer and of enquiry into disputed boundaries within the forest of Knaresborough,[3] he was appointed an executor of the will made by Edward IV on the eve of his departure for France in 1475,[4] and custodian of the lands of William, Lord Hastings, who had joined the king's expedition. As a member of Gloucester's council he acted on behalf on the duke in business concerning the city of York; and as a kinsman of the Plumptons he was one of the feoffees appointed by Sir William for the settlements of 1 June 1464.[5] A man whose services to many masters ensured his independence, in his will he expressed contrition for having 'taken men's money and not done so effectually for it as I ought to have done'.[6]

He is commemorated in a fifteenth-century light in the church of Long Melford, Suffolk. His grandson, Thomas, had a similarly distinguished legal career.[7]

[1] Ives, *CL*, 451, 473; *Test. Ebor.*, i, 331; Pollard, in *Patronage, Pedigree and Power*, 45; Somerville, 239, 473, 524; Kirby, *NH*, xxv, 111–12.

[2] Ives, 473.

[3] Reid, 44–46; *CPR*, *1467–77*, 55, 378, 517, 572 and passim; *ibid.*, *1476–85*, 345.

[4] Hicks, in *Richard III and His Rivals*, 320.

[5] CB 565; BL,Add.MS 6698, fols 1–2.

[6] *Test. Ebor.*, iii, 285–6.

[7] Pollard, *NE England*, 135–7.

Pilkington, Sir John (c.1425–79)

Eldest son of Robert Pilkington of Sowerby, cadet of a Lancashire knightly family, whose elder brother had been made knight-banneret at Agincourt,[1] he married Jane, daughter and co-heiress of William Balderston, whose sister became the wife of Sir Robert Harrington. The brothers-in-law were staunch Yorkists – Pilkington fled with the leaders to Calais in 1459, but returned the following year and was pardoned.[2] His fortunes rose after the Yorkist success in 1461 when he soon became squire of the body, then knight of the household and the recipient of numerous grants, including the tonnage and poundage of the port of London, and of manors and lands in Yorkshire, Lancashire, Lincolnshire, Derbyshire and Ireland from the forfeited possessions of attainted Lancastrians. He made his home at Chevet Hall, near Wakefield, which he crenellated in 1477, together with two other country houses.[3]

Imprisoned during the Readeption, his star rose again with the return of Edward and the northern ascendancy of Gloucester, whose retainer he became. He sat in the packed Parliament of 1478 which prepared the way for the fall of Clarence; possibly as Gloucester's chamberlain he accompanied the duke to the nunnery where Elizabeth, widow of the executed 12th earl of Oxford was living in retirement, to whom Gloucester announced that he had been awarded the custody of herself and her possessions. Sir James Tyrell later deposed that Pilkington forthwith demanded her keys from the weeping countess.[4]

He obtained the constabularies of the castles of Chester, Berkhamsted and Wicklow, the forestership of Sowerby chase, stewardship of Howden, and appointment *ex parte* Gloucester, as one of the two chamberlains of the exchequer.[5] The duke as master forester was also directly instrumental in obtaining for him a valuable messuage and vaccary in the forest of Rossendale. Thus Sir William Plumpton as one of the three sureties for Sir John's payment of the farm must have felt confident that the latter's good offices would be available to him.[6]

JP for the West Riding almost continuously from 1464 until his death, Pilkington was sheriff of Lancashire in 1462–3 and 1464–7, and a frequent commissioner. On 18 June 1471, for example, he and Plumpton were members of a commission headed by Gloucester for the arrest and imprisonment of certain Scottish persons reportedly at large in Yorkshire.[7]

At his death early in 1479 Sir John's lands were valued at £213 a year. In his will he requested burial in his chantry within the parish church of Wakefield, and charged his executors, Gloucester, Robert Chaloner, William Calverly and the Lord Chamberlain, William, Lord Hastings to apply for the wardship and marriage of his young son Edward, and to place him in the Lord Chamberlain's household. A bequest to the monks of Fountains was accompanied by a request that in their memorial they would forgive him 'allowance of bargains had betwene them and me'.[8] His widow's subsequent marriage to Sir Thomas Wortley was dissolved and she took the veil. Edward Pilkington died without issue and the Yorkshire branch of the family continued through Sir John's illegitimate son Robert.[9]

[1] John Pilkington, 'The Early History of the Lancashire Family of Pilkington and its Branches from 1066 to 1600', *Transactions of the Historic Society of Lancashire and Cheshire*, n.s., ix (1893), 158, 186–7.

[2] Gooder, 204–7; Jones, 40.

[3] Ross, *Edward IV*, 328; Arnold, 125; *CPR, 1476–85*, 71; Gooder.

[4] Ross, *Richard III*, 33n.; M. A. Hicks 'The Last Days of Elizabeth, Countess of Oxford', in Idem, *Richard III and His Rivals*, 298.

[5] Gooder; A. Steel, *The Receipt of the Exchequer 1377–1485* (Cambridge, 1954), 3–4, 425; Horrox, *Richard III*, 58; *CPR, 1476–85*, 89.

[6] Horrox, *Richard III*, 45; **28**.

[7] *CPR, 1467–77*, 637–8; *ibid., 1476–85*, 85; Arnold, 128.

[8] *Test. Ebor.*, iii, 238–40.

[9] *CPR, 1476–85*, 158; *ibid., 1485–94*, 90; Gooder.

Plumpton, Edward (d. before Feb. 1501)

Possibly a son of Sir William Plumpton's younger brother Godfrey and his wife Alice Wintringham (Joan Plumpton's sister).[1]

Apparently a young man of some aptitude, he had the good fortune to find favour with his kinsman, Sir Robert, who sent him to Furnivall's Inn for legal training[2] and employed him thereafter as his man of affairs, granting to his first wife, Agnes, thought by Stapleton to have been the sister of David ap Griffith, a jointure of 12m.[3] Employed in the same capacity by George, Lord Strange and by Sir John Weston, Master of St John's Clerkenwell, he was known also to the Cely brothers.[4]

His earnest request to Sir Robert for financial provision to enable him to marry Agnes Drayate seems to have been granted, for on 14 Feb. 1501 a certain Robert Tykhull, of Holborn, gent., having been appealed of murder by Agnes widow of Edward Plumpton, appeared before Sir John Furneaux and was pardoned on the ground that he acted in self-defence.[5]

[1] Stapleton, 44.

[2] R.A. Griffiths, 'Public and Private Bureaucracies in England and Wales in the Fifteenth Century', *TRHS*, 5th ser., xxx (1980), 119–20.

[3] App. II, 49; **82**n.

[4] **86**; C.L. Kingsford (ed.), *The Stonor Letters and Papers* (2 vols, Camden Society, 3rd ser., xxix, xxx, 1919), ii, 159; Alison Hanham (ed.), *The Cely Letters 1472–1485* (Early English Text Society, 1975), nos 99, 106.

[5] **121–3**; *CPR, 1494–1509*, 233.

Plumpton, George, priest (d. after 4 December 1459)

A younger son of William Plumpton (exec. 1405), some of the main events of George Plumpton's life are documented in the Coucher Book. When he was granted a licence by Henry Bowet, archbishop of York and Papal Legate, to receive holy orders, he was already a Doctor of Laws and in receipt of a title and an annual life pension of £10 from the prior and convent of the Augustinians of Landa.[1] Ordained deacon 18 September 1417, and priest the following February by John Fordham, bishop of Ely, he was presented to the rectory of Grasmere in 1438/9 through the patronage of St Mary's Abbey, York.[2] The following year he had a faculty from Richard Arnall, vicar-general of John Kempe, archbishop of York, to hear reserved cases in confession and give absolution to all penitents, save violators of the privileges of the cathedral church of York, and of the collegiate churches of Beverley, Ripon and Southwell, and those stealing game from parks belonging to the archiepiscopal see.[3]

Thanks, perhaps, to the patronage of his kinsman John, Lord Scrope of Masham[4] he was granted the Nottinghamshire rectory of Bingham, to which he was inducted by proxy 2 December 1447.[5] The following June, however, pleading age and infirmity, he applied for a three-year leave of absence and shortly afterwards let the rectory to farm to Sir Thomas Chaworth for 40m. By 11 February 1450/1 he had resigned the living to Sir James Swaledale, whilst retaining an annual life pension of £10 therefrom.[6]

Ill health does not appear to have prevented him from fomenting trouble at Kinoulton in August 1457, for which he and William Plumpton (d.1461) were to be arrested and brought before the king and council.[7]

His brother Richard Plumpton having appointed him a feoffee in properties in York and Ripon designated for the provision of daily masses in perputuity, in his own will, dated 14 November 1450, he conveyed these lands to clerical trustees for the provision of a perpetual chantry priest at the altar of the family's chantry of St Mary Magdalen in Spofforth church, to pray for deceased members of the family and their benefactors, including himself whilst alive and his soul 'after I have taken the universall way'.[8]

He passed the remainder of his life in comfort and seclusion at Bolton Priory where, attended by three servants, he was granted a licence to have masses celebrated in his presence in any suitable oratory within the abbey for a year from the date of issue, 4 December 1459.[9]

Whilst rector of Grasmere in 1431 he described to Thomas Gascoigne the symptoms of the mysterious skin disease said to have afflicted Henry IV after the execution of Archbishop Scrope in 1404.[10]

[1] CB, 380, 312; Stapleton, xxxiv.

[2] CB, 392, 395, 442; *CPR*, *1430–41*, 230, 239; A. Hamilton Thompson (ed.), 'The Registers of the Archdeaconry of Richmond, 1361–1442', *YAJ*, xxv (1920), 226.

[3] CB, 449. Transcript in Stapleton, xxxvn.

[4] **1**.

[5] CB, 515.

[6] CB, 521. After Swaledale's death one of his executors, William Shawe, parson, received a pardon for failure to appear to answer George Plumpton in a matter relating to a debt of 100s and a book worth 4m, 21 Nov. 1458, *CPR*, *1452–61*, 450.

[7] *CPR*, *1452–61*, 370.

[8] CB, 520. Transcript in Stapleton, xxxvii.

[9] CB, 523.

[10] Hughes, *Pastors and Visionaries*, 312, 326.

Plumpton, Robert (d.1507)

The elder of Sir William Plumpton's two illegitimate sons, he was known to the family as 'Robinet',[1] and was probably brought up within the Plumpton household. He must have had some legal training for he practised in York, where he lived in the parish of St Michael, Spurriergate, and served as common clerk of the city from 1490 until his death.[2] His legal and other business took him to London from time to time, and he obviously knew his way around the central courts.[3]

Sir William had provided annuities for Robinet and his brother out of a life interest in certain parcels of land in the Derbyshire manor of

Ockbrook – an arrangement which was affected by the recovery of the Plumpton estate by the heirs general.[4] Robert also held land and houses in York, Dringhouses, Sicklinghall and Pickering.

In his will he remitted £10 of the debt of £21 17s owed to him by Sir Robert Plumpton, the remission to be cancelled if the balance were not paid. In the event of his son's death without issue, houses in York and Sicklinghall were to be vested in trustees, chosen by the churchwardens and parishioners of Spofforth, for the provision of a priest, by appointment of Sir Robert and his heirs, to sing in the family's chantry of St Mary Magdalene in the parish church of Spofforth.[5] His son Richard (d.1544/5) became a freeman, merchant, goldsmith and haberdasher of York.[6]

[1] **26**; Kirby, in *Church and Chronicle*, 226.
[2] Keith Dockray, 'Why did the Fifteenth-Century English Gentry Marry: the Pastons, Plumptons and Stonors Reconsidered', in M. Jones (ed.), *Gentry and Lesser Nobility*, 67; R. Horrox, 'The Urban Gentry in the Fifteenth Century', in J.A.F. Thomson (ed.), *Towns and Townspeople in the Fifteenth Century*, (1988), 28.
[3] **26**.
[4] **182**; CB, 600–2.
[5] *Test. Ebor.*, iv, 258–60.
[6] *Ibid.*, 258n.

Pole, German de la (d.1551/2)

Of Radbourne, Derbyshire, son of John de la Pole, who died in the lifetime of his father, Ralph (d.1492). Through a succession of able lawyers the family gained a high reputation and were in demand as counsellors, administrators and arbitrators.

Ralph de la Pole rose to eminence through service in the affinities, successively of Lord Grey of Codnor, William, Lord Hastings and Humphrey, duke of Buckingham, and as counsellor to Margaret of Anjou, through whom he acquired the stewardship of Tutbury. A justice of the king's bench and chief justice at Lancaster in 1456, during the mid-1430s he and one or two others bore the burden of the work of the sessions of the peace in Derbyshire.[1]

He married Elizabeth, daughter of Sir Reginald Moton of Peckleton, Leicestershire, who, as German's grandmother, administered his estate until he came of age in 1504. Business-like and determined, she seems to have shared a household at Radbourne with her grandson and his wife, Anne, daughter of Sir Robert Plumpton, until German came of age, thereafter moving into semi-retirement.[2] Her daughter Mary married Robert Blackwall (**147**).

Little is known of German, save that he seems to have acted as the

Plumpton's steward in Derbyshire, and was one of the collectors of the subsidy granted in 1523.[3] His grandson and namesake is buried in the parish church of Crich, near Matlock, where the family had a chantry.[4]

[1] Wright, 68, 79, 84–85, 98, 111, 216; Rawcliffe, 221; Somerville, 451; Rowney, 369.
[2] *CIPM Henry VII*, i, 776; *CPR, 1485–94*, 431; Wright, 52, 216; Du Boulay, 108; **138, 159, 193**.
[3] **180**; *L&P*, iii (2), 3283.
[4] *Collectanea*, i, 44–5.

Pullein, John (d.1541)

Described in a pardon dated 25 June 1509 as 'of Kirkby Hall, gent., son and heir of Richard Pullein, late of Killinghall', he was a member of a family numerous in and around Knaresborough forest.[1]

Admitted to Lincoln's Inn as an outer barrister in 1496 at the instance of Percival Lambton (**115**), he and George Emerson were assigned to John Newdigate's chambers (**146**). He appears from time to time in the *Black Books* as being fined for failure to moot in hall or for refusing office, or expelled temporarily from commons for refusal to carry the body of one of his fellows to the graveyard, as ordered by the benchers. By 1516/17 he was a governor, and in 1521/22 Lent Reader.[2]

He obtained office in the Duchy in 1515 as vice-chancellor at Lancaster, steward of the manor of Barnoldswick, 1522, deputy steward of Knaresborough, 1539, commissioner for taking Duchy depositions, 1521,[3] and for examinations in Star Chamber proceedings 1520 and 1536. Active in local government, he became escheator for Yorkshire, 1516–17; JP for the West Riding 1530–41; recorder of York 1534–7; collector of the West Riding subsidy 1523, and commissioner for the muster at Harrogate 1539.[4]

Retained as counsel by the Cistercians of Fountains, he received 60s 8d a year, with a robe and a number of benefits and privileges.[5]

Through his marriage with a daughter of Thomas Roos of Ingmanthorpe, a relation by marriage of the Plumptons, and that of his daughter with William Tancred of Boroughbridge (**55**) he doubtless extended the range of his local clientèle.[6]

[1] *CPR, 1485–94*, 181; Pullein, 145.
[2] *Black Books of Lincoln's Inn*, i, 106, 122, 126, 141, 146, 180, 200; Ives, *CL*, 266, 300.
[3] Somerville, 479–80, 525, 532.
[4] *Yorkshire Star Chamber Proceedings*, i, 105–7; ii, 172; *L&I*, lxxxii, 190.
[5] Ives, *CL*, 139, 308.
[6] Pullein, 146–8; Somerville, 479.

Rocliffe, Brian (d.1496)

Son of the lawyer Guy Rocliffe of Cowthorpe, near Wetherby (d.1460), an estate acquired through marriage.[1] Guy had been escheator for Yorkshire in 1426, JP for the West Riding, a puisne baron of the Exchequer and recorder of York in 1453, when the city submitted under duress to the rebel Lord Egremont whom he afterwards accused of severe maltreatment of himself and the mayor.[2]

In May 1455 Brian Rocliffe, a barrister of the Middle Temple, was awarded an annuity of £20 in addition to the fee of 40m he received as a puisne baron of the Exchequer, as compensation for the drastic reduction in his income occasioned by his being prohibited from taking fees or robes from anyone other than the king. In office as 3rd or 2nd baron, 'one of the lesser plums' of the legal profession, throughout the political changes of the times, he obtained re-appointment during pleasure from Henry VII, 24 Sept. 1485.[3] As a puisne he was automatically put on the commission of the peace in 1454 for that part of the country in which his estates lay, and continued to be re-appointed thereafter to the West Riding bench until the Readeption of 1470, when he was dropped in favour of his son, John, but re-appointed in Feb. 1472 after the reinstatement of the Yorkists.[4]

His commissions included an investigation into the means by which Henry VI might reduce his debts, and appointment to receive the possessions of the Yorkist chieftains attainted in the Coventry Parliament.[5]

During the rebuilding of Cowthorpe church parish services were held in his private chapel. His fine memorial brass shows him holding the church which he had provided. In his will he bequeathed a silver musk ball to his granddaughter, Alice, and to his eldest son, John (d.1533), 112 nobles towards the cost of recovering the inheritance of his wife, Margaret, granddaughter of Sir William Plumpton.[6]

John Rocliffe followed his father in the legal profession. He and his co-parcenors pursued their cause with vigour and ultimate success, doubtless aided by John's legal colleagues and friends Brian and George Palmes, William Babthorpe and Robert Chaloner.[7]

John's great granddaughter, Anne Rocliffe, heiress to the Rocliffe moiety, married Sir Ingram Clifford, younger son of Henry, 1st earl of Cumberland. Dying without surviving children, her estates were divided between George Clifford, 3rd earl, and his younger brother Francis Clifford (later 4th earl).[8]

[1] H. Speight, *Nidderdale and the Garden of the Nidd* (1894), 137.

[2] *List of Escheators*, 188; Lander, 33; R.A. Griffiths, 'Local Rivalries and National Politics', *Speculum*, xliii (1968), 611; Ives, *CL*, 301.

[3] *CPR, 1452–61*, 482; *ibid., 1467–77*, 63; *ibid., 1485–94*, 13, 19; Chrimes, 158; Ives, *CL*, 81–2.
[4] Arnold, 124; *CPR, 1452–61*, 683.
[5] *CPR, 1452–61*, 246, 390, 572.
[6] *Test. Ebor.*, iv, 104–7; *CIPM, Henry VII*, ii, 112. The figure of his wife Jane, daughter of Sir Stephen Hammerton, is missing, Mill Stephenson, 'Monumental Brasses in the West Riding', *YAJ*, xv (1900), 10–12; Joseph E. Morris, *The West Riding of Yorkshire* (1911), 164.
[7] *CPR, 1467–77*, 601; Kirby, *NH*, xxv, 113–19; *Test. Ebor.*, v, 319–23.
[8] Hoyle, *Camden Miscellany* xxxi, 172–3.

Rokeby, Ann, Lady (d.1530/1)

Daughter of Sir Ralph Ellerker of Rusby, Lincolnshire and widow of Sir Ralph Rokeby of Mortham (*fl.*1522/3), her niece Elizabeth Ellerker was the wife of Sir Robert Constable of Everingham.[1]

First mentioned in Rokeby in the North Riding in 1201, the family afterwards settled at Mortham, near Greta Bridge,[2] and in the 15th century, as retainers of Salisbury and Warwick, were strongly Yorkist – Sir Ralph's father, Thomas, received a pardon for participation in Lord FitzHugh's abortive rising.[3] Sir Ralph, himself, was appointed standard-bearer to Henry, Lord Scrope of Bolton at the battle of Flodden.[4]

A vowess by the time of her death, Lady Ann left bequests of silver, clothing and linen to William and Isabel Plumpton and their children, and requested burial in Spofforth church. As Sir Ralph had left no surviving heir, the estate passed to his younger brother William (d.1542).[5]

[1] *Flower's Visitation*, 66, 109. Sir Robert's father, Sir Marmaduke Constable of Everingham was the writer of **225**.
[2] *VCH*, Yorks, *North Riding*, i, 111–12, 122, 138.
[3] Pollard, *NE England*, 89; Idem, 'Lord Fitzhugh's Rising in 1470', *BIHR*, lii (1979), 172–3.
[4] *VCH*, 111–12.
[5] 'Test. Leod.', 45.

Savile, Sir John (d.1504), Sir Henry (d.1558)

The Saviles of Thornhill, near Wakefield, one of the oldest gentry families in the county, established a tradition of public service that provided seven sheriffs between 1380 and 1613. Marriage brought them estates in other counties, including Lancashire and Oxfordshire, Shropshire and the Midlands; fecundity enabled them to produce flourshing branches, notably the Saviles of Howley, Copley, Elland and Lupset.[1]

Sir Henry was the eldest son of Sir John Savile, a Yorkist supporter who succeeded his father and namesake as steward of York's lordship of Wakefield, and was knighted and made banneret by Gloucester at Berwick, August 1481.[2] On his appointment as captain of the Isle of Wight at a fee of £200, he was required to resign the stewardship, the loss of which seems to have rankled. Trusted by Richard III he nevertheless benefited immediately from Henry VII's patronage, through which he was restored to the stewardship, appointed to the West Riding bench, and became Henry's first sheriff of Yorkshire.[3] On his death his son, Henry, was still a minor.[4]

Having proved his dependability by remaining loyal to Henry VIII during the Pilgrimage of Grace, Henry received commensurate rewards: the shrievalty of Yorkshire in 1537–41; the stewardships of Wakefield and Pontefract, and in February 1542 membership of the Council in the North. He was also appointed a JP for all three Yorkshire ridings.[5]

By his wife, Elizabeth, daughter of Thomas Sotehill of Soothill, he had an heir, Edward, but his illegitimate son, Robert, by Margaret Barlaston, a waiting-maid, was obviously dear to him. Robert, who married, first, Anne, sister of Lord Hussey and widow of Sir Richard Thimberley, became the progenitor of the Saviles of Howley. His son Sir John Savile (d.1630) played a key role in West Riding politics, and his grandson Sir Thomas (d.1652) was created Lord Savile and earl of Sussex.[6]

[1] J.T. Cliffe, *The Yorkshire Gentry from the Reformation to the Civil War* (1969), 30, 244.

[2] Somerville, 519; Horrox, *Richard III*, 60; *List of Sheriffs*; Hicks, *NH*, xiv, 105; Arnold, 123.

[3] Horrox, 195; Dockray, in *Kings and Nobles*, 207, 225; Pollard, *NE England*, 374.

[4] *L&P*, iii (3), 2297 (12); *Test. Ebor.*, vi, 139–40.

[5] *List of Sheriffs*; Somerville, 515; Reid, 169; *CPR, 1547–48*, passim; Taylor, *NH*, x, 85; Smith, 66, 148.

[6] *Tonge's Visitation*, 79–80; **241–242**; Thoresby, 152; Clay, 190; Cartwright, 247.

Sheffield, Sir Robert II (1462–1518)

Grandson of Robert Sheffield (1405–84), who was assessed in 1436 as having an income of £40 from land in Lincolnshire, Yorkshire, the city of York and elsewhere.[1] Son of Sir Robert I (1430–1502), who, through marriage with Genette, heiress of Alexander Lounde of Butterwick, Lincolnshire, acquired the property which became the family's principal home.[2] A barrister of the Inner Temple, he was, as an active Lancastrian, obliged to obtain pardons in 1458, 1462 and 1472. Through membership of Northumberland's council he was appointed one of the arbitrators for the first two attempts to settle the Plumpton dispute, which were interrupted, respectively, by the deaths of Sir William Plumpton and of Edward IV.[3] He played a prominent part in government as JP for Lindsay from 1462 until his death; MP for Bedwyn, 1467–68 and Ludgershall, 1472–75; and as counsellor to the Duchy under Edward IV and Richard III.

Sir Robert II added greatly to his estate by marriage with Ellen, daughter and co-heiress of Sir James Delves of Doddington (exec. 1471).[5] A barrister of the Inner Temple, where he gave the autumn reading in 1493, he was pardoned in 1485 as of London, Butterwick and Chilwell, Nottinghamshire,[6] and thereafter remained a dependable servant of the Tudors. In 1493 he was appointed to the stewardship of the manor of Howden during a vacancy in the see of Durham.[7] He became recorder of London two years later, and was frequently MP, either for London or Lincolnshire, and twice elected speaker between 1495 and 1515.[8] He received knighthood on the field after the defeat of the Cornish insurgents at Blackheath in 1497.[9]

At his death he held lands in Lincolnshire and seven other counties; his son Sir Robert III, then aged forty, succeeded him, and his grandson Edmund became the 1st Baron Sheffield.[10]

[1] Gray, 636.
[2] Wedgwood, 759.
[3] Kirby, *NH*, xxv, 114; Reid, 58–9.
[4] *CPR, 1485–94*, 181, 492, 493. Roskell, *Commons*, 312–13; Clay, 205.
[5] **92**.
[6] *Readings and Moots*, p. xvi.
[7] *CPR, 1485–94*, 422, 492.
[8] Ives, *CL*, 106; Roskell, 312–13.
[9] Mackie, 142.
[10] *IPM, Henry VIII to Philip and Mary* (L&I, xxiii), p. 205; Clay, 205.

Sotehill, Sir Henry (d. after 1480)

Although the eldest son of Gerard Sotehill, of Redbourne, Lincolnshire, Henry's endowment in 1457 of a chantry at the altar of St Catherine in the parish church of Wakefield suggests a West Riding origin.[1] He acquired the Leicestershire estate of Stockerston through marriage with the heiress Anne Boyville, and this became the family's home.[2]

A young man of promise, he rose in the service of the Duchy as apprentice from 1456 to 1466, and of the earl of Warwick, who appointed him deputy steward of the North Parts in 1460 and of the honor of Pontefract in 1458,[3] where he was known as the 'learned steward'. In 1466 as king's attorney he took a leading part in the commission of enquiry into the estates of the Harrington heiresses, and in the prosecutions of Henry Courtenay and Thomas Hungerford at Salisbury in January 1468/9.[4]

His most exalted clients included the dukes of York and Clarence, but he also held retainers from the litigious Sir John Fastolf, John Paston I and Sir William Plumpton, with whom he served in 1457 on commissions of array and inquisition into sedition. His legal expertise won him membership of a powerful commission, which included Guy Fairfax and Brian Rocliffe, to investigate concealed royal lands and dues. He was appointed to the quorum of the West Riding commission of the peace in 1454, and afterwards joined the Leicestershire and Rutland benches.[5]

Dismissed from his office as king's attorney in 1475, possibly because he had come under suspicion as a former adherent of Warwick, he retired to the life of a country gentleman.[6] Four years earlier he had founded a perpetual almeshouse at Stockerston for three poor persons, and a chantry within the church, with a priest to celebrate Divine Service daily.[7]

His daughter-in-law Elizabeth Plumpton, aged three when she was contracted to marry Sir Henry's son John, apparently also a lawyer, spent her childhood in his household. Widowed in 1494, her deep affection for her husband and family, including her daughter-in-law Joan Empson, is expressed in her will, proved 17 February 1506/7.[8]

[1] J.W. Walker (ed.), *Yorkshire Pedigrees* (3 vols, Harleian Society, xiv–xvi, 1942–44), ii, 344. Subsequently Henry's great granddaughters and their husbands, Sir William Drury and Sir John Constable, sued for the recovery of this property, *CSPD, 1547–48*, 71; **210**.

[2] *VCH, Leics*, v, 304.

[3] Somerville, 425.

[4] Ross, *Edward IV*, 123; Acheson, 75; Ives *CL*, App. E; Grimble, 54; *CPR, 1467–77*, 128; **16**.

[5] Acheson, 250; Davis, *Paston Letters*, i, 86; ii, 38, 134; *CPR, 1467–77*, 408, 530; *ibid., 1452–61*, 518; Arnold, 120, 127.

[6] C. Richmond, *John Hopton: A Fifteenth-Century Gentleman* (Cambridge, 1981), 183–6.

[7] *CPR, 1467–77*, 113.

[8] CB, 562; PRO, PROB 11/15/19, fol. 151v.

Tunstall, Sir Richard (1427–92)

Eldest son of Sir Thomas Tunstall (d.1457), from whom he inherited Thurland castle in Lancashire, with lands elsewhere in the county and in Yorkshire and Westmorland,[1] Richard entered Henry VI's household in 1452 as one of the king's esquires of the body, receiving knighthood three years later, and appointment as king's knight and carver in 1457. He is reputed to have accompanied his master to Westminster Abbey for a discussion about a projected royal tomb, the king leaning heavily upon his arm during the long and tiring interview with the abbot.[2] Among his many rewards was the control of a number of heiresses and their estates, the mastership of the mints at the Tower and at Calais, and several Duchy stewardships and receiverships.[3] Appointed chamberlain of the household in 1459, he represented Yorkshire in the Coventry Parliament which met the same year.[4]

After fighting on the Lancastrian side at Wakefield and Towton he was for next seven years an attainted fugitive with the royal court in exile.[5] Between 1462 and 1468 he took part in the defence of Dunstanburgh castle, avoided capture after Hedgerley Moor and commanded an epic defence of Harlech castle until lack of money forced its reduction on 14 August 1468.[6] His faithfulness must have impressed Edward IV for he was granted an almost immediate pardon, reinstated as the king's chamberlain and recruited into the royal affinity.[7] Though high in favour during the Readeption he was nevertheless pardoned again and made a knight of the body. In 1475 he accompanied the king to France with a following of 10 spears and 100 archers, and two years later was one of a small group to be granted the wardship, marriage and custody during his minority, of Edward, earl of Wiltshire.[8]

Meanwhile his younger brother Thomas received a pardon after the death of his patron the earl of Warwick at Barnet, and was soon afterwards recruited by Gloucester. Following his brother into the ducal entourage as councillor, Richard was well placed to benefit from the events of 1483.[9] The new king appointed him a KG and lieutenant of Calais with an annuity of 100m. The following year the crew of a ship of which he was part owner came under examination for allegedly attacking and boarding a Spanish vessel.[10]

He seems to have passed easily into the service of Henry VII, for on 25 June 1486, as a king's knight, he was granted the stewardship of Kendal for life. The following August he and Sir Thomas Wortley were commissioned to take sureties from a number of important former Yorkists, including Sir James Harrington, and admit them to the king's obedience. The same year saw his appointment to the royal Council and to the stewardship of the honor of Pontefract.[11] In 1487 his annuity was increased to £117 13s 4d, payable out of the customs of Kingston-upon-Hull. After the assassination of Northumberland in 1489, Tunstall and Sir Henry Wentworth were associated with the earl of Surrey in the lieutenancy of the North.[12] On 19 Feb. 1490/1 he was a commissioner with Thomas Rotherham, archbishop of York, the earl of Surrey, and others, to enquire into a dispute between the citizens of York and the prebendaries and vicars choral of the cathedral over rights of common.[13] The following year he was one of those entrusted with the task of obtaining financial support from the people of Yorkshire for the king's projected expedition to France whose ineffectual result aroused discontent amongst the contributors, who felt their efforts had been to no avail.[14]

He married Elizabeth, daughter of Sir William Franke, but the family estates devolved upon the descendants of his brother Thomas whose illegitimate son Cuthbert became bishop of Durham and president of the Council in the North.[15]

[1] Dorothy J. Clayton, *The Administration of the County Palatine of Chester* 1442–1485 (Chetham Society, n.s., xxxv, 1990), 166–7.

[2] Gooder, 213–16; Goodman, 132; Griffiths, *Henry VI*, 776.

[3] *CPR, 1450–61*, 181, 229, 335, 553, 592; *CCR, 1453–61*, 384; Somerville, 485, 494, 500, 507.

[4] *Return of Members of Parliament*; *RP*, v, 477.

[5] Goodman, 57.

[6] Goodman, 61, 63–4, 98; Pollard, *NE England*, 302; Gillingham, 140.

[7] Morgan, 7; *CPR, 1467–77*, 97, 271.

[8] Horrox, *Richard III*, 50; Goodman, 132; Gillingham, 32; *CPR, 1477–85*, 19, 498.

[9] Horrox, *Richard III*, 50.

[10] Ross, *Richard III*, 57; Dockray, in *Kings and Nobles*, 212–13; *CPR, 1476–85*, 446.

[11] *Anglica Historia*, 5; *CPR, 1485–94*, 95, 133; Somerville, 514; **56**.

[12] *CPR, 1485–94*, 211, 95, 133, 135; **87**.

[13] *CPR, 1485–94*, 320.

[14] *CPR, 1485–94*, 366; Mackie, 109.

[15] *DNB*.

Vavasour, Sir John (d.1506)

Son of John Vavasour of Spaldington in the East Riding, an estate he acquired through marriage with Elizabeth, daughter and co-heiress of Thomas de la Hay. John Vavasour senior, who may have been a lawyer, was JP for the East Riding, MP for Lincoln and probably clerk of estreats in common pleas.[1]

His son entered the Inner Temple and was called sergeant in 1478, having already served as MP for Bridport in the Parliament of 1472.[2] Retained as legal councillor by Gloucester, his appointment as king's sergeant in 1488 was renewed after the duke's accession as Richard III.[3] Like most leading lawyers he seems to have experienced little difficulty in transferring his service to Henry VII, for on his election as recorder of York in 1486, though he defeated the king's preferred candidate he was permitted to exercise the office.[4] As a member of Gloucester's council he had represented the heirs general on the second panel appointed to arbitrate on the Plumpton land dispute.[5]

His marriage with Elizabeth, daughter of Sir Robert Tailboys – a member of Gloucester's circle – ended in separation *c.* 1494. His reputed meanness is said to have provoked a provincial landlady to destroy his judicial robes.[6] Knighted in August 1490, he was in the same year appointed puisne judge of the common pleas – an office he held until 1504 – and in 1502 a justice of assize for the midland circuit. In 1495 he joined the legal establishment of the Duchy as chief justice at Lancaster during pleasure – Empson, who had been attorney general since 1485, was promoted to the chancellorship in 1504.[7] During this period he connived at Empson's conspiracy to recover the Plumpton estates.[8]

He is said to have had £800 in gold in reserve at the time of his death. His charitable bequests therefore amounted to more than £700, including £200 for the foundation of a chantry at Spaldington. His wife was to receive neither goods nor land unless she repaid the £700 she had taken, presumably on leaving the marital home, and he named several locations in and around London where the chests containing his valuables would be found.[9] As he died without issue his estate presumably passed to his nephew, Sir Peter Vavasour.

[1] Ives, *CL*, Apps.

[2] Ives. 451; Wedgwood, 904.

[3] Horrox, in *Richard III and the North*, 87; *DNB*.

[4] D. Palliser, 'Richard III and York', in *ibid.*, 59; A. Raine (ed.), *York Civic Records*, i (YASRS, xcviii, 1939), 29, 106, passim; *ibid.*, ii (YASRS, ciii, 1941), 1–55, passim; He was busily engaged from 1485 until his death, *CPR, 1485–94*, passim.

[5] Kirby, *NH*, xxv, 114.

[6] Ives, *Law Quarterly Review*, 358; Idem, *CL*, App.

[7] Somerville, 469, 392–3; *CPR, 1494–1509*, 278, 291; Ives, *CL*, 311–12.

[8] Kirby, *NH*, xxv, 118. It was in February 1496/7 that Edward Plumpton first heard of Empson's intention to bring an action of novel disseisin, **119**.

[9] Ives, *TRHS*, 5th ser. xviii (1968), 158; *Test. Ebor.*, iv, 89–92.

Warde, Sir Christopher (d.1521)

Son of Sir Roger Warde of Givendale, near York, and his wife Joan, daughter of Sir Richard Tunstall, who survived him and afterwards married Sir William Stapleton of Wighill. To her two sons, Christopher and John, she bequeathed pieces of jewellery and plate.[1]

Christopher married Margaret, sister of Sir William Gascoigne (d.1477) and of Dame Agnes, wife of Sir Robert Plumpton. Knighted by Northumberland in 1481, he was a banneret by the following year and a Percy feedman.[2] Unlike Sir Robert he found favour with Richard III, who entrusted him with authority in the South after the collapse of the rebellion of 1483, as master of the hart hounds, steward of Worplesdon, JP and commissioner of array, sheriff of Surrey and Sussex. Prior to Richard's usurpation Warde had been given a command under Northumberland in the great northern army that marched on London in July 1483 in a show of strength which may have had a decisive effect on events.[3]

Though pardoned after Bosworth (where he was present in Northumberland's contingent), he appears to have played little part in public affairs thereafter, though he was among the great company of knights, headed by Northumberland, which joined Henry VII at Barnsdale on his progress to York in the spring of 1486.[4]

In June 1494 he obtained remission of outlawry for non-payment of two debts amounting to £23 19s 9d.[5] Two years later his daughter Joan was married in the private chapel at Givendale to Edward Musgrove of Kirby Stephen.[6] A loyal kinsman and friend of Sir Robert Plumpton (his sister Margaret was married to another Plumpton ally, Sir John Norton of Norton Conyers), they supped together soon after the trial at York assizes, and he was one of the signatories to the memorandum endorsing Sir Robert's view of the legal proceedings.[7]

Mary Warde (b. 1485), possibly a niece, founded the Institute of the Blessed Virgin Mary, which survived until recently as the Bar Convent at York.[8]

[1] *Flower's Visitation*, 335; *Test. Ebor.*, iv, 274.

[2] Hicks, *NH*, xiv, 92, 106.

[3] Bennett, 11, 67; Hicks, in *Richard III and his Rivals*, 379; *CPR, 1476–85*, 397, 489, 572, 574.

[4] F.J. Furnival (ed.), 'The Battle of Bosworth Field', in *Bishop Percy's Folio Manuscript, Ballards and Romances* (3 vols, 1868), iii, 233–9; *CPR, 1476–85*, 531; *Collectanea*, iv, 186.

[5] *CPR, 1485–94*, 447.

[6] *Test. Ebor.*, iii, 360.

[7] **162**; CB, 824; Stapleton, p. cviii. Sir John Norton's daughter Anne married Sir Robert Plumpton's grandson and namesake, **228–229.**

[8] Peter Anson, *The Call of the Cloister* (2nd edn, revsd, 1964), 15; Bossy, 160. She was brought up in the household of her kinsmen the Babthorpes.

INDEX

a. = abbot; archb. = archbishop; b. = bishop; dau. = daughter; d. = duke; dss. = duchess; e. = earl; s. = son. Figures in **Bold** type refer to the letters. Figures in *Italics* refer to page numbers in the Introduction. Figures in Roman type refer to pages of the Appendices.